## For nearly four decades, a brand and a directory you can count on...

SELECT REGISTRY, Distinguished Inns of North America—the premier guide to exceptional travel and lodging for 36 years—invites you to find that special place that will make your next trip unforgettable.

Whether you're traveling for business or pleasure, by yourself or with your family, this guidebook will help you to locate extraordinary places to stay throughout the U.S. and Canada. And, no matter what the season or the type of property that you find most appealing, SELECT REGISTRY likely has something for you.

Most importantly, you can rest assured that our member properties have been selected as among the most comfortable and welcoming—unique and quality assured lodging alternatives in an increasingly cluttered and impersonal travel marketplace.

In years past, the registry book in the lobby of hotels and inns welcomed guests and provided a connection between innkeepers and travelers. The historical registry "quill"—the original instrument of guest registration—has been incorporated into our Association's graphic identity, and the predicates of hospitality, comfort, and authenticity establish our members as "the best of the best"—select properties that will exceed your highest expectations when it comes to lodging.

Look for the plaque with the quill on it when you visit our members' inns, and you'll know that you are "traveling the SELECT REGISTRY way..."

### SELECT REGISTRY
#### DISTINGUISHED INNS OF NORTH AMERICA

se·lect (sĭ-lĕkt') *v.* **-lect·ed**, **-lecting**, **-lects**. —*tr.* To choose from among several; pick out, —*intr.* To make a choice or selection. —*adj.* Also **se·lect·ed** (-lĕk'tĭd). **1.** Singled out in preference; chosen. **2.** Of special value or quality; preferred. —*n.* One that is select. [Lat. *seligere*, select-: se-, apart+legere, to choose.] —**se·lect'ness** *n.*

SelectRegistry.com

Helen Young, Board President
Inn on the Twenty, Ontario

Keith Kehlbeck, Executive Director

Dear SELECT REGISTRY Guest:

In the late 1960s, one man had an interesting idea. A travel writer named Norman Simpson drove throughout North America in a paneled station wagon, identifying unique places that offered what he called, "good honest lodging, good honest food, and good honest feeling." Hailed as "the Father of Country Inn Travel," Simpson—through his pioneering book, *Country Inns and Back Roads*—introduced an entirely new type of lodging experience to the traveling public. Today, the Association of independent innkeepers started by Norman Simpson includes more than 400 of the "finest country inns, luxury B&Bs, and unique small hotels" from California to Nova Scotia.

Although the Association has its roots in the Country Inn travel movement of the 1960s and 1970s, our membership has continued to evolve. We now include exceptional Bed and Breakfasts, urban inns, boutique small hotels and small resorts as part of our diverse membership. Every year, we add new properties that meet our rigorous Quality Assurance guidelines and that enhance the variety and diversity of our membership. For your convenience in identifying the newest members of the SELECT REGISTRY "family," these properties are highlighted in the indexes in the front and back of the guidebook.

On behalf of the member innkeepers, Board of Directors, and staff of SELECT REGISTRY, we hope that you enjoy this complimentary copy of our directory—which is a gift from your hosts. Use it in good health as you travel; the innkeepers of SELECT REGISTRY look forward to welcoming you along the way!

*"Among all the different ratings existing today, the most coveted innkeeping award should be an eager referral from a satisfied guest to a friend planning a trip."*
–Norman Simpson

*"I could see that all of your guests were being treated like the inspector"*
*—Inc.* Magazine

**Perhaps the most important distinction that sets a SELECT REGISTRY member apart from other inns or B&Bs is our Quality Assurance Program.**

SELECT REGISTRY carries out a quality assurance inspection for each of its more than 400 member properties. This program involves independent inspectors—Quality Consultants, L.L.C.—who are not employees of SELECT REGISTRY and who have handled our inspections for nearly 20 years. The inspectors arrive unidentified, spend the night, and evaluate the inn on a detailed point system, which translates into a pass/fail grade for the inn. Hospitality, the physical plant, and cuisine of the property are all evaluated. Inns applying for membership are inspected, as are existing members on a periodic schedule. Not all properties have what it takes to pass the inspections, and this process provides an assurance to the traveling public that a SELECT REGISTRY inn is in a class of its own.

**No other online directory or organization of innkeepers has a comparable inspection program.**

Guest comments also inform us as we continue to help our member properties meet evolving guest expectations. To look at other Select Registry guest comments on various properties, visit us online at **www.selectregistry.com/advisor**. To add your own comments and feedback on a property, go to **www.selectregistry.com/comments**.

# *How to use this book*

For the convenience of our guests, an index of the properties by state and province is provided at the front of the book. At the back of the book, you'll find an alpha-listing of all member properties.

Each SELECT REGISTRY member property is represented with its own page of information in this guidebook. The page includes two pictures, a brief description of the experience a guest can expect at that property, and contact information. The owners/innkeepers are listed so you know who your hosts will be. ❶

The Rooms/Rates section gives the number of rooms and pricing structure for the property. ❷ Cuisine describes the food and beverage specialties for which our members are famous, including whether the property serves only breakfast or is full service. ❸ The Directions section gives you an easy to follow "road map" to reach the property. Nearest Airport(s) tells you where you might fly in. ❹

Because food and wine are important complements to many of our properties, some members are proud to have received the prestigious **DiRoNA** (Distinguished Restaurants of North America) or *Wine Spectator* Awards.

The guidebook is organized in alphabetical order, by state and province (our Canadian members have a separate section, which begins on page 442). A map of the state or province at the beginning of each section shows the location of each property, relative to major cities and highways. For larger map images, go to the SELECT REGISTRY web site, www. SelectRegistry.com.

Generally speaking, properties are grouped within each state or province by travel area, north to south, east to west. All Camden, Maine properties, for example, are listed together.

These awards are noted on participating Inns' guidebook page(s), as is any AAA Award the inn has received (confirmed by Official Appointment by AAA). SELECT REGISTRY is particularly pleased to co-market with DiRoNA, whose mission statemtn and audience so clearly mirror our own. **5**

Each of our inns has a slightly different mix of food and beverage services. Although these are often described in more detail in the Cuisine section for each inn, we want to give our guests a quick snapshot of what each inn offers in-house. The icons near the top of each page tell you whether the inn serves breakfast, lunch, and/or dinner, and whether or not wine or cocktails are available. **6**

Breakfast   Lunch   Dinner   Wine/Cocktails

Beneath the photos on each page, you'll find a guest quote or some recognition garnered by the property. This tells you something, in particular, for which the property is known. **7**

On our website (www.selectregistry.com) on each individual inn's page, there is an Amenities and Policies grid—a brief indication of the services each SELECT REGISTRY member property offers its guests. The icons stand for:

| ☺ 12+ | Suitable for Children | ●━ | Exercise Facilities |
| ⊘ | Not Suitable for Children | ✕ | Spa Services |
| ⊗ | Non-smoking Inn | 🖋 | Reservations by Travel Agents |
| ♿ | Handicap accessible guestrooms | | |
| 💳 | Credit cards accepted | @ | Internet Access |
| ⓨ | Corporate/Business Rates | 🐕 | Pets Welcome |
| 📁 | Conference Facilities | ≋ | Pool |
| ♥ | Wedding Facilities | 🔥 | Fireplaces |
| ⑤ | Eco-tourism | ◎ | Whirlpool Tubs |
| ☕ | Collectible mug, i.e., Deneen Pottery | ❋ | Air-conditioning |

Please note that these amenity icons appear only online, and not in the guidebook.

For more information on eco-tourism and eco-tourism friendly properties go online at **www.selectregistry.com/ecotourism.**

**We hope these instructions help you utilize our guidebook as you plan your travels. For many additional pages of information on each member property, visit us online at www.selectregistry.com**

## Gift Certificates

The gift of an overnight stay or a weekend at an exceptional inn or B&B can be one of the most thoughtful and appreciated gifts you can give your parents, children, or dear friends. Employers are discovering that a gift certificate for a "getaway" is an excellent way of rewarding their employees, while at the same time giving them some much needed rest. A few ideas:

- **Weddings** • **Anniversaries** • **Holiday & Birthday gifts** •
- **Employee rewards/incentives** • **Retirement**

Our gift certificates are valid at any of our more than 400 member properties. We process orders daily, packaging certificates with our complimentary Association guidebook and your personal message. Certificates may be ordered online or by phone, and expedited shipping is available at an additional cost. The next time you think about gift-giving, think about our Gift Certificate Program—the perfect gift for that special person.

**Toll Free at: 1-800-344-5344 or online at www.selectregistry.com/giftcertificates.**

## The Golden Quill Club: SELECT REGISTRY'S guest loyalty program

Because we value our many return guests, for the past several years SELECT REGISTRY has administered a modest frequent traveler reward—The Golden Quill Club Loyalty Program.

In the back of this book, you'll find a detachable card that serves as a passport *and* a voucher, all rolled into one. Completed cards entitle guests to a value-added reward from our member properties and may qualify you for ongoing SELECT REGISTRY contests and promotions. Rules and instructions are printed on the card and posted online. **Ask your host innkeeper or staff to validate the card during your stay, or contact the Central Office at 1-800-344-5244 for instructions on how to complete your card if you miss getting validation at any Select Registry member property.**

Start collecting Loyalty Rewards today while staying at SELECT REGISTRY inns. We think you'll find that some experiences are worth repeating!

# www.SelectRegistry.com
## www.innbook.com

*"By far, the most attractive, complete directory of top quality inns, B&Bs, and small hotels and resorts on the Internet! Loads of information."*

If you see something you like in the SELECT REGISTRY guidebook, and also look for travel information on the Internet, we encourage you to visit our central Association web site or the home web sites of our individual members. On the SELECT REGISTRY site, you'll find thousands of pages of information all in one place, including recipes, descriptions and photos of individual rooms, area attractions and other details that complement the information contained in this book.

The SELECT REGISTRY web site includes: user-friendly "Find an Inn" search functions, trip planner itineraries, and innovations such as email postcards utilizing the extensive photo archives we have for our inns. Other online features include:

- amenity icons for each property
- inn page translation into several languages (at bottom of the page)
- local weather
- nearby inns
- social networking tools/links, such as: Del.icio.us, Technorati, Digg, FURL, blinklist, reddit, YahooMyWeb, Newsvine, StumbleUpon, Google, and Facebook. Flag your favorite inns for friends and family!

In most cases, you'll also be able to check availability and request a reservation online from our members. And, of course, if you want even more in-depth information on a particular member property, there is a hot-link to the home web page for the inn or B&B of interest to you, as well as links to regional and local portals featuring SELECT REGISTRY members.

On our central web site, you'll also find a place to register for our regular guest e-newsletters, which include featured inns, recipes, stories, and specials. Sign up today, and keep in touch with SELECT REGISTRY on a regular basis!

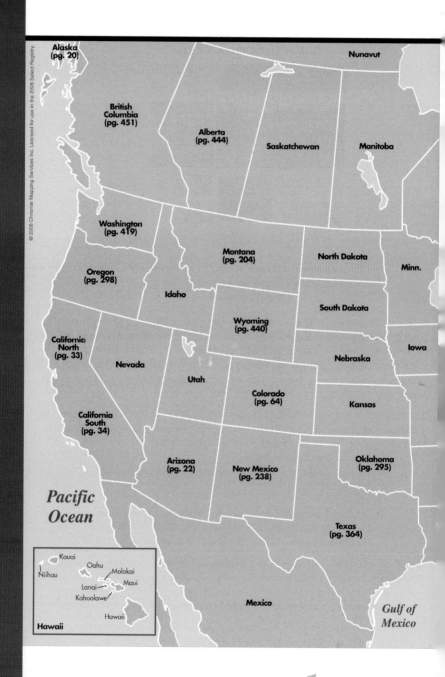

Alaska (pg. 20)

Nunavut

British Columbia (pg. 451)

Alberta (pg. 444)

Saskatchewan

Manitoba

Washington (pg. 419)

Montana (pg. 204)

North Dakota

Minn.

Oregon (pg. 298)

Idaho

South Dakota

Iowa

Wyoming (pg. 440)

California North (pg. 33)

Nevada

Utah

Nebraska

Colorado (pg. 64)

Kansas

California South (pg. 34)

Arizona (pg. 22)

New Mexico (pg. 238)

Oklahoma (pg. 295)

Pacific Ocean

Texas (pg. 364)

Kauai

Niihau

Oahu

Molokai

Lanai

Maui

Kahoolawe

Hawaii

Hawaii

Mexico

Gulf of Mexico

© 2008 Chrismar Mapping Services Inc. Licensed for use in the 2008 Select Registry.

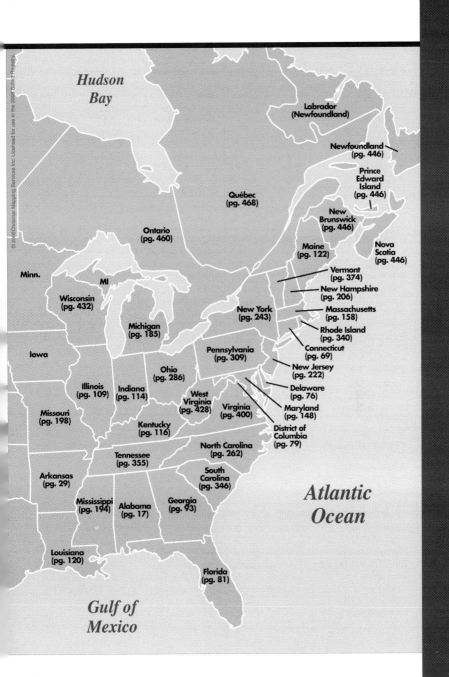

Hudson Bay

Labrador (Newfoundland)

Newfoundland (pg. 446)

Prince Edward Island (pg. 446)

Québec (pg. 468)

New Brunswick (pg. 446)

Ontario (pg. 460)

Maine (pg. 122)

Nova Scotia (pg. 446)

Minn.

MI

Vermont (pg. 374)

New Hampshire (pg. 206)

Wisconsin (pg. 432)

New York (pg. 243)

Massachusetts (pg. 158)

Michigan (pg. 185)

Rhode Island (pg. 340)

Iowa

Pennsylvania (pg. 309)

Connecticut (pg. 69)

New Jersey (pg. 222)

Ohio (pg. 286)

Illinois (pg. 109)

Indiana (pg. 114)

Delaware (pg. 76)

West Virginia (pg. 428)

Virginia (pg. 400)

Maryland (pg. 148)

Missouri (pg. 198)

Kentucky (pg. 116)

District of Columbia (pg. 79)

North Carolina (pg. 262)

Tennessee (pg. 355)

Arkansas (pg. 29)

South Carolina (pg. 346)

Atlantic Ocean

Mississippi (pg. 194)

Alabama (pg. 17)

Georgia (pg. 93)

Louisiana (pg. 120)

Florida (pg. 81)

Gulf of Mexico

# *Index by State or Province*

# Index by State or Province

# Alabama

Famous for: Cotton, Steel, Antebellum Mansions, Confederate Capital (1861), Azalea Trail, U.S. Space and Rocket Center.

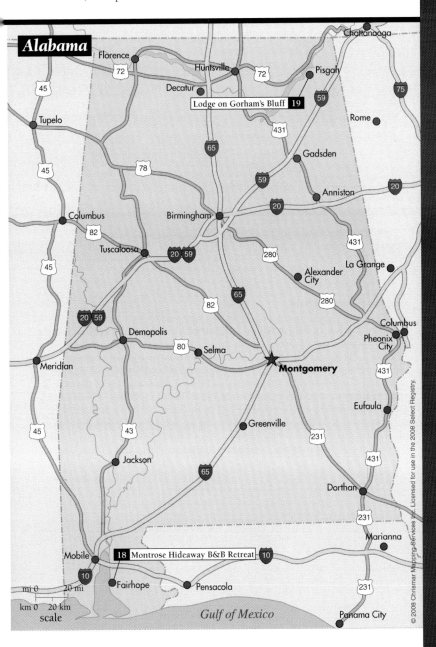

# Montrose Hideaway

www.montrosehideaway.com

P.O. Box 1183, Daphne, AL 36526;, 24437 Main St. (Montrose), Fairhope, AL 36532

**866-443-3299** • 251-625-4868

gandmmcnair@earthlink.net

*Member Since 2008*

*"Thank you for a wonderful stay. What a beautiful location you have here. The chocolate gravy was sublime and the surroundings so peaceful. We will be back."*

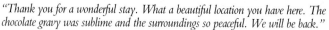

## Greg and Mary McNair

**Montrose Hideaway Bed-and-Breakfast Retreat** is a unique inn located in Fairhope's Montrose Historic District on Mobile Bay's Eastern Shore, next to Daphne. Eleven private acres with a spring-fed pond invite you to retreat to a hidden paradise while remaining convenient to shopping, golfing, bayfront parks with fishing piers and walking paths, restaurants, museums, popular attractions and gulf beaches. Enjoy a middle-of-nowhere feel in the middle of all there is to see and do in Mobile and Baldwin counties. *Coastal Living* magazine selected this inn as one of 15 for its 2006 annual list of favorites after only being open two years. In addition to luxury accommodations, we'd love to help you plan your trip, including customizing in-room packages unique to you. Let us help you with your group event (wedding, reception, business retreat, reunion). Let us help you save with one of our discount offers (weekday frequency and business, military, pastors). We'll customize gift certificates, as well as accept certificates issued through Select Registry, bnbfinder.com and bedandbreakfast.com. Near Carnival Cruise in Mobile.

**Rates**
$150/$295: Weekdays $175/$325: Weekends, holidays, special-events . Number of Rooms: 6

**Cuisine**
Freshly prepared bountiful breakfast served by candlelight. Menus vary daily. Notify of food allergies or dietary restrictions.

**Nearest Airport(s)**
Mobile, Alabama; Pensacola, Florida

**Directions**
From I-10, Exit 35 (Spanish Fort, Fairhope, Daphne): Head south on U.S. Hwy. 98E. Turn right onto Ryan Avenue just past mile marker 41 at corner with Mazda dealership. Go to the stop, then turn left onto Main Street (Scenic Hwy. 98). Our driveway is exactly 2/10 of a mile on the right around a curve. Follow long drive and signs to entrance.

# Lodge on Gorham's Bluff

🍽️ 🍽️ 🍽️

www.gorhamsbluff.com
101 Gorham Drive, Gorham's Bluff, Pisgah, AL 35765
**256-451-VIEW** • 256-451-8439 • Fax 256-451-7403
reservations@gorhamsbluff.com

*Member Since 2003*

*Alabama*

*Pisgah*

*"Gorham's Bluff smoothes the wrinkles of my soul."*
*"Beautiful room, glorious food, marvelous view!"*

General Manager
**Keith Izydore**

The Lodge on Gorham's Bluff is perched high on the bluffs overlooking the Tennessee River Valley. Although the atmosphere is one of mannered Southern charm, the daily routine is low-key and casual dress is encouraged. Furnished in an elegant, traditional country style, the Lodge suites are appointed with antiques, CD/DVD players, in-room snacks, luxurious his/her bathrobes, fine Egyptian cotton linens, feather mattresses, down pillows and remote-controlled fireplaces. Generously sized windows, multiple sets of French doors and private balconies bring the mountain-high views indoors. Amenities include hiking trails, biking, fishing, bird watching, a pool, a fitness center and seasonal events. The Lodge has been recognized by Condé Nast, and *Southern Living* magazine rated Gorham's Bluff as the most romantic destination in Alabama.

**Rates**
6 Suites $175/$210 per evening, double occupancy. Tax and service charge is additional. Number of Rooms: 6

**Cuisine**
A regionally inspired 4-course gourmet meal, prepared with only the freshest locally grown ingredients, is served in the candlelit dining room each evening. Room service available. Our chef will gladly accomodate individual dietary needs. Our full-service restaurant is also available for breakfast and lunch. Reservations are required, and additional charges apply.

**Nearest Airport(s)**
Chattanooga, TN and Huntsville, AL

**Directions**
Directions available on website and from the innkeeper.

# Alaska

Famous for: Glacier Bay, Mendenhall Glacier, Tongass National Forest, Admiralty Island, Grizzly Bears, Humpback Whales, Dog Mushing and World Class Fishing.

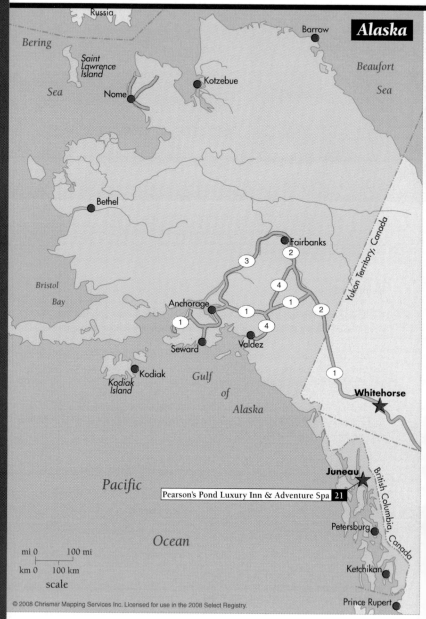

Russia

**Barrow**

## Alaska

Bering

Saint
Lawrence
Island

**Kotzebue**

Beaufort

Sea

**Nome**

Sea

**Bethel**

Bristol

Bay

**Fairbanks** ②

③

④

**Anchorage** ①

① ①

② Yukon Territory, Canada

**Seward** ④

**Valdez**

① **Whitehorse**

**Kodiak**

Kodiak
Island

Gulf

of

Alaska

Pacific

**Juneau** ★

Pearson's Pond Luxury Inn & Adventure Spa **21**

Ocean

mi 0          100 mi

km 0    100 km

scale

**Petersburg**

British Columbia, Canada

**Ketchikan**

**Prince Rupert**

SelectRegistry.com

# Pearson's Pond

www.pearsonspond.com
4541 Sawa Circle, Juneau, AK 99801
**907-789-3772**
book@pearsonspond.com

*Member Since 2005*

*Alaska Juneau*

*"The view of the Mendenhall Glacier from my hot tub will be imprinted on my mind forever... Expert trip planning by the best!... Scenic romantic retreat."*

Innkeepers/Owners
**Diane & Steve Pearson**

**Pearson's Pond Luxury Inn & Adventure Spa** is among Alaska's most picturesque and romantic retreats. Located in Juneau, Alaska's capital city, this relaxed eco mini-resort is tucked in the pristine rainforest and framed by the spectacular Mendenhall Glacier. Guest rooms feature romantic touches like double Jacuzzis, canopy beds, fireplaces and waterview balconies, while providing conveniences like kitchenettes, a well-stocked breakfast pantry and evening refreshments around the fire.

Pearson's is also a great outdoor getaway, and is staffed by adventure-travel specialists prepared to help you plan your escape to the healing calm of the Alaskan wilderness. For unstructured exploration, take a kayak or rowboat out on the lake, hike or bike to the glacier. At the end of the day, relax in the peaceful waterfall gardens, the ideal setting for a wedding, renewal or reception following vows taken atop a nearby glacier. Escape to Alaska and let Pearson's Pond take care of the details. Open year-round.

### Rates
5 Studios, 2 demi-suites w/fireplace, canopy bed, Wi-Fi, DVD, kitchenette, balcony,some w/whirlpool. $199/$499. Weekly & monthly rates. Flexible Breakfast, snacks, afternoon tea, hosted evening reception & unlimited Wi-Fi/laptop. Number of Rooms: 7

### Cuisine
Flexible self-serve extended continental. Fresh baked breads, healthy choices + eggs, cheese, or meat. Breakfast in bed, the Breakfast Nook, Alfresco on a deck or gazebo overlooking the glacier or waterfall.

### Nearest Airport(s)
Juneau International is 8 minutes by car, and a world apart.

### Directions
In Tongass National Forest, near Mendenhall Glacier and Juneau historic district, Glacier Bay National Park, Pack Creek National Monument. Minutes to adventures, attractions, Auke Bay ferry, Juneau airport and cruise dock. See website for specific directions.

# *Arizona*

Famous for: Grand Canyon, Painted Desert, Petrified Forest, Copper Mines, Gila Monster, Lake Mead (largest man–made lake in the world), Tombstone (Wyatt Earp's fight at the OK Corral), Cliff Dwellings.

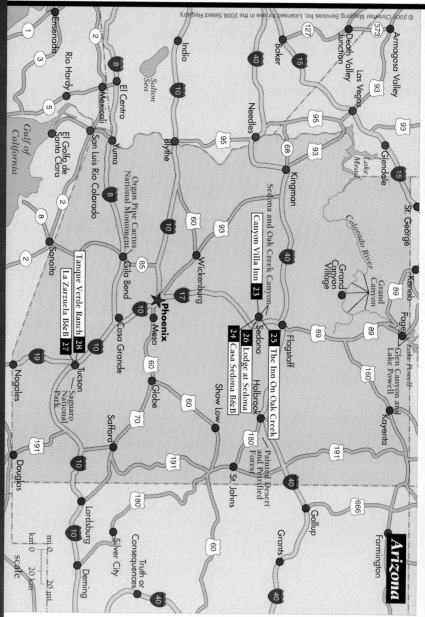

© 2008 Christart Mapping Services Inc. Licensed for use in the 2008 Select Registry.

Canyon Villa Inn  23

The Inn On Oak Creek  25
Lodge at Sedona  26
Casa Sedona B&B  24

Tanque Verde Ranch  28
La Zarzuela B&B  27

# Canyon Villa Bed & Breakfast Inn

www.canyonvilla.com
40 Canyon Circle Drive, Sedona, AZ 86351
**800-453-1166** • 928-284-1226 • Fax 928-284-2114
canvilla@sedona.net

*Member Since 1995*

*"One night is too short to stay in a place as wonderful as Canyon Villa. The views are as spectacular as the warm hospitality and ambiance."*

**Innkeepers/Owners**
**Les & Peg Belch**

Custom built as an elegant Bed & Breakfast Inn, Canyon Villa was designed to showcase the Red Rocks of Sedona from virtually every room in the inn. Guests enjoy unique views of such famous Red Rocks as Bell Rock, Courthouse Butte, Castle Rock, and Lee Mountain. Themed intimate guest rooms and large common areas open through arched French doors onto private balconies and lush garden patios. Guestrooms include cable TV, phone, radio, CD player, and some have gas-log fireplaces. Ceramic baths include jetted tubs and luxurious lounge robes. Guests relax daily in the warm Arizona sun by our salt water glass tiled swimming pool. Hike desert trails from the premises, and stargaze cool evenings outdoors by fireside. Ranked by TripAdvisor in their 2008 Awards as one of the Top Ten "Best Inns and B&Bs" in the U.S. Also a past recipient of the annual elite "Best U.S. Bed and Breakfast" award from Harper's *Hideaway Report*. Highly rated by Frommers and recommended by Exxon-Mobil Travel Guide. Awarded the AAA Four Diamond Award of Excellence for the past 16 consecutive years.

**Rates**
11 Rooms. Red Rock View Rooms $249/$349. Limited-View Room $199. Discounts available for AAA, AARP, and Slower Seasons. Number of Rooms: 11

**Cuisine**
Three course served breakfast, afternoon refreshments, and appetizers included. Coffee, tea, and original light deserts are available throughout the entire evening in the dining area. Guests welcome to bring their own spirits.

**Nearest Airport(s)**
Phoenix PHX

**Directions**
From I-17, use Exit 298 and go N on SR 179 for 8 mi. L on Bell Rock Blvd. After 1 block turn R on Canyon Circle Dr. The Inn is on the R. Please call for directions if arriving from SR 89-A.

# Casa Sedona Inn

www.casasedona.com
55 Hozoni Drive, Sedona, AZ 86336
**800-525-3756** • 928-282-2938 • Fax 928-282-2259
casa@sedona.net

*Arizona*

*Sedona*

*"The surroundings are spectacular, the garden relaxing, the stars are so bright each night from our balcony. Thanks for the memories."*

Innkeepers/Owners
**Paul & Connie Schwartz**
General Managers

Beautifully landscaped acre at the base of Sedona's highest peak, Thunder Mountain. Casa Sedona is an adobe style inn designed by a prot?g? of Frank Lloyd Wright featuring sun terraces with awe-inspiring 180-degree views, a large garden patio, and fountains. Recipient of the AAA 4-Diamond Award of Excellence for 10 years. Each room is unique: choose Contemporary Southwest to Cowboy style to Romantic! Enjoy the tranquil ambiance of the inn, its beautifully landscaped grounds, evening appetizers, a hot tub for stargazing, and bountiful breakfasts served in the garden, or fireside. Casa Sedona is only three miles from the town's center making it the perfect respite from the city just minutes from fine restaurants and shops. Luxury, elegance, privacy, and exceptional cuisine have guests returning time and time again. Featured by The Travel Channel on its "Best of the Best" series.

**Rates**
$189/$299. Amenities include gas fireplaces, king or queen beds, private baths, snuggly robes, whirlpool tubs, TV/VCR's, CD players, wireless Internet, balcony, or porch. Number of Rooms: 16

**Cuisine**
Two course breakfast. Late afternoon hor d'ouevres, beverages and homemade cookies. Guests are welcome to bring their own alcoholic beverages.

**Nearest Airport(s)**
Phoenix Sky Harbor

**Directions**
From Hwy. 89A, N onto Tortilla Dr. then L at the first stop sign (Southwest Dr). Immediate R onto Hozoni Dr.

# The Inn on Oak Creek

www.innonoakcreek.com
556 Hwy. 179, Sedona, AZ 86336
**800-499-7896** • 928-282-7896 • Fax 928-282-0696
theinn@sedona.net

*Member Since 2001*

*Arizona*

*Sedona*

*"This is the way all B&Bs ought to be. You've thought of everything. Thank you! Thank you!"*

Owner/Manager
**Jim Matykiewicz**

Initially built in 1972 as an art gallery, then totally refurbished and transformed in 1995, the Inn perches on a bluff overlooking Oak Creek, one of Arizona's premier year-round spring-fed streams. Within easy walking distance are Sedona's best art galleries, boutique shops, several fine restaurants and Tlaquepaque shopping village. Yet, almost as close, are National Forest trails that will take you to the heart of red rock country. So, while guests are constantly surprised that an Inn so centrally located in Sedona can offer such privacy and relaxation, the luxurious AAA Four Diamond accommodations, professional staff, and culinary delights (Five Star Food!) are what really please them.

### Rates
11 Rooms, $200/$295 DBL; 1 Suite, $350. All rooms feature private marble baths, whirlpool tubs, gas fireplaces, TV/VCR/HBO, Cable, data ports, luxurious bathrobes, hairdryers, phones. Creekside rooms have decks w/dramatic views. Number of Rooms: 11

### Cuisine
Full gourmet breakfast, afternoon beverages, cookies & hors d'oeuvres included. Guests are welcome to bring their own adult beverages. Cooking classes are conducted on Tuesday and Thursday evenings in the owner's quarters.

### Nearest Airport(s)
Flagstaff (40 minutes), Phoenix (2 hours)

### Directions
In Sedona proper on Hwy. 179 just 0.4 mile S of the intersection of Hwy 179 & Hwy 89A.

# The Lodge at Sedona

www.LODGEatSEDONA.com
125 Kallof Place, Sedona, AZ 86336
**800-619-4467** • 928-204-1942 • Fax 928-204-2128
Info@LODGEatSEDONA.com

*Member Since 2003*

*Arizona*

*Sedona*

---

*"The Lodge at Sedona - A Luxury Bed & Breakfast Inn, is a grand setting for Intimate Meetings and Retreats."*

---

Proprietors
**RJ Wachal**

"Romance and Intrigue, Comfort & Luxury, Escape and Adventure - the AAA Four Diamond Lodge at Sedona has it all."- AZ News. Elegant & Secluded Mission/Arts & Craft estate set on two acres of grand seclusion in the very heart of Sedona, Arizona. Awarded Top 10 Inns in US by Forbes.com, Best B&Bs by *Phoenix* Magazine. Recommended by Small Elegant Hotels, Historic Lodging Directory, *Bon Appetit*, Mobil Three Star, Fodors. com, and Frommer's. Close to hiking trails, biking, golf, tennis, galleries and shopping. Spectacular Red Rock views, sculpture gardens, fitness center priviledges and pools adjacent, fountains and a magical labyrinth. King suites with fireplaces, jet tubs, spa robes, large decks, stereo TV, DVD. Massage Services, complete concierge service and full gourmet breakfast and snacks included daily. "The Lodge at Sedona is one of the most romantic Inns in Arizona." - AZ Foothills Magazine.

### Rates
14 Rooms & King Suites: $189/$339 B&B; Kings w/ fireplaces, jet tubs, view decks, stereo TV/DVD. Hot Tubs available.Seasonal Specials Number of Rooms: 14

### Cuisine
Professionally prepared & served gourmet breakfast w/ Sedona Gold coffee & Lodge Granola w/ yogurt. Sunset appetizers, spring water & snacks included daily. Complimentary wine setups. Guest beverages welcome!

### Nearest Airport(s)
Phoenix (PHX) Flagstaff

### Directions
In W. Sedona at 125 Kallof Place, S off Hwy 89A, 2 mi. W of Hwy 179, a block W of Mountain Shadows Dr, or a block E of Coffee Pot Dr. in the very Heart of Sedona. Refer to map on website.

SelectRegistry.com

# La Zarzuela, A Bed & Breakfast Inn

www.zarzuela-az.com

455 No. Camino de Oeste, All Mail to-PO Box  86030, Tucson AZ 85754, Tucson, AZ  85745

**888-848-8225** • 520-884-4824 • Fax 520-903-2617     *Member Since 2004*

*"Exemplary. There simply are no superlatives big enough for the music, the beauty, the food and hospitality. A profoundly wonderful experience."*

Innkeepers/Owners
**Cliff Aberham, Lew Harper & Pauline Spurgiesz**

Imagine that you have a very well-to-do friend, with very good taste, who owns a large, private villa in the Tucson Mountains (think carefree). This friend, being a very good friend, offers you the use of the villa and its staff, who have been instructed to do anything your heart desires: arrange flights, limos, massages, dinner, whatever - anything to make you blissfully happy. That's La Zarzuela, "the operetta," in a nutshell. The Frank Lloyd Wright-inspired architecture resonates Southwestern culture, with scored concrete floors and walls painted in vibrant hues. With five lovely casitas, La Zarzuela is small enough to provide you the personal level of service we are committed to, yet large enough for the vacationer to meet new people, if you wish. Our new Sonoran Desert Terrace is perfect for small group functions and for the enjoyment of our guests.

**Rates**
5 Rooms. $275/$325. 3rd Person in a Rollaway add $75.00. All Casitas with private bathrooms, coffee maker, hair dryer, TV, DVD and CD Players, Balcony or Patio.  Number of Rooms: 5

**Cuisine**
Fresh coffee or tea ready at 7:00am in our pantry. A Full Gourmet Breakfast is Served at 8:00am in our Dining Room. Some guests may choose to have a Continental Breakfast served in their Casita.

**Nearest Airport(s)**
Tucson International Airport

**Directions**
Located in the mountains off Gates Pass only 10 min. from downtown Tucson's historical Presidio District & Convention Center. Refer to website for map & directions or call 884-4824

{||} {||} {||}

# Tanque Verde Ranch
www.tvgr.com
14301 East Speedway, Tucson, AZ 85748
**800-234-3833** • 520-296-6275 • Fax 520-721-9426
dude@tvgr.com

*Member Since 1970*

*Arizona*

*Tucson*

*Voted one of The Top Ten Family Resorts in North America
by The Travel Channel, March 2003!*

Innkeepers/Owners
**Robert and Rita Cote**

Founded on a Spanish land grant in 1868 in the spectacular Sonoran Desert, Tanque Verde Ranch has evolved into one of the Southwest's most complete vacation destinations. A 4-star quality resort, it maintains the cowboy traditions and spirit unique to this western cattle ranch. Sonoran-style with adobe walls, high saguaro rib ceilings, beehive fireplaces and mesquite corrals, the Ranch setting provides expansive desert and mountain views. The facilities are just as remarkable, with 140 horses, tennis courts, indoor/outdoor pools, saunas, spa, guided hiking, mountain biking, nature programs, children's program, outdoor BBQs, breakfast rides and more, in a casual relaxed atmosphere!

**Rates**
Nightly rates include room accommodations, three meals a day & all of the wonderful ranch activities! The Ranch offers 51 charming rooms and 23 spacious suites, is open year round and has three rate seasons. Rates vary by room type & number of people. Number of Rooms: 74

**Cuisine**
In addition to the activities, three delicious meals are included in the rate! Meals are served daily from 8:00-9:00 a.m., 12:00-1:30 p.m. and 6:30-8:00 p.m. 4-star quality, fully licensed.

**Nearest Airport(s)**
Tucson International

**Directions**
From Tucson, east on Speedway Blvd. to the dead-end, in the Rincon Mountain foothills.

{ SelectRegistry.com

# Arkansas

## "The Land of Opportunity"

Famous for: Natural Hot Springs, The Ozarks, Waterfalls, Diamonds, Oil, Aluminum

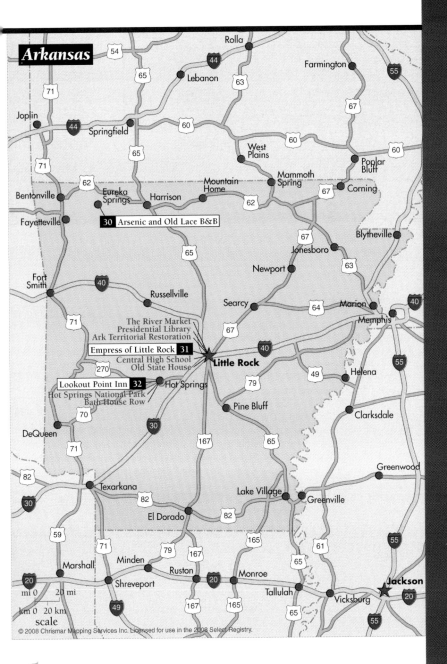

**Arkansas**

- 54
- Rolla
- 44
- Lebanon
- 63
- 65
- Farmington
- 55
- 71
- 67
- Joplin
- 44
- Springfield
- 60
- 65
- 60
- 60
- West Plains
- Poplar Bluff
- 71
- 62
- Mammoth Spring
- 60
- Eureka Springs
- Mountain Home
- 67
- Corning
- Bentonville
- Harrison
- 62
- Fayetteville
- **30** Arsenic and Old Lace B&B
- 67
- Blytheville
- 65
- Jonesboro
- Newport
- Fort Smith
- 40
- 63
- Russellville
- Searcy
- 64
- Marion
- 40
- 71
- 67
- Memphis
- The River Market
- Presidential Library
- Ark Territorial Restoration
- Empress of Little Rock **31**
- Central High School
- Old State House
- 270
- ★ **Little Rock**
- 40
- 49
- Helena
- 55
- Lookout Point Inn **32**
- Hot Springs
- 79
- Hot Springs National Park
- Bath House Row
- 70
- Pine Bluff
- Clarksdale
- DeQueen
- 30
- 167
- 65
- 71
- Greenwood
- 82
- Texarkana
- Lake Village
- Greenville
- 30
- 82
- El Dorado
- 82
- 59
- 165
- 61
- 55
- 71
- Minden
- 79
- 167
- 65
- Marshall
- Ruston
- Monroe
- ★ **Jackson**
- 20
- Shreveport
- 20
- 20
- mi 0   20 mi
- Tallulah
- Vicksburg
- km 0   20 km
- 49
- 167
- 165
- 65
- 55
- **scale**

# Arsenic and Old Lace B&B

www.eurekaspringsromancebb.com
60 Hillside Avenue, Eureka Springs, AR 72632
**866-350-5454** • 479-253-5454 • Fax 479-253-2246
arsenicoldlacebb@aol.com

*Member Since 2006*

*Arkansas*

*Eureka Springs*

*"We can't wait to get back to our Tree Top Paradise, Doug & Beverly and that wonderful little town...a summer weekend away is just calling our name."*

Innkeepers/Owners
**Beverly and Doug Breitling**

Arsenic and Old Lace is located on a heavily wooded hillside in the Historic District of Eureka Springs. The beautiful Ozark Mountains surround this step back to a quieter, more relaxed time. From our Morning Room, or the Chantilly Rose room balcony, guests enjoy the mixed white squirrels, birds, chipmunks and sometimes even deer. A Short walk through a wooded area will bring guests to the shops, historic homes and buildings of the Historic Loop. The mood of the Inn is relaxed luxury, as your hosts strive to make each guest feel as if they are at home. The relaxed feel continues to your room, where you will find comfortable furnishings, jetted tubs, luxury showers, televisions, VCR/DVD players, CD players and Wireless Internet access. Enjoy the video library to watch a movie, curl-up with a good book or your loved one. Relax, unwind. You've stepped back in time without leaving modern necessities. Treat all of your senses to unforgetable experiences!

**Rates**
$115/$259. Rates vary seasonally & midweek. Number of Rooms: 5

**Cuisine**
Enjoy custom blended coffee, tea or hot chocolate; our full gourmet breakfast starts with a delicious fruit course, breakfast breads or scones, & a unique main course. Enjoy homemade snacks all day & a well stocked refrigerator.

**Nearest Airport(s)**
NW Arkansas Regional (XNA)

**Directions**
Exit airport turn L on Hwy 264 to I-540. R on to I-540 S to US 412 exit. L on US 412 through Springdale AR then 18 mi. E on 412 to AR 45. L on AR 45 to AR 12. R on AR 12 to AR 23. L on 23 to Eureka Springs. Lost? Call 1-800-243-5223.

# The Empress of Little Rock

www.theempress.com
2120 Louisiana Street, Little Rock, AR 72206
**877-374-7966** • 501-374-7966 • Fax 501-375-4537
Email: hostess@theempress.com

*Member Since 2001*

*"In over 80 countries on 6 continents, The Empress is the very best B&B we have ever visited."*

Innkeepers/Owners
**Robert Blair and Sharon Welch-Blair**

Stay a century away in the award winning small luxury hotel, THE EMPRESS OF LIT-TLE ROCK. The Four Diamond quality boutique hotel, ranked as a top ten in the US, was built in 1888 as the largest most opulent mansion in Arkansas. Let your senses be lavished with the most modern spa amenities: hydro-massage therapy, steam, aromatherapy, antique Jacuzzi soaking tubs. Work a 1000 piece puzzle by the warmth of firelight in the parlor. Enjoy an elegant two course gourmet breakfast by candlelight in a dinning room fit for Her Majesty, the Queen. Ascend a magnificent double stairwell as Scarlett to the Chatelaine Suite where a night in a canopied featherbed will have you begging for more. If something slightly more daring peaks your interest, retire to the Hemingway Spa Suite with a 1940's "Mogambo" touch, a romantic escape to contemplate the next chapter in your life. Stroll thru the Secret Garden where the fountain drums and a romantic hammock beckons. Ah!!! The Empress?.where unrushed conversation abounds, along with true Southern Hospitality. Two blocks from the Governor's Mansion in the Quapaw Quarter Historic District.

## Rates
9 Rooms, 4 Spa Suites, 3 Mini-Suites, $135/$295 Featherbeds/Cable/DSL/Jacuzzi/Fireplaces Number of Rooms: 9

## Cuisine
Elegant-two course gourmet breakfast by candlelight served 'Before the Queen' w/Victorian pomp & circumstance & a "bow-tied butler". Gourmet coffee, snacks & mineral water available 24/7. Wine social hour & in room complimentary liqueur.

## Nearest Airport(s)
Little Rock

## Directions
From I-30, take I-630 W. Exit Main St. L on Main to 22nd St. R on 22nd-1 block. From Airport: I-440 W to I-30 E to I-630. Follow above directions. I-430: I-430 to I-630. Take Center St. exit thru light to Main to 22nd St.

# Lookout Point Lakeside Inn

www.lookoutpointinn.com
104 Lookout Circle, Hot Springs, AR 71913
**866-525-6155** • 501-525-6155 • Fax 501-525-5850
innkeeper@lookoutpointinn.com

*Member Since 2005*

*"A beautiful blend of water, architecture, comfort and style, Lookout Point embraces the very best of its natural surroundings." Southern Living 2005*

Innkeepers/Owners
**Kristie and Ray Rosset**

Enjoy peace and tranquility, comprehensive pampering and luxury. This newly constructed Arts & Crafts inn is located on the soothing waters of beautiful Lake Hamilton.

Experience an exceptional inn, with a fine attention to detail as its hallmark. Understated luxury invites relaxation, romance, and rejuvenation. The gardens with waterfalls and meditation labyrinth are perfect for small, intimate weddings. Canoe the bay, watch the birds, nap in the hammock, or soak in the nearby historic Hot Springs bathhouses. A well-stocked library and video collection, puzzles, and board games enhance the experience of simplifying life. Come relax, feast, and play!

New! A one or two bedroom lakeside condominium, called Lakeview Terrace, invites guests to enjoy the 36 ft. deck right at waters' edge. Perfect for a family to enjoy all of Hot Springs fun.

Named by National Geographic Traveler (4/08) as one of the Top 150 Hotels in North America & the Caribbean!

**Rates**
$137/$527. Corp. weekday rates available. Wedding, romance and girlfriend getaway packages available. Number of Rooms: 11

**Cuisine**
Fresh and hearty breakfast plus innkeeper's reception features dessert, cheese/crackers, wine & tea. Complimentary snack bar with coffee/tea available. Hot Springs bottled water en suite. Luncheons by reservation.

**Nearest Airport(s)**
Little Rock, 60 miles

**Directions**
From E: I-30 to US 70 (exit 111) to exit 6 (bypass to Mt. Ida). Go to AR Hwy 7 S (exit 4A). South on Hwy 7 3.5 mi. Watch for our blue highway sign, turn left at sign. From W: I-30 to AR Hwy 7 (exit 78). North 24.5 mi. R at blue highway sign.

# *Northern California*   **"The Golden State"**

Famous for: Spanish Missions, Gold Rush, Golden Gate Bridge, Wine Country, Citrus, Sequoia Redwoods, Hollywood, Disneyland, Lake Tahoe, Sierra Nevada, Yosemite National Park, Big Sur, Earthquakes and Death Valley,

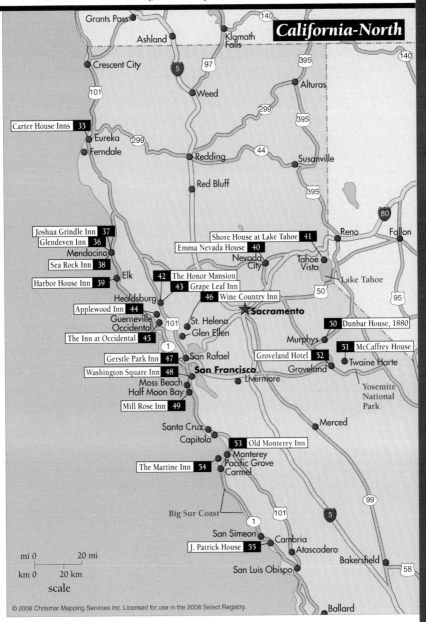

**California-North**

Grants Pass
Ashland
Klamath Falls
140
Crescent City
5
97
Weed
395
Alturas
101
299
395
Carter House Inns 35
Eureka
299
44
Susanville
Ferndale
Redding
Red Bluff
395
80
Reno
Fallon
Joshua Grindle Inn 37
Glendeven Inn 36
Shore House at Lake Tahoe 41
Mendocino
Emma Nevada House 40
Sea Rock Inn 38
Nevada City
Tahoe Vista
Elk
42 The Honor Mansion
Harbor House Inn 39
43 Grape Leaf Inn
Lake Tahoe
Healdsburg
46 Wine Country Inn
50
95
Applewood Inn 44
St. Helena
Sacramento
Guerneville
Occidental
101
Glen Ellen
50 Dunbar House, 1880
The Inn at Occidental 45
Murphys
51 McCaffrey House
1
Gerstle Park Inn 47
San Rafael
Groveland Hotel 52
Twaine Harte
Washington Square Inn 48
San Francisco
Groveland
Moss Beach
Livermore
Yosemite National Park
Half Moon Bay
Mill Rose Inn 49
Merced
Santa Cruz
Capitola
53 Old Monterey Inn
Monterey
The Martine Inn 54
Pacific Grove
Carmel
99
Big Sur Coast
101
5
1
San Simeon
Cambria
J. Patrick House 55
Atascadero
Bakersfield
58
San Luis Obispo
Ballard

mi 0        20 mi
km 0      20 km
scale

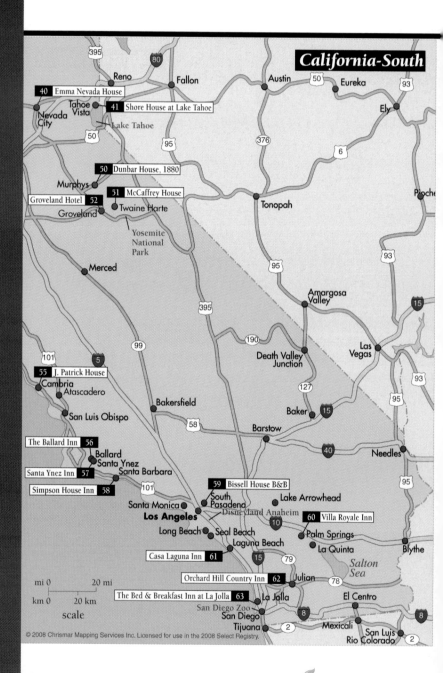

**California-South**

395
80
Reno
Fallon
Austin
50
Eureka
93

40 Emma Nevada House
Tahoe Vista
Ely
41 Shore House at Lake Tahoe
Nevada City
Lake Tahoe
50
95
376
6

50 Dunbar House, 1880

Murphys
51 McCaffrey House
Groveland Hotel 52
Twaine Harte
Tonopah
Pioche
Groveland

Yosemite National Park
95
93

Merced
Amargosa Valley
95
15

99
190
127
Death Valley Junction
Las Vegas
93

101
5
55 J. Patrick House
Cambria
Atascadero
395
Baker
15
95

San Luis Obispo
Bakersfield
Barstow
58

The Ballard Inn 56
Ballard
Santa Ynez
40
Needles

Santa Ynez Inn 57
Santa Barbara
Simpson House Inn 58
101
95

59 Bissell House B&B
Santa Monica
South Pasadena
Lake Arrowhead
**Los Angeles**
Disneyland Anaheim
60 Villa Royale Inn
Long Beach
Seal Beach
10
Palm Springs
Laguna Beach
La Quinta
Blythe

Casa Laguna Inn 61
15
79
*Salton Sea*

Orchard Hill Country Inn 62
Julian
78

The Bed & Breakfast Inn at La Jolla 63
La Jolla
El Centro
San Diego Zoo
8
8
San Diego
Tijuana
2
Mexicali
San Luis Rio Colorado
2

mi 0          20 mi
km 0      20 km
scale

© 2008 Chrismar Mapping Services Inc. Licensed for use in the 2008 Select Registry.

# Carter House Inns

🍽 🍽 🍷

www.carterhouse.com
301 L Street, Eureka, CA 95501
**707-444-8062** • 707-445-1390 • Fax 707-444-8067
reserve@carterhouse.com

*Member Since 2003*

*California*

*Eureka*

*"I'll never forget my stays at the Carter House Inns."*
*Lora Finnegan, Sunset Magazine*

**Innkeepers/Owners**
**Mark and Christi Carter**

Northern California's premier inn is an enclave of 3 magnificent Victorians perched along-side Humboldt Bay in Old Town Eureka. The luxurious accommodations at Carter House Inns and the sumptuous dining at its Restaurant 301 (considered among Northern California's best restaurants) set an indulgent tone for a marvelous visit to the giant redwood forests, rugged Pacific beaches and the other wonders of Northern California's Redwood Coast. Our accommodations and service are unparalleled; our award-winning cuisine is prepared w/local organic products and fresh herbs, greens, and vegetables harvested daily from the Inn's extensive gardens. The Inn also produces its own wine under the label Carter Cellars (WS 96 pts.) and Envy Wines, specializing in limited production cabs & merlots from some of the finest vineyards in Napa. Check out our incredible food and wine lovers' packages, featuring romantic dining and accommodations in the heart of the Redwood Empire! We offer Humboldt County's finest accommodations, an outstanding full-service restaurant, an online wine shop, and information about our scenic region in the heart of the Redwoods.

**Rates**
9 Rooms, $190/$380 B&B,2 Suites, $304/$612 B&B.Open year-round. Number of Rooms: 11

**Cuisine**
Full service award-winning restaurant open nightly, full breakfast, full bar, Wine Shop with 3,880 wine selections. With a recent 96-point rating from James Laube, Carter Cellars wine is quickly becoming a cult classic.

**Nearest Airport(s)**
Eureka-Arcata Airport is 16 miles north of Eureka.

**Directions**
From Highway 101 heading South turn right on L Street. From Highway 101 heading North turn left on L Street. The Inn is located on the corner of 3rd & L Street.

# Glendeven Inn

www.glendeven.com
8205 North Highway One, P.O. Box 914, Mendocino, CA 95460
**800-822-4536** • 707-937-0083 • Fax 707-937-6108
innkeeper@glendeven.com

*Member Since 2002*

*California*

*Little River*

> *"WOW! Glendeven far exceeded our expectations. In all aspects this is one of the most beautiful inns we've visited. The world needs more places like this."*

Proprietors
## John Dixon & Mike Roemmler

Named "One of the 10 best inns in America" by Country Inns magazine, this well appointed inn with its blend of fine antiques and contemporary art, offers wood burning fireplaces, ocean views, full in-room gourmet breakfasts, secluded patios & decks, featherbeds, and a wine and hors d'eouvres hour in the homestead's former barn. Glendeven is a serene, eight-acre, 1867 country estate situated on a headland meadow with grazing llamas, just minutes south of historic Mendocino. Right outside your door, you'll find walking trails to the headlands of the pounding Pacific, to the sand of Van Damme State Park beach, and to our own Forest Trail that takes you into a six-mile fern canyon walk along Little River. The first floor of the original barn of the property has been transformed into The Wine Bar[n] featuring tastings of local Mendocino county varietals in its comfortable garden and watertower-view lounge. The second and third floors comprise a 2,000 square foot vacation rental called The Barn Loft, perfect for couples traveling together. Glendeven's location provides easy access to the Mendocino village just 2 miles to the north, the cliff-side restaurants to the south, and easy access to the outdoor amenities of the area including cycling, river & ocean kayaking, golf, birding, and whale watching, to name a few.

**Rates**
Six rooms, 4 suites in the inn: $145/$300 B&B; King & Queen beds; 2-3 people per room.Open year-round. Number of Rooms: 10

**Cuisine**
Delicious homemade, hot, three-course breakfasts are brought to your room to begin the day.Complementary informal early evening gatherings in the Farmhouse living room with wine & hors d'oeuvres. Coffee, teas and homemade baked goods always available in the living room.

**Nearest Airport(s)**
Sacramento, Oakland and San Francisco

**Directions**
From San Francisco: Hwy 101 N to Hwy 128 W to Hwy 1 N; then 8.2 miles.

🪶 SelectRegistry.com

# Joshua Grindle Inn

www.joshgrin.com
P.O. Box 647, 44800 Little Lake Road, Mendocino, CA 95460
**800-474-6353** • 707-937-4143
stay@joshgrin.com

*Member Since 1996*

*"The hospitality, food & service are among the best we have experienced. Outstanding massage therapy." "No. 1 on TripAdvisor for good reason."*

Innkeepers/Owners
**Charles & Cindy Reinhart**

Experience Mendocino at its best. Our welcoming home sits atop a two-acre knoll overlooking the village and ocean. Park and forget about your car, as galleries, shops, restaurants and hiking trails are just a short stroll away. Tastefully decorated, comfortable, and exceptionally clean rooms await you. Charles and Cindy and our friendly staff will attend to your every need, and serve a full gourmet breakfast. Enjoy chatting with fellow guests over evening refreshments in our parlor, or escape to a private, quiet nook in our gardens. Relax on our front veranda and watch the whales spout in the distance. AAA Four Diamond and Mobil Three Star rated.

**Rates**
10 Rooms Main House, Cottage, Water Tower, $189/$279 B&B. 2 Ocean View, 2 bdrm, Guest Houses $400/++. Number of Rooms: 10

**Cuisine**
Full gourmet breakfast served to inn guests using fresh local ingredients. The highly regarded Cafe Beaujolais is just a two-block stroll from the Inn. Wineshop on premises with selection of premium Mendocino wines. Complimentary wine in room & Cream Sherry in Parlor.

**Nearest Airport(s)**
Little River Airport, Oakland International, San Francisco International, Sonoma

**Directions**
From San Francisco, take Hwy. 101 N to Hwy. 128 West to Hwy. 1 N. From Hwy. 1 turn west onto Little Lake Road. First driveway on your right.

# Sea Rock Inn

www.searock.com

11101 Lansing Street, PO Box 906, Mendocino, CA 95460

**800-906-0926** • 707-937-0926 • Fax 707-676-9008

innkeeper@searock.com

*Member Since 2005*

---

*"Sipping wine-relaxing fireside in our room watching waves crash on the shore...authentic and special inn...we'll cherish all the great memories forever."*

*Three Diamond Award*

**Innkeepers/Owners**
**Andy and Susie Plocher**

One of the few inns in Mendocino with ocean views from every hillside accommodation, The Sea Rock Inn beckons with crashing surf and inviting firelit rooms. From your suite or cottage you will experience the true beauty of the Mendocino Coast with spectacular panoramic views of the ocean and dramatic rocky cliffs of the Mendocino Headlands State Park. The setting is perfect for a memorable getaway. Hand hewn wood treatments accent luxuriously comfortable coastal contemporary design and appointments of virtually every amenity imaginable. Stroll through colorful gardens, curl up by the fire or relax on your deck and watch the sunset from your private oceanview cottage or suite. Hiking trails abound nearby, as does ocean and river kayaking, canoeing and many other outdoor actvities. Gourmet dining is a short walk or minute's drive away, and the charming village of Mendocino is a National Historic Register community laden with special shops and attractions. Great rooms, stunning views and nice people...The Sea Rock Inn.

---

**Rates**
6 Cottages, 4 Jr.Suites, 4 Suites. $179/$395. Number of Rooms: 14

**Cuisine**
Guests enjoy an attractive breakfast buffet with daily changing quiche, hard boiled eggs, yogurt, fresh pastries, juices, fruit and more. Upon check in to the room, guests may relax with a complimentry split of fine local wine.

**Nearest Airport(s)**
SFO or Oakland, 3 1/2 hrs

**Directions**
From SF area take Hwy 101 north to Hwy 128 West (scenic) at Cloverdale-Turn right onto Hwy 1 at ocean & go north (scenic) 10 mi to Mendocino. Turn left on Little Lake Rd & make a right on Lansing - inn is 1/3 mi ahead on right.

# Harbor House Inn by the Sea

www.theharborhouseinn.com
P.O. Box 369, 5600 S. Highway, Elk, CA 95432
**800-720-7474** • 707-877-3203 • Fax 707-877-3452
innkeeper@theharborhouseinn.com

*Member Since 1975*

*"This inn has it all: views, elegant rooms, and meals that alone make the trip worthwhile."*

Innkeeper/Owner
**Edmund Jin & Eva Lu**

Built in 1916, the Harbor House is at the throne of the Redwood Empire, standing vigil on a cliff overlooking Greer wood Cove with its spectacular rock formations and powerful surf. Pathways meander through magnificent seaside gardens and lead to the private beach below. The drama continues throughout the Inn's ten guest rooms, its stately sitting room, and breathtaking ocean-view dining room. Refurbished with luxury in mind, the Inn features antique and classic appointments throughout. Creative California cuisine, fresh daily. *Wine Spectator* 'Award of Excellence.' Prix-fixe four-course dinner included. Distinctive lodging, fine dining and timeless luxury; only three hours from San Francisco.

**Rates**
10 Rooms (6 in Main House, 4 Cottages) $300/$475 MAP.
Open year-round. Number of Rooms: 10

**Cuisine**
Dramatic ocean-view dining. Full breakfast and highly rated 4-course gourmet dinner included in rates. Extensive wine cellar featuring local and international selections.

**Nearest Airport(s)**
Santa Rosa, San Francisco, Oakland

**Directions**
From San Fancisco take 101 N, in Cloverdale take Hwy. 128 W to Hwy. 1, S 5 miles to Elk.

# Emma Nevada House

www.emmanevadahouse.com
528 East Broad Street, Nevada City, CA 95959
**800-916-3662** • 530-265-4415 • Fax none
mail@emmanevadahouse.com

*Member Since 2006*

*California*

*Nevada City*

*"Susan is a world-class chef and baker, and the usual B&B breakfast fare was nowhere to be found at this gourmet oasis."*

Innkeepers/Owners
**Andrew & Susan Howard**

Enjoy Nevada City's four seasons of food, wine and art in California's best-preserved gold country town. Our welcoming home sits in a quiet enclave of unique and elegant Victorians, just on the edge of the most beautiful town in the Sierra Foothills. Park and forget your car, as the historic allure of Nevada City is just a short stroll away. Beyond the fascinating shops, galleries and history, there are also trails alongside boiling river rapids, and nineteen unique and interesting wineries to visit. All this is capped by a proliferation of exceptional restaurants that will delight even the most cosmopolitan of travelers. It is not uncommon to hear favorable comparisons to the most notable restaurants of San Francisco and the Napa Valley. At the Emma Nevada House, you will find large and comfortable rooms characterized by their fine linens, exceptional cleanliness and thoughtful touches. Wrap around porches, beautiful gardens, and a babbling brook invite guests to linger and unwind in this graceful retreat.

**Rates**
$179/$239   Number of Rooms: 6

**Cuisine**
Guests enjoy a sit down three course breakfast that many guests say is worth the trip by itself. Menus are seasonal, with variations on fluffy soufflés and fruit or berry stuffed French toast as frequent choices.

**Nearest Airport(s)**
Sacramento, Reno, San Francisco & Oakland

**Directions**
From Sacramento Take Interstate 80 north to Auburn, then Highway 49 north to the Broad Street exit in Nevada City. Go left on Broad Street and up the hill. We are on the right.

# Shore House at Lake Tahoe

www.shorehouselaketahoe.com
7170 North Lake Blvd., P.O. Box 499, Tahoe Vista, CA 96148
**800-207-5160** • 530-546-7270 • Fax 530-546-7130
innkeeper@shorehouselaketahoe.com

*Member Since 2000*

California
Tahoe Vista

*"The views, the hospitality, the breakfasts, who could ask for more?"*

Innkeepers/Owners
**Barb & Marty Cohen**

The Shore House is the ultimate romantic getaway at the water's edge of spectacular Lake Tahoe. Balconies in front of each room offer fabulous views of the pristine lake and mountains. Relax in the large outdoor lakefront hot tub. Enjoy fine lakefront restaurants, art galleries, and casinos close by. This winter wonderland offers world class downhill and x-c skiing at 29 resorts, ice skating, snowmobiling, and sleigh rides. Summer activities include spectacular hiking, biking, golf, tennis, rafting, parasailing, and lunch cruises on the Shore House 36' cabin cruiser, *Lady of the Lake*. Kayak right from the Shore House. Enjoy a romantic couples' massage in the on site massage studio overlooking the Lake and Mountains. The Shore House specializes in intimate lakefront weddings with marriage license and Minister on site. Wedding and Honeymoon Packages are also offered.

**Rates**
All King or Queen Rooms, $190-$310. Each room has a gas log fireplace, custom-built log furnishings, down comforter, featherbed,and TV. All private baths, most with whirlpool tubs. Number of Rooms: 9

**Cuisine**
Award-winning gourmet breakfasts, wine and appetizers served daily in lakefront dining room or in lakeside gardens. Walk to extraordinary lakefront restaurants.

**Nearest Airport(s)**
Reno International

**Directions**
Take Hwy 80E from San Francisco or 80W from Reno. Take Exit 188B onto Hwy 267 towards Kings Beach & North Lake Tahoe. Turn R on Hwy 28 (N Lake Blvd.). Go 3/4 mile to the Shore House at 7170 N Lake Blvd.

# The Honor Mansion

www.honormansion.com
14891 Grove Street, Healdsburg, CA 95448
**800-554-4667** • 707-433-4277 • Fax 707-431-7173
innkeeper@honormansion.com

*California*

*Healdsburg*

*"Far more than 'First Class'-it's more like 'World Class.'" "Consistent Perfection." "Simply Outstanding." "Fabulous!" "Better than Perfection."*

Owners
## Steve & Cathi Fowler

A Resort Inn...let us pamper you! Built in 1883, this luxuriously comfortable Resort awaits your arrival. Imagine "World-class" amenities and service with hometown hospitality. Spa Services, Pool, Tennis, PGA Putting Green, Bocce, Competition Croquet lawn, Decks, Fountains and Walking Gardens, situated on more than three acres of landscaped grounds, yet a pleasant walk to the downtown square which is replete with terrific shops, bakeries and restaurants. The perfect "special" occasion get-away. Romantic and private. Located in Healdsburg at the confluence of the world-renowned wine growing appellations of Dry Creek, Alexander and Russian River Valleys, with over 100 wineries. Come enjoy our passion for this incredible area and discover some of our boutique wineries, as well as those that have been here for over 100 years. Our fully trained concierge staff is at your service. Plan day trips, picnics, get that special "private" wine tour in some of the world's best wineries right in our back yard. You will never want to leave!

### Rates
13 Rooms, $230/$600, 2 guests per rm. K & Q beds, fireplaces, soaking tubs, garden spa tubs, private decks, rm service menu, comp. resort grounds. Number of Rooms: 13

### Cuisine
Full gourmet breakfast buffet, as well as room service menu, complimentary evening wine and appetizers, sherry, cappuccino machine, & bottomless cookie jar.

### Nearest Airport(s)
Oakland and San Francisco

### Directions
From the South: Take Hwy 101 North to Healdsburg. Take the Dry Creek exit to the R for 1 block, turn R on Grove St. We are the first white picket fence on the R. From the North: Take Hwy 101 South to the Dry Creek exit; go L.

# Grape Leaf Inn

www.grapeleafinn.com
www.grapeleafinn.com, 539 Johnson Street, Healdsburg, CA 95448
**866-433-8140** • 707-433-8140 • Fax 707-433-3140
info@grapeleafinn.com

*Member Since 2004*

*"The Wine Country's beautiful Grape Leaf Inn combines the luxury and amenities of a chic boutique hotel with the romantic charm of a B&B."*

*California*

*Healdsburg*

Innkeepers/Owners
**Richard & Kae Rosenberg**

Surrounded by century-old evergreens and lush award-winning gardens, this luxury wine country Inn is tucked away on a quiet historic street, a short walk from fine shops and restaurants. A ten minute drive takes you to more than 104 world-class wineries and the most picturesque countryside imaginable. This highly acclaimed B&B combines the gracious hospitality of a country inn with meticulous service, fine cuisine and 12 luxurious accommodations. Stylish, contemporary decor paired with timeless antiques meld to create the best of California Wine Country style. The relaxing ambience, attentive staff, and its unmistakable romance have made this B&B one of the most sought after small luxury inns in the Wine Country. The 12 rooms and three cottages, most with king beds, have TV, DVD, CD, Internet wireless service, plush, down bedding and fine pressed linens. Many rooms have fireplaces and phones. Most baths offer two-person spa tubs, and one has a two-person steam shower and Japanese soaking tub. All have Frette linens and Aveda bath amenities.

### Rates
17 Rooms. $265/$575. Number of Rooms: 17

### Cuisine
Breakfast is an exquisite culinary experience, not just another morning meal. From freshly ground coffee to the 4-course gourmet breakfast created from the freshest local produce and herbs grown in our gardens--all is prepared with imaginative flair by the owners/chefs to create a delicious start to your day. Join us nightly in our "Speakeasy" wine cellar, hidden behind a bookcase, for award-winning local wines and cheeses.

### Nearest Airport(s)
SFO and OAK

### Directions
See our website for directions from anywhere.

# Applewood Inn

www.applewoodinn.com
13555 Hwy 116, Guerneville, CA 95446
**800-555-8509** • 707-869-9093 • Fax 707-869-9170
stay@applewoodinn.com

*Member Since 2004*

> *"We have stayed at 3 other B&Bs in the wine country and keep comparing them to Applewood. We just need to stick with the one we love best."*

Owners
**James Caron & Darryl Notter**

A lovely and verdant meadow guarded by towering Redwoods in the heart of Sonoma's Russian River Valley (one of the world's premier growing regions for Pinot Noir & Chardonnay grapes) is home to Applewood Inn and its acclaimed restaurant which is reccommended by both the Zagat and Michelin Dining Guides. Splashing fountains and whimsical statues add texture and interest to the terraced courtyard and gardens that separate the tiled roofed and stuccoed villas of this gracious Mediterranean complex. The old-world atmosphere of a "Gentleman's Farm" is evoked in lovingly maintained orchards and kitchen gardens that supply the restaurant through the Summer and early Fall. Gourmet picnic baskets provided by Applewood's kitchen help make a day of exploring the wine country and dramatic Sonoma Coast all the more enjoyable while Day Spa services add a touch of indulgent pampering. Located within a short drive of wineries in both the Napa and Sonoma Valleys, the Sonoma coast and Armstrong State Redwood Reserve.

**Rates**
$195/$345 Number of Rooms: 19

**Cuisine**
The 4 1/2 star restaurant @ Applewood offers Mediterranean inspired wine country fare paired with an award winning Sonoma County wine list. The inn's romantic dining room features 2 fireplaces & lovely views over a garden courtyard & towering redwoods. Advanced reservations suggested.

**Nearest Airport(s)**
San Francisco/Oakland

**Directions**
Hwy. 101 N from San Francisco to the River Road exit past Santa Rosa. W on River Road 15 mi. to traffic signal @ Guerneville. Turn L at signal, cross Russian River & proceed 1/2 mi. to the inn.

SelectRegistry.com

# Inn at Occidental

www.innatoccidental.com
3657 Church Street, P.O. Box 857, Occidental, CA 95465-0857
**800-522-6324** • 707-874-1047 • Fax 707-874-1078
innkeeper@innatoccidental.com

*Member Since 1995*

*California*

*Occidental*

> *"Simply everything you want at a Country Inn" - Recommended Country Inns.*
> *"Great to be back!! Just as beautiful as the last time."*

Innkeepers/Owners
**Jerry & Tina Wolsborn**

**Inn at Occidental of Sonoma Wine Country**--according to *The Wine Spectator*, "One of the Top Five Wine Country Destinations."

The antiques, original art and decor provide charm, warmth and elegance exceeded only by the hospitality you experience. "Tops our List as the Most Romantic Place to Stay" is what *Bride and Groom* said of the featherbeds, down comforters, spa tubs for two, fireplaces and private decks. The gourmet breakfast and evening wine and cheese reception add to a memorable experience. Excellent boutique wineries, nearby Armstrong Redwoods State Reserve, Russian River, the dramatic coast and scenic drives along country backroads make for a great destination. Hiking, biking, horseback riding and golfing nearby. All reasons why *AAA VIA* says of The Inn "The Best Bed and Breakfast in the West." An *Andrew Harper* Recommendation.

**Rates**
3 Suites, 13 Rooms: Fireplaces, Spa Tubs, Decks $209/$359, 2 BR Vacation House $679. Number of Rooms: 18

**Cuisine**
Full gourmet breakfast. Local wines, cheeses and hors d'oeuvres nightly. Nightly sweets. Concierge service. Wonderful dining nearby. Special Functions: Wedding, Corporate Retreat, Wine Seminar/Dinner.

**Nearest Airport(s)**
San Francisco (SFO), Oakland (OAK)

**Directions**
From San Francisco (101-N) exit at Rohnert Park/Sebastopol. Take 116-W for 7.4 mi to Sebastopol. Turn left onto Bodega Hwy for 6.4 mi, turn Right onto Bohemian Hwy thru town of Freestone for 3.7 mi to Occidental. At 4-way stop, turn right to Inn's parking.

# The Wine Country Inn
www.winecountryinn.com
1152 Lodi Lane, St. Helena, CA 94574
**888-465-4608** • 707-963-7077 • Fax 707-963-9018
romance@winecountryinn.com

*"This stay was simply outstanding. The facilities are wonderful and the staff has been great!!"*

Innkeeper
**Jim Smith**

For over thirty years, three generations of Ned and Marge Smith's family have been welcoming guests to this little slice of Heaven. The stone and wood Wine Country Inn is a tranquil and hidden oasis in the heart of the Napa Valley, America's center for fine wine and eclectic dining. The tree-lined drive, welcoming common room and friendly greeting set the mood for a memorable experience. Smells of freshly baked granola or evening cookies raise expectations of meals to come. Then with the antique-filled guest rooms, panoramic vineyard views, lush gardens, sun-drenched pool with warming hot tub and massage tent almost in the vineyards, guests find it hard to leave the property. But for those who do, the Smiths and their staff are eager to help map out truly memorable days of sampling the finest the area has to offer. At the end of the day guests gather with the innkeepers to compare experiences over more great wine and tables laden with homemade appetizers. To increase enjoyment the Inn offers a Free Evening Restaurant Shuttle servicing twelve of the finest area restaurants as well as guided day-tours they call Inn-Cursions.

**Rates**
20 Rooms 4 Suites 5 luxury cottages. Rates are $220/$610 Off-season and $285/$680 Harvest Season. All rates include a full buffet breakfast, wine social in the afternoon and evening restaurant shuttle. Call for seasonal special packages. Number of Rooms: 29

**Cuisine**
Innovative egg dishes, fresh fruit, juices, home-made granola and nut-breads as well as a fun bagel/waffle bar. Family-recipe appetizers with great local wines in afternoon.

**Nearest Airport(s)**
Sacramento or San Fran

**Directions**
From San Francisco take I-80 (E) to Hwy. 37 follow signs to Napa (Hwy. 29N) 18 miles N to St. Helena. 2 miles N to Lodi Lane R on Lodi 1/3 mile. .

# Gerstle Park Inn

www.gerstleparkinn.com
34 Grove St., San Rafael, CA 94901
**800-726-7611** • 415-721-7611 • Fax 415-721-7600
innkeeper@gerstleparkinn.com

*Member Since 1998*

*California*

*San Rafael*

> "Elegant, yet not stuffy - Marin County enchantment - Really, just lovely - Impeccable in every way - Beyond exquisite - Lovely luxury and attention."

Owners
## Jim & Judy Dowling

Located 15 minutes from the Golden Gate Bridge and 30 minutes from the wine country, the Inn is in the heart of beautiful Marin County. It is the perfect location from which to explore all of the points of interest in the San Francisco Bay area. The Inn has a country setting on several acres with an orchard, a grove of Redwood trees, giant Valley Oaks, Cedar trees and green lawns. Being located at the end of a quiet residential street and backing up to the county open spaces, it creates a secluded, restful environment as if being in the wine country. The historic estate offers a breathtaking example of comfortable elegance and refinement. In the evening, relax on the veranda during wine hour, play croquet, or pick fruit from the orchard. Also, hike in the woods that border the estate. In the morning, enjoy a full hot breakfast to order at your leisure on the veranda or in the breakfast room. Spacious guest rooms are plush in comfort and color, with fine fabrics, antiques, parlor areas and private decks or patios with beautiful views. There is nothing like this in Marin County.

**Rates**
12 Rooms, 4 with Jacuzzi tubs; Cottages and Carriage House Suites with kitchens $189/$245. Open year-round. Meeting facilities up to 20 people conference style. Number of Rooms: 12

**Cuisine**
Accommodations include & extensive breakfast menu offering a full hot breakfast cooked to your order during a two hour period. Self service wine hours in the evening & 24 hour kitchen privileges which include a variety of beverages & snacks.

**Nearest Airport(s)**
SFO-San Francisco and OAK-Oakland A.P., 45 min.

**Directions**
Hwy-101, Exit Central San Rafael, West on 4th St, Left on D St., Right on San Rafael Ave, Left on Grove St. 34 Grove St.

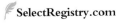

# Washington Square Inn

www.wsisf.com
1660 Stockton Street, San Francisco, CA 94133
**800-388-0220** • 415-981-4220 • Fax 415-397-7242
info@wsisf.com

*Member Since 2006*

> *"As a member of Select Registry, it's almost a guarantee of a great stay. This inn is no exception. Location is fabulous; quiet, near the best restaurants."*

Proprietors
**Maria & Daniel Levin**

Ideally situated in the very heart of San Francisco's legendary North Beach, the Washington Square Inn welcomes its guests with the charm and comfort of a small European hotel. Whether traveling for business or recreation, you will find some of the amenities offered include free wireless Internet access, complimentary breakfast, afternoon tea, evening wine & hors d'oeuvres, and full office services. Rooms feature European antiques, cable TV, soft robes & private baths. Some rooms have sitting areas in bay windows; others offer a cozy atmosphere with fireplaces. Located in the vibrant neighborhood of North Beach-just voted as one of the top ten neighborhoods in the US,our historic hotel boasts beautiful views of Coit Tower, Russian Hill, Washington Square Park & the Cathedral of Saint Peter & Paul. The Inn is one of the best San Francisco hotel deals available, offering exemplary lodging & service. As our guest,you'll have a great location from which to explore one of the most beautiful and exciting cities in the world! It's just a short cable car ride or comfortable walk to some of the most famous San Francisco landmarks.

**Rates**
$179/$329. Number of Rooms: 15

**Cuisine**
Includes breakfast & wine & hors d'oeuvres. Guests will be pleased to discover that the neighborhood has a high concentration of the very best restaurants.

**Nearest Airport(s)**
San Francisco,Oakland,San Jose

**Directions**
From SFO: Take ramp onto US 101 N toward San Francisco & follow US 101 for 8.4 mi. Follow I-280 exit toward Port of SF for 3.2 mi. L on ramp at King St. .9 mi. L on to 3rd Street for approx. .9 mi. 3rd Street becomes Kearny St for the next .7 mi. Bear L onto Columbus Ave for .3 mi. Bear R onto Stockton St for about .1 mi. & Inn will be on the R at the corner of Filbert St.

*48*

# Mill Rose Inn

www.millroseinn.com
615 Mill Street, Half Moon Bay, CA 94019
**800-900-7673** • 650-726-8750 • Fax 650-726-3031
info@millroseinn.com

*Member Since 2008*

*California*

*Half Moon Bay*

*"Wow! I've traveled all over the world and your inn is one of the best, you've thought of everything - don't change a thing! We will be back."*

Innkeepers/Owners
**Eve & Terry Baldwin**

For guests who expect extraordinary personal service, warm hospitality and meticulous attention to detail, the Mill Rose Inn of Half Moon Bay is a destination not to be missed. This award-winning boutique Inn is renowned for an exuberant garden of year round color, sinfully comfortable rooms and suites, decadent culinary treats and an easy five-minute walk to beaches, numerous shops, galleries and restaurants of vibrant Half Moon Bay. The Mill Rose Inn invites you to relax and be pampered for a night or two in the comfortable luxury of an English country garden by the sea. The innkeepers and their staff welcome you into a world of tranquility and romance. Ideally located 30 minutes south of San Francisco and 45 minutes north of the heart of Silicon Valley on the breathtakingly beautiful California coast, the Inn is the perfect venue for a special celebration, a reunion, or a business meeting, as well as an elegant garden wedding and reception. A Mill Rose Inn massage treatment coupled with our spa enhances your total escape. Owned and operated since 1982. Four-diamond AAA rating since 1992.

**Rates**
$175/$360 per night. Number of Rooms: 6

**Cuisine**
Our Lavish gourmet champagne or breakfast with vegan options served to you in your room or dining room gets rave reviews from all our guests. Fresh and homemade emphasized!

**Nearest Airport(s)**
We are 30 minutes from San Francisco International and 45 minutes from Oakland International and San Jose International.

**Directions**
Take Highway 92 westbound to Half Moon Bay. Turn left on Main Street (the first stop light). Turn right on Mill Street (the second stop sign). The Mill Rose Inn is at the end of the block on the right side of the street. GPS coordinates: 37.4647780 -122.4305870

# Dunbar House, 1880

www.dunbarhouse.com
271 Jones Street, Murphys, CA 95247
**800-692-6006** • 209-728-2897 • Fax 209-728-1451
innkeep@dunbarhouse.com

*Member Since 2001*

*California*

*Murphys*

*"The crackling fire was very warm & cozy. Our bed was like sleeping on a cloud. Your staff, breakfast, & yummy goodies made us feel right at home."*

Innkeepers/Owners
**Arline & Richard Taborek**

Step into Dunbar House, 1880 and step back into a piece of history, where homes were beautifully decorated with a casual elegance. This Italianate home is filled with Old World Charm, and offers guests a private haven of relaxation, comfort and ease. Located two hours east of San Francisco, nestled between Lake Tahoe and Yosemite in the Sierra foothills, Murphys remains much the same as it was during the Great Gold Rush. The village is just steps across the bridge over Murphys Creek, and offers fine dining, galleries, wineries, seasonal events, and live theatre. Our lovingly tended historic rose garden and surrounding floral gardens are the jewels of our property. Water fountains and lush greenery abound, surrounded by a white picket fence with many private sitting areas. Get a good book, or take a long nap in our hammock for that ultimate, lazy afternoon. An appetizer plate and local bottle of wine await guests in their rooms each day. Grab a fresh baked cookie, a cup of hot chocolate, or a glass of Rosemary Lemonade, Iced Tea, Sherry or Port, and just sit on our veranda, and watch the world go by.

### Rates
3 Rooms, $190/$260; 2 Suites, $250/$280. TV, DVD, wireless internet, phone, refrigerator, fireplace & AC. Some rooms have private porch & 2 person Jacuzzi. Number of Rooms: 5

### Cuisine
Candlelit breakfast graced w/edible flowers served in dining room by the fire, in the rose garden, or in the privacy of the guest's room.

### Nearest Airport(s)
SFO, SAC, SJC

### Directions
San Francisco: 580 E to Tracy to 205 E to 99 N to Stockton, exit on Hwy. 4 E (Farmington), to Angels Camp. 49 S to Hwy. 4 E again. 9 mi. to Murphys. L at Main St. L at Jones St.

# McCaffrey House

www.mccaffreyhouse.com
23251 Highway 108, P.O. Box 67, Twain Harte, CA 95383
**888-586-0757** • 209-586-0757
innkeeper@mccaffreyhouse.com

*Member Since 2004*

*California*

*"...set off the main road, among trees that reached halfway to heaven...you could leave the windows open and hear the trees whisper. It's a great place!" Al Martinez, columnist - Los Angeles Times*

*Twain Harte*

### Innkeepers/Owners
**Michael & Stephanie McCaffrey**

Pure elegance...in a wilderness setting. This AAA Four Diamond Inn is a delightfully warm and enchanting mountain lodge nestled in the quiet forest hollow of the High Sierras - near Yosemite National Park. Guestrooms are artfully decorated and feature handmade Amish quilts, fire stoves, private bath, TV/VCR, CD players plus exquisite views of the forest that envelops the Inn. McCaffrey House was designed and built by your hosts, Michael and Stephanie McCaffrey. They had one essential theme in mind: refined luxury blended with comfort and modern convenience. General gathering areas are spacious and beautifully decorated, with a fascinating collection of furniture and art acquired by Michael and Stephanie during their extensive travels. All appointments have such a welcoming touch that they extend an invitation to come often and stay a while. In the summer months breakfast is served on the decks which surround the Inn. Enjoy the romance of this mountain lodge, the pleasure of a family vacation, take over the Inn for a reunion or business meeting, schedule a wedding or winemaker dinner...take in the views of the pristine forest, diverse birds and wildlife, rays of sunshine or snowflakes in flight.

### Rates
$139/$200  Number of Rooms: 8

### Cuisine
Awaken to the aroma of fresh brewed coffee. Relax in the beautifully decorated dining room for a full country breakfast, prepared by Stephanie McCaffrey, a master of the culinary arts. Enjoy fresh fruits and juices, hot entres like Italian Eggs, Potatoes, Muffins, Scones, Decadent Bread Pudding, delicious egg casseroles and quiches.

### Nearest Airport(s)
Sacramento Airport

### Directions
11 mi. E of Sonora and one-half mi. above the E. Twain Harte exit on Highway 108. 3 hour drive from San Francisco; 2 from Sacramento; 3 from San Jose; 3 from Monterey area; 5 from LA.

# Groveland Hotel

www.groveland.com
18767 Main Street, P.O. Box 289, Groveland, CA 95321
**800-273-3314** • 209-962-4000 • Fax 209-962-6674
guestservices@groveland.com

*Member Since 2005*

*California*

*Groveland*

*"Most Comfortable Bed I've EVER slept in."* - Bill Bruzy - New Texas
Magazine *"The cuisine is exquisite."* - Elizabeth Kennedy - SF Chronicle

Innkeepers/Owners
**Peggy and Grover Mosley**

Wine Spectator
AWARD
OF
EXCELLENCE

Drive to Yosemite 24/7 - take a picnic and great bottle of wine from our restaurant.
We have it all! Tuolumne Whitewater Rafting, a US Top 10 River, over 100 species of
wildflowers, hiking, golf, tennis, stables, swim at Rainbow Pool or discover God's Bath
on the Clavey River. Four seasons - Spring, with songbirds, incredible flowers and North
America's tallest waterfall. Summer's roses, hydrangeas, lavender and balmy evenings to
herald Fall's brilliant color and crispness in the air. Winter temps suggest hot cider, cozy fireplaces, toboggans, snowshoes and skis. Lots of wildlife - deer, squirrel, possum, skunk, rac-
coon, fox, coyote, cougar, and an occasional bear. Feathered species offer a wide variety of
birds, and an occasional eagle. *Country Inns* Magazine named it one of the US Top 10 Inns,
and *Sunset* Magazine called it 'One of the West's Best Inns.' Romantic parlour dining with
fireplace, music, fresh flowers and candlelight. Upscale linens surround your warm, snuggly
bed. We provide the ambience - you create the memories! A perfect venue for weddings,
receptions, family reunions, company parties, etc. Our Conference Room for 15 people,
has a 1900 Belgian conference table. Full service business amenities and free wireless access.

### Rates
Decadent Suites: $235. Truly Decadent Suites: $275/$285.
Really Nice Rooms: $145. Extremely Nice Rooms: $155/$165.
Luxury Rooms: $175/$185. Rates are for 2 guests. Additional
guests: $25. Pets Welcome - $10/pet per night includes treats
& use of bowls. Number of Rooms: 17

### Cuisine
Gourmet Breakfast, Lunch for Groups and Full Service Dining,
open to the public. Full Service Saloon and Wine List.

### Nearest Airport(s)
Approximately 2.5 hours from Sacramento (SAC), San
Francisco (SFO) or E45.

### Directions
E of San Francisco, and S of Sacramento, on Highway 120.

# Old Monterey Inn

www.oldmontereyinn.com
500 Martin Street, Monterey, CA 93940
**800-350-2344** • 831-375-8284 • Fax 831-375-6730
omi@oldmontereyinn.com

*Member Since 1993*

*California*

*Monterey*

---

*"Old Monterey Inn: elegance, comfort & room decors that read like poetry" - Discovery Magazine "Voted one of California's Top 10 Inns" - ILoveInns.com*

---

**Innkeeper/Owner**
**Patricia Valletta**

'The level of service and accommodations here would rival most any inn or hotel we've visited,' says *The San Francisco Chronicle*. Set amidst an acre of spectacular gardens on a quiet, oak studded Monterey hillside, the Old Monterey Inn exudes romance and warmth. The 1929 half-timbered English Tudor Inn's rooms all overlook the uniquely beautiful gardens. Inside, guests find the attention to detail, which is the hallmark of the Inn--memorably fluffy featherbeds and 24-hour access to mineral waters, juices, tea and coffee. A full gourmet breakfast is served bedside or in our Heritage dining room, or, weather permitting, in our gardens. The owner imbues every element with the extra touches that help the Inn achieve near perfection. Recommended by prestigious Harper's *Hideaway Report*, Condé Nast Gold List, and Travel & Leisure (as seen on a recent Today Show Dream Getaway Segment).

**Rates**
Cottage, 3 Suites & 6 Rooms w/sitting areas - fireplaces, spa tubs, pvt. baths, feather beds, TV/VCR, TEL, WIFI & DSL, safes. $300/$480. Open year-round. Number of Rooms: 10

**Cuisine**
Evening wine and hors d'oeuvres. Extaordinary restaurants nearby. Port and fresh fruit...

**Nearest Airport(s)**
Monterey Airport - 10 min. San Jose Airport - 1 hr. 15 mins. SFO - 2 hrs. 30 mins.

**Directions**
SOUTH on Hwy 1: exit Soledad-Munras Ave, cross Munras Ave, R on Pacific. Go about 1 mile, L on Martin St. NORTH on Hwy 1: exit Munras Ave, L to Soledad, R on Pacific, L on Martin. Continue on Martin St 1 long block, Inn is on the R.

# Martine Inn

www.martineinn.com
255 Oceanview Boulevard, Pacific Grove, CA 93950
**800-852-5588** • 831-373-3388 • Fax 831-373-3896
don@martineinn.com

*Member Since 1992*

*"One of the 10 Most Romantic Inns in the U.S." - Vacations Magazine "It's the kind of place where starry eyed young lovers dream of getting married." - San Francisco Magazine*

Innkeeper/Owner
**Don Martine**

*Three Diamond Award*

Just blocks from Monterey's bustling Cannery Row lies a 24-room Victorian villa that *Bon Appetit* considers "one of the 8 best B&Bs in historic homes" and *Condé Nast Traveler* calls a "spectacular place for a romantic getaway." Welcome to the Martine Inn, built in the 1890s as a lavish private residence just 90 minutes south of San Francisco. Today it's a meticulously renovated resort steps from the water's edge, where every fixture and furnishing is an authentic Victorian-era antique, and every room, many with fireplaces, claw foot tubs and/or ocean views, has its own name and unique decor. Two sitting rooms afford priceless views of the bay, and other inn extras include a library, piano, game room replete with a 1917 nickelodeon and an 1890's billiard table, spa and Don Martine's collection of vintage MG autos. Miles of coastal hiking and biking are accessible literally at the inn's front door. All attractions of California's magnificent Monterey Peninsula are nearby, including the Monterey Bay Aquarium, Monarch butterflies, 17 Mile Drive, Carmel, Cannery Row, Big Sur and Fishermans Wharf.

**Rates**
25 Rooms, 4 Suites. $179/$450. Number of Rooms: 25

**Cuisine**
Morning brings a full breakfast of a hot entre/fresh baked pastry/fruit/fresh juices and Starbucks Coffee, on a background of silver, crystal and lace, while evening presents wine and hot hors d'oeuvres. Group lunches and dinners prearranged from 20 to 50, Victorian dinners up to 12 courses.

**Nearest Airport(s)**
Monterey - 5 miles
San Jose - 70 miles
San Francisco - 90 miles

**Directions**
Hwy 1 to Pebble Beach Pacific Grove exit. Turn on to Hwy 68 toward Pacific Grove. Stay in R lane on Forest Ave. at the water turn R on Ocean View Blvd turn R at 255 Ocean View Blvd.

# J. Patrick House

www.jpatrickhouse.com
2990 Burton Drive, Cambria, CA 93428
**800-341-5258** • 805-927-3812 • Fax 805-927-6759
jph@jpatrickhouse.com

*Member Since 2003*

*California*

*Cambria*

> *"Best On the West Coast and One of the Top 15 B&B/Country Inns."*
> Inn Traveler Magazine

Innkeepers/Owners
**Ann O'Connor and John Arnott**

**J. Patrick House Bed & Breakfast Inn**: Country Elegance in Accommodations.

Cambria's original – and still the finest – Bed and Breakfast Inn, nestled in the tall Monterey pines above Cambria's charming east village. As you enter the front door of this enchanting log home, the warmth of its embrace will welcome you. The aroma of freshly baked cookies, homemade granola, breads and muffins will transport you to a magical place. The main log home has one guest suite. Stroll through the passion vine covered arbor to the charming carriage house with seven "exquisitely appointed" guest rooms. Indulge in wine and hor d'oeuvres in the evening and "killer" chocolate chip cookies and cold milk before bedtime. Each morning a delicious full breakfast is served in the light-filled Garden Room. Enjoy exemplary guest services.

**Rates**
$185/$215  Number of Rooms: 8

**Cuisine**
Enjoy a full gourmet breakfast in our Garden room. Fresh fruit, homemade granola, fresh plump raisins and delicious yogurt for starters. Main entrees such as, Vegetable strata, Blintzes with Raspberry Sauce, Chili Corn Souffl? and Stuffed French Toast with pure Maple syrup to name a few, change daily.

**Nearest Airport(s)**
San Luis Obispo Airport

**Directions**
Midway between Los Angeles & San Francisco on the Central Coast of CA. 6 mi. from Hearst Castle.

# The Ballard Inn

www.ballardinn.com
2436 Baseline Avenue, Ballard, CA  93463
**800-638-2466** • 805-688-7770 • Fax 805-688-9560
innkeeper@ballardinn.com

*Member Since 1993*

*California*

*Ballard*

*The West's Best Small Inns / Sunset Magazine*
*Top 10 Most Romantic Inn / American Historic Inns*

Innkeepers/Owners
**Budi & Chris Kazali**

Voted one of America's Top Ten Most Romantic Inns, our comfortably elegant 4 diamond Country Inn is nestled among vineyards and orchards in the charming township of Ballard. Each of the 15 rooms posesses its own special charm and character reflecing local history. Many of our rooms have fireplaces, creating an especially romantic retreat. Borrow a bicycle and take a picnic lunch for an adventurous tour of the Santa Barbara wine country. A tasting of local wine & hors d'oeuvres, bed turn down service with home made cookies, and a full breakfast are included in your stay. The acclaimed Ballard Inn Restaurant features French-Asian cuisine in an intimate dining room complete with a magnificent marble fire place. Our Restaurant is open to the public Wednesday-Sunday. AAA Four Diamond Award.

**Rates**
15 Rooms, $225/$315 not including tax or service. Closed Christmas Eve & Christmas Day.   Number of Rooms: 15

**Cuisine**
An East meets West, French cuisine with an Asian touch.

**Nearest Airport(s)**
Santa Barbara and Santa Ynez.

**Directions**
From Hwy. 101, take Solvang exit, follow Route 246 E through Solvang to Alamo Pintado; turn L. Drive 3 miles to Baseline Ave. turn R. The Inn is on your R.

# Santa Ynez Inn

www.santaynezinn.com
3627 Sagunto St., Santa Ynez, CA 93460
**800-643-5774** • 805-688-5588 • Fax 805-686-4294
info@santaynezinn.com

*Member Since 2004*

*California*

*"What a delight to find one such a quality country Inn with such charm. We will return!"*

*Santa Ynez*

Innkeeper/Owner - **Douglas Ziegler**
General Manager/Innkeeper - **Rick Segovia**

Our Wine Country Getaway awaits in 14 individually decorated rooms and junior suites. Accommodations feature unique antiques, queen or king-sized beds with Frette linens, remote-controlled gas fireplaces and whirlpool tubs in deluxe marble baths. Most rooms offer a private balcony or patio to savor the beauty and serenity of the Santa Ynez Valley. Take advantage of all that Santa Barbara County has to offer, from wine tasting and antique shopping, to Glider rides and Jeep tours. There's something for everyone in Santa Ynez. After a day of Southern California sightseeing adventures, you may wish to unwind in the heated outdoor whirlpool, lounge on the sundeck, or take a leisurely stroll through the gardens of the Inn. Whatever your needs--whether you wish to arrange for wine tasting tours, shopping, dining, glider rides, bicycle rentals or transportation--our concierge service is eager to assist you.

**Rates**
$285/$475 Number of Rooms: 14

**Cuisine**
Full Gourmet breakfast, Evening Wine & Hors d'oeuvres and Evening Desserts.

**Nearest Airport(s)**
Santa Barbara Airport

**Directions**
From the North: Take 101 South to Highway 246. Take 246 East (left) to the town of Santa Ynez and turn left on Edison and right on Sagunto. From the South: Take 101 North to Highway 154. Take 154 over the San Marcos Pass to Highway 246 and make a L onto 246. R on Edison and R on Sagunto.

# Simpson House Inn

www.simpsonhouseinn.com
121 East Arrellaga Street, Santa Barbara, CA 93101
**800-676-1280** • 805-963-7067 • Fax 805-564-4811
reservations@simpsonhouseinn.com

*Member Since 1993*

*"The staff and Inn completely exceeded our expectations. We had a beautiful stay!"*

Managing Partner
**Nicholas Davaz**

This elegantly restored 1874 Historic Landmark Victorian Estate is the only Five Diamond Bed & Breakfast Inn in North America. It's comprised of six tastefully appointed rooms in the original Victorian estate home, four private cottages and 4 spacious rooms in our historic carriage house. The Inn is secluded within an acre of beautifully landscaped English gardens, yet just a five-minute walk from the historic downtown, restaurants, shopping, theater and a pleasant walk to the beach. All rooms feature antiques, fine art and Oriental rugs. Fireplaces and whirlpool tubs are available. We serve a delicious full gourmet breakfast, to your room, in the gardens or our dining room. Afternoon dessert tea and lavish evening Mediterranean hors d'oeuvres and wine tasting are not to be missed. Additional complimentary amenities include full access to the Athletic Club a short distance from the Inn, bicycles and English croquet. Our Concierge can arrange spa treatments in your guest room, wine country tours, whale watching & dining reservations.

**Rates**
6 Main House and 1 Garden Room $255/$475. Historic Carriage House Rooms $595/$610. Garden Cottages $595/$610. Open year-round. Mid-week and seasonal rates on availability. Number of Rooms: 15

**Cuisine**
Complimentary full vegetarian breakfast, afternoon dessert tea and Mediterranean hors d'oeuvres buffet with local wine tasting each evening.

**Nearest Airport(s)**
Santa Barbara

**Directions**
From San Francisco - Mission St. exit, L. Anacapa St., R. Arrellaga St., L; From Los Angeles - Garden St. exit, R. Gutierrez St., L. Santa Barbara St., R. Arrellaga St., L.

*California*

*Santa Barbara*

# Bissell House Bed & Breakfast

www.bissellhouse.com
201 Orange Grove Avenue, South Pasadena, CA 91030
**800-441-3530** • 626-441-3535 • Fax 626-441-3671
info@bissellhouse.com

*Member Since 2006*

*California*

*South Pasadena*

*"Perfect in every detail...I'm spoiled for any place else!"*

Innkeeper
**Juli Hoyman**

Restful, elegant and romantic, this 1887 classic Victorian estate will exceed your expectations for charm. Bissell House offers intimate accommodations for travelers seeking comfort and relaxation amidst the culture and heritage of Old Pasadena. Nearby are the world-famed Huntington Library & Gardens, Norton Simon Museum, Gamble House and greater Los Angeles. Located in the historic Orange Grove Mansion District, the Bissell House is a perfect location for attending annual garden tours or the New Year's Rose Bowl Parade (walking distance). An upscale neighborhood with tree-lined streets cloisters the inn amongst an old-world setting. Delightful breakfasts are served in the dining room where Albert Einstein was once feted! Complimentary services include: concierge, high speed Internet/wireless access, DVD library, pool/gardens, afternoon tea, desserts, snacks and beverages. Guests may indulge in seclusion or linger with others as we offer as much privacy as you desire. December & New Year's are a special time to enjoyour Victorian Christmas decor. We are minutes from downtown Los Angeles. Voted one of Top Romantic inns for 2006.

### Rates
6 rooms, one with w/Jacuzzi, antiques, featherbeds, robes, claw-footed tubs or showers, DSL/wireless, TV/VCR/DVD available select rooms. $150/$350 all inclusive, no tax rates. Number of Rooms: 6

### Cuisine
Gourmet breakfast served weekends by candlelight on Haviland Limoges china with crystal & Victorian silver. Weekdays guests choose continental or 9 a.m. service. Afternoon dessert tea, wine, treats.

### Nearest Airport(s)
Los Angeles International-30 minutes
Burbank-15 minutes

### Directions
1.25 miles south of Colorado St., Pasadena on Orange Grove Blvd. Corner of Columbia/Orange Grove Ave. Take 110 or 134 or 210 Freeways at Orange Grove exits.

# Villa Royale Inn

www.villaroyale.com
1620 S. Indian Trail, Palm Springs, CA 92264
**800-245-2314** • 760-327-2314 • Fax 760-322-3794
info@villaroyale.com

*Member Since 2006*

*California*

*Palm Springs*

> *"Picturesque...a fountain and beautiful garden entrance, mature trees, meandering brick pathways, stunning mountain views. A very special place to stay."*

Innkeepers/Owners
**Bambi and David Arnold**

Framed by breathtaking mountain views, the Villa Royale's intimate three acres echo an ancient Tuscan estate. Wander through tranquil courtyards overflowing with fragrant citrus, jasmine and lavender, gently cascading fountains, two heated pools and a large jacuzzi. AAA's Westways magazine calls the Villa Royale's AAA Four Diamond Europa Restaurant "a charming hideaway where you'll feel as if you have been transported to an intimate castle in Europe." Europa's bar, with its pool and mountain views, prides itself on its extensive offerings awarded by *Wine Spectator* Magazine. Luxurious full-service amenities, including full complimentary breakfast and fine dining, a daily newspaper, in-room spa services, and an attentive and caring staff make the Villa Royale Inn your ultimate Palm Springs romantic getaway.

### Rates
Seasonal rates. Hideaway Guestrooms $99/$225. Royale Guestrooms $175/$300. The Villas, 1 Bedroom $250/$450; 2 Bedroom $325/$475. Deposit taken at time of booking w/10 day cancellation policy. Number of Rooms: 30

### Cuisine
Superb cuisine served fireside or by trickling fountains. Small private dinning room for up to 12 ideal for a special occasion or intimate wedding celebration.

### Nearest Airport(s)
5 min. from downtown Palm Springs & the Palm Springs International Airport.

### Directions
Driving time subject to traffic & weather. From LA area: approx. 2 hrs. From San Diego: approx. 2 hrs.15 min.

# Casa Laguna Inn & Spa

www.casalaguna.com
2510 South Coast Highway, Laguna Beach, CA 92651
**800-233-0449** • 949-494-2996 • Fax 949-494-5009
innkeeper@casalaguna.com

*Member Since 2004*

*California*

*Laguna Beach*

*"The perfect getaway! A charming and relaxing retreat.
Marvelous setting with wonderful staff."*

Innkeepers/Proprietors
**Paul Blank & Francois Leclair**

Silver Medal winner in the 2007 Inn-Credible Breakfast Cook-ff and voted "Best B&B in Orange County" for nine consecutive years by the OC Register. Terraced on a hillside amid tropic gardens and flower-splashed patios, the historic Casa Laguna Inn & Spa exudes an ambiance of bygone days when Laguna Beach was developing its reputation as an artists' colony and hideaway for Hollywood film stars. The mission style inn set below towering palms framing views of the blue Pacific invites you to slow your pace to that of another, less hurried era. The magnificent Palm Court and the ocean-view pool deck will enchant you with fountains and rare Catalina tiles. Two lovely beaches are a few minutes walk from the hotel. Victoria Beach offers a long stretch of white sand while Moss Point offers tide pools and coves. One and a half miles south of Main Beach, the inn is a short distance from the boutiques, pottery shops, and galleries for which Laguna Beach is famous. A Casa Laguna Spa treatment is an excellent way to enhance your stay at Casa Laguna. Guests are pampered, rejuvenated and renewed.

**Rates**
15 Rooms, 5 suites and a Cottage: $150/$600. All rooms are air-conditioned and feature a 9-layer, deluxe bed, CD & DVD players. Some w/ private patios, jetted tubs and/or fireplaces. Number of Rooms: 22

**Cuisine**
Full gourmet breakfast & afternoon wine & hors d'oeuvres included. Area fine dining.

**Nearest Airport(s)**
Orange County - John Wayne, SNA

**Directions**
From I-5 N: Exit CA-1/Camino Las Ramblas to Beach Cities. Keep L at the fork; merge to CA-1/PCH for 6.7 mi. From I-5 S or I-405 S: Exit CA-133 S to Laguna Beach for 9 mi., then L onto CA-1/PCH for 1.75 mi.

🍽️ 🍽️ 🍽️ 🍷

# Orchard Hill Country Inn

www.orchardhill.com
2502 Washington St., P.O. Box 2410, Julian, CA 92036
**800-716-7242** • 760-765-1700 • Fax 760-765-0290
information@orchardhill.com

*Member Since 1998*

*Top 9 western lodges - Sunset Magazine*
*"....reminiscent of America's great national park lodges."*

Innkeepers/Owners
**Pat and Darrell Straube**

Orchard Hill Country Inn is the premiere four-diamond inn nestled in the heart of Julian's historic district. Visiting Julian is a return to a quiet, simpler time. There are extensive hiking trails and horseback riding for all levels. Springtime brings daffodils and lilacs and autumn brings opportunities to pick apples from Julian's orchards.

The Inn features hilltop views and colorful gardens. Our natural surroundings will bring you peace as you relax in a hammock or watch the brilliant stars in our night sky.

A great room with vaulted ceilings and a large stone fireplace welcomes guests with a blend of comfort and elegence. Cottage rooms have porches and fireplaces, and lodge rooms are cozy and beautifully appointed. The dining experience at Orchard Hill, in which flavor and warm hospitality takes precedence, will complete the perfect get-away experience.

**Rates**
$225/$450. Number of Rooms: 22

**Cuisine**
Full breakfast and afternoon hors d'oeuvres are included. Dinner is served on select nights and picnic lunches are available. An excellent selection of beer and wine is also offered.

**Nearest Airport(s)**
San Diego International

**Directions**
60 mi. NE of SD. IS 15 north to Scripps Poway Pkwy, turn right (East). Approx. 12 mi, left on Hwy 67 (North). Hwy 67 becomes Hwy 78 in Ramona and continues straight into Julian through Santa Ysabel (22 mi.) In Julian, at the four way stop sign, continue straight. Orchard Hill Country Inn is up one block on the left.

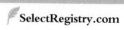
SelectRegistry.com

California
Julian

# The Bed & Breakfast Inn at La Jolla 🍽️

www.innlajolla.com
7753 Draper Avenue, La Jolla, CA 92037
**800-582-2466** • 858-456-2066 • Fax 858-456-1510
BedBreakfast@innlajolla.com

*Member Since 2002*

*California*

*"Delighted we switched from the Hilton!"*

*La Jolla*

Innkeeper
**Gayle Wildowsky**

This elegant historical inn is drenched in sunlight, draped in brilliant bouganvillia and kissed by mild ocean breezes. Located in one of the most beautiful seaside villages in the world, it is only steps to the best beaches and snorkeling in California, as well as the finest shops, restaurants, art galleries, and museums. The inn is central to the main attractions of San Diego, such as the Stephen Birch Aquarium, Sea World, Old Town, Wild Animal Park, and Mexico. After a fun-filled day, return to the peaceful respite of the inn, where, lulled by the melodious garden fountain and surrounded by lush greenery, you will have time to reflect and relax and savor the good life. Each of the thirteen guest rooms and two suites are unique in their personality and decor, embellished with fine antiques and accessories, creating a personalized space you can call your "home away from home." You may like it so much that you may never want to leave. Fine sherry and fresh flowers are in each of the guest rooms to relax the body and delight the senses. Come be our guest and experience all the best that San Diego, and particularly La Jolla, have to offer. "So close yet so far from all!"

## Rates
13 Rooms $199/$329; 2 Suites $359/$459. Deluxe, elegant cottage-style rooms w/fresh flowers & fruit. Open year round.
Number of Rooms: 15

## Cuisine
Full candlelit breakfast. Gourmet entrees served with fresh fruit, muffins, scones, homemade granola topped with honey and vanilla-laced yogurt, rich coffee and exotic teas.

## Nearest Airport(s)
San Diego International

## Directions
From the S: I-5 N; exit La Jolla Parkway to Torrey Pines Rd. W, R on Prospect Pl to Draper Ave., L on Draper. From the N: I-5 S; exit La Jolla Village Dr. W, L on Torrey Pines Rd., R on Prospect Pl to Draper, L on Draper.

# Colorado

"The Centennial State"

Famous for: Gold Rush, Mile-High City, Mesa Verde, Cliff Dwellings, Rocky Mountains, Skiing, and Hiking.

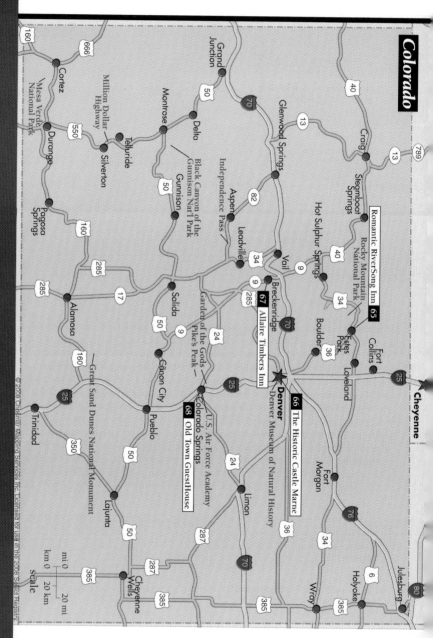

SelectRegistry.com

# Romantic RiverSong Inn

www.romanticriversong.com
P.O. Box 1910, 1766 Lower Broadview Road, Estes Park, CO 80517
**970-586-4666** • Fax 970-577-1336
romanticriversong@earthlink.net

*Member Since 1987*

*Colorado*

*Estes Park*

*"...the most romantic place my wife and I have stayed. The breakfast is delicious... phenomenal service & hospitality. Still the best dinner in Estes Park!"*

Innkeepers/Owners
**Sue & Gary Mansfield**

RiverSong represents the classic country inn rarely found in Colorado. Located on a quiet backroad, the inn was personally chosen by Select Registry's founder Norman Simpson.... his choice for a unique place that offered "exceptional hospitality" and "good honest lodging ". Secluded on 27 wooded acres with towering Blue Spruce and Ponderosa pines, quiet ponds, hiking trails and tree swings. Romantic RiverSong is as much a refuge for guests as well as wildlife. With only ten guest rooms, the inn has achieved a marvelous balance with its luxurious rooms (radiant heated floors, jetted tubs for two by a crackling fire) and nature. These lovely rooms are merely background to the mountain melodies of songbirds and a rushing mountain stream. After a great hike in nearby Rocky Mountain National Park come home to a relaxing "streamside massage." Then, later that evening enjoy our own chef prepared candlelight dinner by fireside. It's our warm hospitality that makes your memories of Romantic RiverSong linger long after you've gone from this little bit of heaven in the Colorado mountains.

**Rates**
4 Rooms, $150/$175 B&B; 5 Cottage Suites, $225/$350 B&B. Tubs for 2; and marvelous packages online.   Number of Rooms: 10

**Cuisine**
Evening dining is reserved for the first four couples that sign up for a marvelous five-course dinner by fireside. The tables are set with fine china and bone handle silver service on white lace linens, while softly in the background the sounds of jazz classics soothe your soul.

**Nearest Airport(s)**
Denver International  - 1 hr. 45 min

**Directions**
Hwy 36 through Midtown of Estes, Hwy 36 to Mary's Lk Rd; L at Mary's Lk Rd; Go 1 bk Cross bridge. Turn R immediately; take country road to the end.

# The Historic Castle Marne Inn

www.castlemarne.com
1572 Race Street, Denver, CO 80206
**800-92-MARNE** • 303-331-0621 • Fax 303-331-0623
info@castlemarne.com

*Member Since 1991*

*Colorado*

*Denver*

---

*Winner of 2004 Condé Nast Johansens Top 3 Inns on the North American continent. "... they pay impeccable attention to details that excite the senses."*

---

Innkeepers/Owners
**The Peiker Family**
**Diane, Jim, Melissa, and Louie**

Denver's grandest historic mansion, listed on both National & Local Historic Registers. Built in 1889, features handhewn lavastone exterior, hand-rubbed woods, balconies, four-story tower and original stained glass Peacock Window. Beautifully blending period antiques and family heirlooms to create a charming Victorian atmosphere. Relax in the English garden beside the bubbling fountain. Full gourmet breakfast served in the original Dining Room. Complimentary Afternoon Tea served in the Parlour. Whirlpool spas and private outdoor hot tubs. Lunch & Private candlelight dinners by reservation. In Denver's Wyman Historic District. Near Museum of Nature and Science, Zoo, Botanic Gardens. Five minutes from Downtown and Cherry Creek Shopping area. Walking distance to many restaurants. Wedding and Honeymoon packages available. Small weddings and elopements a specialty. The AIA says, "Castle Marne is one of Denver's great architectural legacies." Free Parking. WIFI. Business meeting space.

**Rates**
9 Rooms, $105/$260 2 Suites with Jacuzzi tubs. 3 Rooms with private hot tubs. Number of Rooms: 9

**Cuisine**
Full gourmet breakfast Elegant Private 6 course Dinners Afternoon Tea and Luncheons.

**Nearest Airport(s)**
Denver International

**Directions**
From DIA, Pena Blvd. To I-70 W to Quebec. L to 17th Ave. R to York St. L to 16th Ave. R 4 blocks to Race St. From mountains, I-70 E, R onto 6th Ave.Frwy (US 6) E to Josephine St. L to 16th Ave. L to Race St. From Colo Spgs, I-25 N exit R onto University Blvd N, R on 16th Ave. to Race St. From Cheyenne, I-25 S, exit R on Park Ave. R on Broadway, L on 17th Ave. R on Race St. one block to 16th Ave.

# Allaire Timbers Inn

www.allairetimbers.com
9511 Hwy. 9, South Main Street, P.O. Box 4653, Breckenridge, CO  80424
**800-624-4904 Outside CO** • 970-453-7530 • Fax 970-453-8699
info@allairetimbers.com                              *Member Since 1995*

*"Hospitality, comfort and culinary magic." Washington Post*

Innkeepers/Owners
**Sue Carlson and Kendra Hall**

This contemporary log B&B is the perfect Rocky Mountain Hideaway. Located on a
tree filled bluff at the south end of historic Main Street, the Allaire Timbers offers 10 guest
rooms, each with private bath and deck. Two elegant suites offer a special touch of romance
with private hot tub and fireplace. Relax by a crackling fire in the log and beam Great
Room. Enjoy the serenity of the tiled sunroom. Retreat to the reading loft, or unwind in
the outdoor hot tub with spectacular mountain views. Just steps from downtown Victorian
Breckenridge with its many and varied restaurants and shops. Access to the ski area and
Breckenridge Riverwalk arts/music amphitheatre via the Free Ride town bus system.
Featured in Arrington's Inn Traveler and CNN's Travel Guide.

**Rates**
8 Lodge Rooms, 2 Suites $165/$400. Number of Rooms: 10

**Cuisine**
Hearty breakfast of homemade breads and sweets, fresh juices
and fruits, the Inn's special recipe granola and changing
menu of hot entrees. Evenings enjoy fresh baked cookies and
seasonal herbal iced tea or hot citrus cider.

**Nearest Airport(s)**
Denver International

**Directions**
From Denver, I-70 West to exit 203. Hwy. 9 South to
Breckenridge, through town past the traffic light at Boreas Pass
Road (gas station on right). Take next Right, bear right into
private parking lot.

# Old Town Guest House

www.oldtown-guesthouse.com
115 South 26th Street, Colorado Springs, CO 80904
**888-375-4210** • 719-632-9194 • Fax 719-632-9026
Luxury@OldTown-GuestHouse.com

*Member Since 2001*

*"I looked for a fault - I'll have to come back to find it!"*

Innkeepers/Owners
**Shirley and Don Wick**

The three-story brick guesthouse is in perfect harmony with the 1859 period of the surrounding historic Old Town. The urban Inn offers upscale amenities for discerning adult leisure and business travelers. Our elevator allows the entire Inn to be accessible and the African Orchid room exceeds ADA specifications. The soundproof, uniquely decorated guestrooms have private baths and most rooms have fireplaces and/or porches overlooking Pikes Peak.   Relax in the library or out on the umbrella-covered patio for afternoon wine, beer and hors d'oeuvres then walk to some of Old Town's many fine restaurants, boutiques and galleries. End your evening with a soak in your own private two-person Hot Tub or your relaxing ensuite Steam Shower.  Your morning starts with a gourmet 3 course breakfast served in our dining area then it's off to one of the many attractions and activities that the Pikes Peak area has to offer.   The elegance and hospitality of the GuestHouse has earned it its AAA Four Diamond Award for Excellence 11 years running.  Member Pikes Peak Lodging Association and Bed & Breakfast Innkeepers of Colorado.

**Rates**
$99/$235, Corporate and military rates available, Private hot tubs, steam showers, fireplaces, balconies, TV/VCR/DVD, phones, wireless Internet, A/C, International videoconferencing in private conference room. Attractions: Pikes Peak, Garden of the Gods, hiking, biking, climbing and more. Number of Rooms: 8

**Cuisine**
Full 3 course sit-down breakast.Hot entre', fruit in season, muffin or sweet bread. Evening with wine/beer and hors d'oeuvres.

**Nearest Airport(s)**
Colorado Springs

**Directions**
From I-25, exit 141 going West to 26th St. North on 26th, proceed 2 1/2 blocks, turn right into B&B's private parking lot.

*68*

Colorado
Colorado Springs

# Connecticut

Famous for: Inventors (Charles Goodyear, Elias Howe, Eli Whitney, Eli Terry), Inventions, Watchmaking, Typewriters, Insurance, Submarines.

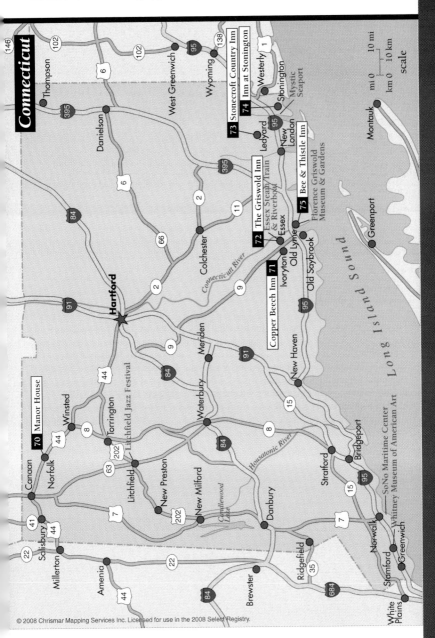

Connecticut

Thompson
West Greenwich
Wyoming
**73** Stonecroft Country Inn
**74** Inn at Stonington
Westerly
Stonington
Mystic Seaport
Danielson
Ledyard
New London
**75** Bee & Thistle Inn
Florence Griswold Museum & Gardens
**72** The Griswold Inn
Essex Steam/Train & Riverboat
Essex
Colchester
Old Lyme
**71** Copper Beech Inn
Ivoryton
Old Saybrook
Hartford
Long Island Sound
Greenport
Meriden
New Haven
Montauk
**70** Manor House
Winsted
Litchfield Jazz Festival
Torrington
Waterbury
Bridgeport
Canaan
Norfolk
Litchfield
New Preston
New Milford
Candlewood Lake
Stratford
SoNo Maritime Center
Salisbury
Millerton
Amenia
Danbury
Ridgefield
Norwalk
Whitney Museum of American Art
Stamford
Greenwich
Brewster
White Plains

Connecticut River
Housatonic River

mi 0   10 mi
km 0   10 km
scale

# Manor House
www.manorhouse-norfolk.com
69 Maple Avenue, Norfolk, CT 06058
**Toll Free 866-542-5690** • Fax 860-542-5690
innkeeper@manorhouse-norfolk.com

*Member Since 2000*

*Connecticut*

*Norfolk*

*"Connecticut's Most Romantic Hideaway" The Discerning Traveler*

Innkeeper/Manager
**Michael W. Dinsmore**

Surround yourself by Victorian Elegance in this 1898 Tudor Estate described by *Gourmet* as "Quite Grand," and designated "Connecticut's Most Romantic Hideaway" by the *Discerning Traveler*. Featured in *National Geographic Traveler, Good Housekeeping*'s "Best Weekend Getaways," and listed as one of the top 25 Inns by American Historic Inns. All rooms offer views of the spacious grounds and perrenial gardens, are furnished with period antiques, and luxurious down comforters. Savour a full breakfast in the elegant dining room, relax by the baronial fireplace in the living room, or read a book in the library, all adorned with Tiffany windows and architectual detail. The Manor House is located at the foot of the Berkshires, and travelers can enjoy an array of outdoor activities, shopping, summer theatre, and music festivals.

**Rates**
8 Rooms, 1 Suite, $130/$255. Four rooms offer wood or gas fireplaces, 3 with whirlpools, and two with private balconies. Number of Rooms: 9

**Cuisine**
Full country breakfast. Complimentary coffee, hot or iced tea, spring water, and hot chocolate available all day, glassware, flatware, ice maker and refrigerator also available.

**Nearest Airport(s)**
Bradley International

**Directions**
NYC: I-84 E to exit for Rte. 8 N in Waterbury. At terminus of highway in Winsted take Rte. 44W R to Norfolk. Boston: I-84 W to exit for Rte. 4 Farmington to Rte. 179 to Rte. 44W to Norfolk.

# The Copper Beech Inn

www.CopperBeechInn.com
46 Main Street, Ivoryton, Essex, CT 06442
**888-809-2056** • 860-767-0330 • Fax 860-767-7840
info@CopperBeechInn.com

*Member Since 2003*

Proprietors
**Ian S. Phillips**
**Barbara C. Phillips**

Named *"The Best Country Inn"* in Connecticut by the readers of *Connecticut* Magazine for 3 consecutive years, and one of *"America's Top 100 Hotel Restaurants"* by the *ZAGAT* Survey and *USA Today*, The Copper Beech Inn in Essex, is minutes from the Connecticut River and Long Island Sound, & is just a 2-hour drive from either New York or Boston. Elegant guest rooms & suites with oversize beds feature Italian marble bathrooms and air-jet thermo-masseur tubs. The Inn has 2 restaurants. The casual French-style Brasserie Pip, selected as the *"Best New Restaurant"* in Connecticut for 2007 complements the *AAA Four-Diamond* Copper Beech restaurant, named in 2006 as the *"Best Overall"* in Connecticut. Both restaurants feature extraordinary food and a *Wine Spectator* award-winning wine list with over 500 selections. Andrew Harper's *Hideaway Report* named the inn as one of the *"The Ten Best in New England"* and, *The New York Times* said "The Copper Beech Inn is a lovely example of what Americans look for in a four-star country inn … the wine list is pretty spectacular ... the dining experience always marvelous." The Connecticut River Valley offers classic unspoiled coastline, countryside and quaint historic villages. "The restaurants alone are worth the 2-hour drive from Boston and New York." *Boston Magazine*.

**Rates**
13 Rooms including 2 suites $150/$395 Full Breakfast. Open Year-Round. All w/private baths. Number of Rooms: 13

**Cuisine**
French with a contemporary flair. Select from an extraordinary menu and 500 plus selection award-winning wine list. "Crystal sparkles, silver shines, Oriental rugs glow on polished floors, antiques & masses of fresh flowers set the scence for the flawlessly elegant dining" *Connecticut Magazine*.

**Nearest Airport(s)**
Hartford 45 mins., Boston 2 hours, New York 2 hours

**Directions**
I-95 to Exit 69 to Route 9. Exit 3. Left off ramp. 1.5 mi on Left.

🍽️ 🍽️ 🍽️ 🍷

# The Griswold Inn

www.griswoldinn.com
36 Main Street, Essex, CT  06426
**860-767-1776** • Fax 860-767-0481
griswoldinn@griswoldinn.com

*Member Since 1974*

*"The 'Gris' is the real deal - authentic and well-preserved - yet the cuisine and amenities are far from dated!"*

Innkeepers/Owners
**The Paul Family**

This 1776 landmark, recipient of Connecticut's highest award for hospitality, is featured in "1000 Places to See Before You Die". It is the only inn located in the heart of Essex village, mere steps from the harbor on the Connecticut River. Savor the atmosphere and acclaimed cuisine in its historic art-filled dining rooms. Relax in the Inn's stunning Wine Bar featuring tapas and a more contemporary dining experience. Step into the award-winning Tap Room where lively music rings out nightly with sea chanteys, swing, blues, banjo, Dixieland, and more. Charming accommodations are furnished in antiques and fine reproductions. Riverboat cruises, shopping, antiquing, hiking, museums and historic homes are just outside the door, while Mystic Seaport and Aquarium, Goodspeed Theatre, shopping outlets, Foxwoods and Mohegan Sun casinos and entertainment complexes are within easy reach.

**Rates**
Seasonal Rates. 14 Guest Rooms, $100/$220 B&B; 16 Suites $160/$370 B&B. Special packages. Open year-round. Number of Rooms: 30

**Cuisine**
Complimentary continental breakfast for inn guests. Lunch, dinner, Sunday Hunt Breakfast. Authentic American Cuisine featuring fresh seafood, aged beef selections and New England favorites. Inspired "small" plates served in Wine Bar. Full service, award-winning Tap Room.

**Nearest Airport(s)**
Hartford's Bradley Airport - 1 hr. Boston, JFK

**Directions**
I-91 S to exit 22 S (left-hand exit). Rte. 9 S to exit 3 Essex. I-95 (N&S) to exit 69 to Rte. 9 N to exit 3 Essex. Two hours from New York and Boston.

SelectRegistry.com

# Stonecroft Country Inn

www.stonecroft.com
515 Pumpkin Hill Road, Ledyard, CT 06339
**800-772-0774** • 860-572-0771 • Fax 860-572-9161
stonecroftinn@comcast.com

*Member Since 2002*

🍽️ 🍽️ 🍷

*Connecticut*

*"A wonderful blend of luxury and simplicity, cared for, pampered." "Kudos to the Chef!" "Married 10 years and coming here for 9." "I want to live here."*

*Ledyard*

Owner
**Joan R. Egy**

Relax in quiet country elegance on an 1807 sea captain's six-acre estate, only ten minutes from Mystic Seaport, Foxwoods and Mohegan Sun casinos. Ancient stone walls and lush green lawns surround the Inn, consisting of The Main House, a sunny Georgian colonial, and The Grange, our recently converted 19th century barn. Romantic guestooms feature French, English and American country decor, with fireplaces, whirlpools and heated towel bars, television and Internet access. Pamper yourself with an on-site massage, and savor an exquisite dinner fireside in our elegant granite-walled restaurant or the candlelit garden terrace. Open year-round.

**Rates**
4 Rooms Main House: AC, 3 with fireplace; 4 Deluxe Rooms Grange: AC, gas fireplace, TV, 2-person whirlpool; 2 Suites Grange: AC, gas fireplace, TV, bidet, 2-person whirlpool, walk-in shower. All rooms $150/$329. Number of Rooms: 10

**Cuisine**
Breakfast included. Dinner in Grange Dining Room or on terrace, contemporary American cuisine, Zagat food rating 27, full service bar. Live guitar on Saturday evening.

**Nearest Airport(s)**
TF Green (Providence)

**Directions**
I-95 N: Exit 89, L off ramp, straight 3.75 mi. I-95 S: Exit 89, R off ramp, straight 3.5 mi.

# Inn at Stonington

www.innatstonington.com
60 Water Street, Stonington, CT 06378
**860-535-2000** • Fax 860-535-8193
www.innatstonington.com

*Connecticut*

*Stonington*

*"There's surely more than one kind of romance in this world, but Stonington Village - and The Inn at Stonington - seem to have most of them covered."*

Innkeeper/Owner - **William Griffin**
General Managers - **Susan Irvine and Anne Starzec Henson**

Named by *Travel + Leisure* as Inn of the Month, this newly constructed 18 room inn is located in the heart of Stonington Borough, one of the last untouched and 'historic' villages in New England. Relax in the privacy of your room, snuggled in front of your fireplace or take a luxurious bath in the soaking Jacuzzi tub. Public rooms include a top floor sitting room overlooking the Harbor, intimate bar with adjoining breakfast room, a cozy living room, and a well equipped gym. During the day stop by one of the local wineries, visit downtown Mystic, or simply take a stroll down Water Street and enjoy the specialty shops and some of the finest antiques in the area. Each evening join us for complimentary wine and cheese before walking to dinner at one of four fabulous restaurants in the village. Area attractions: small beach within walking distance, Mystic Seaport, Mystic Aquarium, Mohegan Sun and Foxwood Casinos, Watch Hill beaches. Come see what *CT Magazine* and *Coastal Living* consider one of New England's most romantic Inns.

**Rates**
18 Guest rooms. Seasonal rates $150/$445. Open Year Round. Number of Rooms: 18

**Cuisine**
Continental breakfast of fresh baked treats. Complimentary wine and cheese hour nightly.

**Nearest Airport(s)**
T.F. Green, Prov. RI

**Directions**
North on I-95 Exit 91 turn right at the bottom of ramp. Proceed 1/2 mile and turn left on North Main St. Proceed to stoplight & cross US Rt. 1. At 1st stop turn left. At next stop, take a right onto Water St. Proceed over bridge, bear left and travel approx. 6/10 ths of a mile to 60 Water St. South on I-95, turn left at bottom of ramp. Use same directions as above.

# Bee and Thistle Inn

www.beeandthistleinn.com
100 Lyme Street, Old Lyme, CT 06371
**800-622-4946** • 860-434-1667 • Fax 860-434-3402
innkeeper@beeandthistleinn.com

🍽 🍽 🍽 ☐

*Member Since 1984*

*"I am grateful to your staff for all that you did to help this be a wonderful memory."*

Wine Spectator
AWARD OF EXCELLENCE

Proprietors - **Linnea and David Rufo**
Chef - **Kristofer Rowe**

This 1756 inn is nestled on five acres bordering the Lieutenant River in the township of Old Lyme, neighboring the Florence Griswold Museum - Home of American Impressionism. The inn is available as a large private guesthouse or by individual room on a bed and breakfast basis. All of our eleven guest rooms are adorned with elegant accents, each individual in design. Therein you will find fine linens, down pillows and a private bath. While you relax as our guest, there are many pleasant diversions just minutes away. You can choose from local museums, galleries, concerts or enjoy our beautiful English gardens. The inn is a perennial favorite thanks to its outstanding New American cuisine and upscale hospitality. It has a well-earned reputation as one of Connecticut's most romantic spots along the shore.

**Rates**
$140 to $275. Country Continental Breakfast. Seasonal midweek rates, packages with area attractions. Eleven guest rooms. Number of Rooms: 11 guest rooms

**Cuisine**
New American cuisine. Intimate spaces offer candle-lit dining overlooking gardens with live music on Saturday evenings.

**Nearest Airport(s)**
Hartford (BDL) Providence (PVD)

**Directions**
I-95 S exit 70 turn R off ramp to 3rd house on L – I-95N L off ramp to 2nd light, turn R to end of road, turn L, 3rd house on L.

# Delaware

## "The First State"

Famous for: Historic Brandywine Valley—Museums and Gardens, Du Pont Family Mansions, Beaches, Fishing, Wildlife, Farmland, Bird-watching, Nascar Races, and No-sales-tax Shopping.

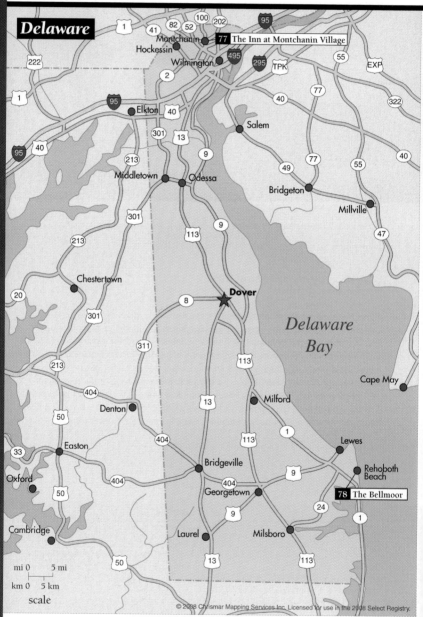

**77** The Inn at Montchanin Village

**78** The Bellmoor

SelectRegistry.com

# The Inn at Montchanin Village

🍽️ 🍽️ 🍽️ 🍷

www.montchanin.com
Rte 100 & Kirk Road, , P.O. Box 130, Montchanin, DE  19710
**800-269-2473** • 302-888-2133 • Fax 302-888-0389
inn@montchanin.com

*Member Since 2002*

*Delaware*

*Received the 2007 Award from Travel + Leisure Magazine for the "Best Value Hotel" under $250 within the Continental U.S. and Canada.*

*Wilmington*

Innkeepers/Owners
**Dan and Missy Lickle**

Listed on the National Historic Register, The Inn at Montchanin Village was once a part of the Winterthur Estate and was named for Alexandria de Montchanin, grandmother of the founder of the Du Pont Gunpowder Company.  One of the few remaining villages of its kind, the settlement was home to laborers who worked at the nearby Du Pont powder mills. In eleven carefully restored buildings dating from 1799 to 1910, there are 28 richly furnished guest rooms/suites appointed with period and reproduction furniture, marble bath with towel warmer and all amenities for the demanding and sophisticated traveller. The Inn's renowned Krazy Kat's Restaurant, once the village blacksmith shop, is known as much for its creative cuisine as its whimsical decor, serving breakfast, lunch and dinner. The Crow's Nest accommodates forty seats in a private and elegant setting. The Village is 100% smoke free. The Inn is located in the Brandywine Valley, four miles Northwest of Wilmington and 25 minutes South of the philadelphia International airport. It is centrally located from all major museums such as Winterthur, Longwood Gardens, Hagley Museum and Nemours Mansion.

**Rates**
28 elegant rooms & suites. $189/$399. Marble baths, nightly turndown, daily paper & imported linens. Internet Packages available. Full Spa to open Summer 2008.   Number of Rooms: 28

**Cuisine**
Krazy Kat's Restaurant is part of the Inn. Modern Continental Cuisine, specializing in fresh/local ingredients. Private dining rooms available for groups of 10-40.

**Nearest Airport(s)**
Philadelphia International

**Directions**
From I-95 North toward Delaware, in Wilmington, take Exit 7a/Delaware Ave. Follow Rte. 52 North/Pennsylvania Ave. for 2.2 miles. Turn right onto Rte. 100 North, continue through 2 traffic lights. At the 3rd light make a right.

# The Bellmoor

6 Christian Street, Rehoboth Beach, DE 19971
**800-425-2355** • 302-227-5800 • Fax 302-227-0323

*Member Since 2004*

*Delaware*

*Rehoboth Beach*

*"...like visiting the seaside manor of a longtime friend."*

Proprietors
**The Moore Family**

Quiet moments in the garden...sunrise on the beach...the crackle of the fire in the Jefferson Library...a leisurely walk to unique boutique shopping and fine dining restaurants...a favorite book in the Sunroom. Our Day Spa offers over 30 services to restore and rejuvenate body and spirit. Whether you choose a sea-weed wrap, hot stone pedicure or a soothing springtime facial, you can leave the world behind and experience refined relaxation and well-being. Additional complimentary services: concierge, bellman, high speed Internet access, wireless access on first floor and in garden, guest computer room, two pools, hot tub, fitness room. Enjoy complete relaxation in our beautifully appointed accommodations of unsurpassed comfort combining the warm, residential feel of a B&B with the efficient, professional service of a small European hotel.

**Rates**
55 rooms, $125/$465 B&B. 23 suites, $150/$695 B&B; suites include marble bath, fireplace, whirlpool, wet bar. Adult concierge floor available. Rates change seasonally. Packages available, see website or call. Number of Rooms: 78

**Cuisine**
Full breakfast in Garden Room or in garden. Afternoon refreshments. 24 hour coffee service. Many fine dining options within walking distance. Entire property non-smoking.

**Nearest Airport(s)**
Philadelphia and Baltimore

**Directions**
Downtown Rehoboth Beach, residential setting 2 blocks from the ocean. See website or call for detailed directions.

SelectRegistry.com

# Washington, DC

**"The Nation's Capital"**

Famous for: The White House, the Capitol, Arlington Cemetery, Cherry Festival, the Smithsonian, Washington Monument.

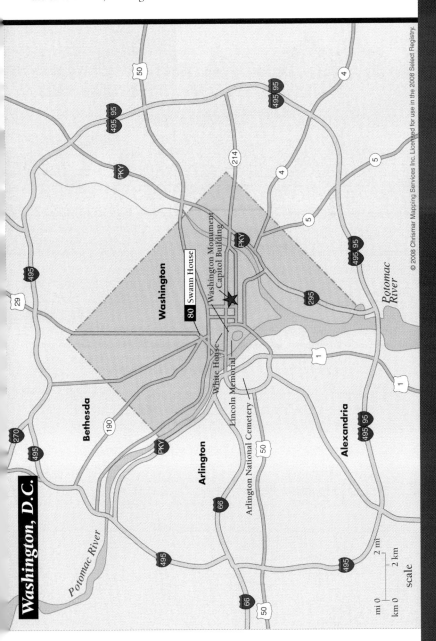

# Swann House

www.swannhouse.com
1808 New Hampshire Ave. N.W., Washington, DC 20009
**202-265-4414** • Fax 202-265-6755
stay@swannhouse.com

*Member Since 2002*

District of Columbia

Washington

*"Romantic, comfortable, welcoming - all the ingredients for a perfect getaway!
A truly wonderful experience!"*

Innkeepers/Owners
**Mary & Richard Ross**

Located on a tree-lined avenue in the heart of the Dupont Circle Historic District, Swann House welcomes you to the Nation's Capital and our 1883 Richardson Romanesque gem. Crystal chandeliers, elaborately carved fireplaces and original plaster moldings reflect just a portion of the nineteenth century craftsmanship that can be seen throughout our inn. Each individually decorated guestroom comes well appointed with sumptuous bathrobes, sateen sheets, down featherbeds and luxurious bath amenities. Select rooms include whirlpool baths, fireplaces and private decks for added luxury. Dozens of restaurants and cafes are just steps away allowing our guests to experience one of Washington's most vibrant and beautiful neighborhoods. Just 12 blocks from the White House and close proximity to several universities, galleries and conference venues, Swann House makes for a wonderful respite whether here for a romantic escape, business meeting or well-deserved getaway. "the Inn that launched 1,000 marriages" *Frommer's*"Fodor's Choice" *Fodor's Guide* "Top 10 Most Romantic Inn" in the country *American Historic Inns*.

### Rates
8 Rooms $165/$365; 4 Suites $265/$365. Each room is unique; all private baths, 6 with fireplace,4 Whirlpool.Cable TV, AC, WiFi. Massage available. Open year-round. Number of Rooms: 12

### Cuisine
Deluxe continental breakfast daily w/gourmet entree on weekends, afternoon refreshments, evening sherry, dozens of fine restaurants within walking distance.

### Nearest Airport(s)
Reagan National (DCA) 6 miles Dulles International (IAD) 26 miles

### Directions
Centrally located, just 12 blocks north of the White House. From Dupont Circle, take New Hampshire Ave. north. Swann House is located between S st & T st at the corner of Swann.

# *Florida*

Famous for: Disney World, Busch Gardens, St. Augustine (the oldest city in the U.S., founded 50 years before Plymouth), Florida Keys, Everglades, Space Shuttles, Beaches, Alligators, Oranges, Grapefruit, Wildlife.

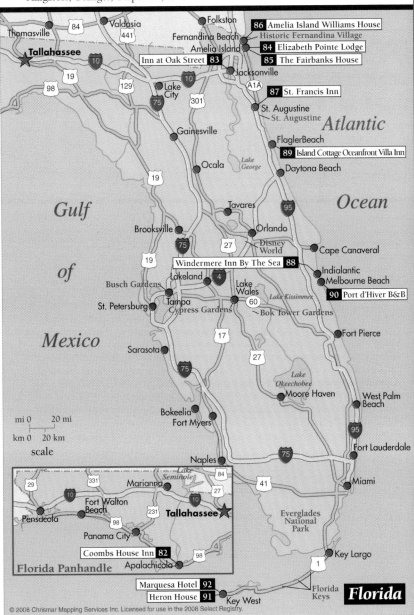

Thomasville
Valdosia
Folkston
84
441
**86** Amelia Island Williams House
Fernandina Beach
Historic Fernandina Village
**Tallahassee**
Amelia Island
**84** Elizabeth Pointe Lodge
10
Inn at Oak Street **83**
**85** The Fairbanks House
19
Jacksonville
98
129
10
A1A
**87** St. Francis Inn
Lake
City
75
301
St. Augustine
St. Augustine
*Atlantic*
Gainesville
FlaglerBeach
*Lake George*
**89** Island Cottage Oceanfront Villa Inn
Ocala
Daytona Beach
19
*Ocean*
Tavares
95
Brooksville
Orlando
75
27
Disney
World
Cape Canaveral
19
Windermere Inn By The Sea **88**
Indialantic
4
Melbourne Beach
Busch Gardens
Lakeland
Lake
Wales
**90** Port d'Hiver B&B
St. Petersburg
Tampa
60
*Lake Kissimmee*
Cypress Gardens
Bok Tower Gardens
*Gulf*
*of*
*Mexico*
17
Fort Pierce
Sarasota
27
75
*Lake Okeechobee*
mi 0    20 mi
Moore Haven
West Palm Beach
km 0    20 km
Bokeelia
scale
Fort Myers
95
Naples
75
Fort Lauderdale
*Lake Seminole*
Marianna
84
Miami
29
331
27
10
41
Fort Walton Beach
10
*Everglades National Park*
Pensacola
231
**Tallahassee**
98
Panama City
4
**Coombs House Inn 82**
98
Key Largo
*Florida Panhandle*
Apalachicola
1
**Marquesa Hotel 92**
*Florida Keys*
**Heron House 91**  Key West
**Florida**

© 2008 Chrismar Mapping Services Inc. Licensed for use in the 2008 Select Registry.

# Coombs Inn

www.coombshouseinn.com
80 Sixth Street, Apalachicola, FL 32320
**888-244-8320** • 850-653-9199 • Fax 850-653-2785
info@coombshouseinn.com

*Member Since 2006*

*"An elegant, romantic, perfect getaway, a memorable experience."*

Owners
**Lynn Wilson and Bill Spohrer**

The 1905 Coombs House Inn, located in Apalachicola on Florida's "Forgotten" Gulf Coast, occupies three elegant Victorian mansions in the historic district of this quaint seaside fishing village, adjacent to St. George Island with its white pristine beaches. Each of the 23 distinctively decorated rooms feature antique furniture and paintings, has its own full bath, cable TV, telephone and wireless access. Our seven luxury suites have romantic Jacuzzi tubs. Guests enjoy complimentary gourmet breakfasts, afternoon tea with home-baked cookies and weekend wine receptions. Choose complimentary bicycles for a tour of the Historic District or select beach chairs, umbrellas and towels for a visit to the nearby beaches. Camellia Hall, a spacious meeting room enhanced by gardens and a classic gazebo, provides the ideal setting for weddings and business meetings. *Travel + Leisure* Magazine recognized us as one of the "30 Great US Inns." Discover this enchanting town, established in 1831 and rich with maritime history. Relax on the many verandas, enjoy a walk to charming restaurants, taste our delicious oysters, visit our museums and theatre, or go fishing or kayaking on the famous Apalachicola River.

**Rates**
16 luxury rooms $99/$159. 7 jacuzzi suites $159/$229. Wedding Gardens seats 150. Number of Rooms: 23

**Cuisine**
An elegant breakfast of culinary delights such as Eggs Benedict, homemade Quiche, biscuits, fresh fruit, juice and Starbucks' coffee.

**Nearest Airport(s)**
Tallahassee & Panama City or private planes at Apalachicola Regional Airport.

**Directions**
Scenic US98 into town. 3 short blocks SW of flashing traffic light, corner of US98 and 6th St.

# The Inn at Oak Street

www.innatoakstreet.com
2114 Oak Street, Jacksonville, FL  32204
**904-379-5525** • Fax 904-379-5525
innatoakstreet@yahoo.com

*Member Since 2005*

*Florida*

*Jacksonville*

> *"A Jewel in Jacksonville…rooms combine comfort with couture."*
> *Travel + Leisure*

Proprietor
**Robert Eagle**

Bordering downtown Jacksonville, the Inn is located in the Riverside National Register Historic District, one of the most diverse collections of historic residential architecture in Florida. The Inn provides luxurious accommodations and superb amenities in the heart of this beautiful neighborhood, just steps from the St. Johns River. Built in 1902, and meticulously renovated by the owners, the Inn offers a vibrant and stylish interior in an urban historic environment. Spacious guestrooms, elegantly furnished, provide modern comforts including flat screen TV with DVD/CD player and wine refrigerator. Business travelers enjoy wireless Internet while lounging on the wraparound porch, while leisure guests relax with a massage in our tranquil spa room. Indulge in our complimentary wine hour, full gourmet breakfast and 24-hour coffee bar. Experience local boutiques, outstanding eateries and art museums, or enhance your stay with a variety of our special packages. Our personal service, fine details and amenities make your visit a memorable one.

**Rates**
$120/$180. Open year-round. Feature flat screen TV with DVD, wine refrigerator, plush robes. 3 rooms with spa tubs and balconies, 1 room with fireplace.  Number of Rooms: 6

**Cuisine**
Full gourmet breakfast included. Complimentary wine hour and 24 hour coffee bar. We offer a variety of Special Packages which include menu selections for dining at the Inn. Excellent dining within walking distance and a short drive.

**Nearest Airport(s)**
Jacksonville International Airport

**Directions**
15 minutes from airport, two miles from downtown Jacksonville. Easily accessible from I-95 North and South, and I-10.

# Elizabeth Pointe Lodge

www.elizabethpointelodge.com
98 South Fletcher Avenue, Amelia Island, FL  32034
**888-757-1910** • 904-277-4851 • Fax 904-277-6500
info@elizabethpointelodge.com

*Florida*

*Amelia Island*

*"One of the ten great places to sit on the porch" USA Today*

Innkeepers/Owners
**David and Susan Caples**

Rated "One of the 12 best waterfront inns" in America, the Pointe sits directly on the beach overlooking the Atlantic Ocean. Focusing upon individualized attention, the inn is Nantucket "shingle style" with an oversized soaking tub in each bath, USA Today and NY Times Digest delivered to your room daily, full seaside breakfast and a staff that wants to exceed your expectations. A selection of soups, salads, sandwiches, dessert, and room service available 24 hours. Complimentary WiFi DSL internet services available everywhere on the property. Only a short bike ride to the historic seaport of Fernandina. Many choices available of outstanding restaurants within 15 minutes of the Lodge. Concierge assistance available for 'day trips', bicycle touring, horseback riding, tennis, golf, sailing, charter fishing, boat rentals, birding, kayak and Segway tours and Spa experiences. Custom packages may be developed for Honeymoons, anniversary and birthday celebrations, golf instruction, 'all girl getaways' and small corporate meetings. AAA Three Diamond.

**Rates**
20 Rooms, $185/$295; 4 Oceanhouse deluxe rooms $240/$395; 1 Cottage, $425/$450 B&B. Open year-round. Number of Rooms: 25

**Cuisine**
A complete and tended buffet breakfast in the Sunrise Room or outside on the deck overlooking the ocean. A light fare menu available 24 hours. Complimentary social hour each evening at 6 p.m. Wine and beer available. Our culinary staff welcomes special dietary requests.

**Nearest Airport(s)**
Jacksonville International Approximately 35 minutes away.

**Directions**
From I-95 take exit 373 and follow Route A1A to Amelia Island. Our address on A1A is 98 S. Fletcher Avenue, on ocean side.

⨍ SelectRegistry.com

# The Fairbanks House

www.fairbankshouse.com
227 South 7th Street, Amelia Island, FL 32034
**888-891-9880** • 904-277-0500 • Fax 904-277-3103
email@fairbankshouse.com

*Member Since 1998*

*Florida*

> *"I've stayed in lots of 'hotels' but never in one that made me feel like I was home until I came here." "Your packages made our trip-planning so simple."*

*Amelia Island*

Innkeepers/Owners
**Bill & Theresa Hamilton**

Featured in *The Best Romantic Escapes in Florida* and built in 1885, Fairbanks House is an 8000 sq. ft. Italianate villa rising above a quiet Victorian village on Amelia Island. Surrounded by soaring magnolias and live oaks with dripping Spanish moss, the mansion, its cottages and pool rest on a strikingly landscaped acre where guests enjoy a serene 100% smoke-free stay. Rooms are casually elegant with period antiques, romantic reproductions and comfortable seating. Numerous upscale amenities are designed for a carefree getaway, honeymoon or vacation. King beds, Jacuzzis, robes, bikes, beach gear and full concierge service are but a few examples of our attention to detail. Many of our rooms are quite spacious and give honeymooners and vacationers plenty of room to spread out for a bit more seclusion and independence. Walk to shops, restaurants, carriage and boat tours; bike to secluded beaches and 1100 acre state park. Ask for details on seasonal specials, Romance Packages, Thanksgiving and Christmas packages and Girls Just Wanna Have Fun Getaways. If you don't see it on the website, just ask. We're happy to accommodate.

**Rates**
6 Rooms $175/$230, 3 Cottages $230/$365, 3 Suites, $265/$395 B&B. Open year-round. Number of Rooms: 12

**Cuisine**
Sumptuous gourmet breakfast served in our formal dining room, or on piazzas and patios amid our hidden gardens by the pool. Lively daily social hour with beverages, hot/cold hors d'oeuvres. Three minute walk to casual cafes, taverns and fine-dining restaurants.

**Nearest Airport(s)**
Jacksonville, FL

**Directions**
Use exit 373 East from I-95 and follow the signs for Fernandina Beach along Highway A1A, 200. After bridge go 3.3 miles to Cedar. L onto Cedar and R onto 7th. 25 minutes from JAX, FL airport, 15 minutes from I-95.

# Amelia Island Williams House

www.williamshouse.com
103 South Ninth Street, Amelia Island, FL 32034
**800-414-9258** • 904-277-2328
info@williamshouse.com

*"Your home is enchantingly beautiful, the breakfasts amazing and the hospitality unforgetable. Our stay was a time we'll always remember."*

Innkeepers/Owners
**Deborah and Byron McCutchen**

This beautiful circa 1856 antebellum mansion is one of Amelia Island's oldest residences. We have ten elegantly appointed guest rooms, each with its own unique decor, private bath and century old antique furnishings. Some guest rooms feature beautiful fireplaces with hand carved mantels and unique European tiles. Sweeping verandahs, fountains, and luscious gardens invite you to come and relax. Enjoy a delicious gourmet breakfast served in our opulent red and gold dining room on antique china, shimmering crystal, and sterling silver. Sip wine beneath 500 year-old oak trees covered with Spanish moss. The Williams House is located in the quaint seaside village of Fernandina Beach, where incredible buildings, wonderful shopping and world class restaurants abound. Experience warm hospitality and personal attention in one of the South's most romantic Bed and Breakfasts.

**Rates**
10 guest rooms, $219/$279. Specials & getaway packages available. Midweek discounts. Open year round. Number of Rooms: 10

**Cuisine**
Breakfast is served each morning in our elegant dining room and consist of two courses with fresh ground coffee and juice. At sunset each evening enjoy wine and hors d'oeuvres on our sweeping verandahs or in winter by the fire.

**Nearest Airport(s)**
Jacksonville, Florida

**Directions**
Take A1A/200,exit 373, from I-95 east toward Amelia Island. Stay on A1A until it becomes 8th St. Turn right on Beech St., then left on 9th St. The Williams House will be on your left.

# St. Francis Inn

www.stfrancisinn.com
279 St. George Street, St. Augustine, FL 32084
**800-824-6062** • 904-824-6068 • Fax 904-810-5525
info@stfrancisinn.com

*Member Since 2002*

*"Your hospitality was great! We liked the small details - mints, sherry, fresh flowers, etc. Thank you for a great place for peace and quiet."*

**Innkeepers/Owners**
**Joe and Margaret Finnegan**

Come visit the past! Guestrooms and suites with antiques, balconies with rocking chairs and swings, fireplaces and whirlpools add to the tranquil ambiance. Walk to everything from the Inn's Old City location. This historic Inn overflows with hospitality, set in a lush tropical courtyard on brick paved streets with horse-drawn buggies passing by. A historic treasure, but modern comforts abound! Great value, with many guest amenities: swimming pool, gourmet Southern breakfasts, bicycles, social hour, evening sweets, DVD, wi-fi, courtesy local transportation, health club privileges, private parking, free and discounted attractions tickets, coffee and inn-baked cookies, sherry and flowers in your room. The Inn provides guest facilities for an afternoon at St. Augustine beach. Add inroom massages, gift baskets, inroom breakfasts, picnic baskets, flowers, champagne and other ala carte extras. Tropical setting provides endless outdoor activities, plus sightseeing, historic landmarks, cultural events and celebrations steps away. Many packages available to enhance your stay with added value and savings, themed for romance, history, and more.

### Rates
12 Rooms $129/$279; 4 Suites $169/$279; 2-BR Cottage $249/$329 for 4. Many superb amenities included. Special packages and extras. Number of Rooms: 17

### Cuisine
Homemade breakfast entrees and more, enjoyed in our dining room, your room, on a private balcony or in the garden courtyard! Appetizers & beverages at social hour; evening sweets; homemade cookies all day. Mimosas, Bloody Marys at weekend breakfast.

### Nearest Airport(s)
St. Johns County (SGJ); Jacksonville Internat'l (JAX)

### Directions
I-95 to exit 318 St. Augustine SR16, to US 1, south to King St, go L. 2/3 mi to St. George St, turn R. Inn is 3 blocks on L, park on R

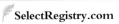

# Windemere Inn By The Sea

www.windemereinn.com
815 S. Miramar Avenue (A1A), Indialantic, FL 32903
**800-224-6853** • 321-728-9334
stay@windemereinn.com

*Member Since 2005*

*Florida*

*Indialantic*

*"Our stay far exceeded our expectations. You made our 12th Anniversary very special. We will be back before our 13th."*

Innkeeper
**Elizabeth G. Fisher**

Imagine ... a luxury, oceanfront bed and breakfast, only an hour east of Orlando. Guest rooms and suites are furnished with antiques and fine linens, most with ocean views, some with balconies, porches, whirlpool tubs or TVs. Start each morning with a full, gourmet breakfast, enjoy pastries and sherry at "tea time." Windemere is the ideal spot for your corporate retreat, small wedding, honeymoon or special getaway, for watching a rocket launch form Kennedy Space Center, or witnessing sea turtles nest and hatch. The grounds have several gardens, including herbs for cooking. The central point is a lily pond alive with marine plants and animals. Sit on our Beachside Pergola and watch dolphins and surfers play in the waves, or the moon rise. The Inn has private beach access and provides beach gear. We are able to cater to most dietary needs upon request. Windemere is 45 minutes south of Kennedy Space Center, an hour east of Orlando and 10 minutes from Historic Downtown Melbourne with shopping, arts and entertainment and casual and fine dining. To view our rooms please visit www.windemereinn.com. Open year round.

**Rates**
7 Guest Rooms. $157/$275. 2 two bedroom suites $355 and $410. AAA and pre-registered corporate discounts offered. Number of Rooms: 9

**Cuisine**
Start each morning with sunrise over the Atlantic, and a full gourmet breakfast. A fruit course is followed by alternating sweet and savory dishes and a bread basket. Home made pastries and desserts are served at "tea time" daily.

**Nearest Airport(s)**
Melbourne Int'l 15 minutes, Orlando Int'l 1 hour

**Directions**
I-95, exit #180 (Hwy. 192) East to A1A, Right/South 1/4 mi. on Left/ocean side.

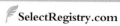

# Island Cottage Oceanfront Inn

www.islandcottagevillas.com
2316 S. Oceanshore Blvd., Flagler Beach, FL 32136
**87-ROMANCE-2** • 386-439-0092 • Fax 386-439-7009
icv@bellsouth.net

*Member Since 2008*

*"The service is amazing, the restaurant is 5 star (seriously), and this place cannot be more adorable."*

Owners/Innkeepers
**Toni and Mark Treworgy**

Tucked away in a tiny beach community along the Atlantic shoreline rests this quaint jewel of the coast appreciated for its warmth, tranquility & romanticism. From the moment you enter the courtyard, you'll want to kick off your shoes & relax as gentle island music mentally transports you to a secluded tropical paradise. Embracing the charm of the Caribbean, the rooms are tastefully decorated in a casually romantic style offering amenities such as private decks, ocean views, fireplaces & Jacuzzis for two - all accented with quality linens, bath robes & other fine luxuries.

Plan to indulge in a couples massage package at the Inn's exclusive Tropical Breeze Spa or just sit back and enjoy the sparkling pool, the sounds of the surf & the scent of fresh sea air. The Inn also offers an elegant Mediterranean style cafe' replete with pressed table linens, simmering silver, sparkling crystal & soft candlelight ... serving gourmet hot breakfasts each morning and offering a prix fixe, 6 course extremely romantic fine dining experience most Saturday evenings - often accompanied by live music and dancing. Advanced reservations are required.

**Rates**
2 cozy rooms $199 to $249 - 4 luxury studios $229 to $399
3 villa suites $299 to $450 - Open Thurs. thru Mon. year round
except Thanksgiving & Christmas weeks. Number of Rooms: 9

**Cuisine**
Gourmet hot breakfast including fresh locally grown fruit,
home grown herbs, coffee, tea & chilled juice served by
candlelight on elegantly appointed individual tables. 6 Course
prix fixe dinner offered most Saturday evenings; $85pp +
beverage, tax & gratuity.

**Nearest Airport(s)**
Daytona Beach International

**Directions**
From I-95 take exit #284. Go east 3 miles to the ocean. Turn
right on SR A1A. Travel 2 miles to #2316.

**Awards**
Environmentally friendly, official "Green Lodging" facility
recognized by the State of Florida for the conservation and
protection of our planet's natural resources.

# Port d'Hiver Bed & Breakfast

www.portdhiver.com
201 Ocean Avenue, Melbourne Beach, FL 32951
**866-621-7678** • 321-722-2727 • Fax 321-723-3221
info@portdhiver.com

*Member Since 2008*

*Florida*

*Melbourne Beach*

*"...waking up with the sunrise, scrumptious breakfast in bed, relaxing soaks in the spa and mints on the pillows at dusk! A wonderfully romantic experience."*

**Linda and Michael Rydson,
Valerie Garofalo**

The historic Port d'Hiver Bed and Breakfast Inn is old Florida luxury at its finest. A comfortable yet elegant retreat just 200 feet from the Atlantic Ocean, Port d'Hiver has gorgeous ocean views, large private porches, a bubbling spa pool and winding brick paths through a private compound of four Island style buildings surrounded by lush tropical landscaping. Soak away the world in a large spa tub in one of our spacious new cabana rooms or watch the sunrise over the ocean from the deck of your beautifully restored historic room. In the morning, enjoy a full breakfast either on your private porch or at individual tables in our cheerfully inviting dining room. At Port d'Hiver we also offer refreshments at five in the main house, full complimentary concierge services, wireless internet, flat screen TVs, evening turn down service and the finest amenities. Fish, surf, dine, or watch the sea turtles... Melbourne Beach is a barrier island only .7 miles across from the ocean to the Indian River Lagoon. On historic Ocean Avenue, Port d'Hiver brings history, nature, privacy and comfort together in one luxurious retreat.

**Rates**
$200/$525. Number of Rooms: 11

**Cuisine**
Elegant and relaxing three course breakfast served individually in our sunny dining room or in your room. Enjoy wine and hors d'oeuvres at 5:00, cookies, coffee and fully stocked snack room available 24 hours a day. Evening treats at bedtime.

**Nearest Airport(s)**
Melbourne International - 7 miles; Orlando International - 69 miles

**Directions**
Port d'Hiver is located 70 miles southeast of Orlando. From Interstate 95, take exit 173. Proceed east on FL192 eight miles to State Highway A1A. Turn right (south) and proceed 2 miles. Follow A1A left, and end at 201 Ocean Avenue.

# Heron House

www.heronhouse.com
512 Simonton Street, Key West, FL 33040
**888-265-2395** • 305-294-9227 • Fax 305-294-5692
heronkyw@aol.com

*Member Since 2002*

*Florida*

*Key West*

*"Unique…quiet and romantic; a lover's paradise!"*

Proprietors/General Manager
**Roy & Christina Howard, Jeffrey Brannin**

The Heron House is located on Simonton Street in the Historic District of Old Town Key West, only one block from the main street known as Duval. The Heron House is a 23-room small romantic Inn, comprised of three historical conch-style homes. An elegantly tiled swimming pool is nestled between two of the homes. Beautifully landscaped, Heron House features an orchid nursery, as well as exotic tropical plants. Centrally located, the Heron House provides easy access to numerous restaurants and beaches. Winner of *American Bed & Breakfast Association* 4-Crown award. Winner of AAA's Four Diamond award.

**Rates**
23 Rooms, $159/$389; 4 poolside, 2 Premium Poolside, 4 Garden, 7 Deluxe Garden, 4 Garden Terrace Junior, and 2 Honeymoon Junior Suites. Newly renovated, tropically furnished, AC, phones, color cable TV. Number of Rooms: 23

**Cuisine**
Full expanded hot and cold continental breakfast; wine and cheese served nightly before sunset on weekends.

**Nearest Airport(s)**
Key West International Airport

**Directions**
Take Truman Ave (US 1) S. Head W on Simonton St. The Heron House is on the S side, between Southard and Fleming.

🍽️ 🍽️ 🍷

# The Marquesa Hotel

www.marquesa.com
600 Fleming St., Key West, FL 33040
**800-869-4631 Reservations Only** • 305-292-1919 • Fax 305-294-2121

*Member Since 1991*

info@marquesa.com

*"Bravo! Beautifully appointed, gorgeous setting, accomodating and knowledgeable staff."*

Innkeeper/Owner
**Carol Wightman**

In the heart of Key West's Historic District, The Marquesa Hotel and Cafe is a landmark 120-year-old home, restored to four-diamond status. Floor-to-ceiling windows, exotic orchids, two shimmering pools and lush gardens are Marquesa trademarks. Rooms and suites are luxurious with private marble baths, bathrobes, and fine furnishings. Located one block from Duval Street for shops, galleries, restaurants and nightlife. *The Miami Herald* rated it as one of Florida's top 10 Inns, and Travel & Leisure Magazine's Reader Poll ranked The Marquesa in the "World's Best Hotels." Zagat Survey members rated Cafe Marquesa as the highest rated restaurant in Key West for 2007. Named an "Orvis-Endorsed Lodge" for fishing expeditions.

**Rates**
14 Rooms, $190/$385; 13 Suites, $300/$495. Open year-round. Number of Rooms: 27

**Cuisine**
Poolside or room service dining for breakfast; fine dining in Cafe Marquesa with an innovative and delicious menu. Excellent wine list and full bar. Fresh local seafood, quality grilled meats. Named one of Key West's Top Five Romantic Restaurants by KeyTV. AAA 4-Diamond Award. Favorites include Conch-Blue Crab Cake, Rack of Lamb, Key-Lime Napoleon.

**Nearest Airport(s)**
Key West International Airport - 3 miles

**Directions**
US 1, R on N Roosevelt Blvd, becomes Truman Ave. Continue to Simonton, turn R, go 5 blks to Fleming. Turn R. Hotel on R.

# Georgia

**"The Peach State"**

Famous for: Stone Mountain, Okefenokee Swamp, Live Oak Trees, Islands, Beaches, Peaches, Historic Savannah.

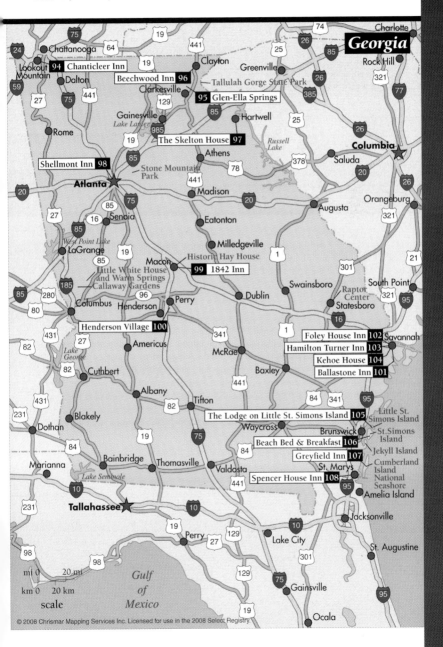

Georgia

**94** Chanticleer Inn
Beechwood Inn **96**
**95** Glen-Ella Springs
The Skelton House **97**
Shellmont Inn **98**
**99** 1842 Inn
Henderson Village **100**
Foley House Inn **102**
Hamilton Turner Inn **103**
Kehoe House **104**
Ballastone Inn **101**
The Lodge on Little St. Simons Island **105**
Beach Bed & Breakfast **106**
Greyfield Inn **107**
Spencer House Inn **108**

© 2008 Chrismar Mapping Services Inc. Licensed for use in the 2008 Select Registry.

# Chanticleer Inn

www.stayatchanticleer.com
1300 Mockingbird Lane, Lookout Mountain, GA 30750
**866-777-7999** • 706-820-2002 • Fax 706-820-7976
info@stayatchanticleer.com

*Member Since 2003*

*Georgia*

*Lookout Mountain*

> *"You are such wonderful hosts! This was so relaxing.*
> *We cannot wait to return. Thank you."*

Innkeepers
**Kirby & Judy Wahl**

THIS HISTORIC INN combines the ambiance of yesteryear with the comfort and amenities of today. Built in 1927, Chanticleer Inn offers 17 luxurious guest rooms each decorated with antiques and classic fabrics. Nestled among gardens and stone walkways, the cottage rooms have modern conveniences and some extras such as fireplace, Jacuzzi,steam shower or patios. Perfect for romance, relaxation, sightseeing, business, or weddings, the Chanticleer Inn caters to each guest with gracious hospitality. Located high atop Lookout Mountain near all Chattanooga attractions, Chanticleer Inn is convenient yet tranquil. Guests enjoy national military parks, waterfalls, golf, shops, spas, and many nearby restaurants.

**Rates**
$120/$220 per night includes full breakfast. King, queen, or 2 queen beds. Rates based on room size and amenities such as whirlpool tub, steam shower or gas fireplace. Suites available. Number of Rooms: 17

**Cuisine**
Breakfast is freshly prepared each day. We recommend local restaurants for lunch and dinner. We also host weddings, conferences, & meetings, see www.meetatgrandview.com.

**Nearest Airport(s)**
Chattanooga

**Directions**
From Atlanta/Knoxville: I-75 to I-24W or Nashville/Birmingham: I-24E. Exit 178 off of I-24 "Lookout Mountain" exit - follow signs to Lookout Mountain and Rock City. 10 min. from Chattanooga.

# Glen-Ella Springs

www.glenella.com
1789 Bear Gap Rd, Clarkesville, GA 30523
**888-455-8886** • 706-754-7295 • Fax 706-754-1560
info@glenella.com

*Member Since 1990*

*Georgia*

*"Delicious food, beautiful scenery, fine hospitality." "God smiles on Glen-Ella." "The Inn and grounds are absolutely awesome - food superior!"*

*Clarkesville*

Innkeepers/Owners
**Ed and Luci Kivett**

Wander down the gravel road at the southernmost tip of the Blue Ridge Mountains and discover the peaceful setting of Glen-Ella Springs Country Inn. Listen to the birds sing while you rock on the porch. Stroll around the extensive perennial and herb gardens, and eighteen acres of meadow bordered by Panther Creek. Relax by the massive stone fireplace in our century-old inn, a rare example of the traditional small hotels that once dotted the North Georgia Mountains. Relish the comfort of the inn's tasteful decor. Savor the outstanding food, from bountiful country buffet breakfasts to elegant dinners. The constantly changing menu in our award-winning restaurant, named one of Georgia's Top Ten Dining Destinations in 2004 through 2007, guarantees a memorable dining experience in an atmosphere of casual elegance. Spend leisurely days fishing world class trout streams, hiking numerous scenic trails, boating on nearby rivers and lakes, or exploring charming historic villages filled with fine art and crafts by local artisans.

**Rates**
16 Rooms, $150/$265 B&B. Open year-round. Number of Rooms: 16

**Cuisine**
Bountiful country breakfasts. Dinner by reservation from a constantly changing menu of upscale southern-American cuisine prepared by our professional staff, guaranteeing a memorable dining experience.

**Nearest Airport(s)**
Greenville, SC or Atlanta, GA

**Directions**
At the edge of the Blue Ridge Mtns, 90 miles north of Atlanta. 3 miles off 4-lane US 441 between Clarkesville & Clayton; Go west on T. Smith Rd. at mile marker 18, then N. on Historic Old 441. Take the first left on Orchard Rd., then follow the signs.

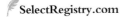

# Beechwood Inn

www.beechwoodinn.ws
220 Beechwood Dr, P.O. Box 429, Clayton, GA 30525
**866-782-2485** • 706-782-5485 • Fax 706-782-7644
david-gayle@beechwoodinn.ws

*Georgia*

*Clayton*

> *"The inn is simply beautiful. You will receive superb service and food on par with either the Ritz or Four Seasons, and at a much more reasonable rate."*

**Innkeepers/Owners**
## Gayle and David Darugh

Georgia's Premier Wine Country Inn offers luxury lodging in a rustic mountain setting. Nestled among 100 year-old terraced gardens overlooking Black Rock Mountain, it is a place where all elements add up to a culinary and wine-oriented journey. The Inn features Northeast Georgia's only Wine Spectator Award of Excellence restaurant. It offers Saturday Prixe Fixe dining by advance reservation featuring fresh California and Mediterranean-style meals using the best of local, organic and sustainable products from nearby farms, vineyards and orchards. Peggy McBride says: "Beechwood Inn is like fine wine itself, aging beautifully on fertile ground, romantic and sensuous with a hint of peach and rosemary bouquet. The innkeepers are protecting this land through eco-friendly practices and a genuinely people-friendly attitude. The results are smiling guests upon departure yearning to return for another taste of that special ingredient. It is the very essence of Beechwood Inn ? true Southern hospitality." Explore mountain villages, raft the Chattooga River, hike to a waterfall or drive along bucolic country lanes.

### Rates
2 rooms, 5 suites, 1 cottage $189/$229 B&B. Private baths, Fireplaces, views. Complimentary afternoon "Wine-Thirty. Number of Rooms: 8

### Cuisine
Beechwood Bountiful Breakfast daily. Multi-course Prix Fixe dinners w/wine on most Saturdays by advance reservation. Extensive wine list & wine cellar. Visit our website for information on gourmet wine events, wine tastings & special weekend packages.

### Nearest Airport(s)
Atlanta, GA and Asheville, NC each 90 minutes; Greenville, SC 50 minutes.

### Directions
In Clayton, Georgia, at intersection of Hwys 441 & 76, turn E on 76. Go 1/10 mi., turn L on Beechwood Dr. Follow inn signs.

**SelectRegistry.com**

# The Skelton House

www.theskeltonhouse.com
97 Benson Street, Hartwell, GA  30643-1991
**877-556-3790** • 706-376-7969 • Fax 706-856-3139
t.skeltonhouse@comcast.net

*Member Since 2001*

*"You delivered...just as promised...real Southern Hospitality!"*

Innkeepers/Owners
**Ruth and John Skelton**

The Skelton House is an 1896 National Register Victorian Inn, located in the historic downtown area of the small town of Hartwell. The charm, grace and hospitality of the original Skelton family and their grand home has been retained by today's generation of Skeltons. Celebrating its 11th year as a bed and breakfast, the doors welcome you into our spacious rooms. Whether sitting on the porches or strolling the 2 acres of gardens, you will feel that you have stepped back into a more relaxed time. Ruth's cheese nubbins or John's chocolate chip cookies add to the homelike atmosphere.Located only 13 miles South of I-85 in the NE corner of GA. Less than 2 hours from the metro Atlanta area or 1 hour from the local Greenville/Spartanburg airport. The perfect getaway for vacationers and business travelers alike. Come experience what many believe to be the ultimate in Southern Hospitality

**Rates**
$100/$135. Antiques, room tvs/hbo, private phones, wi-fi, room thermostats, ceiling fans, queen beds, luxury linens, private baths/hairdryers.  Number of Rooms: 7

**Cuisine**
Creative full service hot breakfasts made fresh daily with the best seasonal and local ingredients. Nearby casual dining with a lunch & dinner menu of southern regional cuisine and a full service bar (closed Mondays)

**Nearest Airport(s)**
Greenville, SC (GSP) 65 miles.

**Directions**
I-85 to GA exit 177. 13 mi. S on GA Hwy 77 to Hartwell. Stay on Hwy 77 as it turns R at the 5th traffic light. Look for us on the immediate L past the Presbyterian Church.

# Shellmont Inn

www.shellmont.com
821 Piedmont Ave. N.E., Atlanta, GA 30308
**404–872–9290** • Fax 404–872–5379
innkeeper@shellmont.com

*Member Since 1994*

*Georgia*

*Atlanta*

*"A jewel in the heart of Atlanta. Southern hospitality at its finest. Exquisite!"*

Innkeepers/Owners
**Ed and Debbie McCord**

The Shellmont Inn is an impeccably restored 1891 National Register mansion in Midtown Atlanta's "Miracle Mile", our theatre, restaurant and cultural district. The Inn is a treasure chest of stained, leaded and beveled glass, intricately-carved woodwork and hand-painted stenciling. Guest rooms are furnished with antiques, oriental rugs and period wall treatments. Wicker-laden verandas overlook manicured lawns and gardens,including a Victorian fishpond. The experience is unforgettable. National Register of Historic Places Property. City of Atlanta Landmark Building. Recipient of Mayor's Award for Excellence for Historic Preservation.

**Rates**
Standard Rooms $160/$225; Deluxe Rooms $215/$275; Carriage House $245/$350. Open year-round. Number of Rooms: 5

**Cuisine**
Full gourmet breakfast, complimentary beverages, fresh fruit basket, evening chocolates, evening turn-down service. Fully licensed and inspected. Atlanta's smallest Historic Hotel.

**Nearest Airport(s)**
Hartsfield-Jackson Int'l - 8 miles

**Directions**
From airport, I-75/85 N, exit 248-C (International Blvd), turn L at 2nd traffic light (Ellis St), turn R at next traffic light (Piedmont Ave). Go N 1 1/4 mile. Located at the intersection of Piedmont Ave and 6th. Street on the R.

# 1842 Inn

www.the1842inn.com
353 College Street, Macon, GA  31201
**800-336-1842** • 478-741-1842 • Fax 478-741-1842
management@1842inn.com

*Member Since 1994*

*Georgia • Macon*

*Zagat top 50 US Inns and Resorts.*

Innkeeper
**Nazario Filipponi**

The 1842 Inn boasts 19 luxurious rooms and public areas tastefully designed with fine English antiques, tapestries and paintings. A quaint garden courtyard and garden pool greet guests for cocktails or breakfast. Nightly turndowns, shoeshines and fresh flowers enhance many other gracious grand hotel amenities. Rooms available with whirlpool tubs and fireplaces. High level of service. Valet parking on request. Considered 'One of America's Top 100 Inns in the 20th Century' by the International Restaurant and Hospitality Rating Bureau.

**Rates**
19 Guest Rooms, $139/$280 B&B. (Rates subject to change without notice.) Open year-round.  Number of Rooms: 19

**Cuisine**
Full breakfast and hors d'oeuvres included. Dinner at Marco Ristorante Italiano and complimentary transportation. Full service bar.

**Nearest Airport(s)**
Macon, Atlanta

**Directions**
Exit 164 on I-75 turn L fm N; R fm S go to College St; turn Left; Inn is 2 blocks on left.

🍽️ 🍽️ 🍽️ 🍷

# Henderson Village

www.hendersonvillage.com
125 South Langston Circle, Perry, GA 31069
**888-615-9722** • 478-988-8696 • Fax 478-988-9009
info@hendersonvillage.com

*Member Since 2002*

*Georgia*

*Perry*

*"This is my kind of country living! Great food, great service, great place. Thank you."*

Assistant Manager
**Vicki Mosteller**

Authentic Southern Hospitality awaits, with twelve historic homes beautifully restored and relocated to create a most charming country resort with thousands of acres to relax, unwind and recuperate in traditional southern style. Delight in our gourmet restaurant voted 'The absolute best dining experience in Georgia,' by *Georgia Trend* Magazine. Unwind as you ride horses alongside the cotton fields and through our pecan orchards. Test your skills shooting sporting clays or spend a lazy day in the sun fishing for bass. Rejuvenate your spirit with massage and an afternoon by the pool. Henderson Village is a rare find. Top Ten Most Romantic Inn for 2003.

**Rates**
24 Rooms/Suites $159/$297, includes full village breakfast. Cottages are elegantly rustic; houses are subtly refined. Office hours are 7 a.m. to 10 p.m. EDT. Number of Rooms: 24

**Cuisine**
Excellent a la carte breakfast, lunch and dinner menu, hot country breakfast, homemade pastries, fruit; room service available. Full bar and extensive wine list.

**Nearest Airport(s)**
Atlanta International

**Directions**
I-75 to Exit 127; Hwy. 26 W 1 mile. Henderson Village is at the crossroads of GA Hwy. 26 and US Hwy. 41. 40 miles south of Macon, 10 miles south of Perry.

# Ballastone Inn

www.ballastone.com
14 East Oglethorpe Avenue, Savannah, GA 31401
**800-822-4553** • 912-236-1484 • Fax 912-236-4626
inn@ballastone.com

*Member Since 2005*

*Georgia*

*"If there were a hall of fame for bed and breakfasts, Ballastone would be at the top." "The word 'no' does not exist here!"*

*Savannah*

Innkeepers/Owners
**Jennifer and Jim Salandi**

The four-story Italianate Ballastone Inn, built in 1838 and located in the heart of Savannah's historic district, offers 16 exquisite rooms and suites, most with fireplaces. "Table for Two Privacy," a handsome Victorian bar, 24/7 concierge services, elevator, and limited off-street parking distinguish the Ballastone Inn, a nine-year AAA four-diamond property. Details including softly-scented Egyptian 400 thread count linens, French down blankets, fresh flowers, Gilchrist and Soames English Spa Collection amenities and distinctive antiques are why the Ballastone Inn has been voted "Most Romantic Inn" by *Savannah Magazine* and in 2006 "Most Romantic" by *Coastal Living Magazine*. Rates include a full Southern breakfast; formal afternoon tea served on a sterling silver tea service and fine china; hors d'oeuvres. Full service bar featuring premium boutique wines. A National Register historic site, The Ballastone is a 2005 Andrew Harper's Hideaway Grand Award Winner and is recommended by Conde Nast Johansens, Fodor's, and Frommer's.

### Rates
$235/$395 Double occupancy. Courtyard, deluxe, and superior rooms, plus luxury suites which overlook the lush garden.
Number of Rooms: 16

### Cuisine
An elegant, personally prepared, "table for two", made-to-order breakfast; afternoon high tea on sterling silver tea service, enjoyed with fragrant antique linens; pre-dinner hors d'oeuvres; and private bar with premium liquors and boutique wines. Smoking is permitted outdoors.

### Nearest Airport(s)
Savannah-Hilton Head Intl

### Directions
East on I-16 to Savannah. Exit on Montgomery St. R on Oglethorpe Avenue to Drayton Street. U-turn L around the median to the Inn.

# Foley House Inn

www.foleyinn.com
14 West Hull Street, Savannah, GA 31401
**800-647-3708** • 912-232-6622
info@foleyinn.com

*Member Since 1998*

**Georgia**

**Savannah**

*"One of the top ten romantic inns in all of North America!" - Vacation Magazine*

Innkeepers/Owners
**Allisen & Grant Rogers**

An upscale AAA 4-diamond Southern B&B with a European appeal. Common areas & guest rooms decorated with British period decor and stunning architecture. Gas fireplaces in most rooms; canopied and four-poster beds. Some rooms with oversized Jacuzzi baths and private balconies. Enjoy a complimentary gourmet breakfast, afternoon tea with sweets, and hors d'oeuvres with wine in the evening...all prepared by our critically-acclaimed chef. Our concierge will make dinner and tour reservations. Amazingly short walk to restaurants, theatres, antique stores, art galleries, etc. from this perfectly central location. Some rooms have private balconies overlooking historic Chippewa square, the site where "Forrest Gump" was filmed eating chocolates and waiting for the bus. Our park-like setting leads to Bull Street and one of the most historic walks in America. All the luxor of the 1800s without sacrificing modern conveniences. Wireless internet connections and spa services are available complete with a fitness room.

**Rates**
$225/$395 Off season discounts offered. Number of Rooms: 19

**Cuisine**
Complimentary gourmet breakfast, afternoon tea with sweets, and hors d'oeuvres with complimentary wine in the evening... all prepared by our critically-acclaimed chef. Treats w/ turndown service. Premium wines & champagnes for sale by the bottle or glass at any time. Short walk to fine restaurants.

**Nearest Airport(s)**
Savannah/Hilton Head International

**Directions**
From I-95 to I-16 to end at Montgomery St. Right at 2nd light onto Oglethorpe St., R onto Bull St., R onto Hull St. 1st red brick building on R. Beautiful Chippewa Square is our front yard.

# Hamilton Turner

www.hamilton-turnerinn.com
330 Abercorn Street, Savannah, GA 31401
**888-448-8849** • 912-233-1833 • Fax 912-233-0291
innkeeper@hamilton-turnerinn.com

*Member Since 2003*

*Georgia*

*Savannah*

> *"We now know what true Southern Hospitality is.
> The food and service at your B&B is exceptional."*

**Innkeepers/Owners**
**Jim and Gay Dunlop**

Experience the gracious Southern hospitality of Savannah at the elegant Hamilton-Turner Inn. The mansion, built in 1873 as a family residence for Samuel Hamilton, retains a 19th century grandeur infused with modern day sophisticated comforts and amenities. Nestled among the live oaks on beautiful Lafayette Square the Inn is ideally situated in the center of the Historic District. Fine cuisine and other points of interest are within a short stroll. Our knowledgeable concierge staff is poised to offer recommendations and secure reservations for touring, restaurants and leisure activities.

Choose from grand suites overlooking the moss-draped oaks in the park; luxuriously appointed rooms; garden-view courtyard rooms with private entrances; and three carriage house rooms with shared parlor. Some accommodations offer fireplace, whirlpool spa bath, and bay windows.

Whether you are looking for a reunion with longtime friends, romantic honeymoon getaway, business travel retreat or golf vacation, the Inn has a package to exceed your desires. Featured in *Southern Living* and *Conde Nast Traveler.*

**Rates**
11 bedrooms, 6 suites from $189 to $369 per night, double occupancy. King, 2 queen, queen, & 2 twin beds available. Carriage house offers 3 guestrooms and parlor. ADA room & pet friendly rooms. Number of Rooms: 17

**Cuisine**
Complimentary cuisine features full southern mansion breakfast, afternoon iced-tea and sweets, evening wine and hors d'oeuvres, late evening port, turndown sweet.

**Nearest Airport(s)**
Savannah/Hilton Head Intl, SAV, 8 mi.

**Directions**
I-95 to I-16. I-16 East to Savannah. Exit on Montgomery St. R on Liberty St. R on Abercorn St. to Lafayette Square. Round the square, park on Charlton or Macon.

# Kehoe House

www.kehoehouse.com
123 Habersham Street, Savannah, GA 31401
**800-820-1020** • 912-232-1020 • Fax 912-231-0208
info@kehoehouse.com

*Member Since 2003*

*Georgia*

*Savannah*

*"Truly a Savannah treasure! ...a gorgeous home with a fascinating history and excellent service. Our stay was a very enjoyable experience!"*

Owner
**Bed and Breakfasts of Savannah.com**

The Kehoe House is the crowning jewel in Savannah's premier group of exquisitely restored historic inns, BedandBreakfastsofSavannah.com. Once home to the William Kehoe family, the Inn features 13 original guest rooms appointed with fine linens, antiques, intriguing art and elegant furnishings. World-class service and amenities include gourmet cooked-to-order breakfast, complimentary afternoon tea and a wine and hors d'oeuvres reception. While the Kehoe House's turn-of-the-century ambience has been preserved, guests also enjoy modern conveniences such as wireless Internet and private, luxurious baths. Known as one of the nation's most romantic bed and breakfast inns, The Kehoe House's elegance and sophistication have made it popular for special wedding nights and anniversary celebrations. Bed and Breakfasts of Savannah.com affiliated Inns in Savannah: The Kehoe House, The Gastonian, The Marshall House, The Eliza Thompson House, East Bay Inn and Olde Harbour Inn.

**Rates**
Low Season $249/$379, High Season $299/$429. Special Packages Available. Specialties include Romantic Celebrations.All-white Q or K-size bedding w/contrasting colors, armoire, wireless high-speed Internet access, CD player, TV/DVD player & private bath.Turndown Service. Number of Rooms: 13

**Cuisine**
Gourmet made-to-order breakfast, afternoon tea service, & evening hors d'oeuvres w/wine. Coffee and tea available 24

**Nearest Airport(s)**
Savannah Airport

**Directions**
I-95 to I-16 to end at Montgomery. Right on Liberty, left on Habersham to Columbia Square.

# Lodge on Little St. Simons Island

🍽️ 🍽️ 🍽️ 🍷

www.LittleSSI.com
P.O. Box 21078, Little St. Simons Island, GA 31522-0578
**888-733-5774** • 912-638-7472 • Fax 912-634-1811
Lodge@LittleStSimonsIsland.com

*Member Since 1993*

*"Great getaway, perfect balance of seclusion and comfort, relaxation and activity."*

General Manager
**Joel Meyer**

Nature prevails on this pristine Georgia island where 10,000 acres are shared with no more than 30 overnight guests at a time. Accessible only by boat, Little St. Simons Island unfolds its secrets to those eager to discover a bounty of natural wonders. Seven miles of shell-strewn, private beaches meet acres of legendary moss-draped live oaks, glistening tidal creeks, and shimmering salt marshes to provide an unparalleled setting for a host of activities and total relaxation. Guests enjoy interpretive tours, birding, canoeing, kayaking, fishing, hiking, and bicycling. Creature comforts include gracious accommodations, delicious regional cuisine, and warm Southern hospitality. The Lodge on Little St. Simons Island was recently voted #1 Resort in the Mainland US ~ Condé Nast Traveler's Readers' Choice Awards.

**Rates**
Open year-round. Children of all ages are welcome May - September; children over 8 years old are welcome October - April. All inclusive rates $450-$675 per couple, per night. Suites, Full House, and Exclusive Full Island rentals also available. Visit www.LittleSSI.com for specials. Number of Rooms: 15

**Cuisine**
Delicious regional cuisine served family-style. Rate includes 3 meals daily, beverages, snacks, and a complimentary cocktail hour. Picnics are available.

**Nearest Airport(s)**
Brunswick, GA (BQK), Savannah, GA (SAV), and Jacksonville, FL (JAX).

**Directions**
Accessible only by boat with departures twice daily from St. Simons Island, GA.

# Beach Bed & Breakfast

www.beachbedandbreakfast.com
907 Beachview Drive, St. Simon's Island, GA 31522
**912-634-2800** • 912-638-5042 • Fax 912-634-4656
reservations@beachbedandbreakfast.com

*Member Since 2003*

*Georgia*

*St. Simon's Island*

*"The St. Simon's Suite would make the most discerning mermaid come in from the sea and stay ashore!" "Absolutely the Best."*

Innkeeper/Owner
**Joe McDonough**

The Beach Bed & Breakfast is a beautiful 13,000 square feet oceanfront Spanish-Mediter-ranean villa. Its seven suites are furnished with exquisite d?cor and detail. Guests can take advantage of ocean-front decks for a hot served breakfast, pool, Jacuzzi and home theatre, and the property is perfectly located within walking distance of ten of the island's best restaurants. In-Suite Complimentary beverages and snacks are an added bonus, along with complimentary bicycles and local airport pickup. Site-seeing tours, golf, tennis, boating, fishing and dinner boat tours are available through the B&B. A full-service staff awaits your arrival. 10 top Romantic Inns.

**Rates**
7 Suites, $240/$500. Southern breakfast served at your ocean-front table each morning along with Capt Joe's internationally famous fresh fruit bowl. Number of Rooms: 7

**Cuisine**
Delightful full breakfast served on an oceanfront deck.

**Nearest Airport(s)**
Brunswick

**Directions**
Take exit 38 (I-95) towards US17 Brunswick. Take US17 S and turn L onto St. Simons Causeway (Torres Causeway). Coming off the last bridge, take R at traffic light. Go to yield sign and turn L onto King's Way. Go straight thru 2 traffic lights, then .4 mi. Turn R onto 5th Street around the 90 degree curve. 2nd unit on the L.

# Greyfield Inn

www.greyfieldinn.com
P.O. Box 900, Fernandina Beach, FL 32035, Cumberland Island, GA 32035
**888-243-9238** • 904-261-6408 • Fax 904-321-0666
seashore@greyfieldinn.com

*Member Since 1982*

*Georgia*

*"We took away memories that will last a lifetime...we felt right at home."*

**Innkeepers/Owners**
**The Ferguson Family**

This turn-of-the-century Carnegie mansion is on Georgia's largest and southernmost coastal island. Miles of trails traverse the island's unique ecosystems along with a beautiful, undeveloped white sand beach for shelling, swimming, sunning and birding. Exceptional food, lovely, original furnishings, and a peaceful, relaxing environment provide guests with a step back into another era. Overnight rate includes an island outing with our naturalist, bicycles and kayaks for exploring the island, round-trip boat passage on our private ferry, and meals.

*Cumberland Island*

**Rates**
16 Rooms, $395/$575 AP. Open year-round. Number of Rooms: 16

**Cuisine**
Hearty southern breakfast, delightful picnic lunch, gourmet dinner. Full bar; wine, beer, liquor, cocktail hour with hors d'oeuvres.

**Nearest Airport(s)**
Jacksonville, Florida

**Directions**
I-95 to Highway A1A (Exit 373) to Amelia Island. 14.8 miles to Centre St. Turn left and go to waterfront. Meet at Dock 3 at the "Lucy R. Ferguson/Greyfield" sign. Call for parking instructions.

# Spencer House Inn

www.spencerhouseinn.com
200 Osborne Street, St. Marys, GA  31558
**877-819-1872** • 912-882-1872 • Fax 912-882-9427
info@spencerhouseinn.com

*Member Since 2003*

*Georgia*

*St. Marys*

*"Your hospitality is outstanding, we're already looking forward to our next stay." "Your personal service is an asset & distinguishes you from the rest."*

Innkeepers/Owners
**Mary and Mike Neff**

Spencer House Inn, built in 1872, is located in the heart of the St. Marys Historic District within walking distance to restaurants, shops, museums and the ferry to Cumberland Island National Seashore. We can make your ferry reservation and pack a picnic lunch for you as you head off for your adventure on a beautiful, undeveloped and pristine barrier island - the beach was voted "one of the best wild beaches" by *National Geographic Traveler* magazine - and we're on the Colonial Coast Birding Trail! You'll enjoy relaxing in the cypress rockers on the Inn's verandahs. For your convenience, the Inn has an elevator and an outside ramp. Take a leisurely stroll around the historic village to the waterfront park, fishing pier, boat ramp and marsh walk. There are golf courses nearby and also an outfitters shop for a kayak trip. Okefenokee Wildlife Refuge is 45 minutes away. The beaches of Jekyll, St. Simons and Amelia Islands are a short drive. We are nine miles east of I-95 by the St. Marys River on the Georgia/Florida border.

**Rates**
$125/$235. Rates subject to change. All private baths. Elevator & outside ramp. Complimentary wireless access. Open year-round.  Number of Rooms: 14

**Cuisine**
Full buffet breakfast. Picnic lunches available. Walk to restaurants for lunch and dinner. Guest refrigerator. Afternoon iced tea, coffee and homemade treats.

**Nearest Airport(s)**
Jacksonville, FL

**Directions**
On Georgia/Florida border. From I-95 take Georgia Exit 3, turn L at stop light and travel 9 miles E on Highway 40 which becomes Osborne Street. The Inn is on the L at the corner of Osborne & Bryant Streets. Ample parking & lobby entrance are on Bryant St.

# Illinois

## "The Prairie State"

Famous for: Hogs, Pigs, Cattle, Electronics, Chemicals, Manufacturing, Ancient Burial Mounds, Lake Michigan, Chicago "Windy City," Sears Tower, Wrigley Building.

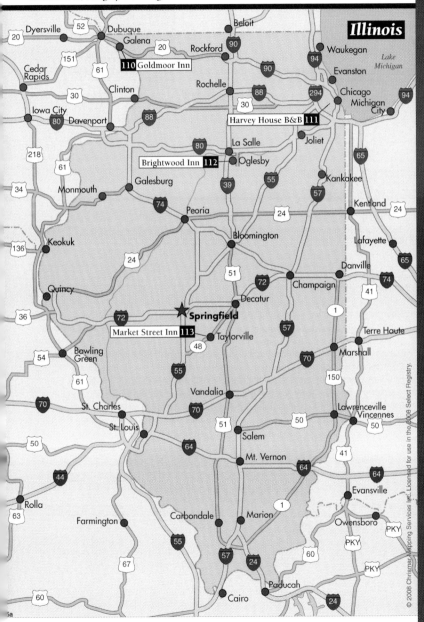

© 2008 Christmas Mapping Services Inc. Licensed for use in the 2008 Select Registry.

# Goldmoor Inn

www.goldmoor.com
9001 W. Sand Hill Road, Galena, IL 61036
**800-255-3925** • 815-777-3925 • Fax 815-777-3993
goldmoor@galenalink.com

*Member Since 2001*

*"The inn is no-expense spared luxurious. Dinner was an amazing experience and astonishing value with personal attention...beautiful, intriguing and tasty."*

Innkeeper
**Patricia Goldthorpe**

Magnificent full service country inn overlooks the Mississippi River, 6 miles South of historic Galena. The Goldmoor is the perfect setting for weddings, honeymoons, romantic getaways, anniveraries, family reunions and business retreats. All luxurious accommodations feature king size beds, whirlpools, fireplaces, galley kitchens, and private baths with beautifully appointed old world decor. Many accommodations overlook the Mississippi. We pamper you with first class amenities: full gourmet breakfast with free room service, European terry robes, fine linens, heated towel bars, refrigerator stocked with complimentary beverages, VCR/DVD stereo systems, free wireless Internet, free long distance calling and complimentary use of mountain bikes. Our restaurant offers an exceptional dining experience with a diverse wine cellar and a seven course menu which compliments the creative cuisine of Chef Dion, who was one of the top 5 finalists in the Select Registry's "Inn-Credible Breakfast Cook-off" in 2007. Relax and rejuvenate with a massage in our spa or in the comfort of your suite. The Goldmoor has been the top rated ABBA Illinois Inn since 1993.

**Rates**
12 Suites $215/$345, 3 Cottages $275/$345, 2 Cabins $255/$295. Number of Rooms: 17

**Cuisine**
Evenings: seven course gourmet dining service with extensive wine cellar; available for events; full breakfast included with every stay.

**Nearest Airport(s)**
Dubuque, IA, 25 minute; Chicago, 2.45 hours.

**Directions**
6 miles S of Galena on Blackjack Rd to Sand Hill Rd:(follow signs on Blackjack Rd.) Turn R on Sand Hill, go 1/4 mi. on the L.

# Harvey House Bed & Breakfast

www.harveyhousebb.com
107 S. Scoville Ave., Oak Park, IL 60302
**888-848-6810** • 708-848-6810
harveyhousebb@gmail.com

*Member Since 2008*

*"The kind of place that makes B&B aficionados gush."*
*Chicago Magazine, May 2008 issue "Urban Oases"*

Innkeeper/Owner
**Beth Harvey**

On Chicago Tribune's Year's Best Hotel List for 07! Selected as one of five for May issue of Chicago Magazine's Best Neighborhood Boutique Hotels/Inns! Chicago area's most luxurious romantic Inn featuring fireplaces and oversized luxury baths with Jacuzzi tubs, gourmet breakfast till noon, late checkouts. Combines the best of luxury hotels and boutique Inns. Perfect location with superb access to downtown and airports. Walk to dozens of shops and restaurants. WIFI, garage parking, great for romantic getaways, mini breaks, and also ideal for the discriminating business traveler that prefers great furnishings, great mattresses and great food. This upscale 6,000 sq. foot brick and limestone Victorian B&B in historical Oak Park is acclaimed by the press as an architectural and design triumph and consistently exceeds expectations. Oak Park is full of interesting shops, galleries and fine restaurants offering a diversity long gone from the average city street. Tour the internationally famous Frank Lloyd Wright Home and Studio. Visit Ernest Hemingway's birthplace. With superb access to Chicago, explore Millennium Park and Navy Pier. Listen to the Chicago Symphony Orchestra, the Lyric Opera, Chicago Jazz or Blues. Appreciate the magnificent Art Institute of Chicago, or take a trip to the top of the John Hancock Center or Sears Tower. The list goes on and on...

### Rates
5 suites all with private baths, 4 with fireplaces, 3 with fireplaces and jucuzzi tubs. Off Season: $165 - $325. In Season: $210 - $350. Number of Rooms: 5

### Cuisine
Offering a warm and friendly atmosphere in which to enjoy delicious food incorporating the best of what is freshest and in season. A full gourmet breakfast is served daily and we accommodate most dietary requests. Guest can choose what time they want breakfast.

### Nearest Airport(s)
Chicago, IL (ORD-O'Hare) 10 miles or Midway Airport also 10 miles.

### Directions
From O'Hare Airport: 11 miles: Start out going N on DEPARTURES. .03 miles. Merge onto I-190 E. .70 miles. Take the exit toward US-12/ US-45 S/ MANNHEIM. .28 miles. Merge onto US-45 S/ MANNHEIM/ US-12 E toward MANNHEIM. 1.09 miles. Turn L onto LAWRENCE. .78 miles. Turn R onto RIVER RD. .94 miles. RIVER RD becomes DES PLAINES RIVER RD. 2.84 miles. Turn SLIGHT R onto N 1ST AVE/ IL-171. 1.90 miles. Turn L onto LAKE ST. 2.39 miles. Turn R onto N SCOVILLE AVE. .11 miles.

# Brightwood Inn

www.brightwoodinn.com
2407 N. IL Rt. 178, Oglesby, IL 61348
**888-667-0600** • 815-667-4600 • Fax 815-667-4727
brtwood@starved-rock-inn.com

*Member Since 2000*

*Oglesby*

*"Where do we start? AMAZING! The food, atmosphere,
...a perfect romantic getaway."*

Innkeepers/Owners
**Jo and John Ryan**

Newly constructed in 1996 and nestled on 14 acres of meadow within the confines of Matthiessen State Park, the Brightwood Inn was designed to resemble a vintage farmhouse complete with a wraparound veranda and rocking chairs. The Inn will provide you with a romantic, peaceful and luxurious stay amid the beauty of nature. All rooms have seasonal gas fireplaces, TV & DVD, phones and free wireless internet connection. Six rooms have large Jacuzzi tubs and three have private balconies. Starved Rock State Park and the I&M Canal National Heritage Corridor are located just two miles north. Hiking, biking, cross-country skiing, river rafting/canoeing/fishing, horse-back riding, golfing and skydiving are just minutes away. Bird watching, wild game spotting and star gazing are less strenuous,but equally popular pastimes. Intimate dining room with seasonally adjusted menu features herbs fresh-picked from our garden. Small business conferences, weddings and family reunions are welcomed. The entire inn is smoke-free and pets are not allowed. Open year around.

**Rates**
7 Rooms, $115/$210; 1 Suite, $225/$255. Each of the eight rooms features its own unique personality and style with great views of the surrounding countryside. All rooms have private bath. Number of Rooms: 8

**Cuisine**
Complimentary hearty breakfast daily. Elegant 4-course dinner on weekends. Simple suppers available Sun-Thur. Reservation required. Beer, wine & liquor. Lunch totes available.

**Nearest Airport(s)**
Midway & O'hare/Chicago

**Directions**
From I-80 take exit 81, go S on IL Rte 178 for 6 mi. Inn will be on R side. From I-39 take Tonica exit. Go E to 2nd stop sign; turn L on IL Rte 178. Follow for 3 mi., Inn on L side.

 SelectRegistry.com

# Market Street Inn

www.marketstreetinn.com
220 E. Market Street, Taylorville, IL 62568
**800-500-1466** • 217-824-7220 • Fax 217-824-7229
jhauser@chipsnet.com

*Member Since 2002*

*"Peaceful! I lost all sense of time while soaking in the hot tub just talking for 2 1/2 hours."*

*Illinois*

*Taylorville*

Innkeepers/Owners
**Myrna & Joseph Hauser**

Rich in architectural detail, this romantic 1892 Queen Anne Victorian jewel boasts six original fireplaces and mantels, ornate woodwork, fretwork over pocket doors and beveled glass windows. Sit by the parlor fireplace and feast your eyes upon the antiques, semi-antiques and Oriental rugs to appreciate the blend of history, luxury, charm and hospitality. In the main inn, the grand oak staircase beckons one to unwind in one of the 8 guest rooms--each with delightfully different decor. Our CARRIAGE HOUSE has two rooms: a King Grand Deluxe with two fireplaces, a wet bar, a double whirlpool and separate shower & HANDICAP SUITE. Modern amenities include central air, private baths--most with double whirlpool tubs/showers, fireplaces, cable TV, in-room phones and wireless DSL. At day's end stroll through the perennial gardens to view over 200 hostas & relax in the gazebo of the Victorian wrap-around porch. Lincoln Library and sites are 30 minutes away. Lincoln Prairie Bike Trail is six blocks away. Golfing & skydiving in area.

**Rates**
10 Rooms, $125/$275. 2 King Jr. Suites with dbl whirlpools, most with fireplaces. Number of Rooms: 10

**Cuisine**
Full hearty candlelight breakfast served daily. Complimentary wine served each evening and hors d'oeuvres on weekends. Complimentary: coffee, tea, soda & bottled water. Fine dining 2 blocks away.

**Nearest Airport(s)**
Springfield Airport

**Directions**
3.5 hrs. from Chicago. I-55 to Springfield: Rt. 29 S to Taylorville; R on Walnut, L on Market. From Decatur: Rt. 48 W to Taylorville, L on Walnut, L on Market. 90 minutes from St Louis: I-55 north, exit 63 onto Rt. 48 go 25 miles, exit L at 1 mile sign for Taylorville; R on Market.

# Indiana

Famous for: Farmlands, Cornfields, Wildflowers, Indiana Dunes National Lakeshore, Indianapolis 500.

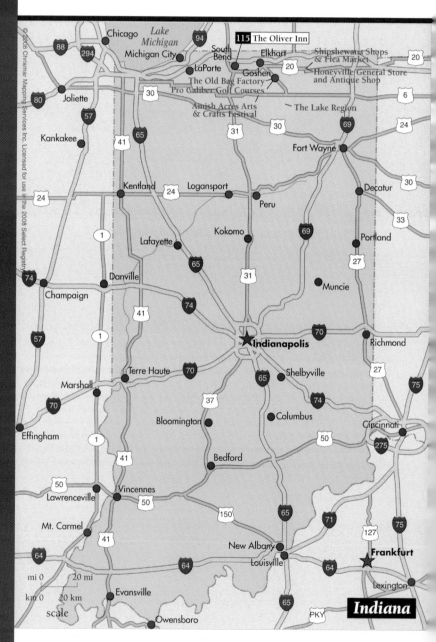

115 The Oliver Inn

Shipshewana Shops & Flea Market

Honeyville General Store and Antique Shop

The Old Bag Factory
Pro Caliber Golf Courses

Amish Acres Arts & Crafts Festival

~ The Lake Region

Lake Michigan

Chicago
Michigan City
South Bend
Elkhart
Goshen
LaPorte
Joliette
Kankakee
Kentland
Logansport
Peru
Lafayette
Kokomo
Fort Wayne
Decatur
Portland
Danville
Champaign
Muncie
Terre Haute
Indianapolis
Shelbyville
Richmond
Marshall
Bloomington
Columbus
Cincinnati
Effingham
Bedford
Lawrenceville
Vincennes
Mt. Carmel
New Albany
Frankfort
Louisville
Evansville
Lexington
Owensboro

mi 0    20 mi
km 0    20 km
scale

## Indiana

© 2008 Chrismar Mapping Services Inc. Licensed for use in the 2008 Select Registry

# The Oliver Inn

www.oliverinn.com
630 W. Washington Street, South Bend, IN 46601
**888-697-4466** • 574-232-4545 • Fax 574-288-9788
oliver@michiana.org

*Member Since 2000*

*Indiana*

*South Bend*

*"We haven't been this relaxed in a long time."*
*"Beautiful house; gracious hospitality far exceeded our expectations."*

Innkeepers/Owners
**Tom and Alice Erlandson**

Experience turn-of-the-century Victorian elegance at The Oliver Inn Bed & Breakfast. This historic 24 room mansion is surrounded by a lush acre of manicured gardens, with a gazebo, hammock, and lawn swings. The Oliver Inn features large, comfortable common areas, 11 fireplaces, nine beautiful guest rooms in the main house, private baths, two-person whirlpool tubs, A/C, CD players, sound machines, hairdryers, luxurious robes. Enjoy candlelight breakfast by the fire to live piano music and complimentary snacks, gourmet coffees and soft drinks from the Butler's Pantry. Experience the ultimate in relaxation, luxury and serenity in our Carriage House Suite. This second floor suite features two queen bedrooms, two bathrooms, (jetted marble shower, double Jacuzzi tub), a living room with fireplace and entertainment center, a full kitchen and a screened in veranda. For dinner, stroll next door to Tippecanoe Place Restaurant in the Studebaker Mansion. Come discover why The Oliver Inn was voted the Michiana area's 'Best Bed & Breakfast'.

**Rates**
8 Rooms plus 2 two-BR suites, $90/$339, King/Queen beds, A/C, telephone, hairdryers, High Speed Internet, cable TV. Some with fireplace, balcony, or 2-person jetted tubs. Number of Rooms: 10

**Cuisine**
Full candlelight breakfast with live piano music. Complimentary drinks and snacks from Butler's Pantry. Dine at Tippecanoe Place Restaurant in the Studebaker Mansion right next door.

**Nearest Airport(s)**
South Bend (SBN)

**Directions**
From the North: Indiana Toll Road (I-80/90), exit 77, right at light on 31/933, 2 miles to Washington St. Turn right 4 blocks. From the South: North on Hwy 31 into downtown South Bend, Left on Washington.

# Kentucky

## "The Bluegrass State"

Famous for: Horses, Kentucky Derby, Tobacco Farms, Fine Bourbon, Lakes, Hardwood Forests, Daniel Boone, Bluegrass music, "My Old Kentucky Home."

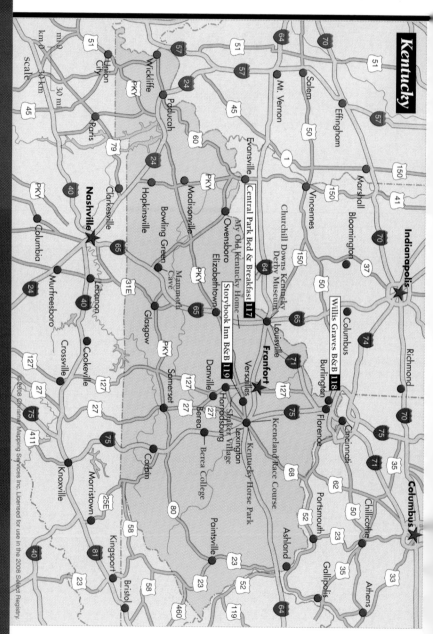

Central Park Bed & Breakfast 117
My Old Kentucky Home 117
Storybook Inn B&B 119
Willis Graves B&B 118

© 2008 Chrisman Mapping Services Inc. Licensed for use in the 2008 Select Registry.

# Central Park Bed & Breakfast

www.centralparkbandb.com
1353 South Fourth Street, Old Louisville Historic District, Louisville, KY 40208
**877-922-1505** • 502-638-1505 • Fax 502-638-1525
centralpar@win.net

*Member Since 2006*

*Kentucky*

*Louisville*

> *"Relaxing in the parlor with the grand piano and stain glass window; walking in the garden and listening to the fountain; I need to do this again soon."*

Proprietors
**Nancy and Kevin Hopper**

Come and bask in the ambiance of a Gilded Age mansion facing Central Park. We are located in one of the largest Victorian neighborhoods in America. Relax and have a glass of wine on the veranda or sip a cup of tea by the 19th century grand piano in the parlor. We have created a bit of a Victorian dream for a romantic get away for any special couple wanting to soak in a tub for two or lounge in a king size bed dressed in luxury linens by the fireplace. It can be a romantic interlude or a corporate retreat. Whether you are a traveler searching for a luxurious respite or the business traveler looking for more than a hotel, we have the place for you. We prepare a delicious three course breakfast daily. Our coffees are specially blended for the inn and we always have specialty teas and treats. We have a wine and cheese reception each evening to welcome our guests. We are centrally located close to downtown, the Expo Center, Churchill Downs, or the airport. All rooms have a private ensuite bathroom, a fireplace, television, comfortable sitting area, and internet access. The inn/antiques are of Victorian period.

**Rates**
Queens $125/$135; Kings/suites $165/$185; Carriage House (kid & pet friendly) $175.00 Corp. rates for single bus. travelers Call General Manager for Corp.Rates. Number of Rooms: 7

**Cuisine**
Creative 3-course breakfast served in dining room or on the veranda overlooking the courtyard. Fresh roasted coffee, teas, juices, & fresh baked pastries. Afternoon beverages & desserts. Fine & casual dining less than 2 blocks from inn.

**Nearest Airport(s)**
Louisville International, 10-min.

**Directions**
I-65 to exit W. Saint Catherine St, Lf on 3rd St to 3rd lt, Rt on Magnolia, Rt on South 4th St, to 1353 South 4th Street.

# Burlington's Willis Graves Bed & Breakfast Inn

www.willisgraves.com
5825 Jefferson Street, Burlington, KY 41005
**888-226-5096** • 859-680-5096 • Fax 859-689-0528
inn@willisgraves.com

*Member Since 2007*

*Kentucky*

*Burlington*

*"I've stayed in 5-star hotels all over the world, but would hail this as the best any day. If genius is in the details, you, Bob and Nancy, are geniuses."*

Innkeepers/Owners
**Nancy and Bob Swartzel**

Experience sophisticated charm and relaxed country living at this award-winning inn on the edge of a small town, just twenty minutes from Cincinnati. Choose between two masterfully restored early and mid-1800s buildings, the Willis Graves Federal brick homestead and William Rouse log cabin, furnished with appropriate antiques and reproductions. Attention to detail and luxurious touches are obvious everywhere. For your comfort and relaxation, we offer whirlpool baths, steam showers, plush robes and towels, fireplaces, triple sheeting with fine linens, down comforters, top quality mattresses, and fresh baked cookies. Guests may also enjoy in-room massage, high speed wireless Internet, cable television, DVD and CD players, a comprehensive movie collection, and our inviting porches. Each morning, a full gourmet breakfast is served at individual tables set with white tablecloths, cloth napkins, and fine china. Gracious hospitality and beautiful surroundings create the perfect setting for your next romantic getaway, reunion, or business retreat.

**Rates**
All rooms have whirlpools, steam showers and fireplaces in suites. $95-$195, special rates available. Number of Rooms: 5

**Cuisine**
Full gourmet breakfast at individual tables begins with a fresh fruit course. French roast coffee, assorted teas, juices, breads, and made from scratch entrees are served daily. Suites offer in-room dining. Each afternoon, a plate of fresh baked cookies is left on your pillow.

**Nearest Airport(s)**
Cincinnati/Northern Kentucky International Airport

**Directions**
4.5 miles off I-71/75 at exit 181. Travel west on Rt.18 for 4.5 miles. At stop sign turn right, we are situated in the second bend in the road.

# A Storybook Inn

www.astorybookinn.com
277 Rose Hill Avenue, Versailles, KY 40383
**877-279-2583** • 859-879-9993 • Fax 859-873-0332
stay@storybook-inn.com

*Member Since 2007*

*"Beautiful inn, superb breakfast, great innkeeper, 5 stars." "What a fabulous B&B! Wonderful, gourmet food & hospitality. Lovely weekend/Innkeeper!"*

Innkeeper/Owner
**C. Elise Buckley**

"A delight to the senses!" "Elegant" "Amazing!" "A Real treasure!" are all words used by our discerning guests to describe beautiful, historic Storybook Inn. We all long for a special place where we feel welcomed and pampered in an unobtrusive way. Your search is over for an incredible destination that skillfully combines elegance with a gracious, tangible sense of calm. A Storybook Inn is not your "garden variety" Bed and Breakfast. It is more like a small European luxury hotel, say guests who have lived abroad. Every detail for our discerning guest's comfort has been considered; from fresh squeezed orange juice, premium fresh ground coffee, painstakingly hand-selected furnishings, quality antiques, hi-thread count bedding, unique accessories, acres of beautifully landscaped grounds, down to the custom "natural" toiletries is for our guest's enjoyment. Minutes from Keeneland, Midway [one of a kind fine dining and shops!], world class horse farms, area attractions, airport and downtown Lexington. Close to everything! Worlds apart!

**Rates**
Low Season Rates are: $179-$250 (except holidays). High Season Rates are: $199-$345. Number of Rooms: 5

**Cuisine**
The emphasis is on "fresh!" Fresh squeezed orange juice, fresh ground coffees, fresh fruit prepared beautifully, assortment of teas, fresh, "from scratch" entrees and baked goods. Special dietary needs considered.

**Nearest Airport(s)**
Lexington

**Directions**
From Lexington: Take Versailles Rd into Versailles. L on Main Street. Take the next R onto Rose Hill. Go 0.3 mi. up the hill; turn R at the stone pillars with the Storybook Inn signs. We are the large white Colonial that sits back from the street. From Louisville: Take I-64E to the Frankfort exit and turn R.

# Louisiana

**"The Pelican State"**

Famous for: Mardi Gras, Dixieland Jazz, French Quarter, Bayou, Crayfish, Pirates, Creole, Cajun Cooking, Salt (#1 salt-producing state), Rice, Sugar, Oil, Gas.

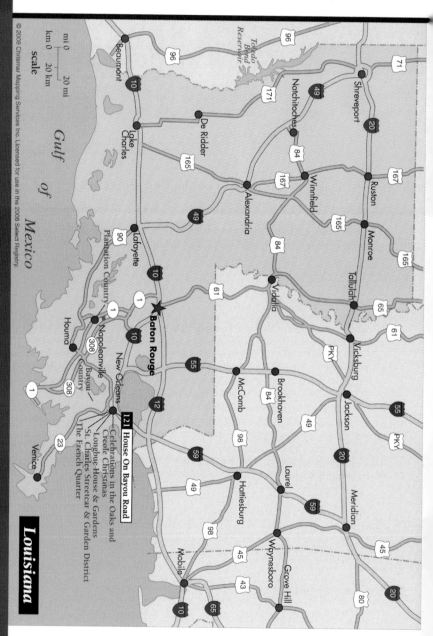

© 2008 Christmas Mapping Services Inc. Licensed for use in the 2008 Select Registry

121 House On Bayou Road
Celebrations in the Oaks and Creole Christmas
Longue House & Gardens
St. Charles Streetcar & Garden District
The French Quarter

# House on Bayou Road

www.houseonbayouroad.com
2275 Bayou Road, New Orleans, LA 70119
**504-945-0992** • Fax 504-945-0993
stay@houseonbayouroad.com

*Member Since 2002*

*"The Inn creates a good balance between genuine, unpretentious hospitality, gracious service and an atmosphere that is elegant and down to earth."*

Innkeeper/General Manager
**Jane Katner**

Circa 1798. Romantic guest rooms, and two acres of grounds await guests at this Creole plantation home. Built as the main house to an Indigo plantation, the lush surroundings are a distraction from city life. Yet this restful inn is just minutes from the historic French Quarter. The guest quarters are appointed with fine linens and elegant furnishings. Breakfast is a 'don't miss' event. Our fun and delicious cooking classes are taught in the historic house kitchen. The attentive staff is ready to help plan a memorable stay with lots of 'inside info.' House on Bayou Road creates a captivating oasis from which to tour New Orleans.

**Rates**
4 Rooms, 4 suites $155/$320. Jacuzzis and fireplaces in some rooms, rooms individually decorated with antique and designer touches. Number of Rooms:

**Cuisine**
Mini-bars in rooms stocked with beer and soft drinks. Breakfast features Louisiana favorites, such as Eggs Benedict and Pan Perdu, among others.

**Nearest Airport(s)**
Louis Armstrong International (MSY), 8 miles

**Directions**
From W: Take I-10 to Metaire Rd Exit. L on City Park Ave. to Carrollton. L on Carrollton, R on Esplanade. 1/4 mile to L on Tonti. Immediate L on Bayou Rd. The inn is on the R of the first block.

# Maine

Famous for: Lobsters, Lighthouses, Rocky Coastlines, Potatoes, Pines, Ports, Paper.

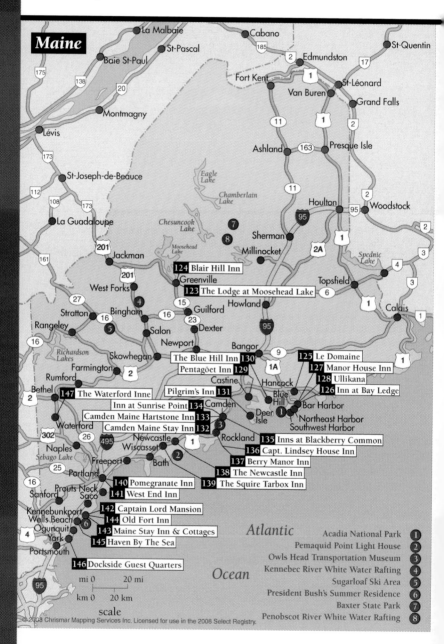

**Maine**

La Malbaie
Cabano
185
St-Quentin
St-Pascal
Edmundston
2
17
Baie St-Paul
Fort Kent
175
St-Léonard
138
20
Van Buren
1
Grand Falls
Montmagny
11
2
Lévis
Ashland
163
Presque Isle
173
St-Joseph-de-Beauce
Eagle Lake
Chamberlain Lake
11
Houlton
2
Woodstock
112
108
173
Chesuncook Lake
95
2
La Guadaloupe
Moosehead Lake
7
Sherman
1
201
161
8
Millinocket
2A
Spednic Lake
3
Jackman
Topsfield
4
201
124 Blair Hill Inn
6
3
West Forks
Greenville
123 The Lodge at Moosehead Lake
27
15 Guilford
Howland
1
Calais
Stratton
16
Bingham
16
95
1
Rangeley
4
23 Dexter
16
5
Salon
Richardson Lakes
Newport
Bangor
Skowhegan
9
125 Le Domaine
The Blue Hill Inn 130
127 Manor House Inn
Farmington
1A
128 Ullikana
Rumford
2
Pentagöet Inn 129
Castine
Hancock
126 Inn at Bay Ledge
Bethel
147 The Waterford Inne
Pilgrim's Inn 131
Blue Hill
Inn at Sunrise Point 134
Camden
Bar Harbor
2
Camden Maine Hartstone Inn 133
Deer Isle
1
Northeast Harbor
Waterford
Camden Maine Stay Inn 132
3
Southwest Harbor
302
26
495
Newcastle
Rockland
135 Inns at Blackberry Common
Naples
Wiscasset
1
136 Capt. Lindsey House Inn
25
Freeport
2
137 Berry Manor Inn
Sebago Lake
Bath
138 The Newcastle Inn
16
Portland
139 The Squire Tarbox Inn
Sanford
140 Pomegranate Inn
Prouts Neck
141 West End Inn
Kennebunkport
Saco
142 Captain Lord Mansion
Wells Beach
6
144 Old Fort Inn
Ogunquit
143 Maine Stay Inn & Cottages
4
York
145 Haven By The Sea
Portsmouth
146 Dockside Guest Quarters
95

**Atlantic**

**Ocean**

| | |
|---|---|
| Acadia National Park | 1 |
| Pemaquid Point Light House | 2 |
| Owls Head Transportation Museum | 3 |
| Kennebec River White Water Rafting | 4 |
| Sugarloaf Ski Area | 5 |
| President Bush's Summer Residence | 6 |
| Baxter State Park | 7 |
| Penobscot River White Water Rafting | 8 |

mi 0    20 mi
km 0    20 km
scale

SelectRegistry.com

# Lodge at Moosehead Lake

www.lodgeatmooseheadlake.com
368 Lily Bay Road, P.O. Box 1167, Greenville, ME  04441
**800-825-6977** • 207-695-4400 • Fax 207-695-2281
innkeeper@lodgeatmooseheadlake.com

*Member Since 1995*

*"You have done the State of Maine a great service by creating this experience.
We depart relaxed, pampered, and impressed. Anxious to return."*

Proprietors
**Dennis and Linda Bortis**

One of the world's most captivating hideaways in inland Maine overlooks the breathtakingly beautiful, pristine waters of Moosehead Lake. The Lodge is an ultra-private, four-season luxury inn considered to be the epitome of "rustic sophistication" - once one has experienced the first-class accommodations, pampering hospitality and attention to detail within its doors, this description is easily grasped.   The Lodge at Moosehead Lake is nestled in the wilderness of Maine's North Woods perched high atop Blair Hill. Its 1917 Cape Cod Colonial appeal has been preserved and treasured, from cozy natural stone fireplaces to the vibrant red stained shutters that accent the front façade. The moment guests arrive they see the warm and welcoming inn, feel the fresh air fill their lungs and have a joyful tranquility wash over them.  BEST of MAINE, January 2008 Down East Magazine, editor's picks for Lakeside Romance. Distinguished in Karen Brown's guide as Most Romantic Inn 2007 and 2005 Grand Award winner in the Andrew Harper's Hideaway report.  Inland Maine's only AAA Four Diamond for thirteen consecutive years.

**Rates**
5 Lodge Rooms, 4 Carriage House Suites, $250/$680. King or Queen luxurious beds. Open year around except April.
Number of Rooms: 9

**Cuisine**
Hearty North Woods Breakfast each morning included. Fine dining offered Friday - Monday from June through October. Bistro pub menu May, November-March. Enjoy dining room with magnificent sunsets over Moosehead Lake; open to lodging and public. Bar and wine list. 24 hour guest pantry.

**Nearest Airport(s)**
Bangor

**Directions**
95N to Newport; 7N to Dexter; 23N to Guilford; 15N to Greenville; go through yellow light 2.6 miles. The Lodge is on the left, lake side. Make sharp left down drive.

🍽️ 🍽️ ♀

# Blair Hill Inn at Moosehead Lake

www.blairhill.com
351 Lily Bay Road, Greenville, ME 04441
**207-695-0224** • Fax 207-695-4324
info@blairhill.com

*Member Since 2005*

> *"This first class Inn is on par with 5 star hotels. We felt we had stayed in the most special inn of New England & will return for the rest of our lives."*

**Innkeepers/Owners**
## Dan and Ruth McLaughlin

It's hard to imagine that such a beautiful place exists. Rising up from a hillside atop massive stone walls, Blair Hill Inn will take your breath away. Surrounded by 15 acres of gardens, meadows and ponds, the 1891 landmark is renowned for soaring views of Moosehead Lake and the mountain wilderness beyond. With a perfect blend of warmth and elegance, the inn is stripped of pretense and brimming with genuine beauty. Its relaxed atmosphere is complimented by service that speaks thoughtfully to your needs. A bright and spacious 9,000 sq. foot. mansion, Blair Hill Inn has the air of a country-house hotel. The decor reflects pedigree but is unpretentious. It is a rare, refreshing find. Beautiful guest rooms, wood burning fireplaces, gorgeous baths, breathtaking views, abundant flowers, award-winning dining and summer evening concerts await you. Sitting on the broad porch as the sun sets across the lake you'll realize this is the hidden gem you've been looking for. Honored as one of America's Top Ten Most Romantic Inns, 2007!

**Rates**
8 Beautiful Guest Rooms $275/$495  Number of Rooms: 8

**Nearest Airport(s)**
Bangor International

**Cuisine**
Dinner here is wonderful; a highlight of one's vacation. Lavish menus feature freshly picked bounty from the inn's gardens & greenhouse. An indoor, wood-burning grill adds delicious, earthy flavors: a hallmark of the inn's cuisine. The georgeous dining room with HUGE lake views, sets the stage for this elegant, yet lively restaurant. Open weekends June-Oct. Breakfast is equally impressive!

**Directions**
95N to Newport; 7N to Dexter; 23N to Guilford; 15N to Greenville. 1.5 hours from Bangor, 2.5 from Portland, 4.5 from Boston.

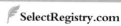

# Le Domaine

www.ledomaine.com
P O 519, Hancock, ME  04640
**800-554-8498** • 207-422-3395
info@ledomaine.com

*Member Since 2002*

*"Le Domaine was a unique experience that transported me back to my days in Provence. Now it is a happily anticipated destination when visiting Maine."*

Manager
**Beth Clark**

The colorful, sun-soaked atmosphere of Provence surrounds you when you step into Le Domaine. The scent of lavender and fresh flowers, French furnishings, cheerful prints, antiques and art create a truly unique atmosphere. There are many delights to savor... breakfast overlooking the garden, the elegant dining room, selecting from the delicious dinner offerings, studying our award-winning list of French wines, the waft of wonderful aromas, delectable desserts. However you choose to spend your days - at a concert, hiking in Acadia National Park or shopping for treasures in this lively area of Coastal Maine - Le Domaine makes any visit truly memorable.

**Rates**
3 Rooms, 2 Suites $150./$225. June 20 to November 1.
Number of Rooms: 5

**Cuisine**
Renowned French restaurant named 'One of the Best Restaurants in the World for Wine' by *Wine Spectator*. French provencal cooking using the finest Maine seafood, local produce & meats.

**Nearest Airport(s)**
Bar Harbor/Trenton 20 minutes. Bangor 40 minutes

**Directions**
Located on U.S. Rte 1, in Hancock, ME. Just 10 min. E of Ellsworth, 45 min. from Bangor. From I-95 in Bangor, take I-395, follow signs to Ellsworth, then rt.1 E. to Hancock. From Bar Harbor Airport or Cat Ferry from Nova Scotia, take Rte. 3 N to Ellsworth, then U.S. Rte.1 E. to Hancock.

*Maine*

*Hancock*

# Inn at Bay Ledge

www.innatbayledge.com
150 Sand Point Road, Bar Harbor, ME  04609
**207-288-4204** • Fax 207-288-5573
bayledge@downeast.net

*Maine*

*Bar Harbor*

> *"We don't want to leave...can't wait to return. This is one of the prettiest places on earth!"*

Innkeepers/Owners
**Jack and Jeani Ochtera**

Amidst the towering pines, The Inn at Bay Ledge literally clings to the cliffs of Mt. Dessert Island, which is locally and aptly referred to as "The Eden of New England." The veranda, appointed with comfy wicker, overlooks the spectacular coastline and is extremely inviting. Guests may enjoy a swim in our pool, relax in a hammock or take a stroll along our private beach. The elegant bedrooms compliment the style of the inn which was built in the 1900s and possesses an upscale country ambiance.  Beautifully decorated with antiques, all rooms are unique with views of Frenchmen Bay. King and queen beds are covered with designer linens, down quilts and feather beds. The Summer Cottage sits just 25 feet from the cliff's edge, and every room has a bay view! Fireplace flanked by French doors with panoromic views of Frenchmen Bay. Air conditioned for your comfort! For your special holiday, the Summer Cottage will make it perfect.

**Rates**
8 rooms, $110/$375 low season; high season $160/$475. 4 cottages $125/$375 low season; high season $175/$475. All rooms are king or queen with private baths. All rooms are air conditioned. Inn rooms have bay view. Cottages,Bear, Deer and Moose enjoy a pine view. Summer Cottage is on the bay. Number of Rooms: 12

**Cuisine**
Full gourmet breakfast served in the sunroom overlooking the bay. Afternoon tea & refreshments on the porch.

**Nearest Airport(s)**
Bar Harbor 15 minutes, Bangor 1 hour,  Portland 3 hours

**Directions**
From the head of the island follow Rt. 3 for 5 mi. L onto Sand Point Rd. The inn is on the L overlooking the bay.

# Manor House Inn

www.barharbormanorhouse.com
106 West Street, Bar Harbor, ME 04609
**800-437-0088** • 207-288-3759 • Fax 207-288-2974
manor@me.acadia.net

*Member Since 1998*

*"Wonderfully cozy room, superb staff and food, and peaceful surroundings.
We're counting the days until our return!"*

*Maine*

*Bar Harbor*

Innkeepers/Owners
**Stacey and Ken Smith**

Manor House Inn was built in 1887 as the 22 room Cottage "Boscobel". It has been authentically restored to its original splendor and is listed on the National Historic Resgister. The Inn now includes the victorian era Chauffeur's Cottage, 2 airy Garden Cottages and the Acadia Cottage. The moment you step into our front entry a romantic Victorian past becomes your present. Enjoy casual comfort, convenience, and privacy while staying within easy walking distance, along historic West Street, of Bar Harbor's fine shops, restaurants, and ocean activities. Wake each morning to the smell of sea air and a delicious homebaked breakfast. After a day spent enjoying the natural beauty of Acadia National Park and exploring Mount Desert Island return to the Inn and take tea with us in the gardens or on one of our many wicker filled porches and enjoy some sweets from the kitchen. We look forward to welcoming you.

**Rates**
18 Rooms/Suites $148/$237. Off-season $80/$200.
Open Mid April - Late October. Number of Rooms: 18

**Cuisine**
Full breakfast and afternoon tea.

**Nearest Airport(s)**
Hancock County Airport; Trenton, Maine, 20 miles

**Directions**
As you approach Bar Harbor on Route 3, turn Left onto West Street. Manor House Inn will be 3 blocks down, on the right.

# Ullikana & A Yellow House

www.ullikana.com
15 The Field, Bar Harbor, ME 04609
**207-288-9552** • Fax 207-288-3682

*Member Since 2000*

*Maine*

*Bar Harbor*

*"When in Bar Harbor, I always stay at Ullikana!" (Roy's Mom)*

Innkeepers/Owners
**Helene Harton and
Roy Kasindorf**

Ullikana, a secluded, romantic haven, overlooking the harbor, and our sister Inn, A Yellow House, only steps away, are two of the few remaining cottages from the 1800s in Bar Harbor. Only a minute walk from the center of town, our quiet location offers a haven of hospitality. Watch the lobster boats in the harbor from the garden or the patio, where sumptuous breakfasts are served. Relax in the casual elegance of these historic Inns, where art is an important part of our decor. We invite you to share the history and hospitality of Ullikana and A Yellow House with us.

**Rates**
16 Rooms, high season: $175/$330; low season: $100/$250.
All our rooms have king or queen beds. All have private baths.
Some have porches overlooking harbor. Some rooms have fireplaces. Number of Rooms: 16

**Cuisine**
We serve a full breakfast on our patio, looking out on the water.
Also we have afternoon refreshments on the patio.

**Nearest Airport(s)**
Bangor and Bar Harbor

**Directions**
Rte 3 to Bar Harbor. L onto Cottage St. R onto Main St. L after Bar Harbor Trust Company building. Take gravel road towards water.

# Pentagöet Inn

www.pentagoet.com
P.O. Box 4, Castine, ME  04421
**800-845-1701** • 207-326-8616
stay@pentagoet.com

*Member Since 2005*

*Maine*

*Castine*

---

*"And the best place for travelers to abandon their cares? The Pentagoet Inn…"*
*Editor's Choice Award, Yankee Magazine 2007*

---

Innkeepers/Owners
**Jack Burke & Julie Van de Graaf**

"Overlooking Penobscot Bay, this picturesque little town is one of the most authentic New England fishing villages you will ever encounter", noted National Geographic. The Pentagöet is a whimsical, Queen Anne Victorian with a wraparound porch and three story turret; it is one of Maine's authentic steamboat era "summer hotels". The inn has been lovingly restored and you will feel at home with the charming mix of antiques and collectibles. Just being here in this vintage seaside village is often all our guests desire. We are centrally located for daytrips to Camden, Belfast, Blue Hill, Deer Isle, Stonington, Acadia National Park and Bar Harbor. We can plan itineraries for kayaking, sailing, hiking, antiques, art galleries and there are bikes for guests for a sunset pedal to the lighthouse. We invite you to dinner; it's casual by candlelight, with Ella and Louie in the background. Enjoy our exceptional home cooking that honors the classic in its soulful simplicity and bow to the seasons. Have a nightcap in our cozy old world bar, the inn's "utterly fascinating Passports Pub," according to Andrew Harper's Hideaway Report.

### Rates
16 Rooms, all private baths, mostly kings, $95-$245. Open May-October. Number of Rooms: 16

### Cuisine
Full country breakfast and afternoon refreshments. Dinner served nightly featuring lobster and local shellfish, native fish and game, New England specialities and fine desserts. There is a well stocked wine cellar and a full bar. "One of the best meals on the coast of Maine for ambience, service and great food." Nancy English, *'Chow Maine'*

### Nearest Airport(s)
Bangor International Airport

### Directions
From I-95 to Augusta, Rte 3 to Belfast, Rte 1 N to Bucksport, Rte 175/166 to Castine, left on Main Street

# The Blue Hill Inn

www.bluehillinn.com
40 Union Street, P.O. Box 403, Blue Hill, ME 04614
**800-826-7415** • 207-374-2844 • Fax 207-374-2829
sarah@bluehillinn.com

*Member Since 1994*

*"Extraordinary inn & extraordinary hospitality."*
*"Wonderful place, wonderful staff, wonderful time."*

Innkeeper/Owner
**Sarah Pebworth**

The coastal village of Blue Hill wraps around the head of Blue Hill Bay and is centrally located for exploring Acadia National Park, Deer Isle, Castine, and the Blue Hill Peninsula. Visitors enjoy the rugged coastlines, blueberry barrens, clear blue waters, lobster, light-houses, and villages filled with fine galleries and restaurants. Evening skies are brilliant with stars. The inn, situated in the historic district, is a short walk to the Bay, Kneisel Chamber Music Hall, Blue Hill Mountain, many restaurants, and art and antique galleries. The 1830 clapboarded inn retains many original features, and the fireplaces, gleaming 19th C. floors, and antique furnishings contribute to an intimate atmosphere. After a day of hiking, kayak-ing, bird-watching, gallery hopping, or reading in the garden, guests return to be pampered with a perfect pot of tea or espresso and sweet treat. Evening hors d'oeuvres, fine wines, down comforters, turn-down service, air conditioned rooms, wireless internet service, and attention to detail add to the amenities. The inn has been designated an Environmental Leader and is committed to green business practices.

**Rates**
11 Rooms, $155/$205 B&B; Cape House luxury suite, $275/$295 B&B. Fpls, AC. Inn opened mid-May to Nov. 7. Cape House available as self-catering Nov-May - $175. 7% tax. Number of Rooms: 12

**Cuisine**
Multi-course breakfasts with several entrees, afternoon refresh-ments, evening hors d'oeuvres. Locally grown organic produce and Maine seafood featured. Fine wines and liquors. Fine and casual dining within walking distance.

**Nearest Airport(s)**
Bangor-1 hour, Portland-3 hours.

**Directions**
From S, ME 95N to 295N to Augusta exit 113, 3E to 15S to Blue Hill. In BH, right at High St. From N, 95S to Bangor. Exit 395W to 15S.

# Pilgrim's Inn

www.pilgrimsinn.com
P.O. Box 69, 20 Main Street, Deer Isle, ME  04627
**888-778-7505** • 207-348-6615
innkeeper@pilgrimsinn.com

*Member Since 1980*

*Maine*

*Deer Isle*

*"The Inn is splendid and everything was absolutely out of this world, from our room to the meals. A wonderful seaside getaway."*

Innkeeper/Owner
**Tony Lawless & Tina Oddleifson**

Overlooking Northwest Harbor and a tranquil pond, this 1793 colonial is surrounded by the unspoiled beauty of remote Deer Isle in Penobscot Bay. Glowing hearths, colonial colors, pumpkin pine floors and antique furnishings; combined with warm hospitality and flavorful meals in the cozy Whale's Rib Tavern have pleased many contented guests. Day-trips to picturesque seaside villages and Acadia National Park make it an ideal location for an extended stay.  The area is a kayaking, sailing and hiking paradise and is home to many artists, writers and the world renowned Haystack Mountain School of Crafts.  The Inn is listed on the National Register of Historic Places; has been chosen as an Editors' Choice in Yankee Magazine's Travel Guide to New England; and as of one of the Country's Best B&Bs by Forbes.com. It has been designated as an Environmental Leader by the State of Maine and recently featured in the US edition of "1000 Places to See Before you Die."  In addition to 12 rooms in the inn, three cottages on the property are perfect for families with children and pets.

**Rates**
12 Rooms and 3 cottages; $89/$249, B&B. Most rooms have views of thepond or Northwest Harbor. All rooms have private baths. Open Mid-May through Mid-October. Cottages open through November.  Number of Rooms: 15

**Cuisine**
Full Country Breakfast; Afternoon refreshments; and Dinner at the Whale's Rib Tavern featuring American Heritage cuisine and creative daily specials.

**Nearest Airport(s)**
Bangor International Airport

**Directions**
I-95 to Augusta. Exit 113 to Rte 3E to Belfast. Route 1N to Bucksport then Rte 15 S. Go 25 miles, over bridge, then 5 miles to Village. Rt onto Main St, Inn on left. Approx. 2hr drive from Augusta.

# Camden Maine Stay

www.camdenmainestay.com
22 High St., Camden, ME 04843
**207-236-9636** • Fax 207-236-0621
innkeeper@camdenmainestay.com

*Member Since 1995*

*Maine*

*Camden*

*"I've stayed in 40 B&B's (including Europe) and the Maine Stay is, by far, the best. Perfect, absolutely perfect...."*

Innkeepers/Owners
**Bob and Juanita Topper**

Relaxed, warm, romantic, and very friendly the Maine Stay is located in the historic district of one of America's most beautiful seaside villages. A short walk down tree-lined streets brings you to the harbor park, shops and restaurants. Built in 1802, the striking main house, attached carriage house, and four-story barn are outstanding examples of early American architecture and old New England taste and charm. Spacious common areas with an eclectic collection of furnishings and artwork, exquisite guestrooms, and a big country kitchen, enchant and delight. A perfect getaway for any season. Chosen by *Frontgate* as one of *America's Finest Homes.* In the words of *Vacations Magazine,* "Down east hospitality at its very best." *Frommer's* comments, "Camden's premier Bed and Breakfast," and *Fodor's* agrees, "Camden's best B&B."

**Rates**
8 Rooms, all with private baths, $150$295 Spacious and tastefully decorated common areas with wood burning fireplaces. Open year-round. Number of Rooms: 8

**Cuisine**
Full breakfast, which may be taken at our antique harvest table in the dining room or at a table for two on our sun porch overlooking our beautifully landscaped one-acre garden. Tea is served in the afternoon and nearby restaurants offer fine dining and casual harbor settings...lobster at its best.

**Nearest Airport(s)**
Rockland (RKD); Bangor (BGR); Portland (PWM)

**Directions**
US Rte 1 (High Street) 3 blocks N of the village.

# Camden Maine Hartstone Inn

www.hartstoneinn.com
41 Elm Street, Camden, ME  04843
**800-788-4823** • 207-236-4259 • Fax 207-236-9575
info@hartstoneinn.com

*Member Since 2002*

*"Blossoming orchids, gourmet cuisine and the attention to detail will bring us back!"*

Wine Spectator
AWARD
OF
EXCELLENCE

Owners
**Mary Jo Brink and Michael Salmon**

An enchanting hideaway in the heart of Camden village that *Fodor's* considers "An elegant and sophisticated retreat and culinary destination," this Mansard style Victorian built in 1835 offers a unique experience in pampered luxury. "From Quimper faince and luscious linens in the guest rooms to the world-class cuisine in the dining room and the collection of 400 live orchids in the common areas, Mary Jo and Michael Salmon get absolutely everything right," says the *Maine Explorers Guide*. Each air conditioned guestroom combines carefully chosen furnishings and original artwork to create a mood of lavish comfort and romance. Luxurious amenities include: on site massage room, WiFi, gas fireplaces, Jacuzzi Tubs, soft robes, fine linens, Flat Screen TV, MP-3 players and a guest computer. Reward yourself and your taste buds with our sumptuous multi-course breakfast presented on the sunny dining room porch. In the late afternoon don't miss our happy hour with specialty cocktails and complimentary hors d'oeuvres. Elegant china, fine crystal and internationally award winning cuisine make dinner a truly memorable experience.

**Rates**
6 rooms, 8 suites,$105/$275 B&B.Gourmet Getaway, Chef for a Day, Cooking Class and Spa packages available. Open year-round. Tour our rooms & check availability at hartstoneinn.com  Number of Rooms: 14

**Cuisine**
Sumptuous multi-course breakfast, afternoon cookies & tea, happy hour w/specialty cocktails & complimentary hors d'oeuvres. Our memorable five-course dinner is available nightly by reservation. Full bar and *Wine Spectator* list.

**Nearest Airport(s)**
Bangor or Portland

**Directions**
US Rt. 1 into Camden, the Inn is on your left as you enter the village from the South.

# Inn at Sunrise Point

www.sunrisepoint.com
P.O. Box 1344, Camden, ME 04843
**207-236-7716** • Fax 207-236-0820
info@sunrisepoint.com

*Member Since 2005*

*Maine*

*Camden*

*"Heaven on Earth! We were lulled to sleep by the sound of waves on Penobscot Bay. Wake up to a gourmet delight each morning. Sheer Luxury! Wonderful!"*

Proprietor/Host
**Daina H. Hill**

A pampering seaside haven, this Andrew Harper Best Hideaways-recommended bed and breakfast inn offers spectacular ocean views and all the luxuries you can expect from a AAA Four-Diamond property. Set within a secluded four-and-a half-acre oceanfront hideaway and just minutes from picturesque Camden. Sleep soundly in the wonderful sea air, comforted by the gentle murmur of waves outside your window. Awaken to the breathtaking sight of the sunrise across Penobscot Bay before enjoying a complimentary gourmet breakfast in the inn's bright conservatory or ocean room. Later, browse in the cherry-paneled library with a glass of fine wine and select a good book. Stay in an elegantly furnished room in the main house, a wonderfully restored 1920s shingle-style Maine summer "cottage," or in one of the beautifully furnished cottages or suite at the water's edge. Perhaps a romantic loft above all of the cottages and high in the trees will let you dream with the birds. A luxurious, romantic and elegant retreat for discerning travelers. All accommodations with ocean views, fireplaces, private decks, free wireless and flat screen TV/DVD/mp3 dock.

**Rates**
3 rooms $300/$395. 5 cottages $335/$595. Loft/ suite $350/$745. Open Mid-April to Mid-November.  Number of Rooms: 9

**Cuisine**
Gourmet Breakfast

**Nearest Airport(s)**
Portland - 80 miles

**Directions**
From S: I-95 N to Portland. Joins Rte 295 N to Rte 1/Coastal Exit 31 at Topsham. Make right from the off-ramp and continue until signs directing you to Rte 1 N to Bath. Follow Rte 1 N through Camden.Inn is 4 miles N of Camden.Turn right off of Rte 1 N onto Sunrise Point Road and drive to road's end at water's edge.

# Inns at Blackberry Common

www.innsatblackberrycommon.com
82-84 Elm Street, Camden, ME  04843
**800-388-6000** • 207-236-6060 • Fax 207-236-9032
innkeepers@blackberryinn.com

*Member Since 2006*

*Maine*

*Camden*

*"Top notch…Best of the rest." "Casual elegance, lovely gardens & breakfast is
ambrosia for the gods!" "Hospitality spoken here."*

Innkeepers/Owners
**Jim and Cyndi Ostrowski**

Just three blocks to the picturesque schooner filled harbor, our Inns are a quiet romantic
oasis surrounded by over an acre of Maine gardens. Maine Explorer's Guide says "the prettiest interior in Camden." Three gracious parlors of the 1849 Victorian boasting original
tin ceilings and ornate moldings welcome guests to enjoy afternoon refreshments or a quiet
read before the fire. Our extensive gardens, complete with a blackberry patch, are a quiet
retreat after a day of sailing, hiking or kayaking. Selection of fine wines, local microbrews
& cocktails. Each air-conditioned guestroom is tastefully appointed. Choose an elegant
guestroom in Maine's only authentic "Painted Lady" Victorian Inn. Select a suite room in
our restored Carriage House tucked amid the gardens. Or stay in a stately guestroom in our
Federal Colonial or in the delightful Tinker's Cottage. Amenities include lavish featherbeds,
fine linens, gas fireplaces, cable tv and soaking clawfoot or whirlpool tub for extra pampering. WiFi throughout. Create a special memory! Seasonal Dinner and Culinary packages
exclusively for guests! Lighthouses are our specialty!

**Rates**
$99/$269. Open all year. Fireplaces, whirlpools, luxury linens.
Seasonal lighthouse & special dining packages.  Number of
Rooms: 18

**Cuisine**
Multi-course gourmet breakfast, brimming with local Maine
specialties and our fresh garden herbs & berries served in our
candlelit dining room or on the garden patio. Complimentary
afternoon refreshments. Gourmet dinner for guests.

**Nearest Airport(s)**
Portland Jetport; Bangor International

**Directions**
I-95 N to Portland Exit 44 on to I-295N. Take Exit 28
Brunswick, on to Rte 1 N for about 40 miles. Left on Rte 90 W
toward Camden. Left on Rte 1 N again. Inns are on R entering
Camden from S.

# Captain Lindsey House Inn

www.lindseyhouse.com
5 Lindsey Street, Rockland, ME  04841
**800-523-2145** • 207-596-7950 • Fax 207-596-2758
lindsey@midcoast.com

*Member Since 1998*

*Maine*

*Rockland*

*"Great hosts, you made us feel like old friends. The service, beds and breakfast were first class and your inn is beautiful!"*

Innkeepers
## Capts. Ken & Ellen Barnes

The Captain Lindsey House is an elegantly restored sea captain's home located in the heart of Rockland's Waterfront District. This historic inn offers old world charm with all modern amenities and features private baths in each guest room. Our location affords a great place from which to walk to the many fine restaurants, galleries and unique boutiques along Main street. Antiques and artifacts from around the world grace our spacious guest rooms, cozy parlor and library. Linger by the fire or relax outside on our garden terrace. Guests are welcome to gourmet breakfast each morning, afternoon refreshments & homemade cakes, cookies and pies. Close by you'll enjoy the Farnsworth Art Museum, fine galleries and a taste of "Down East" coastal life. Friendly, genuine hosts await you.

**Rates**
$105/$150 off season (Oct 15th to June 15th), $160/$230 in season. Business rates available year-round. Many packages available. Open year-round.   Number of Rooms: 9

**Cuisine**
Lunch and dinner in the Waterworks Restaurant. Pub favorites, local fare and seafood. Microbrewed beers, wines and spirits.

**Nearest Airport(s)**
Portland Jetport, Portland, ME Bangor International

**Directions**
From Boston: Rte. I- 95 N to Rte. I-295N to Rte. I-95N to exit 28 (Coastal Rte. 1) into Rockland, Main St. to L. Summer St (by Ferry terminal), L on Union, 1st L to Lindsey.

# Berry Manor Inn

www.berrymanorinn.com
81 Talbot Avenue, P.O. Box 1117, Rockland, ME 04841
**800-774-5692** • 207-596-7696 • Fax 207-596-9958
info@berrymanorinn.com

*Member Since 2007*

*Maine*

*"You've done a magnificent job of creating a showplace, yet showing guests hospitality & warmth of a home. You should have named it the 'WOW' house!"*

*Rockland*

Innkeepers/Owners
**Cheryl Michaelsen & Michael LaPosta, Jr.**

Honored to receive the 2008 TripAdvisor Travelers'Choice award as 1 of 10 "Best Inns and B&Bs in the US." The Berry Manor Inn was built in 1898 with all the grandeur of the Victorian age and today it remains one of Rockland's most stately homes. Each of the twelve spacious guest rooms are uniquely decorated in the colors and tones of the Victorian era with a pleasing balance of elegance and comfort. All guest rooms have luxury baths, many with oversized whirlpool tubs and body jet showers and 11 rooms with fireplaces. The inn prides itself on providing a range of guest services and amenities to enhance each guest's stay in a comfortable and relaxed atmosphere including homemade pie made by the MOMs! The inn is located in a quiet, historic residential neighborhood away from Route 1, but within walking distance to the harbor, downtown shops, art galleries, Farnsworth Art Museum, Maine Lighthouse Museum and an array of great restaurants. We invite you to enjoy Midcoast Maine's only AAA Four Diamond Historic Bed and Breakfast inn and enjoy our nearby lighthouses, renowned museums, lobsters and a little slice of real Maine hospitality!

**Rates**
$165/$265 In season; $115/$175 Off season. Suite $380/$240. Open Year Round. All private luxury baths (8 w/ whirlpool tubs), fireplaces, high speed Internet, indiv. heat/ac. Packages available. Number of Rooms: 12

**Cuisine**
Delicious multi-course breakfast featuring homemade breads and sweet or savory seasonal entrees that vary daily. Dietary restrictions accommodated with advanced notice. Guest Pantry area available with ice, soda, & homemade pies!

**Nearest Airport(s)**
Rockland (RKD); Portland (PWM)

**Directions**
95N to Exit 44 (295N);to Exit 28 (Rt 1) for ~55 miles to Rockland. Take L on Broadway, R on Talbot. Inn will be on L.

# The Newcastle Inn

www.newcastleinn.com
60 River Road, Newcastle, ME 04553
**877-376-6111** • 207-563-5685 • Fax 207-563-6877
info@newcastleinn.com

*Maine*

*Newcastle*

*"What a find! Gracious host, enjoyable conversation and outstanding food."*

Innkeeper/Owner
**Julie Bolthuis**

The Newcastle Inn, located in Maine's Mid-Coast region, has been welcoming guests since 1911. The individually decorated guestrooms offer warmth and details such as gas fireplaces or stoves, four poster beds, Jacuzzi tubs or views of the harbor. Several of the guestrooms are dog friendly and we look forward to welcoming your canine companion with special treats just for them. A delicious, made-from-scratch breakfast is served in the dining room, or weather permitting, outside on the deck which overlooks the gardens and the river. The variety of common areas provide opportunity to mix and mingle with other guests, or if you prefer more solitude, there are spaces for you to find your own "private corner." After a day of exploring the area with its beaches, lighthouses, art galleries and antique shops, our pub is the perfect place to relax and enjoy a cocktail, glass of wine or a Maine microbrewed beer while planning your next day's adventures. However you choose to spend your time, the Newcastle Inn is the vacation destination you deserve for your romantic getaway.

### Rates
14 guest rooms all with private baths, air-conditioning and WiFi. Open Year-round. Rates: $155 - $255. Number of Rooms: 14

### Cuisine
Breakfast features local and regional ingredients and everything is made from scratch.Every afternoon an assortment of fresh baked treats is available for guests to enjoy.

### Nearest Airport(s)
Portland Jetport, Portland, ME - 1 hour

### Directions
I-95 North to I-295 North to Exit 31. Take 196 to Rte. 1. Stay on Rte. 1 and after the Wiscasset bridge go 6 miles and turn right on River Rd. We are a 1/2 mile ahead on the right.

# The Squire Tarbox Inn

www.squiretarboxinn.com
1181 Main Road, Westport Island/Wiscasset, ME 04578
**800-818-0626** • 207-882-7693 • Fax 207-882-7107
innkeepers@squiretarboxinn.com

*Member Since 1974*

*"Fantastic food. Very friendly caring innkeepers. Beautiful quiet location. Excellent place."*

Innkeepers/Owners
**Roni and Mario De Pietro**

Once upon a time, there was a Country Inn conspicuous from all others. After a restoration for your comfort, this colonial farm created an alternate luxury, amidst the splendor of nature. Set within fields, stone walls, and woods, and with kindness to all creatures great and small, pristine barns are filled with gentle animals. The Inn offers you peace and tranquility, away from tourist crowds, but convenient to coastal adventures. Relax with a drink on our screened in deck while watching the wild life or the beautiful sunsets. Dine leisurely & enjoy the ambiance in our 1763 dining room or on the deck with meals created by our Swiss/owner chef Mario, using all local organic vegetables from our own farm. Take a row or just daydream in the boat on the salt water marsh. Sleep with the luxury of down duvets and pillows and the comfort of Posturepedic mattresses. On the National Register of Historic Places.

**Rates**
$115/$199 double occupancy. Open mid April - Dec. 31.
Number of Rooms: 11.

**Cuisine**
A mouthwatering hot breakfast with eggs from our own chickens is served. Fresh goat cheese at the cocktail hour, chocolate chip cookies all day, & a full liquor license. A la carte dinner menu served daily.

**Nearest Airport(s)**
Portland Jetport

**Directions**
From south I-295 to exit 28/Brunswick; Rt. 1 N through Brunswick & Bath; from Bath bridge 7 miles on Rt. 1; turn R on Rt. 144 & go 8.5 miles, it twists & turns but is well marked; you can't miss us - The Rambling Colonial Farmhouse on R. From South look for sign after Wiscasset.

# Pomegranate Inn

www.pomegranateinn.com
49 Neal St., Portland, ME 04102
**800-356-0408** • 207-772-1006 • Fax 207-773-4426

*Member Since 1995*

*"There's a very special place to stay in Portland, Maine...the Pomegrante, a place with a sense of peace and privilege."*

Owner
**Kim Swan**

Portland's beautiful Western Promenade District, an historic residential neighborhood, is the location of this special city inn. It is a small sophisticated hotel which offers a quiet haven from the tensions of travel. The bustle of downtown is forgotten when you step through the Pomegranate's doors. Antiques and modern art abound in the eclectic atmosphere as featured in the *New York Times, Boston Globe* and *Travel + Leisure* Magazine. For real seclusion, the carriage house offers a first floor guest room with its own private terrace (seasonal). The main house also has a lovely urban garden. A lot of elegance with a touch of panache.

**Rates**
8 Rooms, 1 Suite, 1 Garden Room, $105/$225 off season. $185/$295 in season. Open year-round. Number of Rooms: 10

**Cuisine**
Full, served breakfast included in price. Complimentary tea and drinks upon request.

**Nearest Airport(s)**
Portland International Jetport

**Directions**
Fr. South: I-95N. ex. 44 to I-295N ex. 4 ex. 5 to 22E. R Bramhall St. immediate L Vaughan St.4th L Carroll St. Inn at intersection Neal and Carroll St. From North: ex. 6A onto Rte.77 (State St.). R on Pine L on Neal.

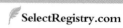

# West End Inn

www.westendbb.com
146 Pine St., Portland, ME 04102
**800-338-1377** • 207-772-1377
innkeeper@westendbb.com

*Member Since 2004*

Maine

Portland

*"It is great to find another B&B that is doing things right!"*

### Innkeepers/Owners
**Kim Swan**

Located in the Western Promenade Historic District, this Georgian style brick townhouse is one of a collection of Victorian-era homes, all reflecting a wealth of architectural detail. The comfort and elegance of the West End Inn creates an oasis within the city and is located in one of the best preserved Victorian neighborhoods in the country. A quiet location and six comfortable guest rooms invite an exceptional night's sleep. The sumptuous breakfast is served in the beautiful dining room with its twelve-foot decorative ceilings and afternoon tea is served in the adjoining library. The residential location provides convenience to the downtown, Arts District and Museums, professional hockey and baseball venues, Old Port, Ferry, Civic Center, and Financial District, while offering a refuge and an opportunity for quieter contemplation and a walk on the Promenade. Enjoy city life the Maine way!

### Rates
6 Rooms Queen/King/Twin beds $139/$209, quiet season $89/$189. All with cable TV and wireless internet. Number of Rooms: 6

### Cuisine
Sumptuous full breakfast, afternoon tea, many exceptional restaurants within short walk.

### Nearest Airport(s)
Portland International (PWM)

### Directions
From South: I-95 exit 44 onto I-295. Exit 6A, Forest Ave South, before first light bear R onto Rte 77, State St, continue up hill cross Congress St (Longfellow statue on your left), immediate R onto Pine St, several blocks corner Neal St and Pine. From North: I-295 to Exit 6A then same directions as above.

# Captain Lord Mansion

www.captainlord.com
6 Pleasant Street, P.O. Box 800, Kennebunkport, ME 04046-0800
**800-522-3141** • 207-967-3141 • Fax 207-967-3172
innkeeper@captainlord.com

*Member Since 1975*

*Maine*

*Kennebunkport*

*"An experience of hospitality at its finest!"*

Innkeepers/Owners
**Bev Davis and Rick Litchfield**

Come enjoy an unforgettable experience with us! Your comfort, serenity and relaxation are important to us. Our warm hospitality, personal service, central location, extensively landscaped grounds, and our large, beautifully-appointed guest rooms are dedicated to your complete satisfaction. Each guest-room offers such amenities as an oversize four-poster bed, a cozy gas fireplace and a heated marble bath floor. Several baths have multiple body-jet showers; 9 have double jacuzzi-style tubs. Find fresh flowers, freshly-prepared breakfasts, afternoon refreshments and lots of personal attention. The Inn is situated at the head of a sloping green, overlooking the Kennebunk River. Our picturesque, quiet, yet convenient, location affords you a terrific place from which to walk to explore the shops, restaurants and galleries in this historic village.

**Rates**
15 Rooms, $175/$475 B&B; 1 Suite $375/$499 B&B. Open year-round. Number of Rooms: 16

**Cuisine**
Full 3-course breakfast. Afternoon tea and refreshments. Also, the Inn offers a selection of fine wines and champagne for purchase.

**Nearest Airport(s)**
Portland, ME

**Directions**
ME Tpke (I-95) to Exit #25. L onto Rte. 35S, go 1.7 mi. to light, cross over Rte.1, bearing R, continue on Rte. 35S/9A for 3.5 miles. At light, turn L onto Rte. 9 E, In Dock Square, @ monument, turn R onto Ocean Ave. Go .3 mile, turn L on Green St. Mansion on 2nd block on L. Parking behind inn.

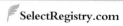

# Maine Stay Inn & Cottages

www.mainestayinn.com
34 Maine Street, P.O. Box 500A, Kennebunkport, ME 04046
**800-950-2117** • 207-967-2117 • Fax 207-967-8757
innkeeper@mainestayinn.com

*Member Since 1996*

*"One of the most relaxing and enjoyable places we have ever stayed."*
*"We cannot wait to return!"*

Innkeepers/Owners
**Judi & Walter Hauer**

Step back in time to a place where exceptional warmth and hospitality will make your visit to the Southern Maine coast a most memorable experience. Listed on the National Register of Historic Places, the Maine Stay Inn and Cottages at the Melville Walker House offers a charming and comfortable ambiance within the quaint seaside village of Kennebunkport. Choose the Victorian romance of a 19th century Inn Room, or the private intimacy of an English Country Cottage Suite. Relax around a cozy fire or enjoy a double whirlpool Jacuzzi tub. Perfectly located in the quiet residential Historic District, you are just a short stroll along tree-lined streets to the fine shops, galleries and restaurants of Kennebunkport's Dock Square. Sandy beaches and quiet coves provide the tranquility that will soothe your soul.

**Rates**
4 Inn Rooms, $109/$269; 2 Inn Suites, $169/$319; 11 Cottage Rooms/Suites, $109/$319. Open year-round. Number of Rooms: 17

**Cuisine**
Awaken to a full New England breakfast served in our dining room or, in summer, on the porch. Guests staying in our charming cottage suites may opt to have their breakfast delivered in a delightful wicker basket! Join us for Afternoon Tea on the sunny porch, or in cooler weather, around a cozy fire.

**Nearest Airport(s)**
Portland

**Directions**
ME. Tpke., Exit 25 (formerly Exit 3). L on Rte. 35, 6 mi. to Rte. 9. Turn L on Rte. 9, Go over bridge, thru village to stop sign. Turn R on Maine St. Go 3 blks.

# Old Fort Inn

www.oldfortinn.com

P.O. Box M, 8 Old Fort Avenue, Kennebunkport, ME 04046
**800-828-3678** • 207-967-5353 • Fax 207-967-4547
info@oldfortinn.com

*Member Since 1976*

> *"To recommend your Inn to our friends requires
> only one word, IMPECCABLE."*

Innkeepers/Owners
**Sheila & David Aldrich**

One of Maine's exceptional Country Inns. Tucked away on 15 acres of immaculately maintained grounds and woodlands; the Inn has been described as "sophisticated, elegant, complete tranquility two minutes from the activities of downtown Kennebunkport"★. Just 1 block from the ocean, The Old Fort Inn offers the visiting guest a quiet atmosphere. The antique appointed guest rooms, rich in nostalgic ambience, are located in a turn-of-the-century carriage house of red brick and ocal stone. Done with a meticulous eye for detail, guest rooms are tastefully decorated with wonderful wall coverings and elegent fabrics, with either four-poster or canopy beds and down comforters. Some rooms have fireplaces and Jacuzzis. Amenities include A/C, phones, cable TV, enclosed honor bars, heated tile floors in all baths, a scrumptious buffet breakfast, afternoon treats, heated pool, tennis court and Antique Shop. The Inn is just 1-1/4 miles from the village and 5 minutes from two 18-hole golf courses. ★S. Schatzki–guest

**Rates**
16 Rooms, $175/$395 B&B. Open April to mid-December.
Number of Rooms: 16

**Cuisine**
Buffet breakfast, fresh fruit, cereals, homemade breads croissants, quiche, waffles, and other hot entrees. Afternoon treats. Wine is available for purchase or guests are welcome to bring their own alcoholic beverages.

**Nearest Airport(s)**
Portland-30 miles

**Directions**
I-95/Maine Turnpike to Exit 25(Kennebunk exit), turn L on Rte. 35 for 5 1/2 mi. L at light on Rte. 9 for 3/10 mi. R on Ocean Ave. for 9/10 mi. to Kings Hwy@Colony Hotel. Turn L. Follow road to "T" intersection go R up hill to Old Fort Avenue-3/10 mi. Inn on L.

# Haven By The Sea

www.havenbythesea.com
59 Church Street, Wells Beach, ME 04090
**207-646-4194** • Fax 207-646-4194
jarvis@havenbythesea.com

*Member Since 2006*

*Maine*

*Wells Beach*

Coastal. *Relaxed*. Desired. *"You're A Stranger Here But Once."*

Innkeepers/Owners
**John & Susan Jarvis**

There are places so charming, so welcoming, so relaxing, so perfect, you want to return time and time again. Haven By The Sea is one of those places! The Inn itself was once a seaside church located in a quiet residential neighborhood and now uniquely restored as one of Southern Maine's destination spots. Enjoy our multi-level dining--once the old altar-- and/or enjoy the terrace with its breeze from the ocean and surrounding marshlands. The original hardwood floors give the building a sense of history, warmth and old-world charm. Three large common areas, all with fireplaces, offer guests a comfortable setting to relax and enjoy their favorite drink at Haven's full bar called "Temptations." All common areas and guestrooms treat the eye to beautiful historical colors, tasteful decor and unique ambiance. Walk outside the front of the Inn, and you are just steps back from one of Maine's most beautiful beaches--Wells Beach. The Inn is conveniently located between the historic towns of Ogunquit and Kennebunkport. Come and enjoy!

**Rates**
5 Rooms, $179/269 1 Suite, $259 Guestrooms offer King/ Queen/Twin beds Private baths, cable tv, wireless internet, and central a/c. Number of Rooms: 6

**Cuisine**
Innkeepers prepare and serve a 3-coursebreakfast with endless coffee/tea/juices. Afternoon/Evening-Full bar service available.

**Nearest Airport(s)**
Portland, ME 45 Min. Manchester, NH 1 Hr./15 Min. Logan, MA 1 Hr./30 Min.

**Directions**
Maine Turnpike (1-95) to Exit 19 Wells. At light take L onto Route 109.2nd light, take R onto Route One South.Continue to 3rd light, turn L onto Mile Road to Beach. Take 2nd R onto Church St. Inn is two blocks on R.

# Dockside Guest Quarters

www.docksidegq.com
22 Harris Island Rd., York, ME 03909
**800-270-1977** • 207-363-2868 • Fax 207-363-1977
info@docksidegq.com

*Member Since 1975*

*Maine*

*York*

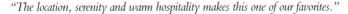

*"The location, serenity and warm hospitality makes this one of our favorites."*

Innkeepers/Owners
**The Lusty Family**

The Dockside is a special place that captures the essence of the Maine seacoast, with its natural beauty, gracious hospitality, abundant sights, recreation and activities. Uniquely situated on a private peninsula overlooking York Harbor and the Atlantic Ocean, each room has a panoramic water view. Accommodations are in the Maine House, a classic New England Cottage, furnished with antiques and marine art. The large wrap around porch, complete with wicker rocking chairs and iced tea, offers great views of the harbor activities. The multi-unit buildings at the water's edge offer several different room types, all with privates decks and water views. Each room is tastefully and individually decorated. Warmth and charm are found throughout. There is plenty to do on site and close by; pristine beaches, nature walk, golf, boat rentals, art galleries and antique shops. The Dockside Restaurant boasts a water view from every table. Our creatively diverse menu and extensive wine list will ensure a truly memorable dining experience. You can also, dine or enjoy your favorite beverage from the screened porch.

**Rates**
19 water-view rooms;$98-229. 6 suites $197-$276. Most have private decks.Off season rates, Packages offered year-round. Number of Rooms: 25

**Cuisine**
Dining on porch, overlooking York Harbor, a favorite of locals & visitors. Specialties: roast duckling, bouillabaisse, lobster dublin lawyer. Lunch & Dinner are served in the restaurant, breakfast in the Maine House.

**Nearest Airport(s)**
Manchester, NH 1 hr. Boston, MA 1.5 hrs.

**Directions**
From I-95 exit at York, ME (exit #7). Go S on Rt 1. First traffic light, turn L on Rte 1A. Follow 1A through York Village and turn R on Rte 103. Take the 1st L immediately after bridge, follow signs.

# The Waterford Inne

www.waterfordinne.com
Box 149, 258 Chadbourne Road, Waterford, ME  04088
**207-583-4037** • 207-542-3630 • Fax 207-583-4037
inne@gwi.net

*Member Since 1979*

*Maine*

*Waterford*

*"The best meal we had in this country!"*
*"Our balcony room, the zabaglione, can't wait to return to our favorite retreat."*

Innkeeper/Owner
**Barbara Vanderzanden**

A 19th century farmhouse on a country lane midst 25 acres of fields and woods, distinctively different, a true country inn offering uniquely decorated guest rooms, a charming blend of three centuries - the warmth of early furnishings combined with contemporary comforts. An air of quiet simple elegance pervades the common rooms rich with antiques and art, pewter and primitives. An intimate library with an eclectic collection to appeal to all tastes--travel, nature, history... Step outside to explore the pleasures of country simplicity, to listen to the quiet or the songbirds, to smell the freshness of a summer morning or perhaps the winter fragrance of a woodburning fire. Wander through the gardens which provide a colorful array of flowers and a bounty of fresh fare for your dining table. Return inne-side to pamper your palate with country chic cuisine. The road to the Waterford Inne is traveled by hikers and cyclists, antiquers and skiers, discriminating travelers who delight in the charm and personal attention of a country inn.

**Rates**
$110/$200 B&B; Open year-round.  Number of Rooms: 8

**Cuisine**
Breakfast included. Fine dinners available with advance reservation. Guests are welcome to bring their own spirits.

**Nearest Airport(s)**
Portland, ME

**Directions**
From ME Tpke: take Exit 63 to Rt. 26A to Rt 26 N for 28 mi. into Norway, then Rt. 118 W for 9 mi. to Rt. 37. Turn L, go 1/2 mi. to Chadbourne Rd. Take R and go 1/2 mile up hill. From Conway NH: Rt. 16 to Rt. 302 E to Fryeburg, ME. Rt. 5 out of Fryeburg to Rt. 35 S, continue to left fork onto Rt. 118 E. for approx. 5 miles to Rt. 37. Turn R, go 1/2 mi. to Chadbourne Rd. Turn R and go 1/2 mile up hill.

# Maryland

**"The Old Line State"**

Famous for: Maryland Crabs, Chesapeake Bay, Ocean City, Atlantic Coast, River Valleys, Rolling Hills, Forests, Appalachian Mountains, Fort McHenry, Tobacco.

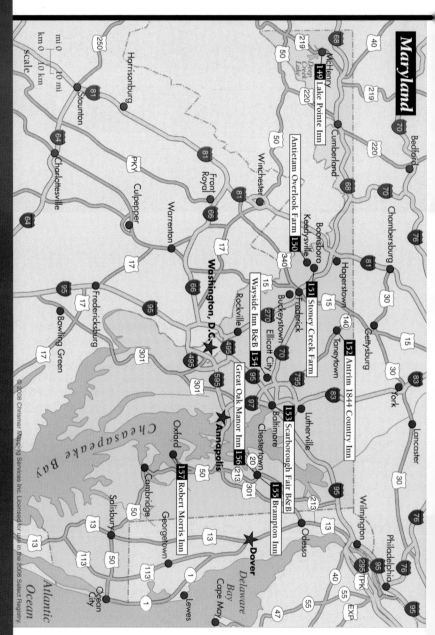

149 Lake Pointe Inn

150 Antietam Overlook Farm

151 Stoney Creek Farm

152 Antrim 1844 Country Inn

153 Scarborough Fair B&B

154 Wayside Inn B&B

155 Brampton Inn

156 Great Oak Manor Inn

157 Robert Morris Inn

© 2006 Chrismar Mapping Services Inc. Licensed for use in the 2008 Select Registry

SelectRegistry.com

# Lake Pointe Inn

www.deepcreekinns.com
174 Lake Pointe Drive, Deep Creek Lake, MD 21541
**800-523-LAKE** • 301-387-0111 • Fax 301-387-0190
relax@deepcreekinns.com

*Member Since 2000*

Maryland

Deep Creek Lake

> *"This is the most relaxing place I have ever been...
> Simply put, EXCEPTIONAL!"*

Innkeeper
**Caroline McNiece**

The Lake Pointe Inn decorated in the Arts & Crafts style, embraces you with an exceptionally warm welcome when you enter the chestnut paneled Great Room with it's Mission Style furnishings. Nestled in the Lake Pointe Community in Western Maryland, the Inn is perched just 13 feet from water's edge. The wraparound porch invites you to relax in a rocking chair, read or watch the waterfowl frolic. It is easy to enjoy Garrett County's 4 season activities while staying at the Inn. Golf, skiing and snowboarding await you at the Wisp Resort, adjacent to the Lake Pointe Community. Tour the area using our complimentary canoes, kayaks and bicycles or hike in the 5 nearby State Parks. The outdoor fireplace, herb garden and hammock provide a perfect haven for private conversation or stargazing. Frank Lloyd Wright's Fallingwater and Kentuck Knob are nearby. Lake Pointe Inn is a perfect getaway in any season for any reason! Voted one of the Top Ten Romantic Inns by American Historic Inns/iLove Inns for 2008.

**Rates**
10 Rooms $188/$279; Some amenities include: Fireplaces, Spa Tubs, Steam Shower, Sauna, CAC, TV/DVD, Bose CD player/alarm (MP3 aux.), Wireless internet, Private Telephone. Massage available. Closed Dec. 24, 25  Number of Rooms: 10

**Cuisine**
Full breakfast & light hors d'oeuvres included in daily rate; dinners served to Inn guests on 3-day holiday weekends. Meeting space available 8-20 persons.

**Nearest Airport(s)**
Pittsburgh International

**Directions**
From I-68 in Western MD, take Rte 219 S for 12.5 mi.; R onto Sang Run Rd; 2 blocks, L onto Marsh Hill Rd., go 1/4 mile; L onto Lake Pointe Dr just past Wisp Resort.

# Antietam Overlook Farm

www.antietamoverlook.com
4812 Porterstown Rd., Keedysville, MD 21756
**800-878-4241** • 301-432-4200 • Fax 301-432-5230
Reservations@antietamoverlook.com

*Member Since 1992*

*"95 Gorgeous acres, Unbelievable food and quiet seclusion…ah!"*
*Visit us on-line at www.AntietamOverlook.com*

Owner - **Mark Svrcek**
Innkeeper and Chef - **David Lori**

Our 95-acre mountaintop country manor inn overlooking Antietam National Battlefield has extraordinary views of four states. You will marvel at the hand-hewn timber framing and rough-sawn craftsmanship. Cozy fireplaces, fabulous furnishings and fine crystal create a warm, comfortable atmosphere. In the winter months, guests are invited to spend time in front of the grand fireplace where interesting conversation adds to the warmth. The views are spectacular year round, but in the spring, summer and fall our large "Overlook" porch is wonderful. Spacious suites include fireplaces, sumptuous queen and king beds, stress relieving bubble baths, and private screened porches. Enjoy a soak in the outside Hot Tub under the stars. While our seclusion and tranquility are unparalleled, many guests also enjoy visiting The Antietam National battlefield, Harpers Ferry, Shepherdstown WV and Gettysburg. Fine dining is nearby. For an additional fee, schedule our Chef at the Inn to create a Five Course meal paired with five wines. It will be a meal you will remember as one of the best.

### Rates
6 Suites, $145/$225 B&B. Generals Quarters $450. Open year-round. Attractions: Antietam National Battlefield, Harpers Ferry, antiquing, Charlestown horse races, hiking, biking & relaxing. Complimentary beverages, wine & liqueurs. Number of Rooms: 6

### Cuisine
3 course breakfast included. Dining nearby. House Chef available for added fee.

### Nearest Airport(s)
Reagan National, BWI & Dulles are 1 Hour. Hagerstown airport is 25 minutes away.

### Directions
Located in the Western Maryland Mountains about one hour from Baltimore and Washington, D.C. Call or check on-line for availability and booking. Directions sent with booking confirmation.

 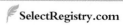

# Stoney Creek Farm

www.stoneycreekfarm.com
19223 Manor Church Road, Boonsboro, MD 21713
**301-432-6272**
innkeeper@stoneycreekfarm.com

*Member Since 2007*

*"What an oasis! Beautiful home, breath taking scenery, spectacular breakfast,
not to mention welcoming host and lovable pups. We will be back."*

Innkeepers
**David Kempton & Denise Lawhead**

Stoney Creek Farm awaits your arrival and welcomes you home to our historic bed and breakfast farmhouse situated on the rolling hills of beautiful Washington County, Maryland. Lovingly restored in 2005, Stoney Creek Farm spares no comfort and affords every modern amenity to eclectic travelers from near and far. Come to the inn to relax, unwind and explore this beautiful region of the country steeped in American history. Stoney Creek Farm is an ideal setting for your special event, be it a wedding or commitment ceremony, a company retreat, or a meditation weekend...we will be happy to help. Please call us directly for more details.

**Rates**
Mon.-Thurs., $195/$225/nightly. Number of Rooms: 4

**Cuisine**
Gourmet breakfast offered. Wine and cheese served nightly. Specialty dinners available upon request.

**Nearest Airport(s)**
Baltimore, Washington Dulles

**Directions**
From Washington D.C.: Take I-270 N to Frederick, then I-70 W toward Hagerstown. Take US Alt 40, exit 49. Continue on US Alt 40 for 12.4 miles to Boonsboro. Turn L at third light (W) onto SR 68, Lappans Rd for 1.6 miles & turn L on Mill Point Rd (2 miles). Continue on Mill Point Rd for 0.8 miles to intersections of Wheeler Rd & Monroe & Manor Church. Turn R on Manor Church Rd & drive 0.6 miles & turn L into farm.

# Antrim 1844 Country Inn

www.antrim1844.com
30 Trevanion Road, Taneytown, MD 21787
**800-858-1844** • 410-756-6812 • Fax 410-756-2744
info@antrim1844.com

*Member Since 1993*

*"Perfection in every way," "magnificent," "opulent," "superb."*
Zagat Survey

Proprietors
**Dorothy and Richard Mollett**

One of the most prestigious inns in the country, Antrim 1844 is near Baltimore and Washington, D.C., and just 12 miles from historic Gettysburg. Set on 24 acres of rolling Maryland countryside, Antrim's mansion, dependencies and other outbuildings have been restored to their antebellum grandeur. Each guestroom or suite is individually appointed with feather beds and antique furnishings. Fireplaces, Jacuzzis, decks, high speed internet and luxurious baths abound. Expect exquisite dining and incredible wines in an old-world setting. Enjoy outdoor swimming, tennis and croquet amid Antrim's elaborate formal gardens. Golf, historic tour and special getaway packages are also available.

**Rates**
40 Guest Rooms and Suites, $160/$400. Open year-round. Activities: Gettysburg, Baltimore & Washington attractions, golfing, antiquing, hiking, biking, swimming, tennis. Number of Rooms: 40

**Cuisine**
Afternoon tea. Evening hors d'ouevres. Elegant 6-course prix fixe dinner $68.50. Morning wake up tray at your door, plus full country breakfast. Full bar and 1800-selection wine list.

**Nearest Airport(s)**
BWI

**Directions**
From Wash D.C.: I-495 to I-270W; 15N to 140E to Taneytown through light; 1 block & bear R on Trevanion Rd. From Balt/BWI: I-695N to I-795W to 140W to Taneytown; L on Trevanion Rd.

# Scarborough Fair Bed & Breakfast

www.scarboroughfairandb.com
One East Montgomery Street, Baltimore, MD 21230
**877-954-2747** • 410-837-0010
innkeeper@scarboroughfairandb.com

*Member Since 2008*

*Maryland Baltimore*

*"From the warm welcome, beautiful clean rooms to the luxury linens, toiletries, flowers and amenities, it was the best B&B experience yet."* - TripAdvisor.com

Innkeepers/Owners
**Barry Werner & Jeff Finlay**

Scarborough Fair Bed & Breakfast invites you to explore historic luxury amid modern adventure. We offer city convenience with the warmth of a small neighborhood in a community that is a quiet and relaxing retreat. Our close proximity to downtown Baltimore and tourist attractions makes us ideally situated for visits of both business and pleasure. Just down the street, rising above the Inner Harbor, lies Federal Hill Park, with a panoramic view of the city skyline. Steps from our front door you will visit the many family owned boutiques, taverns and fine restaurants that comprise our diverse neighborhood. Be surrounded with "Euro-Americana" ambiance that makes our locality a favorite hidden treasure of visitors the world over. We offer experiences that surpass the common visit, including trapeze lessons, picnics in the park, and indulgent spa treatments, among many others. We can also create a customized package to fit any of your varied interests.

**Rates**
6 rooms: $175/$215 a night. All private baths, some with fireplaces & whirlpool tubs. Flat screen TVs with DVDs. Open year round. Number of Rooms: 6

**Cuisine**
Full gourmet breakfasts freshly prepared using local, seasonal & organic ingredients whenever possible. We rotate sweet meals with more savory ones every other day, striving to never repeat the same meal during your stay. Special diets accommodated if notified in advance.

**Nearest Airport(s)**
Baltimore/Washington International and Reagan National Airport

**Directions**
Directions available on our website, or via phone or e-mail.

# Wayside Inn Bed & Breakfast

www.waysideinnmd.com
4344 Columbia Road, Ellicott City, MD 21042
**410-461-4636**
bnbboy@verizon.net

Member Since 2008

*"Thank you so much for what you do! The whole experience (our first B&B) was simple GRAND! The bed...great, the shower...heavenly, and the breakfasts...WOW!"*

Innkeepers/Owners
**Susan and David Balderson**

Step back in time to a gentler way of living. Two hundred years of history await you at the Wayside Inn. Conveniently located in historic Ellicott City, Maryland, and within a short drive of either Baltimore or Washington, D.C., the Wayside Inn is the perfect place for you to escape into the past. Guests of the Inn enjoy outstanding, home-away-from-home hospitality. Your Room or Suite is filled with fine antiques or reproductions, the finest linens, and too many ammenities to list here. A perfect blend of the old and new. Your comfortable night's sleep in one of our exquisite rooms is followed by a full, gourmet breakfast, created fresh that morning by the innkeepers. Then spend the day exploring the area: shopping in Historic Ellicott City, antiquing in Frederick, touring our nation's capital, meandering through Annapolis, cruising on the Chesapeake Bay, or experiencing Baltimore's famous Inner Harbor. In the evening, treat yourself to a fabulous dinner at one of our area's many restaurants, wine bars or micro-breweries. In fact, there are five of Baltimore Magazine's Top 50 restaurants within a five mile radius of the Wayside Inn.

**Rates**
$155.00 to $225.00  Number of Rooms: Three Rooms, Three Suites

**Cuisine**
A full, upscale breakfast is served each morning between 7:30 AM and 9:30 AM.

**Nearest Airport(s)**
Baltimore /Washington Intl. Travelers also come into National and Dulles Airports.

**Directions**
Directions from DC/VA/MD and areas south or North: Take RT.95 to 100 west (Exit 43B), toward Ellicott City. At US 29 (approx. 5 1/2 miles), take the left exit onto US 29 south. Move to the right and take the first exit (Exit 21B, Clarksville) onto Route 108 west. Take your first right (at a traffic light) onto Columbia Road. Drive 1.5 miles to 4344 Columbia Road. The Inn is on your left.

SelectRegistry.com

# Brampton Inn

www.bramptoninn.com
25227 Chestertown Road, Chestertown, MD  21620
**866-305-1860** • 410-778-1860 • Fax None
innkeeper@bramptoninn.com

*Member Since 2001*

*Maryland*

*Chestertown*

*"The staff is outstanding, the food exceptional, the rooms most comfortable and elegant. Thank you to all who make Brampton a magical place."*

Innkeepers/Owners
**Danielle and Michael Hanscom**

The Brampton Bed and Breakfast Inn is the Eastern Shore's romantic oasis. Located on 25 wooded and landscaped acres, one mile outside the charming town of Chestertown, Maryland, Brampton beautifully blends the grand elegance of a historical estate with the comfort and amenities today's travelers demand. Ignite or rekindle romance in a spacious, private and well-appointed guest room or cottage, offering wood-burning fireplaces, whirlpool tubs and glorious views. Enjoy a full breakfast graciously served at individual tables in Brampton's beautiful dining room. Afternoon tea features delectable treats. Attention to detail, personal service, and friendly innkeepers will make your visit a memorable one. Chestertown is a colonial village with abundant activities, unique shops and great restaurants. It serves as a perfect base for exploring all that the Eastern Shore has to offer. Brampton Inn was the only Maryland property selected by National Geographic Traveler for it's first-ever, annual "Stay List". The editor's list, which debuted in April 2008, includes just 150 properties in the United States, Canada, and the Caribbean.

**Rates**
5 rooms, $215-$265; 2 suites, $275; 5 Cottage Suites, $295-$435; Spacious guest and public rooms, simple elegance, wood-burning fireplaces, spa-tubs, steam showers, Japanese soaking tubs. Open year-round.  Number of Rooms: 12

**Cuisine**
Full breakfast served in dining room or delivered to your room and daily afternoon tea. Freshly prepared, using the finest ingredients, preferably from our garden for our guests enjoyment. Treats and complimentary beverages available 24/7.

**Nearest Airport(s)**
Baltimore (BWI) and Philadelphia (PHL)

**Directions**
291 West to 20 West. Brampton is located 0.9 miles outside of Chestertown on 20 West.

# Great Oak Manor

www.greatoak.com
10568 Cliff Road, Chestertown, MD 21620
**800-504-3098** • 410-778-5943 • Fax 410-810-2517
innkeeper@greatoak.com

*"Gracious, lovely ambiance. Thank you for your peaceful refuge
that catered to all of our senses."*

Innkeepers/Owners
**Cassandra & John Fedas**

F. Scott Fitzgerald wrote of blue lawns and country houses such is Great Oak Manor. From the estate's walled garden bordered by 65-year old boxwoods and its circular drive on the estate side, to its magnificent view of the Chesapeake Bay and private beach on the water side, this country estate provides the appropriate setting for a relaxing getaway or a romantic weekend. Our guest and public rooms are spacious and beautifully furnished. Built at a time when grandeur was more important than cost, guests are swept away by the majesty of the house. This is a true Manor House with fine details, beautiful furnishings, Orientals, and an 850 volume library to browse. We offer complimentary 9-hole golf, tennis, a swimming pool, and a private beach. The Manor will meet your every need, with 1,200 ft. of waterfront lawn on the Chesapeake Bay, and the most beautiful sunsets on the Eastern Shore of Maryland. Our newest addition, the "Conservatory," which overlooks the Bay, is popular for small business retreats or family reunions.

**Rates**
9 rooms, $170/$310, 3 suites, $235/$310. Elegant spacious rooms, fireplaces, gracious public rooms. Massage therapy available. Internet access available, Number of Rooms: 12

**Cuisine**
Scrumptous Breakfast. Individual Egg dishes or French Toast daily, "Manor" baked muffins, & fresh fruits year round. Afternoon refreshments, snacks, & complimentary coffee, tea, water, & soda. Evening Port & Sherry.

**Nearest Airport(s)**
BWI (90 min.) PHL (90 min.)

**Directions**
8.5 mi. from High St., Chestertown, MD From High Street, take a right on Rt. 514 N. past pastoral fields until you reach the Chesapeake Bay.

# Robert Morris Inn

www.Sandaway.com
7 Miles From St. Michaels, 314 N. Morris St., Oxford, MD 21654
**888-726-3292** • 410-226-5111 • Fax 410-226-5744
select@sandaway.com

*Member Since 1970*

*Maryland*

*Oxford*

*"A place to fall in love again, Great river views, Romantic...a walk back into a more relaxed time."*

Innkeeper/Active Owners
**Ben Gibson, Wendy & Ken Gibson**

Come to our country romantic (1710) inn and step back in time. Explore the Chesapeake Bay and all the unique things the Eastern Shore of Maryland has to offer. We are indeed the "Land of Pleasant Living." Guests staying overnight can choose between accommodations at our historic Main Inn or Sandaway where many rooms have porches overlooking the river and beach. We tell guests they have two choices for activities. One, you can take the scenic car ferry across the river for a short-cut to St. Michaels (6 mile drive) and then explore the nearby towns of Tilghman and Easton. We call this "doing the loop." Second choice is to find yourself a lounge or adirondack chair at the Sandaway property to linger away the day watching workboats, sailboats, yachts and wildlife go by. After seeing a fabulous sunset, dine in one of the many fine restaurants in Oxford and Talbot County.

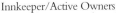

**Rates**
$130 to $350 Historical & Waterfront. Mid-week reduced rates.
Number of Rooms: 34

**Cuisine**
Fresh brewed coffee is ready at 7:15 a.m., and a light breakfast is served from 8:00 a.m.-9:30 a.m.

**Nearest Airport(s)**
BWI & National - 1.5 hours. Dulles - 2 hrs. 15 min.

**Directions**
Hwy 301 to Rte 50 E. Turn R on Rte 322 for 3.4 mi, turn R on Rte 333 for 9.6 mi. 1 hr from Annapolis, 1 1/2 hrs from DC, 1 3/4 hrs from Baltimore, 2 1/2 hrs from Philadelphia. Speed limit in Oxford 25 mph and is strictly enforced.

Famous for: Pilgrims, Thanksgiving, Salem Witch Trials, Boston Tea Party, Birth of the American Revolution, Minutemen, Freedom Trail, Swan Boats, Cape Cod, Education, Arts, Technology, and Medicine.

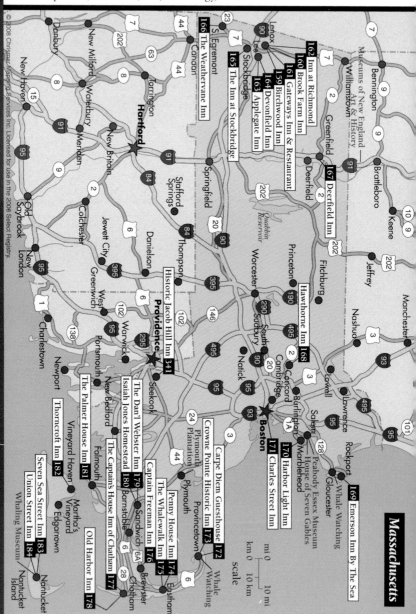

# Birchwood Inn

www.birchwood-inn.com
7 Hubbard Street, P.O. Box 2020, Lenox, MA 01240
**800-524-1646** • 413-637-2600 • Fax 413-637-4604
innkeeper@birchwood-inn.com

*Member Since 2003*

*Massachusetts*

*Lenox*

*"Wonderfully romantic! Thank you for memories we will cherish forever."*

Innkeeper/Owner
**Ellen Gutman Chenaux**

Imagine... a warm welcome... the wag of a friendly tail... hot-from-the-oven chocolate chip cookies... Imagine... awakening to the aroma of freshly baked bread... savoring our sumptuous and creative breakfasts... Imagine... New England stone-fenced gardens... our tranquil front porch, enjoying afternoon tea and the Berkshire breezes... curling up next to a crackling hearth with a good read and a steaming cup of mulled cider... Imagine... a hammock and spring blossoms... autumn's vibrant foliage... fireflies in the summer twilight... firesides when snowflakes fall... snow angels... Imagine...hiking, biking or snowshoeing on neighboring Kennedy Park's trails... a short walk to the shops, restaurants and galleries of historic Lenox... picnicking at Tanglewood... exploring historic homes... indulging your passion for food with a Fun for Foodies experience... de-stressing in a yoga class... luxuriating in a spa day... all at our doorstep.

**Rates**
$150/$310. Rates change seasonally. Distinctly & comfortably decorated guestrooms, 6 w/ fireplaces (seasonal) & TV, antiques, all with private bath, air-conditioning (seasonal), hairdryer, outgoing telephone. Free WiFi. Open year-round.
Number of Rooms: 11

**Cuisine**
Fireside "best breakfast in New England," featuring seasonal fruit dishes, homemade breads, & hot entrees served at individual tables. Afternoon tea w/homemade pastries.

**Nearest Airport(s)**
Albany and Hartford airports

**Directions**
Mass Pike (I-90), Exit 2, Rte. 20W for 4 mi., L at 2nd light (183/7A), bear R at monument, up the hill, R on Hubbard.

# Brook Farm Inn

www.brookfarm.com
15 Hawthorne Street, Lenox, MA 01240
**800-285-7638** • 413-637-3013 • Fax 413-637-4751
innkeeper@brookfarm.com

*Member Since 2001*

*Massachusetts*

*Lenox*

*"'There is poetry here' is indeed a most fitting expression of what the Inn and the innkeepers are all about...beauty and romance, warmth and hospitality."*

Innkeepers/Owners
**Linda and Phil Halpern**

There is poetry here.... This Victorian Berkshires treasure is nestled in a wooded glen, surrounded by award-winning gardens.Brook Farm Inn is just a short walk to historic Lenox village. Built in 1882, and furnished with antiques, the inn features a library filled with poetry, history and literature, where the sounds of classical music can be heard. Brook Farm is close to Tanglewood and all Berkshire cultural and outdoor attractions. The combination of cultural and outdoor activities is unique to the Berkshires. Your friendly hosts offer gracious hospitality and assistance in planning a memorable Berkshires vacation. The sumptuous buffet breakfasts are unsurpassed. Afternoon tea and scones are served daily in the library. Seasonal activities include downhill and xc-skiing, hiking, biking, theater, concerts, antiquing and museum tours. The foliage season is spectacular, and special winter packages are offered. Attractions: Tanglewood, Berkshire Theatre Festival, Rockwell Museum, Shakespeare & Co., Hancock Shaker Village, Clark Art Institute, Barrington Stage Co., Ventfort Hall.

**Rates**
$130/$425 B&B. Furnished w/antiques, canopy beds. 9 w/fireplaces, some w/whirlpool tubs, all with A/C, hairdryers, phones. Heated outdoor pool. Open year-round. WIFI access. Number of Rooms: 15

**Cuisine**
Full buffet breakfast and afternoon tea with homemade scones. Well-stocked guest pantry with refrigerators, ice, instant hot water, tea, coffee, hot chocolate, and homemade cookies.

**Nearest Airport(s)**
Albany, NY and Hartford, CT

**Directions**
Mass. Tpke. (I-90), exit 2, R on Rte. 20W 5 miles, to L on Rte. 183, 1 mile to Town Hall, sharp L on Old Stockbridge Rd., 2/10 mi then R on Hawthorne St.

 SelectRegistry.com

# Gateways Inn

iOi iOi iOi ♀

www.gatewaysinn.com
51 Walker Street, Lenox, MA  01240
**888-492-9466** • 413-637-2532 • Fax 413-637-1432
innkeeper@gatewaysinn.com

*Member Since 2001*

*"A touch of Europe in New England. A warm and inviting atmosphere
...we'll surely be back!"*

Innkeepers/Owners
**Fabrizio and Rosemary Chiariello**

Gateways Inn is a stately neoclassical mansion, built for the Procters of Procter & Gamble as a summer home in picturesque Lenox. The mansion later became an inn. Today the Gateways Inn owners and staff welcome guests from the world over, providing gracious hospitality in a European manor home atmosphere. The 12 guest rooms are each unique in decor, all with private baths, as well as modern comforts and amenities. La Terrazza Restaurant & Bar showcases a Classic Italian & Modern American Menu. We proudly use local fresh farm and artisanal ingredients. Lunch and Late Night dining are also served in Summer. High Tea is served mid-afternoon. Our award-winning bar offers an impressively large collection of Single Malt Scotches and Grappas. Business travelers welcomed. The Inn's spacious common rooms are ideal for meetings. Customized weddings and private parties are our specialty. Tanglewood, the summer home of the Boston Symphony Orchestra, is closeby. Our Tanglewood picnics are a unique experience! The Inn is a short stroll to town center with many fine shops and galleries. The nearby natural parks offer the best in hiking and nature sport.

### Rates
11 Rooms.1 Suite,$150/$515, depending upon season. Peak season minimum stay may apply. Open year-round.Low season packages.  Number of Rooms: 12

### Cuisine
Full Breakfast served daily. La Terrazza Restaurant offers all meals daily in summer, including Afternoon High Tea,and Late-Nite Menu. Full bar service. Extensive wine list. *Wine Spectator* Award. Special menus for Holidays.Custom menus for weddings, and private parties.

### Nearest Airport(s)
Albany,NY

### Directions
Boston: I-90W to Lee, exit 2. Right on Rt. 20 to intersection Rt 183. Left onto Rt 183-Walker St.The Inn is 1 mile on Rt. NYC: Taconic Pkwy to I-90E, exit 2 Lee..(as above)

*Massachusetts*

*Lenox*

# The Inn at Richmond
www.innatrichmond.com
802 State Road (Route 41), Richmond, MA 01254
**888-968-4748** • 413-698-2566 • Fax 413-698-2100
innkeepers@innatrichmond.com

*Member Since 2006*

*Massachusetts*

*Richmond*

> *"Charming, hospitable, beautifully decorated, and delicious breakfasts. With the Berkshire Equestrian Center, the inn offers a unique experience."*

Carl M. Dunham, Jr.
**Innkeeper/Owner**

A relaxing and gracious four season's country Inn. This 1770s Inn is nestled in the countryside just west of Tanglewood and Lenox on 27 exquisite acres with gardens, meadows, and woodlands. Come and enjoy a wide range of outdoor adventures: kayaking, hiking, horseback riding, road cycling, mountain biking, white water rafting, fly fishing, downhill skiing, snow shoeing, cross country skiing, or experience the Berkshire's wide spectrum of world renowned cultural activities. Stroll historic barns on our alleyway of maple trees to visit The Berkshire Equestrian Center, where horse events, training and lessons are happening every day, all year round. The casual country elegance of this historic home make it a perfect setting for family celebrations, intimate weddings, honeymoons, corporate retreats or just a weekend getaway. Further indulgences might include massage or hydrotherapy treatments at our new spa. Be a part of the harmonious blend of scenic natural beauty, outdoor adventures, luxurious amenities, and true New England hospitality. Minutes from Tanglewood, The Norman Rockwell Museum, and Jiminy Peak Resort, it is the perfect Inn for all seasons.

### Rates
9 Rooms, Suites, Cottages. $180/$380. Weekly rates, special packages. A/C, Cable TV & VCR/CD, wireless internet access; phones; some fireplaces, whirlpools, kitchens, decks. Open year-round  Number of Rooms: 9

### Cuisine
The innkeeper/staff prepares a sumptuous country continental plus breakfast featuring locally grown foods and innovative seasonal specialties. Complimentary beverages and sweets are offered.

### Nearest Airport(s)
Albany and Hartford

### Directions
NYC-Taconic Pkwy Rte 295 Exit, right to Rte 41, left 1 mile to inn. Boston-I90 Exit 1, N 7 mi. on Rte 102/41 to inn.

# Applegate Inn

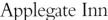

www.applegateinn.com
279 West Park Street, Lee, MA 01238
**800-691-9012** • 413-243-4451 • Fax 413-243-9832
lenandgloria@applegateinn.com

*Member Since 2002*

*"A lovely place for relaxation and gracious hospitality - a perfect 10!"*

Owners/Innkeepers
**Gloria and Len Friedman**

Once inside the iron gate, the circular drive, lined with lilac bushes reveals this elegant 1920s white-pillared Georgian mansion. It is situated on a 6 acre country estate across the road from a golf and tennis club one-half mile from the historic town of Lee and about 3 miles from Stockbridge. The inn's spacious public rooms are furnished with antiques and antique reproductions. The 11 guest accommodations are uniquely decorated and luxuriously appointed. From the screened porch look beyond the heated swimming pool to the lawns, towering trees and gardens. This is tranquility itself?a relaxing place to rejuvenate while pampered with attentive service, candlelit breakfasts, and wine and cheese served each afternoon. Explore Tanglewood, theater, dance, Norman Rockwell Museum, golf, tennis, hiking, swimming, boating, skiing, antiquing, shopping and other natural and cultural wonders of the Berkshires, or linger at the inn by a roaring fire, rest in a hammock for two under an old apple tree, or stroll the perennial gardens.

**Rates**
Rooms $150/$270; Suites $260/$385; Cottage $260/$365. Central AC,TV,VCR/DVD,CD, many with fireplace, jacuzzi, mini-fridge, balcony and patio. One room has a steam shower for two. All have robes, hair dryer, phone, fresh flowers, brandy & chocolate. Gift shop. Number of Rooms: 11

**Cuisine**
Multi-course gourmet candlelit breakfast served on china & crystal. Wine & cheese served in the afternoon. Fruit bowl, cookie jar & guest pantry always available.

**Nearest Airport(s)**
Albany Int'l & Bradley Airports

**Directions**
I-90 to Exit 2 (Lee); Rte. 20 W to stop sign. Go straight .5 mile on L, across from Greenock Country Club.

# Devonfield Inn B & B

www.devonfield.com
85 Stockbridge Road., Lee, MA 01238
**800-664-0880** • 413-243-3298 • Fax 413-243-1360
innkeeper@devonfield.com

*Massachusetts*

*Lee*

*"From the moment we stepped in to this elegant English country inn, we felt at home. The innkeepers were welcoming and warm."*

Innkeepers/Owners
**Ronnie & Bruce Singer**

Centrally located, yet a world apart, Devonfield Inn is set on a 32 acre pastoral meadow shaded by graceful birch trees, with the rolling tapestry of the Berkshire Hills beyond. This 200 year old historic estate home has been graciously updated and is filled with fine antiques. It is sophisticated, yet comfortable and inviting. Devonfield's upscale suites and bedrooms are all beautifully appointed, spacious and offer modern private baths. Quilts, down comforters, plush sheets, towels, CD players and TV/VCRs enhance every room along with handmade chocolates and bottled water. Many have wood-burning fireplaces, Jacuzzis and fine terry robes. For your comfort, the Inn is completely air conditioned and provides wireless Internet. The guest pantry is always open and is stocked with treats. There is a refrigerator and a microwave as well. Follow breakfast with a stroll through the flower-filled gardens, play tennis, or take a dip in the heated pool, and then enjoy the best in cultural and recreational activities in all seasons. Or, just relax and enjoy the sights and sounds of nature, snooze in a hammock (or by a roaring fire), have afternoon refreshments or a complimentary cordial in the living room. Whatever you choose, you'll find warm hospitality, relaxation, and rejuvenation to be the hallmark of your stay in this romantic country home.

**Rates**
6 Rooms; 3 Suites; 1 Guest Cottage. Off Season: $160/$325.
In Season: $225/$350  Number of Rooms: 10

**Cuisine**
A fireside (fall and winter) candlelit gourmet breakfast is served on fine china accompanied by classical music. Breakfast includes a bountiful buffet of fresh baked goods, fruits, granola, yogurt, juices and more, followed by a specially selected hot entree served tableside each day.

**Nearest Airport(s)**
Bradley, CT (63 mi); Albany (45)

**Directions**
From NY & points S: Taconic Pkwy. OR New York Thruway to Route 90. Head East to the Mass. Pike- Take Exit 2 and follow directions below. From Mass. Pike & points E & W: Take Exit 2 off the Mass. Pike. After toll, bear R toward town of Lee, (Rte. 20 W/Housatonic St.). Follow to first stop sign. (Landmarks: park on R and Carr Hardware on L) Go straight to West Park St. (becomes Stockbridge Rd.). Continue for .9 mile. We are on the L.

# The Inn at Stockbridge

www.stockbridgeinn.com
RTE 7N, Box 618, 30 East St, Stockbridge, MA 01262
**888-466-7865** • 413-298-3337 • Fax 413-298-3406
innkeeper@stockbridgeinn.com

*Member Since 1986*

*Massachusetts*

*Stockbridge*

> *"Wonderful as always. Great hospitality, breakfast and a wonderful time.*
> *Loved the poodle. Excellent, elegant, beautiful, comfortable & delicious."*

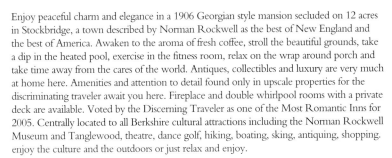

Three Diamond Award

Innkeepers/Owners
**Alice & Len Schiller**

Enjoy peaceful charm and elegance in a 1906 Georgian style mansion secluded on 12 acres in Stockbridge, a town described by Norman Rockwell as the best of New England and the best of America. Awaken to the aroma of fresh coffee, stroll the beautiful grounds, take a dip in the heated pool, exercise in the fitness room, relax on the wrap around porch and take time away from the cares of the world. Antiques, collectibles and luxury are very much at home here. Amenities and attention to detail found only in upscale properties for the discriminating traveler await you here. Fireplace and double whirlpool rooms with a private deck are available. Voted by the Discerning Traveler as one of the Most Romantic Inns for 2005. Centrally located to all Berkshire cultural attractions including the Norman Rockwell Museum and Tanglewood, theatre, dance golf, hiking, boating, skiing, antiquing, shopping. enjoy the culture and the outdoors or just relax and enjoy.

**Rates**
8 Rooms $150/$290-8 Fireplace and/or Whirlpool Suites $250/$375 Rates vary by room and season. Number of Rooms: 16

**Cuisine**
Multi course candlelit breakfast surved buffet style featuring local products. Wine and cheese served in the afternoon. Butlers pantry with snacks and beverages.

**Nearest Airport(s)**
Albany, NY - Hartford, CT

**Directions**
MA Pike to exit 2, W on Rte 102 to Route 7N 1.2 miles to Inn on Rt. From NYC: Saw Mill Pkwy N to Taconic Pkwy N to Rte 23E to MA to Rte 7N past Stockbridge village 1.2 m N. From NJ: NYS Thruway (RT 87N) to exit 17 to Rt 84E to Taconic State Parkway N. Follow above from NY.

# The Weathervane Inn

www.weathervaneinn.com
17 Main Street, Route 23, South Egremont, MA 01258
**800-528-9580** • 413-528-9580 • Fax 413-528-1713
innkeeper@weathervaneinn.com

*Member Since 1984*

*Massachusetts*

*South Egremont*

*"Thank you all very much for your hospitality, thoughtfullness and attention to detail."*

Innkeepers/Owners
**Jeffrey and Maxine Lome**

Nestled in the quaint and historic village of South Egremont, this charming landmark Country Inn has been offering gracious hospitality to visitors to the Berkshires for over 18 years. The Lome family invites you to enjoy all the Berkshires has to offer in the comfort of our ten charming and beautifully-appointed guest rooms. We offer a bountiful country breakfast to start your day and a fireside tea for your relaxation after a full day of activities. The Berkshires offer four seasons of cultural and recreational activities including Tangle-wood summer stock, historic homes, hiking, skiing and antiquing. Our newly renovated barn offers Yoga, Chikitsa, and Swadhyaya classes. You can also schedule a private Body-work or Massage session. Please call for more details. Rekindle your romance and get away from it all at the Weathervane.

**Rates**
Guestrooms: $115/$200. Suites: $225/$300. Number of Rooms: 10

**Cuisine**
Full Country Breakfast each morning and afternoon tea. Dinner available to parties of ten or more by prior arrangement. We have a Liquor License and sell and serve a variety of beverages.

**Nearest Airport(s)**
Albany, NY - 1 hour
Hartford/Bradley, CT - 90 miles

**Directions**
From NYC: Taconic Pkwy to Rte. 23 E 13 miles to Inn on R. From Mass Tpke: exit 2 to Rte. 102 to Rte. 7 S to Rte. 23 W to Inn on L.

SelectRegistry.com

# Deerfield Inn

www.deerfieldinn.com
81 Main Street, Deerfield, MA  01342-0305
**800-926-3865** • 413-774-5587 • Fax 413-775-7221
frontdesk@deerfieldinn.com

*Member Since 1996*

*"Visiting Deerfield is like stepping back in time. We love the inn, our home away from home."*

DiRōNA

Innkeepers
**Karl Sabo & Jane Howard**

An original country inn, this classic hostelry opened its doors in July 1884, despite a plague of grasshoppers devouring its way across a drought-stricken county. Located along a mile-long street, known as the loveliest in New England, the Deerfield Inn is still the centerpiece of Old Deerfield. We have 11 rooms in the main inn and 13 in the carriage barn - all of individual size and style. A National Historic Landmark, this unspoiled 350-year-old village is a perfect destination for those looking for the real New England. Enjoy Deerfield's farms, museums, attractions, country walks, area boutique shops, friendly folk, and beautiful scenery. Dinner at the Inn is a well-deserved reward after a busy day of touring, antiquing, and browsing. We look forward to welcoming you here.

### Rates
$155/$250 room. Rates include afternoon tea and cookies, an extensive continental breakfast, taxes. Rates, availability, reservations, packages, available on our website. Online discount. Open year-round except Dec. 23-26  Number of Rooms: 23

### Cuisine
Relaxed fine dining using local, seasonal produce fresh from the field, orchard, and stream. Convivial tavern, single malts, local beers, 101 martinis, supper menu. Open Thursday-Monday.

### Nearest Airport(s)
Bradley Field, CT

### Directions
FROM NYC: 3.5 hrs. I-91 N to exit 24. Follow signs to Historic Deerfield. FROM BOSTON 2 hrs. I-90 W to Exit 4 & I-91 N to exit 24.

# Hawthorne Inn

www.concordmass.com
462 Lexington Road, Concord, MA  01742-3729
**978-369-5610** • Fax 978-287-4949
Inn@ConcordMass.com

*Member Since 1980*

*Massachusetts*

*Concord*

*"Everything about our stay was wonderful, with beautiful accommodations and gracious hosts."*

Innkeepers/Owners
**Gregory Burch and Marilyn Mudry**

Just 30 minutes from Boston, three rivers wend through a Colonial landscape of Minutemen's fields where moss-covered walls embrace the homes of Hawthorne, Alcott, Thoreau and Emerson. Here you'll find the Hawthorne Inn, an intimate refuge filled with artworks and archaic artifacts, coverlets to snuggle on a crisp autumn eve and burnished antiques that speak of home and security. Vibrant Guestrooms, inspired by tradition and an artist's whimsy, offer abundant amenities, including; wireless Internet, TV/CD/DVD player, bottled water, snacks and robes. Since 1976 we have made welcome business travelers, lovers, pilgrims and families to our historic 17th century village. As you amble in the footsteps of Patriots and Poets you will savor the Inn's unique location near the Author's homes, Walden Pond, Minuteman National Park and the Old North Bridge, where was fired, "the shot heard 'round the world". Many choose the Hawthorne as a base for day-trips, to explore Boston, Cambridge, Sturbridge, Salem, Marblehead and the near ocean beaches. Then enjoy our evening gardens with a leisurely sip of wine or inhale the sweet aroma of fine tea. Our hallmark is heartfelt hospitality. Our goal is that you'll depart wanting one more day at the Hawthorne Inn.

### Rates
Seven graciously appointed guestrooms offering Canopy or Four-poster Bed.$155.-$305. Recognized by Forbes Magazine "10 Best Inns of New England" Number of Rooms: 7

### Cuisine
Breakfast served each morning, around a convivial common table, on hand-painted Dedham Pottery. Guests enjoy a robust selection of fresh-baked breads, pasteries, specialty jams, seasonal fruit offerings and fresh-roasted organic, Fair-Trade coffee.

### Nearest Airport(s)
Logan/Boston, Hanscom/Bedford

### Directions
From Rte 128-95: Exit 30 B (Rte 2A West) for 2.8 miles. Bear Right at fork (towards Concord) for 1.5 miles. Inn is opposite Hawthorne's home.

# Emerson Inn By The Sea

www.EmersonInnByTheSea.com
One Cathedral Avenue, Rockport, MA 01966
**800-964-5550** • 978-546-6321 • Fax 978-546-7043
info@EmersonInnByTheSea.com

*Member Since 1973*

*"Lovely view of sunrise, comfortable bed, lots of pillows;
...it was perfectly wonderful."*

### Innkeepers/Owners
**Bruce and Michele Coates**

Ralph Waldo Emerson called the Inn "Thy proper summer home." Today's guests enjoy the relaxed 19th Century atmosphere from our broad oceanfront veranda, but can savor the 21st Century amenities of a heated outdoor pool, room phones, data ports, high speed wireless internet, air conditioning, cable television, private baths and spa tubs. Nearby are hiking trails along the oceanfront, tennis, golf, sea kayaking, scuba diving and the always popular whale watches. Halibut Point State Park features the history of the Rockport Quarries and downtown Rockport is famous for shops and art galleries. The historic Emerson is the ideal ocean front location for weddings, retreats and conferences. "Editors Pick," *Yankee Travel Guide to New England*. And as featured in 1000 Places To See in the USA Before You Die and in Zagat's *2005 & 2006 Top U.S. Hotels, Resorts, and Spas*. Mobil Three Star, AAA Three Diamond rated.

### Rates
36 Rooms, $99/$379 B&B; Rooms with ocean views, spa tubs, fireplaces. Two Seaside Cottages, each accommodates 8, available for a weekly rental. Open all year. Number of Rooms: 36

### Cuisine
Award-winning Restaurant. 'Unparalleled ambiance' - *The Boston Globe*. Outdoor oceanfront dining and elegant turn-of-the-century dining room serving breakfast daily; dinner and live music schedules vary by season.

### Nearest Airport(s)
Boston Logan International Airport

### Directions
Rte. 128 N to traffic light in Gloucester L on Rte.127 to Pigeon Cove. R at our sign on Phillips Ave.

# Harbor Light Inn

www.harborlightinn.com
58 Washington Street, Marblehead, MA 01945
**781-631-2186** • Fax 781-631-2216
info@harborlightinn.com

*Member Since 1996*

*"Impeccable accommodations out done only by the staff and their eagerness to please!"*

Innkeepers/Owners
**Peter & Suzanne Conway**

Winner of numerous national awards for excellence, including *Vacation* magazine's "America's Best Romantic Inns." The Inn offers first-class accommodations and amenities found in the finest of lodging facilities. Elegant furnishings grace these two connected Federalist mansions. Formal fireplaced parlors, dining room and bed chambers, double Jacuzzis, large high definition TV's, WIFI, sundecks, patio, quiet garden and outdoor heated pool combine to ensure the finest in New England hospitality. Located in the heart of historic Harbor District of fine shops, art galleries and restaurants. Intimate Pub opening June 08!

**Rates**
20 Rooms, $145/$365; Suites, $195/$365 B&B. Open year-round. Number of Rooms: 20

**Cuisine**
Breakfast buffet. Wine, beer and cordials in new pub (June 08) along with limited pub menu. 7 restaurants within 2 blocks of Inn.

**Nearest Airport(s)**
Boston Logan International

**Directions**
From Boston & airport: take Rt. 1A N to Rt. 129 E to Marblehead. Take first R at Hunneman Caldwell Banker Real Estate, onto Washington St. Follow approx 1/3 mile to Inn.

# Charles Street Inn

www.charlesstreetinn.com
94 Charles St., Boston, MA  02114
**877-772-8900** • 617-314-8900 • Fax 617-371-0009
info@charlesstreetinn.com

*Member Since 2004*

*"A business executive, tired of waiting for elevators in larger chain hotels might find solace here." Washington Post*

Innkeepers/Owners
**Sally Deane & Louise Venden**

A luxury inn located in historic Beacon Hill within blocks of Boston's shopping, touring, and subway stops, the Charles Street Inn offers unique comfort and privacy in nine spacious rooms with elevator access. Each room features a private bath with whirlpool tubs, working marble fireplaces, fresh flowers, BOSE radio/CD player, Cable TV, VCR, DVD, HVAC controls, DSL and Wireless Internet, and Sub-Zero refrigerator. Authentic Victorian-era antiques, king & queen size canopy and sleigh beds, and rich imported linens complete each elegant setting. Relax in front of a fire or enjoy any of the fabulous restaurants that are literally steps from the inn. Recognized among Boston's Best by *Travel + Leisure, Boston Magazine*, and as one of the top 10 romantic inns in the US by America's Historic Inns. Concierge services available.

**Rates**
9 Rooms. $225/$425 depending on room, season, and day of the week. Call for rates (US toll-free 877-772-8900) or visit "Reservations" on our web site.   Number of Rooms: 9

**Cuisine**
Arrive to sweets, fresh fruit, snacks and refreshments in the lobby and in your room (kitchenette w/dishes, tea kettle, coffee pot and mini-fridge). Then, schedule your in-room breakfast with so many choices we call it "deluxe continental".

**Nearest Airport(s)**
Boston

**Directions**
Find Storrow Drive & take Gov't Ctr Exit. Turn S onto Charles Street and go 2 blocks.

# Carpe Diem Guesthouse & Spa

www.carpediemguesthouse.com
12 - 14 Johnson Street, Provincetown, MA 02657-2312
**800-487-0132** • 508-487-4242
info@carpediemguesthouse.com

Member Since 2003

*Massachusetts*

*Provincetown*

*"A perfect paradise, it will stay in our memories forever--a wonderful place to wake up in."*

Innkeepers/Owners
**Rainer Horn, Jürgen Herzog,
Hans van Costenoble**

"Carpe Diem" - Seize the day - is not only the life motto of innkeepers Rainer, Jürgen and Hans but for years a trademark for hospitality, luxury and friendliness on Cape Cod. Located in the heart of Provincetown the Carpe Diem is an oasis of peace and tranquility close to the tasteful shops, gourmet restaurants and fun yet sophisticated nightlife Commercial Street has to offer. The secluded gardens and patios of the inn invite guests to rest, meet interesting people or simply enjoy life. The newly created spa is a year-round retreat where you can pamper yourselves with a rejuvinating massage, a relaxing steam bath, a stimulating hot sauna or some lazy time in the outdoor Jacuzzi. The guestrooms are decorated with exquisite taste, many feature fire-places and whirlpool-tubs. Breakfast at Carpe Diem is a social event when the varied guests gather all morning in the sun lit dining area of the inn. Food aficionados can start their day with a wonderful hot cup of Carpe Diem Coffee, homemade breads and pastry, egg dishes and weekend specials like Belgian Waffles, French Crepes or Austrian Kaiserschmarrn.

**Rates**
18 rooms and suites, $95/$425. Open year round. Number of Rooms: 18

**Cuisine**
Jürgen's homemade German-style breakfast is famous. Out&About: "Imagine a cross between Martha Stewart cozy and cool European design. Similarly, the breakfasts are classic American gourmet meets German bounty. One of the most tasteful inns in town." Afternoon wine & cheese hour and refreshments.

**Nearest Airport(s)**
Boston & Providence

**Directions**
Entering Provincetown on Rt. 6 take the second L at the street light. Go down Conwell Street which ends at Bradford Street. Take a R and Johnson Street is your first L.

# Crowne Pointe Historic Inn & Spa

www.crownepointe.com
82 Bradford Street, Provincetown, MA 02657
**877-276-9631** • 508-487-6767 • Fax 508-487-5554
welcome@crownepointe.com

*Member Since 2003*

*Faaaabulous-Eartha Kitt*

Innkeepers/Owners
**David M. Sanford & Thomas J. Walter**

A prominent Sea Captain built this historic mansion, which has been fully restored to its 19th Century glory. The inn's stunning Victorian architecture includes two-story wrap around porches complete with turret and harbor views. The *New York Daily News* raves "Five Star Luxury Without the Cost." Revive at our full service on-site Shui Spa featuring many treatments and massage options. Shui Spa offers guests an intimate spa experience. Crowne Pointe is a AAA Four Diamond property located in the center of town, walk to everything. Our signature gourmet hot breakfast and afternoon wine and cheese social are included. Heated in-ground pool, two hot tubs, fireplaces and in-room whirlpools are offered. Spa packages are available. Our restaurant captures our guests with exquisite gourmet cuisine, and our hotel bar is a treasured place to socialize. The finest menu creations from our talented chefs, carefully selected labels from our wine cellar, and excellent service in a charming setting are waiting for you to indulge.

**Rates**
40 Rooms. $110/$465 depending upon season. Min stay req's may apply. Many special packages available, call for details.
Number of Rooms: 40

**Cuisine**
The freshest regional ingredients arriving daily, our distinctive full hot breakfasts are unsurpassed. The main selections change daily and special dietary needs are accommodated.

**Nearest Airport(s)**
Provincetown Airport (PVC) or Boston Logan Airport

**Directions**
Rt 6 E. 63 m. to Provincetown. Turn L at the 2nd Provincetown exit onto Conwell St. Take Conwell St. to the end & make R onto Bradford St. Follow Bradford to 82. Inn sits on a bluff.

# Penny House Inn & Spa

www.pennyhouseinn.com
4885 County Rd (Route 6), Eastham, MA 02642
**800-554-1751** • 508-255-6632 • Fax 508-255-4893
pennyhouse@aol.com

*Member Since 2003*

Massachusetts

Eastham

*"A great escape, the perfect stressbuster. A wonderful place to relax and reconnect with my husband. We felt truly pampered."*

Innkeepers/Owners
**Margaret & Rebecca Keith**

A little slice of heaven hides behind a large hedge on the Outer Cape, just minutes away from breathtaking beaches and sand dunes of the Cape Cod National Seashore. Relax, rejuvenate and reconnect at this 1690 restored sea captain's home. Guestrooms at the inn are characterized by their own personal charm. Modern bathrooms, AC, TV/VCR/DVD, phone, fireplaces, whirlpool tubs, suites, WIFI, seasonal, heated, outdoor pool, high thread count sheets, fluffy towels and comfortable beds are among the many modern amenities the inn offers. Several rooms are perfect for romantic escapes and honeymoons. For complete pampering our day spa offers massage, manicures, body wraps & facials plus a full menu of spa services specially designed for couples. A short walk away is a full service health club with indoor tennis, steam, sauna, nautilus, pilates and indoor pool.

**Rates**
Season: May 25-October 10 $215/$375 Off-Season: $189/$325  Number of Rooms: 12

**Cuisine**
Traditional full breakfast with a gourmet flair. Specialties: Eggs Benedict, French Toast Croissants & Pecan Waffles w/fresh fruit. Special dietary needs accommodated (Vegetarian, Diabetic, Gluten-free) with advance notice.

**Nearest Airport(s)**
Boston & Providence

**Directions**
Cross Cape Cod Canal and take RT 6 towards Provincetown. Past exit 12, highway ends at traffic circle, take 2nd exit (Rt6) thru 3 lights, exactly 5 mi. from circle on L (cnr of Bayside Dr & Rt6) across from St.Aubin's Nursery.

# The Whalewalk Inn and Spa
www.whalewalkinn.com
220 Bridge Road, Eastham, Cape Cod, MA 02642
**800-440-1281** • 508-255-0617 • Fax 508-240-0017
reservations@whalewalkinn.com

*Member Since 1993*

*Massachusetts*

*Eastham, Cape Cod*

*"We discovered many treasures on the Cape, but none as treasured as The Whalewalk Inn. Another fabulous visit! Thank you for making Cape Cod so memorable."*

Innkeepers
**Elaine and Kevin Conlin**

Abandon every day life. Rekindle your romance and rejuvenate your body and mind. Relax at Cape Cod's most romantic country Inn and Spa. Secluded, but centrally located to all the attractions which make Cape Cod so special. After a gourmet breakfast, walk the "Outer Cape" beaches, listening to the soothing sound of the waves, lapping on Cape Cod Bay or crashing at the National Seashore. At the end of a day on the beach, riding the Rail Trail, kayaking, shopping or museum hopping, restore your inner balance and harmony at The Spa, a very special place with your comfort and exercise regime in mind. Forget the weather; you can pamper your mind and body with a massage or facial package; feel the heat of the dry sauna; or workout in the indoor resistance pool or on the cardiovascular machines. Stay in the luxurious Spa Penthouse or in another of our beautiful accommodations. All rooms are individually decorated, have air-conditioning, TV/VCR, CD players and phones. Come and enjoy our impeccable service and heartfelt hospitality.

**Rates**
$220/$420. Call for off-season rates. Open March to December 31. Number of Rooms: 16

**Cuisine**
Full-service gourmet breakfast with fresh home-baked delights and entrees including: Pecan Waffles, Eggs Benedict, Corn Pancakes with Dill Shallot Sauce and Salmon Rosettes, Grand Marnier Oatmeal Pie, Frittata Primavera, and Captain Harding Omelet. Evening hors d'oeuvres are served.

**Nearest Airport(s)**
Boston, MA; Providence, RI

**Directions**
Rte. 6 to Orleans Rotary, Rock Harbor Courthouse Exit off Rotary, L on Rock Harbor Road (1/4 mile), R on Bridge Road (1/4 mile). Driving time, Boston or Providence 2 hours. GPS-N41'48.108' W69'59.556'

# The Captain Freeman Inn

www.captainfreemaninn.com
15 Breakwater Road, Brewster, Cape Cod, MA 02631
**800-843-4664** • 508-896-7481 • Fax 508-896-5618
stay@captainfreemaninn.com

*Massachusetts*

*Brewster, Cape Cod*

*"A honeymoon made in heaven! We were in awe when we entered our room."*

Innkeepers/Owners
**Donna and Peter Amadeo**

Built just a short stroll from beautiful Breakwater Beach, The Captain Freeman Inn is a lovingly restored Victorian sea captain's mansion furnished with canopy beds and period antiques. Luxury accommodations include fireplace, two-person whirlpool, garden and pool views. Breakfast is served poolside on the wraparound porch overlooking lush perennial gardens. In cooler winter weather you will dine fireside in the garden-view dining room. Bicycles are provided to our guests. Venture out to watch humpback whales at play or bike miles of wooded trails. Return for a glass of wine and a dip in our heated pool. See sunset on Cape Cod Bay. Sail, surf, fish, golf, or rock on our wraparound porch.

**Rates**
12 Rooms, 6 w/fireplaces, whirlpool tubs and TV's, $150/$250 B&B. Open year-round. Number of Rooms: 12

**Cuisine**
Full gourmet breakfast, afternoon tea, winter weekend cooking school with wine-tasting and dinner.

**Nearest Airport(s)**
Providence Boston Logan International

**Directions**
From route 6 (Mid Cape Highway) take exit 10 (route 124) toward Brewster. At the end of 124 go Right on Route 6A, then Left on Breakwater. Our driveway is the first one on the Left.

# The Captain's House Inn

www.captainshouseinn.com
369-377 Old Harbor Rd, Chatham, MA 02633
**800-315-0728** • 508-945-0127 • Fax 508-945-0866
info@captainshouseinn.com

*Member Since 1989*

*Massachusetts*

*Chatham, Cape Cod*

*"Fantastic service and accommodation. Can't wait to tell our friends."*

Innkeepers/Owners
**Jill and James Meyer**

Perhaps Cape Cod's finest small Inn, this historic 1839 sea captain's estate on two acres is the perfect choice for a romantic getaway or elegant retreat. Gourmet breakfasts, English afternoon teas, beautifully decorated rooms with king and queen size four-poster beds, fireplaces, seating areas, telephones with data ports, WI-FI capability and TV's with DVD players; some with whirlpool tubs. Enjoy uncompromising service from our enthusiastic international staff and enjoy the Inn's many gardens and fountains, heated outdoor pool, fitness centre, and savor the scenic beauty of the historic seafaring village of Chatham with its spectacular views of the ocean. The Captain's House Inn of Chatham has been a AAA Four Diamond award winner since 1987.

**Rates**
12 Rooms, $250/$360; 4 Suites, $250/$475 Summer
$185/$250; $185/$305 Winter. All rooms are air conditioned.
Open year-round. Number of Rooms: 16

**Cuisine**
Breakfast, poolside lunches, afternoon tea, evening snacks.

**Nearest Airport(s)**
Providence or Boston

**Directions**
Rte. 6 (Mid-Cape Hwy) to exit 11(S) Rte. 137 to Rte 28, L approx. 3 miles to rotary. Continue around rotary on Rte. 28 toward Orleans 1/2 mile on L.

# Old Harbor Inn

www.chathamoldharborinn.com
22 Old Harbor Road, Chatham, MA 02633
**800-942-4434** • 508 945-4434 • Fax 508 945-7665
info@chathamoldharborinn.com

*Member Since 2004*

*Massachusetts*

*Chatham*

*"You have met and exceeded all of our expectations." "Wonderful, restful, stay." "Breakfast to die for!" "Perfection… we will return."*

Innkeepers/Owners
**Judy & Ray Braz**

Designer decorated rooms with king or queen sized beds, some with fireplaces or jacuzzis help create a casually elegent ambiance. We often hear that, "I haven't slept like this in months" from our guests. WiFi,TV/VCR/DVD units add to the enjoyment of the rooms. Ideally located steps from the major attractions that Chatham offers. Many visiters enjoy not having to use their cars for several days as they explore the village. Judy, Ray and their experienced and knowledgeable staff are always available to help you plan your days. Our award winning, professionally designed gardens always delight. Our most popular outdoor feature is our two tiered koi ponds and their connecting waterfall. Chatham serves as a centralized base for exploring all of Cape Cod and the Islands. Itineraries for day trips to Sandwich or Provincetown or anywhere in between can be arranged based on what activities you enjoy the most. Explore the natural beauty of Cape Cod. Discover the breathtaking vistas of the National Seashore. Be pampered at The Old Harbor Inn. Whether you are planning a romantic getaway or an elegant retreat, every day you get our best.

### Rates
Rates are: $239/$319 summer - $179/$259 spring and fall - $149/$209 winter. Peak season minimum stays may apply. Special romantic packages always available. Number of Rooms: 8

### Cuisine
The full breakfast includes fresh juices, gourmet teas and coffees, seasonal fresh fruit, assorted breads and cereals, plus a fresh prepared entre and a fresh bakery specialty.

### Nearest Airport(s)
Boston or Providence

### Directions
Rte 6 (Mid Cape Hwy) to exit 11 S to Rte 137 go 3 mi. to Rte 28 S approx. 3 mi. to rotary stay on 28 around rotary. We are immediately on the right. Please call for directions from Boston, Providence or New York.

# The Dan'l Webster Inn & Spa

www.DanlWebsterInn.com
149 Main St., Sandwich, MA  02563
**800-444-3566** • 508-888-3622 • Fax 508-888-5156
info@DanlWebsterInn.com

*Member Since 1994*

*The Romance of a canopy bed, fireplace, whirlpool … The Elegance of Award-Winning cuisine and wines … The Tradition of 23 years of family ownership!*

Innkeeper/Owner
**Catania Family**

This award-winning Inn set in the heart of Historic Sandwich, offers guests the romance of the past with today's conveniences.  Canopy and four-poster beds, fireplaces, Keurig coffee makers and oversized whirlpool tubs await your arrival.  Each guest room and suite has been individually appointed with exquisite period furnishings.  The Beach Plum Spa at The Dan'l Webster offers the ultimate in luxury for Men and Women...from completely organic Body Treatments and relaxing Massages to soothing Facials, Hand and Foot Rituals and more, we will pamper your mind, body and soul!  Enjoy a romantic dinner in one of our distinctive dining rooms. Savor delicious award-winning cuisine and creative chef's specials complemented by an acclaimed wine selection, or relax in our casual Tavern at the Inn and enjoy lighter fare and always a warm, friendly atmosphere. All suites are furnished with purifing e-showers, 300 ct. Pima cotton triple sheeting, selection of high quality pillows, photo-catalytic ionization air purifiers and silky micro fiber robes.

**Rates**
35 Traditional/Deluxe/Superior Rooms, $109/$249; 13 Suites, $179/$379. Open year-round. Closed Christmas.  Number of Rooms: 48

**Cuisine**
Breakfast, lunch, dinner, & Sunday Brunch. Dining Al Fresco. Afternoon Tea. Tavern on premise. Fine & casual dining menus available serving contemporary and traditional American cuisine.

**Nearest Airport(s)**
Logan Airport (Boston)

**Directions**
From Boston, MA: Rte. 3 S to Rte. 6 to exit 2 turn L on Rte. 130 approx. 2 miles-R at fork. Inn will be on L.

# Isaiah Jones Homestead

www.isaiahjones.com
165 Main Street, Sandwich, MA 02563
**800-526-1625** • 508-888-9115 • Fax 508-888-9648
info@isaiahjones.com

*Member Since 1989*

Massachusetts

Sandwich

*"You dream of places like this." "We will never forget such a special place."*
*"Pure pleasure."*

Innkeepers/Owners
**Don and Katherine Sanderson**

Relax in pampered elegance in this 1849 Italianate Victorian Inn. The main house has five exquisitely appointed guest rooms with private baths featuring queen beds, antique furnishings, oriental carpets, all with fireplaces or glass-front stoves and two with oversize whirlpool tubs. The unique Carriage House includes two spacious junior suites each with a fireplace and whirlpool bath, one with a king bed. Located in the heart of Sandwich village, the inn is within easy walking distance of many shops, restaurants and attractions of Cape Cod's oldest town. Unwind by strolling the meandering garden paths around the goldfish pond, by sitting in comfortable Adirondack chairs placed around the well-manicured yard or by relaxing by the original antique-tiled fireplace in the gathering room. A full breakfast, served in our cherry-paneled dining room, sets a warm tone to start your day. Chosen Editors Choice, *Cape Cod Travel Guide*, Spring, 2005. Selected as "Insider Pick" for Romantic Getaways by *Destination Insider*. Featured in "Checking In," Boston Sunday Globe, April 6, 2008.

**Rates**
Seven rooms, $150/$275, including a full, three course breakfast. Air conditioned. Open year-round. Number of Rooms: 7

**Cuisine**
Breakfast is served in our sunny, cherry paneled dining room. Enjoy a full three-course breakfast of fresh fruit, juices, creative hot entrees, home-baked scones and muffins, and our special blend of gourmet coffee.

**Nearest Airport(s)**
Logan Airport, Boston, MA; TF Green, Providence, RI

**Directions**
Rte. 6 (Mid-Cape Hwy.) Exit 2, Left at the end of the ramp onto Rte.130 to the village center. Bear right at the fork, go 2/10 mile, Inn is on the Left - 165 Main.

# Palmer House Inn

www.palmerhouseinn.com
81 Palmer Avenue, Falmouth, MA 02540
**800-472-2632** • 508-548-1230 • Fax 508-540-1878
innkeepers@palmerhouseinn.com

*Member Since 2001*

*"How visually appealing everything is…the decor, the gardens, the porches.
We loved it!"*

Innkeepers/Owners
## Pat and Bill O'Connell

On a tree-lined street in the heart of the Historic District, The Palmer House Inn is an elegant Victorian home. Stained glass windows, rich woodwork, gleaming hardwood floors and antique furnishings create an overall sense of warmth and harmony. Beautiful beaches, quaint shops, ferry shuttles, and excellent restaurants are only a short stroll away. The innkeepers pamper you with meticulous housekeeping, fresh flowers, extra pillows, fluffy robes, fine linens and good reading lights. The Palmer House Inn is the perfect place to stay, in splendid comfort and gracious care. Local activities include golf, swimming, cycling on the Shining Sea Bike Path, fishing, charter sailing, kayaking, hiking, bird watching and more.

**Rates**
16 Rooms, $109/$259; 1 Cottage Suites, $245/$299. K,Q,DBL beds, AC, cable TV & phones. Some have whirlpools, fireplaces. Open year-round. Number of Rooms: 17

**Cuisine**
Full gourmet breakfast served with candlelight and classical music. Afternoon and evening refreshments. Early morning coffee.

**Nearest Airport(s)**
TF Green (Providence) Logan (Boston)

**Directions**
After crossing the Bourne Bridge, follow Rte. 28 S for approximately 15 miles. A half-mile past the only traffic light at Jones Road/Ter Heun Drive, Rte. 28 turns left into Falmouth Village. The Inn is on the L just after the turn.

# Thorncroft Inn

www.thorncroft.com
460 Main St., P.O. Box 1022, Martha's Vineyard, MA  02568
**800-332-1236** • 508-693-3333 • Fax 508-693-5419
innkeeper@thorncroft.com

*Member Since 1994*

> *"Thorncroft is the kind of place, where we find ourselves falling in love all over again. The perfect place to escape the real world for a time."*

Proprietors/Innkeepers
**Lynn and Karl Buder**

Thorncroft Inn is situated in three restored buildings on 2 1/2 acres of quiet, treed grounds on the Island of Martha's Vineyard. It is secluded, exclusively couples-oriented and first-class. All rooms have phone, TV/VCR, high-speed wireless internet access, air-conditioning, deluxe bathrobes and an array of amenities. Most rooms have working, wood-burning fireplaces and canopied beds. Some have two-person whirlpool bathtubs or private 250-gallon hot tubs. Several offer private exterior entrances or furnished private porches or balconies. Full country breakfast served in our dining rooms or breaksfast delivered to the room, afternoon tea and pastries and evening turndown service are included in our room rates. Our concierge service is renowned and focuses on the specific needs of each couple. Thorncroft Inn is an ideal setting for honeymoons, anniversaries, engagements, birthdays or any romantic getaway for couples. Thorncroft also specializes in intimate, two-person weddings. The American Automobile Association has awarded Thorncroft Four Diamond for 19 consecutive years.

## Rates
14 antique appointed rooms, 10 with working wood burning fireplaces, some with two person whirlpools or private hot tubs. $225/$600 B&B with seasonal variations. Number of Rooms: 14

## Cuisine
Full country breakfast served in two dining rooms at individual tables for two or an ample continental breakfast delivered to room; Traditional or healthful entrees. Afternoon tea and pastries.

## Nearest Airport(s)
Martha's Vineyard Airport (MVY) 5 miles

## Directions
Year-round car & passenger Steamship Authority Ferry at Woods Hole, MA. (508-477-8600) Take left off dock and right at stop sign. Take next right onto Main St. Inn is 1 mile on left.

*Massachusetts*

*Martha's Vineyard*

# Seven Sea Street Inn

www.sevenseastreetinn.com
7 Sea Street, Nantucket, MA 02554
**800-651-9262** • 508-228-3577 • Fax 508-228-3578
innkeeper@sevenseastreetinn.com

*Member Since 1996*

*Massachusetts*

*Nantucket*

*"We loved every moment of our stay at your beautiful Inn.
Our room was perfect; thanks!"*

**Innkeepers/Owners**
**Matthew and Mary Parker**

Enjoy Seven Sea Street Inn, a truly charming Nantucket bed and breakfast Inn, where we pride ourselves on the attentive service and elegant accommodations that will make your stay with us a fond memory. Our Inn is distinguished by its beautiful red oak post and beam style, designed and constructed with an authentic Nantucket ambiance in mind. We are the only Inn on the Island which offers guests both a relaxing Jacuzzi Spa and a stunning view of Nantucket Harbor from our Widow's Walk deck. All of our guest rooms are furnished with luxurious Stearns and Foster queen or king mattresses, the world's finest bedding. Each Main house guest room and suite is furnished with rainshower showerheads, ACs, high definition TVs, high speed wireless connectivity and a bow box of Nantucket's famous chocolate covered cranberries. Our location, nestled on a quiet tree-lined side street and less than a five-minute walk from Main Street shopping, restaurants, museums and the beach, couldn't be better. Indulge yourself at our lovely Inn this year.

**Rates**
13 Guest Rooms, $99/$299 B&B; 2 Suites, $159/$389 B&B.
Seasonal rates. Number of Rooms: 15

**Cuisine**
Expanded Buffet Continental Breakfast served daily. Two seatings, 8 a.m. and 9 a.m. Gourmet coffee, tea, soda, bottled water and homemade cookies available anytime.

**Nearest Airport(s)**
Nantucket Memorial Airport

**Directions**
Flights available from Boston, NYC, Providence, & Hyannis. Ferry service from Hyannis to Steamboat Wharf in Nantucket. Less than a 5 minute walk from the wharf to the Inn. Take your 1st right onto South Beach Street then your 2nd left onto Sea Street. The Inn is on the left at 7 Sea Street.

# Union Street Inn

www.unioninn.com

7 Union Street, Nantucket, MA 02554

**888-517-0707** • 508-228-9222 • Fax 508-325-0848

unioninn@nantucket.net

*Member Since 2005*

*Massachusetts*

*Nantucket*

*"Over the years we had stayed in various B&B's in Nantucket. Then we found this gem and have been here five times."*

Innkeepers/Owners
**Deborah & Ken Withrow**

Nantucket's boutique inn. "This mint 1770 house in the middle of town has more style than most--not a surprise, given the previous careers of proprietors Ken (ex-GM of the Royalton in New York City) and Deborah (a display manager at Henri Bendel). They've decorated the 12 rooms in impeccable New England-by-way-of-France style--Pierre Deux wallpaper, high-poster beds, polished original floorboards, and a few non-fusty antiques. Six also have fireplaces. Add to the mix delicious breakfasts served on the outside patio (try the challah-bread French toast with fresh berries), a concierge to score hard-to-get dinner reservations, and just-baked cookies served every afternoon, and you'll see why this place has return guests every summer."- Conde Nast Traveler. Rooms have private baths, cable TV, Frette and Matouk bedding, Fresh bath amenities and complimentary Wi-Fi. Restaurants, shops, galleries, and museums are a short stroll. Walk or bicycle to Nantucket's beautiful beaches.

**Rates**
12 Rooms. High Season: $365/$550; Shoulder Seasons: $160/$495. Closed November through March. Number of Rooms: 12

**Cuisine**
Full Country Breakfast. Afternoon Treats. Coffee, Tea, Bottled Spring Water always available.

**Nearest Airport(s)**
Nantucket Memorial Airport-10 minute taxi ride.

**Directions**
Year round flights from Boston, NYC, New Bedford & Hyannis. High season from Providence, Washington D.C. Year round ferry service from Hyannis-short walk from ferries.Click on "Directions" on our home page for more details and links.

# Michigan

**"The Wolverine State"**

Famous for: Great Lakes,(borders on four of the five Great Lakes), Fishing, Swimming, Water Sports, Holland (Tulip Center of America), Cherries, Farmland, Auto Manufacturing.

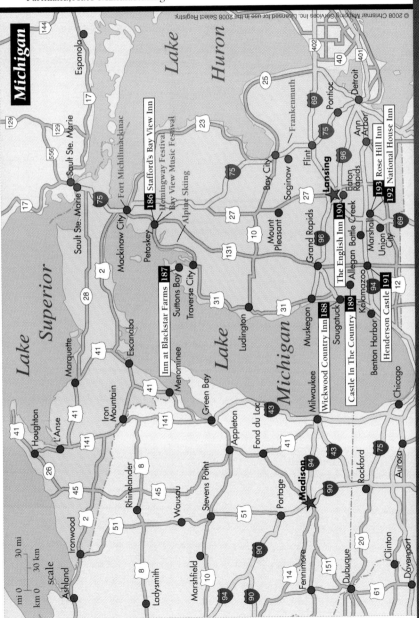

Michigan

© 2008 Chrismar Mapping Services Inc. Licensed for use in the 2008 Select Registry.

186 Stafford's Bay View Inn

Hemingway Festival
Bay View Music Festival
Alpine Skiing

187 Inn at Blackstar Farms

188 Wickwood Country Inn

189 Castle In The Country

190 The English Inn

191 Henderson Castle

192 National House Inn

193 Rose Hill Inn

Lake Huron

Lake Superior

Lake Michigan

🍽️ 🍽️ 🍽️ 🍷

# Stafford's Bay View Inn
www.staffords.com
2011 US 31 N, P.O. Box 657, Petoskey, MI 49770
**800-258-1886** • 231-347-2771 • Fax 231-347-3413
bayview@staffords.com

*Member Since 1972*

*Michigan*

*Petoskey*

> *"Perfect! The staff-decor-food! The view! Everything at this charming inn is wonderful! Warm caring smiles, yummie cookies, and unsurpassed cuisine."*

Proprietor
**Stafford Smith**

Bay View Inn was purchased by Stafford and Janice Smith in 1961. Stafford and his family has owned, operated, and lovingly restored, this grand Victorian Country Inn on the shores of Lake Michigan's Little Traverse Bay. Built as a rooming house in 1886 in the Historic Landmark District of Bay View, this Inn sets the standard in country inn dining and gracious service. Each beautifully appointed guest room features a private bath, and individual climate controls. Visitors to the area enjoy summer Chautauqua programs, championship golfing, paved bike paths just out our front door, our fall color tours, winter ski packages, and sleigh rides around the Bay View cottage grounds. Petoskey's Historic Gaslight Shopping District and marina are located nearby. Our inn is an exquisite place to hold weddings, rehearsal dinners, receptions and reunions. Many quiet corners offer a wonderful environment for company meetings and conferences. Landmark Hospitality where yesterday and today come together. Voted 'Michigan's Best Brunch' by *Michigan Living*. *This Inn is the flagship property of Stafford's Hospitality.*

**Rates**
21 Victorian rooms $95/$180 10 spa & fireplace Suites $130/$250. Number of Rooms: 31

**Cuisine**
Breakfast & Dinner: May-Oct. and winter weekends. Lunch: Late May-Oct. Sunday Brunch: June-Oct. & Holidays. Visit www.staffords.com for menus, dining schedules and info on full-service, year-round, innkeeper-owned properties nearby.

**Nearest Airport(s)**
Pellston (PLN) - 17 miles Traverse (TVC) - 65 miles

**Directions**
From Detroit: I-75N to Gaylord exit 282, Rte. 32W to US 131N to Petoskey. From Chicago: I-94 to I-196N to US 131N to Petoskey. From the North: I-75S across Mackinac Bridge to Petoskey Exit, US 31S.

# Inn at Black Star Farms

www.blackstarfarms.com
10844 E. Revold Rd., Suttons Bay, MI 49682
**877-466-9463** • 231-271-4970 ext. 150 • Fax 231-271-6321
innkeeper@blackstarfarms.com

*Member Since 2003*

*Michigan*

*Sutton's Bay*

*"Thanks for making our third visit to Black Star even more delightful than our first. Each time we return you've found a new way to surprise and pamper us."*

Proprietor - **Don Coe**
Inn Manager - **Corey Wentworth**

Our year-round Inn is nestled below a hillside of vineyards in the heart of Leelanau Peninsula wine country. Its eight contemporary guestrooms, each with private bath and some with fireplaces and spa tubs, have fine furniture, luxurious linens, and down comforters. Amenities include a bottle of our Red House Wine, cozy robes, and satellite TV/VCR. Massage services and sauna are available. A full gourmet breakfast is prepared for you daily using local seasonal products. You can sample our award-winning wines and spirits at our on site tasting room - also home of the artisanal Leelanau Cheese Co. The farm also features boarding stables and wooded recreational trails that are great in any season. Meetings, reunions and receptions welcomed.

**Rates**
May 25-October 27, 2007: $280/$395. October 28-May 22, 2008: $215/$295. Number of Rooms: 8

**Cuisine**
Our breakfasts feature fresh fruit and juices, homemade baked goods, a seasonal gourmet entree using local products, and coffee & tea.

**Nearest Airport(s)**
Cherry Capitol Airport (TVC)

**Directions**
From Traverse City: Follow M-22 N toward Northport. The Inn will be on your L after approx. 12 mi. L on Revold Rd. and L again into our driveway. From Cherry Capital Airport: Exit the airport and turn R. At Garfield Rd. turn R. At Front St. (M-72) turn L. Follow M-72 to M-22 and proceed as above.

# Wickwood Inn

www.wickwoodinn.com
510 Butler Street, Saugatuck, MI 49453-1019
**800-385-1174** • 269-857-1465 • Fax 269-857-1552
innkeeper@wickwoodinn.com

*Michigan*

*Saugatuck*

*"Every time we visit, now twelve times and counting, we marvel at all of Wickwood's efforts to make our stay ever more memorable during every season."*

Innkeepers/Owners
**Julee Rosso Miller and Bill Miller**

*Travel + Leisure* says, "Wickwood is one of America's most romantic Inns, a jewel with delicious food!!" Foodlovers, romantics and art connoisseurs gather at Silver Palate Cookbook author Julee Rosso's Inn in this charming art village on the shores of Lake Michigan. "She changed the way American eats," New York's Newsday compliments. Everyday terrific "surprises" are served including Chocolate Strawberries, lush Evening Hor's d'ouvres, great Champagne Brunch, Biscotti & Vin Santo. This exquisite getaway has a sophisticated décor, stunning artwork, antiques, gazebos and gardens. Guest rooms are appointed with featherbeds, fireplaces, cozy robes, stereos, books and spa secrets. "The décor is breathtaking–the food perfection," raves Zagat. The villages feature one of the "World's Top Ten Beaches," nature and bike trails, antique shops, 50 art galleries, berry and apple orchards, wineries, 150 shops and boutiques, four golf courses, theater, music and film festivals. The Inn is exquisite all year, especially magical at The Holidays.

**Rates**
7 traditional rooms, 4 suites with sitting areas, fireplaces & private baths. $155/$355 K & Q or twin. Number of Rooms: 11

**Cuisine**
She changed the way America eats-*New York Newsday*. Great eclectic food is evident in a warm complimentary Country Breakfast, daylong Serendipity Sips & Sweets, Candlelight Evening hor's d'ouvres & Brandies & Chocolate finalé.

**Nearest Airport(s)**
Grand Rapids

**Directions**
Southwestern Michigan, downtown in Village of Saugatuck on Lake Michigan. Two and one-half hours from Chicago and Detroit. Take I-96 to Exit #36 from the S, Exit #41 from the N on to the Blue Star Highway into Village to Butler Street.

# Castle in the Country

www.castleinthecountry.com
340 33rd. st. (M-40 S.), Allegan, MI 49010
**888-673-8054** • 269-673-8054
info@castleinthecountry.com

*Member Since 2008*

*Michigan · Allegan*

*"We made the right choice for our getaway-beautiful grounds, incredible decor, romantic ambiance, amazing breakfasts and outstanding hospitality! Thanks!"*

Innkeepers/Owners
**Herb and Ruth Boven**

Your perfect escape from the ordinary awaits you at Castle in the Country. Walk hand in hand through our wooded forest trails, sip a glass of wine in the screened porch beside our private lake or close the door to your own romantic suite with a whirlpool tub for two, fireplace and gourmet breakfast. Schedule a side-by-side couple's massage in our secluded Royal Retreat Spa Area. Gaze up into the star-studded sky and celebrate you! Awarded "Most Romantic Hideaway in North America!" by *Inntraveler Magazine*. When you choose Castle in the Country, you choose a Michigan getaway with extraordinary decor, amenities, and service! Scenic countryside provides a peaceful pastoral & wooded setting for your getaway. We offer ten individually decorated Rooms/Suites within the timeless beauty of our century-old Victorian Castle and in our contemporary country manor house, the Castle Keep. Whether you're looking for a romantic getaway for two to celebrate a birthday, anniversary or honeymoon or, an all-inclusive event venue for a Destination Wedding & Reception, our Innkeepers will help you create an experience that will exceed every expectation.

**Rates**
10 Rooms; 7 whirlpool/fireplace suites $155-$245 3 rooms fireplaces $115-$185 Midweek discounts; Spa & Dinner Packages;Wedding Packages; Business Retreats. Number of Rooms: 10

**Cuisine**
Full breakfasts are artfully presented & served daily in our dining rooms overlooking the pond. Picnic baskets filled with fresh baked bread, and creative Dinner Packages may be added by advanced reservation.

**Nearest Airport(s)**
Kalamazoo/Battle Creek International

**Directions**
From Detroit Take I-94 west to exit 60 or From Chicago Take I-94 east to exit 60; then North for 16 miles to the Inn. From Allegan Take M-40 South 6 miles to the Inn.

# The English Inn

www.englishinn.com
677 S. Michigan Rd., Lansing/Eaton Rapids, MI 48827
**517–663–2500** • Fax 517–663–2643
englishinn@comcast.net

*Member Since 1991*

*Michigan*

*Lansing/Eaton Rapids*

*"The Inn is a 'magical' place - thanks for the memories!"*

Innkeepers/Owners
**Gary and Donna Nelson**

A former auto baron's residence, this 1927 Tudor mansion will make you feel as though you've been transported to the English countryside. Perched on a hillside overlooking the Grand River, the Inn is part of a 15-acre estate that includes formal gardens and wooded nature trails. The main house has six well-appointed bedrooms named for English towns or the royal family, a cozy pub, library and two cottages include 4 bedrooms w/fireplaces and Jacuzzi tubs, common sitting areas. The Inn's award-winning restaurant includes a wine list bestowed with the Award of Excellence by *Wine Spectator*. A perfect setting for get-aways, executive retreats and family gatherings. In addition, a 200-seat, 10,000 sq.ft. banquet facility sits adjacent to the main house.

**Rates**
10 Rooms, $105/$175 B&B; includes 6 Inn Rooms, Two Cottages include 4 bedrooms w/jacuzzi tubs and fireplaces. Open year-round. Number of Rooms: 10

**Cuisine**
Breakfast w/room, Lunch M-F, Dinner 7 days. Continental-French cuisine, daily chef specials. Specialty of House; Chateaubriand for Two, carved tableside. Authentic English pub. Wine, beer, ale, liquor. Banquet Facilities 15-200+.

**Nearest Airport(s)**
Lansing Capitol City

**Directions**
From I-96 in Lansing, take M-99 S (exit 101) 8 mi. From I-94, take M-99(N) 22 mi. Ninety miles W of Detroit, 15 miles S of State Capitol (Lansing), and Michigan State Univ.

 SelectRegistry.com

# Henderson Castle

www.hendersoncastle.com
100 Monroe Street, Kalamazoo, MI 49006
**269-344-1827**
info@hendersoncastle.com

*Member Since 2008*

*"Everything was just perfect. The hot tub overlooking the city at night, the steam room and breakfast were all just fabulous."*

Proprietors
**Peter and Laura Livingstone-McNelis**

There is simply no place like it. Anywhere. Step through the leaded-glass doors of this elegant inn. And enter another world--a world of beauty, comfort and quiet refinement. Since its construction in 1895, Henderson Castle has been one of Kalamazoo's most prominent local landmarks and is listed on the National Registry of Historic Places. High atop a hill, commanding a panoramic view of the city and over 37 miles beyond, the Henderson Castle has served as much as a symbol as it has a building; refined, dignified, embodying old-world values of craftsmanship and appreciation for beauty. The Castle has kept up with the times however and includes modern amenitites such as wireless internet, heated marble floors and a hot tub on the roof. Conveniently located only 6 blocks from downtown and one block from Kalamazoo College, the Castle is private but accessible making it the perfect place to get away but have it all.

**Rates**
$150-$300/night based on double occupancy. Number of Rooms: 6

**Cuisine**
Full hot breakfast daily

**Nearest Airport(s)**
Kalamazoo/Battle Creek International Airport

**Directions**
US-131, exit 38A, 2.9 miles East to 100 Monroe St., or I- 94, exit 75, North on Westnedge, West on Lovell, North on Monroe to 100 Monroe St.

# National House Inn

www.nationalhouseinn.com
102 S. Parkview, Marshall, MI 49068
**269-781-7374** • Fax 269-781-4510
innkeeper@nationalhouseinn.com

*Member Since 1978*

*Michigan*

*Marshall*

*National House Inn has been featured in Midwest Living - April 2004*

Innkeeper/Owner
**Barbara Bradley**

Nestled in the heart of Historic Marshall, National House Inn is Michigan's oldest operating Inn. The first brick building in the county, National House has been restored as a warm, beautifully furnished, hospitable Inn with lovely gardens. Marshall--nicknamed "The City of Hospitality"--has many citations for its 850 19th Century architectural structures, and is included on the National Register of Historic Places, where the Inn is also listed. In 2004, Marshall was chosen as one of 12 distinctive destinations for the National Trust for Historic Preservation, has a prestigious National Historic Landmark District designation and is home to Schuler's Restaurant and the annual fall Historic Home Tour. Come join us for afternoon tea at a turn of the century pace in a turn of the century Inn.

**Rates**
15 Rooms, $105/$115 B&B; 2 Suites, $145. Number of Rooms: 17

**Cuisine**
Breakfast, afternoon tea, catered dinners for receptions.

**Nearest Airport(s)**
Kalamazoo

**Directions**
I-94 to exit 110 Rte. 27(S) 2 miles to Michigan Ave (SW corner of circle, located in downtown Marshall).

# Rose Hill Inn

www.rose-hill-inn.com
1110 Verona Road, Marshall, MI 49068
**269-789-1992** • Fax 269-781-4723
rosehillinnkeeper@cablespeed.com

*Member Since 2004*

*Michigan*

*Marshall*

> *"Rose Hill is the standard for B&Bs. First cabin all the way."* *"The Rose Hill Inn reminds one of a Tuscan villa."* New York Times Travel Section

Innkeepers/Owners
**Gerald & Carol Lehmann**

The Rose Hill Inn is an elegant 1860 Victorian mansion, once the summer home of William Boyce, flamboyant self-made millionaire and founder of the American Boy Scouts. Twelve-foot ceilings, tall windows, lovely views, fireplaces, and fine antiques combine to create a mood of tranquility and escape from the modern world. Guest rooms are decorated in luxurious nineteenth century style with vintage art work, period decor, and antique lighting but feature all the contemporary conveniences: A/C, private baths, cable TV, and wireless Internet. A card room and billiard room are also available for your enjoyment. Situated on three acres of landscaped grounds, Rose Hill offers a private swimming pool, tennis court, porches, patios, gardens, and fountains. Guests may use pool or tennis court without fees. Located in historic Marshall, Michigan, within walking distance of fine dining, museums, and shops. The Rose Hill Inn provides the rare opportunity to step back into the Gilded Age and create a unique memory--the perfect choice for your wedding, family reunion, or corporate event.

**Rates**
$99/$260. Other rates may apply for special events/holidays, off-season & business travel. Some discounts available. Queen beds, some fireplaces. Number of Rooms: 6

**Cuisine**
Full breakfast served fireside on Haviland China includes a hot specialty d'jour, seasonal fruit, juice, yogurt, & home-baked goods. Complimentary snacks, coffee/tea, bottled water & soft drinks always available.

**Nearest Airport(s)**
Kalamazoo/Battle Creek Regional Airport

**Directions**
From I-94: Exit 110, S to Mansion St., W .8 mi. From I-69: Exit 36, E to Fountain St., N 2 blks. to Verona Rd. W 100 ft

# Mississippi

Famous for: Mississippi River, Fertile Soil, Cotton, River Boats, Catfish, Old South, Red Bluff, Civil War Sites, Antebellum Mansions.

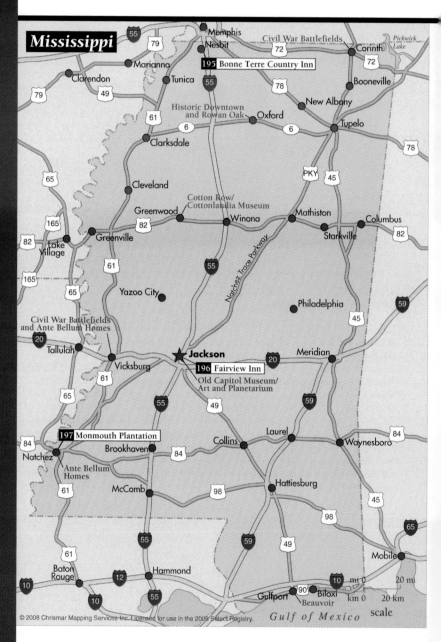

**Mississippi**

Memphis
Nesbit
Civil War Battlefields
Corinth
Pickwick Lake
**195** Bonne Terre Country Inn
Marianna
Tunica
Clarendon
Booneville
New Albany
Historic Downtown and Rowan Oak
Oxford
Tupelo
Clarksdale
Cleveland
PKY
Cotton Row/ Cottonlandia Museum
Greenwood
Winona
Mathiston
Columbus
Greenville
Starkville
Lake Village
Natchez Trace Parkway
Yazoo City
Philadelphia
Civil War Battlefields and Ante Bellum Homes
Tallulah
★ **Jackson**
Meridian
Vicksburg
**196** Fairview Inn
Old Capitol Museum/ Art and Planetarium
Laurel
**197** Monmouth Plantation
Brookhaven
Collins
Waynesboro
Natchez
Ante Bellum Homes
McComb
Hattiesburg
Baton Rouge
Hammond
Mobile
Gulfport
Biloxi
Beauvoir
mi 0        20 mi
km 0     20 km
scale
*Gulf of Mexico*

© 2008 Chrismar Mapping Services Inc. Licensed for use in the 2009 Select Registry.

SelectRegistry.com

# Bonne Terre Country Inn

www.bonneterre.com
4715 Church Rd. West, Nesbit, MS 38651
**662–781–5100** • Fax 662-781-5466
info@bonneterre.com

*Member Since 2003*

*"It's the most beautiful place I've ever seen.
A romantic, peaceful retreat beyond compare."*

Innkeepers/Owners
**Charles and Kimbel Orr**

Bonne Terre, French for the "good earth," is a 14-room Country Inn nestled in Nesbit, Mississippi just 15 minutes south of Memphis. Our 23 beautifully wooded acres of Mississippi highlands are within a short drive from anywhere in the Mid-South. In our restaurant, a double sided fireplace is a romantic focal point while the indoor veranda paints a beautiful portrait of the woods and one of our picturesque lakes. Bonne Terre also includes a New England-style Wedding Chapel, a gazebo, and Ashley Hall, our grand Colonial Williamsburg-style reception and banquet hall where countless memorable weddings, receptions and special occasions are held. Bonne Terre is ranked as the premier bed and breakfast property in the Memphis area, consistently rated #1 in readers polls for both dining and lodging.

**Rates**
14 Rooms, $165/$250. Special rates are available for corporate groups. All rooms are decorated with fine antique decor and feather beds. Special touches in most rooms include fireplaces, whirlpool tubs, and balconies Number of Rooms: 14

**Cuisine**
Cafe Bonne Terre, the heart of our lovely inn, presents an exquisite fine dining experience for our guests. Chefs prepare an array of American Continental cuisine set in an elegant, intimate setting.

**Nearest Airport(s)**
Memphis International

**Directions**
Just 25 minutes S of Memphis off I-55. Take Church Rd. exit(#287) and go W 4.4 miles to Bonne Terre. 3 hours north of Jackson, Ms.

# Fairview Inn

www.fairviewinn.com
734 Fairview Street, Jackson, MS 39202
**888-948-1908** • 601-948-3429 • Fax 601-948-1203
fairview@fairviewinn.com

*Member Since 1994*

*"This is a place to sustain the body and rest the soul."* Jane Goodall

Proprietors
**Peter and Tamar Sharp**

Fairview Inn & Restaurant, located downtown in the Belhaven Historic District of Jackson, Mississippi, offers luxury accommodations with all modern amenities such as high speed Internet access and voice mail. Enjoy its well-stocked library, replete with military history and many first editions, its formal garden, flowering magnolia and crepe myrtle trees, and the relaxed ambiance of a two-acre estate on the National Register of Historic Places. Named a Top Inn of 1994 by *Country Inns* magazine, cited "Southern hospitality at its best" by *Travel + Leisure* in 1998, selected by the National Trust for Historic Preservation for inclusion in the 1998 wall calendar featuring Historic Bed & Breakfast Inns and Small Hotels, named a Top Ten Romantic Inn of 2000 by American Historic Inns, featured in *Southern Living* in 2001, winner of Condé Nast Johansens "Most Outstanding Inn 2003, North America."

**Rates**
3 Rooms and 15 Suites, $139/$349 B&B. Open year-round.
Number of Rooms: 18

**Cuisine**
Full breakfast each morning. Fine Dining Tuesday-Thursday 5:30 p.m. to 9:30 p.m., Friday and Saturday 5:30 p.m. to 10:00 p.m. Sunday Brunch 11:00 a.m. to 2:00 p.m. Banquet and meeting facilities for groups from 10-800pp. Wine and liquor available.

**Nearest Airport(s)**
Jackson International

**Directions**
I-55 exit 98A on Woodrow Wilson, L at second traffic light at North State, L one block past second traffic light at Fairview St., Inn is first on L.

 SelectRegistry.com

# Monmouth Plantation

www.monmouthplantation.com
36 Melrose Avenue, Natchez, MS  39120
**800-828-4531** • 601-442-5852 • Fax 601-446-7762
luxury@monmouthplantation.com

*Member Since 1993*

*Monmouth has been honored with "The Travel and Leisure 500 - The World's Best Hotels" award, and was placed on the Condé Nast Gold List*

Owners
**Lani & Ron Riches**

Monmouth Plantation, a National Historic Landmark (circa 1818), is a glorious return to the Antebellum South, rated "one of the ten most romantic places in the USA" by *Glamour* magazine and *USA Today*. It waits to enfold you in luxury and service. Walk our beautifully landscaped acres. Thirty rooms and suites in the mansion and the seven other historic buildings hold priceless art and antiques while providing every modern comfort. Mornings begin with a delightful complimentary Southern breakfast. Nights sparkle under candlelight during 5-course dinners.

**Rates**
17 Rooms, $195/$235 13 Suites, $260/$290. Open year-round.  Number of Rooms: 30

**Cuisine**
Breakfast and dinner, lunch for private parties only. Wine, liquor, and beer.

**Nearest Airport(s)**
Jackson, MS. Baton Rouge, LA. New Orleans, LA.

**Directions**
E on State Street, 1 mile from downtown Natchez on the corner of John Quitman Parkway and Melrose Avenue.

# Missouri

## "The Show-Me State"

Famous for: Center of Continental United States, "Gateway to the West," Livestock, Ozark Plateau, Cottontail Rabbits, Dairy, Corn, Wheat, Cotton, Lead, Zinc, Lime, Cement, Timber, Aircraft, Automobiles, Spacecraft.

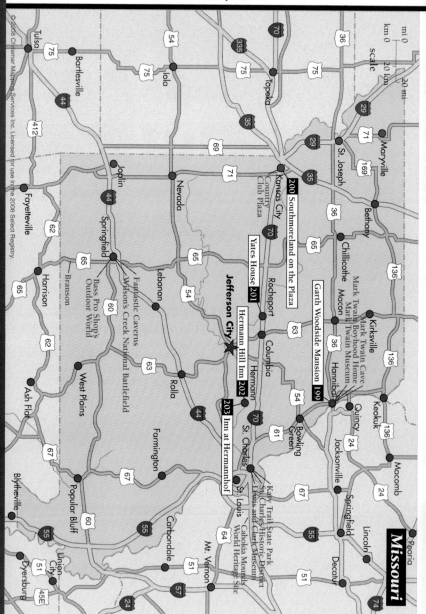

# Garth Woodside Mansion

www.garthmansion.com
11069 New London Road, Hannibal, MO 63401
**888-427-8409** • 573-221-2789 • Fax 573-221-9941
innkeeper@garthmansion.com

*Member Since 2001*

*"This has become a wonderful tradition for us, please always be there!"*

Innkeepers/Owners
**Col. (Ret.) John and Julie Rolsen**

For years Garth Mansion has been rated the #1 B&B in Missouri. Only 8 minutes from historic downtown Hannibal, yet secluded on 39 acres. Walking/hiking trails throughout the woodlands, ponds, a pasture with llamas, and rolling lawns. Take advantage of the estate and enjoy dinner at the onsite restaurant, The Woodside, where you may enjoy a six course chef feature paired with wines or a casual dinner on the garden patio. Nominated for a Wine Spectator Award, you may also enjoy local wines from Missouri. All three cottages offer their own private hot tub on their deck, and each have fireplaces. Your breakfast is still made fresh for you at your desired time. No frozen meals here! The Dowager's meals are even brought to you. The mansion rooms each have private baths and most have fireplaces. Jetted tubs available. The charm of an 1871 historic mansion will lure you to a getaway to remember. You may sleep in the same room Samuel Clemens stayed many times. Our toll free number is to ask questions or reservations. 888-427-8409.

**Rates**
8 Rooms $139/$225; 3 Cottages $280/$395. Original antiques, hypo-allergenic Queen and King feather beds, central heat/air. 2 rooms offer oversized two-person whirlpool tubs. Open all year. Number of Rooms: 11

**Cuisine**
The breakfast will bring you back and entice you to enjoy the local cuisine at the onsite restaurant. Full dinner menu, many items from onsite garden.

**Nearest Airport(s)**
STL: 99 mi. Chicago 295 mi.

**Directions**
From St. Louis: N. SR 61, 75 mi. N of I-70. R on Warren-Barrett, R on New London. Follow signs. From SR 36 or I-72 S on SR 61, L on Warren-Barrett, R on New London. Use GPS of 39.40 -91.24 instead of address.

*Missouri*

*Hannibal*

# Southmoreland on the Plaza

www.southmoreland.com
116 East 46th St., Kansas City, MO 64112
**816-531-7979** • Fax 816-531-2407
innkeeper@southmoreland.com

*Member Since 1992*

*Missouri*

*Kansas City*

> *"Southmoreland on the Plaza is as restful and alluring a place as I've ever experienced." - Southern Living Magazine. "Gem of the Midwest."*

## Innkeepers/Owners
**Mark Reichle and Nancy Miller Reichle**

Southmoreland on the Plaza-an Urban Inn sets the standard for B & B hospitality and comfort. Located just one and one-half blocks off of the Country Club Plaza and two blocks from the Nelson Atkins Musuem of Art, the Inn blends classic New England Bed and Breakfast ambiance with small hotel amenities. Twelve guestrooms and the Carriage House suite offer private baths, telephones, and off-street parking. Guests enjoy individually decorated rooms featuring decks, fireplaces or Jacuzzi baths. Business travelers find respite at Southmoreland. We are pleased to offer corporate rates and a rare mix of services conducive to business travel: in-room phones, Wi-Fi, fax, copier, voice mail, 24-hour access and switchboard, and guest privileges at two full-service fitness centers. Southmoreland on the Plaza is an Inn of national reputation, worthy of its Plaza locale; warm and accommodating like Kansas City itself. Featured on the Food Network's "Barbecue with Bobby Flay." Visit us at www.southmoreland.com.

**Rates**
12 Rooms in Main House, $135/$200 Summer $130/$215 Winter $250 Carriage House (less $20 SGL.) Number of Rooms: 13

**Cuisine**
Gourmet breakfast served daily. Complimentary afternoon wine & hors d'oeuvres, with hot beverages and sweets served in the evening. Courtyard breakfast BBQ served Saturdays, Apr 15-Oct 15.

**Nearest Airport(s)**
Kansas City International

**Directions**
From I-70, I-29 or I-35 in downtown KC, take Broadway (S) to Cleaver II Blvd. (47th St.), L on Cleaver II Blvd, L on Main, R on E 46th St. About 1.5 blks down E 46th on the lefthand side.

# Yates House Bed & Breakfast

www.yateshouse.com
305 Second Street, Rocheport, MO 65279
**573-698-2129**
yateshouse@socket.net

*Member Since 2005*

*Missouri*

*Rocheport*

*"Unpretentious hospitality, superior breakfasts, and lovely accommodations."*

Innkeepers/Owners
**Dixie and Conrad Yates**

Located in "One of America's Top Ten Coolest Small Towns" Frommers Budget Travel Guide. Everything you'll need for luxurious and relaxing enjoyment is provided or within easy walking distance. All rooms are large, beautifully furnished, and well equipped. King beds, jetted tubs, and fireplace are available. Wireless Internet and other business services are provided. Twenty-four seat dining/meeting room available and catered for small groups. Individual table or inroom breakfast provided. Famous for seasonal, gourmet breakfast menu and cooking classes. "Dixie can flat cook," observed *Southern Living* magazine. Within a block of most scenic section of Katy Trail State Park. Photogenic trails, bluffs, tunnels, and Missouri River within short walking distance. Vineyards, winery, shops and restaurants nearby. Voted "Favorite Day Trip" by readers of the Kansas City Star. Fortunately located midway between Kansas City and St.Louis and fifteen minutes from University of Missouri town of Columbia.

### Rates
5 rooms, $149/$254. 1 suite $249/$289. Business rates and cancellation available. Premium quality Queen and King beds. Two jetted tubs. One fireplace. Digital cable/DVD. Wireless DSL. Plentiful outdoor seating in garden areas and on multi-level brick patio. Open year-round. Number of Rooms: 6

### Cuisine
Full, seasonally changing, gourmet breakfast menu with individual table or inroom service. Afternoon cookies and beverage.

### Nearest Airport(s)
Columbia Regional, 30 min.

### Directions
I-70 to Exit 115 (Rocheport) at Missouri River Bridge. 2 miles N on BB. L one block on Columbia St to 305 Second St.

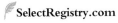

# Hermann Hill Vineyard & Inn

www.hermannhill.com
P.O. Box 555, 711 Wein Street, Hermann, MO 65041
**573-486-4455** • Fax 573-486-5373
info@hermannhill.com

*Member Since 2005*

*Missouri*

*Hermann*

*"Hermann is a B&B town... but a trip to the region would not be complete without a stay at Hermann Hill Vineyard & Inn." Southern Living Magazine*

Innkeepers/Owners
**Peggy and Terry Hammer**

Enjoy the ultimate country inn experience at Missouri's most popular Bed and Breakfast. While both properties were built just for upscale lodging, you can choose the Inn's traditional bed and breakfast amenities and service or opt for more privacy and even higher amenities at our Hermann Hill Village cottages. The Inn's eight exquisitely appointed guest rooms offer you spectacular views from your own balcony or patio, luxurious private baths with Jacuzzi-style tubs for two, and the privacy and freedom to set your own pace. Sited on a bluff and surrounded by a vineyard, the inn rooms create the backdrop for your stay in an ever-changing panorama of Hermann and the Missouri River Valley. Sleep late, have breakfast in bed, or walk to a nearby winery. Our riverbluff cottages offer even higher amenities, including personal and private outdoor hot tubs overlooking the Missouri River, aroma threapy fireplaces, kitchens, outdoor gas grills, steam showers, and laundry facilities. We supply your cottage with breakfast entrees prior to your arrival and provide daily make up service and also samples of our Port Chocolate Raspberry sauce.

**Rates**
2008 rates $166/351,for all eight Inn rooms and all 12 cottage rooms.All 20 rooms have king beds, fireplace, large jacuzzi and shower, TV,DVD,and WIFI  Number of Rooms: 20

**Cuisine**
A full country breakfast with choice of entree served either to your room, or in kitchen, dining room, or outside deck.

**Nearest Airport(s)**
70 miles west of St. Louis Lambert Airport

**Directions**
From Exit 175 of I-70, take Hwy 19 south into Hermann, continue south on Hwy 19 to West 6th St. Turn right on W. 6th St., then left on Washington St. At West 10th St., turn right and go 3 blocks up hill, around sharp right turn and watch for our sign on right.

# Inn at Hermannhof

www.theinnathermannhof.com
237 E. First Street, Hermann, MO  65041
**888-268-1422** • 573-486-5199
theinn@hermannhof.com

*Member Since 2008*

Innkeepers
**James and Mary Dierberg**

For a truly memorable experience, join us for a historic vacation in Hermann Missouri. The Inn At Hermannhof features spacious, historically decorated Suites with luxurious amenities and a full breakfast. The Inn offers 8 Suites in the Festhalle and 6 Haus Wineries with 20 Suites. The Inn is located in the heart of the historic district, placing you in the center of Hermann activities. Our Haus Wineries are located on East Hill and are former working wineries. Each Haus was thoughtfully reconstructed with attention to detail. Though no two Suites are alike, the highest standard of excellence is evident in all. Each Suite is designed with exquisite style to offer guests pencil post tiger maple beds, luxury linens, lustrous carpets over wood floors, wine cellars, sitting rooms, fireplaces, deep soaking and whirlpool tubs, oversized jetted and steam showers, Missouri River views and more. High speed Internet service and a flat screen cable TV make your stay convenient and relaxing.

Everything has been selected with you, our guests, and your comfort as our top Priority. Hermann Lodging at it's best!

**Rates**
Rates vary by season and day, from $126 to $364.  Number of Rooms: 28 Suites

**Cuisine**
Enjoy a complimentary full breakfast with locally made sausage or country ham, fresh eggs, biscuits, and other American and German favorites. We also offer lighter fare if requested.

**Nearest Airport(s)**
Lambert St. Louis International Airport

**Directions**
Hermann is on the Missouri river at the crossroads of Highways 19 and 100. The Inn is located at First and Gutenberg.

# *Montana*

Famous for: Majestic Mountains, The Great Plains, Ponderosa Pines, Glacier National Park, Battle of the Little Bighorn, Lewis and Clark Historic Site.

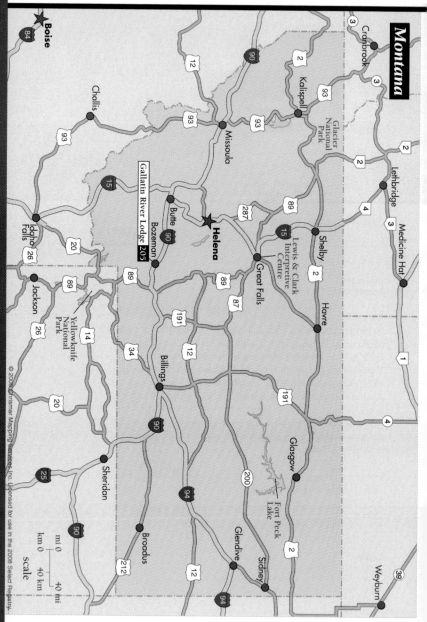

# Gallatin River Lodge

www.grlodge.com
9105 Thorpe Road, Bozeman, MT 59718
**888-387-0148** • 406-388-0148 • Fax 406-388-6766
info@grlodge.com

*Member Since 2007*

🍽️ 🍽️ 🍽️ 🍷

*Montana*

*Bozeman*

*"...what a finely crafted, well-appointed and charming lodge you have built. Equally important, we found that the staff was terrific."*

Wine Spectator
AWARD
OF
EXCELLENCE

Innkeeper/Owner
**Steve Gamble**

Welcome to the Gallatin River Lodge. We are just minutes from Bozeman, Montana and Yellowstone National Park. We are open year-round and are in the best location to experience southwest Montana. We also offer fly fishing guide service on the Madison, Gallatin and Yellowstone Rivers nearby. Our services include creative fine dining, elegant accommodations, conference and wedding services. Room amenities include fireplaces, Jacuzzi tubs, Satellite TV and high-speed wireless Internet. The Lodge is in a secluded, quiet location just six miles west of Bozeman and 30 miles from the Big Sky resort. Our restaurant, The Grill, is recognized as the finest dining facility in the region and dinner is served seven nights a week. We offer creative American cuisine, a full bar and an extensive wine list. Contact us for special packages and last minute discounts. Free airport transportation available.

**Rates**
High Season: May 1st - October 31st A three night minimum stay is requested during the above dates. See our web site for more information on our packages. One night stays are offered if reserved within 2 weeks of arrival. Double $270 Single $250 Low Season: November 1-April 30 Reservations accepted anytime. Double $170 Single $150 Rates do not include state bed tax (7%) Number of Rooms: 6

**Cuisine**
Our menu reflects influences from many cuisines.

**Nearest Airport(s)**
Bozeman, Montana (BZN)

**Directions**
Please Visit Mapquest or GoogleMaps.

# New Hampshire

### "The Granite State"

Famous for: Granite, White Mountains, Lakes, Beaches, Prime Primary '(the first state to hold presidential primary elections).

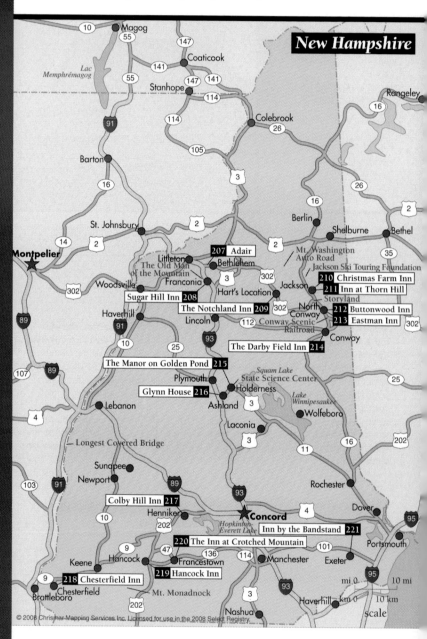

New Hampshire

207 Adair
210 Christmas Farm Inn
211 Inn at Thorn Hill
Sugar Hill Inn 208
212 Buttonwood Inn
The Notchland Inn 209
213 Eastman Inn
The Darby Field Inn 214
The Manor on Golden Pond 215
Glynn House 216
Colby Hill Inn 217
Inn by the Bandstand 221
220 The Inn at Crotched Mountain
218 Chesterfield Inn
219 Hancock Inn

© 2008 Chrismar Mapping Services Inc. Licensed for use in the 2008 Select Registry.

SelectRegistry.co

# Adair Country Inn & Restaurant

www.adairinn.com
80 Guider Lane, Bethlehem, NH 03574
**888-444-2600** • 603-444-2600 • Fax 603-444-4823
innkeeper@adairinn.com

*Member Since 1995*

*New Hampshire*

*Bethlehem*

*"Our whole experience here was glorious: the smells, sights, sounds that soothe the soul, we have never stayed anywhere that has been so hard to leave."*

Innkeepers/Owners
**Ilja and Brad Chapman**
**Betsy and Nick Young**

"Adair Country Inn & Restaurant is everything you dreamed a New England country inn would be." - USA Today. Get away from it all and unwind at this peaceful country inn. Enter a woodland oasis via a long winding drive surrounded by stone walls, stately pines, ponds, gardens and 200 acres. The inn's scenic grounds were originally created by the Olmsted Brothers. This elegant inn sits atop a knoll and enjoys magnificent views of the Presidential Range and comfortably appointed guest rooms with fireplaces, antiques, reproductions and air conditioning. Adair serves as an intimate, romantic retreat for adults who enjoy observing wildlife, hiking, golfing, skiing and more in the nearby White Mountains. The inn's relaxing ambiance and casual dress belie uncompromising attention to detail, highly personalized, warm service and award-winning New England style cuisine. Adair is within a short drive of Franconia Notch, Mt. Washington, Mt. Lafayette, The Flume, superb hiking, numerous cross-country venues and major ski areas. Deliberately small... Naturally quiet! Come make a treasured memory year round.

## Rates
$195/$325 B&B. Spacious rooms all w/private baths, 7 w/fireplaces, 3 w/2-person tubs. Complimentary wireless internet. German, Dutch and Spanish spoken. Number of Rooms: 9

## Cuisine
Breakfast features fresh fruit, steaming popovers and hot entree. Afternoon tea with homemade pastries. New England style cuisine in a cozy fireside restaurant with seasonal patio seating. Full beverage service.

## Nearest Airport(s)
Manchester NH 95 miles, Boston MA 155 miles, Montreal 180 miles

## Directions
From I-93 N/S take Exit 40/Route 302. Turn R then sharp L at Adair sign. From the E, take Rt 302 W 3 miles past Bethlehem, turn R at Adair sign.

# Sugar Hill Inn

www.sugarhillinn.com
116 Scenic Route 117, Sugar Hill, NH 03586
**800-548-4748** • 603-823-5621 • Fax 603-823-5639
info@sugarhillinn.com

*Member Since 2001*

*New Hampshire*

*Sugar Hill*

*"Extraordinary in all categories! Meals - four stars, accommodations - luxury level. Enjoyed our stay to the max. Can't wait to return!"*

Innkeeper/Owner
**Steven Allen & Theresa Spear**

Nestled in New Hampshire's White Mountains, Sugar Hill Inn is a romantic getaway known for culinary adventure and warm, inviting guest rooms and cottages. You'll be immersed in country inn ambiance, New England hospitality and all the recreation of the Franconia region. Impeccably restored, this country inn ranges from charming and cozy to sophisticated and distinctive. This 18th Century classic farmhouse is perched on a hillside on acres of woodlands, rolling lawns and perennial gardens, enhanced by unparalleled views of the White Mountains. All rooms have air-conditioning, and many have fireplaces, whirl-pool tubs, and private decks. The new Dream Cottage with a cathedral ceiling, stone fire-place, wide plank floors, whirlpool and sauna has been featured in "Everyday with Rachael Ray" magazine. Whether you seek a convenient base for the many wonderful attractions and outdoor activities of Franconia Notch and the White Mountains or a special private hideaway to snuggle in front of a fireplace...come share the good life at the Sugar Hill Inn... your destination of choice. 2008 Yankee Magazine Editors' Choice.

**Rates**
Classic Rooms $140/$225; Cottages, $150/$360; Luxury Rooms, $175/$360. Open year-round. Number of Rooms: 14

**Cuisine**
Full breakfast and afternoon tea and sweets daily. Dinner Thursday-Monday by reservations. Relax in the Tavern with your favorite cocktail before dinner. Excellent wine list.

**Nearest Airport(s)**
Manchester Airport - 100 miles.

**Directions**
From I-93 N: Take exit 38, left at bottom of ramp. Right turn onto Rte. 18 N. Travel .5 (1/2) miles. Left at bridge Rte 117. The Inn is .5 (1/2) miles up the hill on R. From I-91 N or S: Take exit 17 onto Rte. 302 E 20 miles on R is Rte. 117. The inn is 8 miles on the left.

# The Notchland Inn

www.notchland.com
US Route 302, Hart's Location, NH 03812
**800-866-6131** • 603-374-6131 • Fax 603-374-6168
innkeepers@notchland.com

x

# The Notchland Inn

www.notchland.com
US Route 302, Hart's Location, NH 03812
**800-866-6131** • 603-374-6131 • Fax 603-374-6168
innkeepers@notchland.com

*Member Since 1996*

*New Hampshire*

*Hart's Location*

*Chosen one of America's 54 Best Inns
by National Geographic Traveler magazine.*

Innkeepers/Owners
**Les Schoof and Ed Butler**

Get away from it all, relax and rejuvenate at our comfortable granite manor house, completed in 1862, within the White Mountain National Forest. Settle into one of our spacious guest rooms, individually appointed and each with woodburning fireplaces and private baths. Children and pets are welcome in our newly completed river or mountain view cottages, ranging in size from 1 to 2.5 bedrooms and all with whirlpool baths. A wonderful 5-course dinner and full country breakfast are served in a fireplaced dining room overlooking the gardens. Nature's wonders abound at Notchland. We have 8,000 feet of Saco River frontage on our property and two of the area's best swimming holes! Top off an active day, in any season, with a soak in our wooden hot tub, which sits in a gazebo by the pond. Visit with Crawford and Felonie, our Bernese Mountain Dogs. Secluded, yet near to all the Mt. Washington Valley has to offer. Notchland...a magical location.

**Rates**
8 Deluxe Rooms, 5 Suites, 3 Cottages $199/$395, B&B.
Open year-round. Number of Rooms: 16

**Cuisine**
5-course distinctive dinners Weds-Sun, hearty country breakfast daily. Fully licensed: wine/spirits/beer. At Notchland, the table is yours for the evening. Dinner is a leisurely affair, taking about 2 hours. $38 per person for in-house guests. $40 Wed, Thur, Sun and $45 Fri, Sat & Holidays for others.

**Nearest Airport(s)**
Manchester, NH, approx. 125 miles
Burlington, VT, approx. 130 miles

**Directions**
Take Rt 93N to exit 35, Rt 3N, go 10 miles to Rt 302, turn R, continue 16.5 miles E on 302 to Inn on R.

# Christmas Farm Inn

www.christmasfarminn.com
3 Blitzen Way, Jackson, NH 03846
**800-HI-ELVES** • 603-383-4313 • Fax 603-383-6495
info@christmasfarminn.com

*New Hampshire*

*Jackson*

*"Excellent food, charming rooms, wonderful staff, perfect location! Be it a romantic getaway or a family vacation the Christmas Farm is the place to stay."*

Wine Spectator
AWARD
OF
EXCELLENCE

## Your Hosts, the Tolley & Belcher Familes

AN INN FOR ALL SEASONS. Nestled in the majestic White Mountains on 14 breath-taking acres, the Christmas Farm Inn & Spa offers a taste of the good life. Accommodations include charming colonial guestrooms w/prvt. baths in the Main Inn, hand-crafted cottages with fplc. on the wooded hillside, and 2-room Luxury Suites with gas fplc, Jacuzzi tubs, pvt. balconies, wet bars & more. Stroll through award winning gardens, enjoy indoor & outdoor heated swimming pools, work out in our health & fitness center, or soak in our hot tubs after a day of XC-skiing. Enjoy full service state-of-the-art SPA & steam room. Sell-out Medical, Health & Wellness Seminars featured throughout the year; book early. 'Fresh & Healthy' Eating Choices always available. The Inn's New American Cuisine menu served in the Plum Pudding Restaurant, recently featured on Ed Hitzer's Table For One radio program, is complimented by a thoughtful, award winning wine list. Conference, Seminar and intimate Wedding accomodations. Featured on the cover of "Top 100 Inns in America", 2008. Member of the Environmental Lodging Program, doing our part for a Sustainable Future.

### Rates
42 Units. $159 & up. Hearty Country breakfast/buffet included. MAP plans available. Taxes and gratuities are additional. Seasonal packages, personally designed itinerary service available. Family owned and operated, Open year round. Number of Rooms: 42

### Cuisine
Culinary Style is 'Fresh Farm Fusion'. Start each day with a Hearty Country Breakfast, home baked pastries, including the inn's famous Sugar Plum Donuts.

### Nearest Airport(s)
Portland, ME Manchester NH

### Directions
Once in Jackson turn right at the red covered bridge & drive through village. Bear Rt. at the school on Rt. 16B/Black Mtn. Road. We are half a mile up the hill.

# Inn at Thorn Hill

www.innatthornhill.com
Thorn Hill Road, P.O. Box A, Jackson Village, NH  03846
**800-289-8990** • 603-383-4242 • Fax 603-383-8062
stay@innatthornhill.com

*Member Since 1998*

*"Nobody does it better and we look forward to being in your home again very soon."*

**Innkeepers/Owners**
**James & Ibby Cooper**

Situated grandly on a knoll overlooking Jackson Village and the Presidential Mountains, the Inn offers 25 uniquely decorated guestrooms, suites, and cottages. The Main Inn features four suites and 12 luxury rooms, all with fireplaces, spa baths, and TV/DVDs, some with steam showers, wet bars, and mountain views. Common areas include a wrap-around porch with views and dining; a lounge with a separate, casual menu; library; and spa level. Spa Facilities include an exercise room, sauna, yoga, manicure/pedicure and three treatment rooms. Activities are available in all seasons at the Inn and throughout the White Mountains. Outdoor pool, year-round outdoor hot tub, cross-country skiing, and tobogganing at the Inn-hiking, golf, tennis, shopping, skiing, and sleigh rides are all nearby. Only AAA Four Diamond Inn and Restaurant in Mt.Washington Valley. *Condé Nast Traveler's* Gold List 2006. *Travel & Leisure's* World's Best Awards 2006.

**Rates**
Main Inn: 4 suites, 12 luxury rooms; Carriage House: 6 North Country rooms; 3 Cottages; Open year round. Breakfast, tea & three-course dinner included. $195/$430. Off Season Spa Packages.  Number of Rooms: 25

**Cuisine**
New England Cuisine with Mediterranean influences & mountain views. Separate lounge menu. Well stocked bar with over thirty single malt scotches & the wine list has over 1300 selections.

**Nearest Airport(s)**
Portland, ME

**Directions**
Boston: I-95 to Spaulding Turnpike Rt.16N to Jackson; Portland: Rt.302 to Rt.16N; Montreal, Canada: Can 55 to I-91/I-93, Exit 40-Rt. 302 to Rt.16N to Jackson. Follow signs to Inn.

# The Buttonwood Inn on Mt. Surprise

www.buttonwoodinn.com

P.O. Box 1817, 64 Mount Surprise Road, North Conway, NH 03860-1817

**800-258-2625** • 603-356-2625 • Fax 603-356-3140

innkeeper@buttonwoodinn.com

*Member Since 1999*

*New Hampshire*

*North Conway*

*"Our hosts couldn't have been more accommodating." "Quiet & Pleasant, very clean, beautifully decorated. Delicious breakfasts."*

Innkeepers/Owners
## Bill and Paula Petrone

The Buttonwood Inn on Mt. Surprise, a North Conway, New Hampshire country inn bed and breakfast, is nationally recognized for our quality of innkeeping providing the best in service, hospitality, and attention to detail. Situated on more than five secluded acres of field and forests, two miles from the village of North Conway, The Buttonwood Inn on Mt. Surprise offers a peaceful, rural setting and the convenience of being close to everything. An 1820s farmhouse, the inn retains its comfortable country atmosphere with wide pine floors, antiques, quilts, and stenciling. Unwind with afternoon tea and home baked treats in front of one of our traditional wood burning fireplaces in either our large living room or the Mt. Surprise Room when days are cool. You can select a spot in the sun or shade in one of our Adirondack chairs or take a dip in our heated pool or soak in our open air hot tub with a view of the mountains and forest by day or stars by night. You can watch outside for the appearance of deer, wild turkeys, moose, hawks or hummingbirds.

**Rates**
All rooms have private baths and amenities. $99/$270.
Number of Rooms: 10

**Cuisine**
Full gourmet breakfast with delicious starter and entree changes daily served at individual tables. Special dietary requests honored.

**Nearest Airport(s)**
Portland, ME - 65 miles; Manchester, NH - 100 miles

**Directions**
From SOUTH: I-95 to Rte. 16 N (Spaulding Tpke.) to North Conway. In North Conway Village, at light, turn R on Kearsarge Rd. and continue 1.2 mi. to stop sign. Straight across intersection, up Mt. Surprise Rd. 3/10 mi. From NORTH: Rte. 302 S, L to Hurricane Mountain Rd., L to Mt. Surprise Rd., travel 3/10 mi.

# Eastman Inn

www.eastmaninn.com
2331 White Mountain Highway, P.O. BOX 882, North Conway, NH  03860
**800-626-5855** • 603-356-6707 • Fax 603-356-7708
BePampered@eastmaninn.com

*Member Since 2004*

*"Our stay at the Inn was the best! Food was excellent, rooms were nice and our hosts very gracious. Dining and outdoor activities were nearby."*

Owners/Innkeepers
**Arthur & Marta De La Torre**

Built in 1777 by the Noah Eastman family, the Inn, one of the oldest homes in North Conway, boasts a history rich in tradition in the development of the social and economic growth of the Mt. Washington Valley. The 1930 edition of the New Hampshire Guidebook described the Eastman Inn as "...an all-season house, where hospitality is extended to guests desiring mountain vacations in the quiet comfort of a private home." Over seventy-five years later, hospitality remains our priority. Join us for a relaxing, vacation in a home steeped in tradition either for pleasure or on business, and let us treat you to warm, attentive bed and breakfast hospitality in the splendor and style of a bygone era. An eclectic mix of antiquity and modern conveniences makes your journey to an earlier time far more comfortable than our ancestors perhaps imagined! 2005 Winner of the "Best Breakfast" category, Best of BedandBreakfast.com Award.

**Rates**
$110/$240 w/private baths. Some with fireplaces, whirlpool and antique soaking tubs. Cable TV and A/C  Number of Rooms: 14

**Cuisine**
Gourmet breakfast with the menu changing daily. Dietary restrictions available. Fine dining within minutes in surrounding North Conway area.

**Nearest Airport(s)**
Portland, ME - 60 miles Manchester, NH - 100 miles

**Directions**
1/2 mile S of Schouler Park in the Village of North Conway on Rte 16/302.

🍴 🍴 🍷

# The Darby Field Inn

www.darbyfield.com
185 Chase Hill Road, Albany, NH 03818
**800-426-4147** • 603-447-2181 • Fax 603-447-5726
marc@darbyfield.com

*Member Since 1981*

*"What a wonderful place nestled away in the mountains. We only meant to stay one night but after three days it's still hard to leave and getting harder!"*

AAA Three Diamond Award

Innkeepers/Owners
**Marc & Maria Donaldson**

Only 6 miles from North Conway, yet right in the middle of nowhere, overlooking the Mt. Washington Valley and White Mountains of New Hampshire, the Darby Field Inn quietly surprises and delights wanderers adventurous enough to leave the beaten path. The Darby Field Inn is much more than just a little bed and breakfast. It is a romantic B&B with fireplace and Jacuzzi rooms and suites, candlelight gourmet dining, a sophisticated wine list, and moonlit sleigh rides. It's a full service country inn for those looking to relax by the fireplace in the living room, on the mountain-view patio, in the fully stocked sunroom Tavern, in our award winning gardens or by the crystal clear, heated swimming pool. The inn also has miles of private nature trails for x-c skiing, snowshoeing, mountain biking or just walking. Why not start or end your day with a soothing theraputic massage for two or a rejuvenating yoga class? Whether you are looking for romance, relaxation or a more active adventure, The Darby Field Inn has it all!

**Rates**
$140-205: 7 rooms w/private bath, mountain view and most w/AC. $240/290: 6 deluxe rooms w/fireplace, jacuzzi, AC, mountain view & 2 w/balconies. Number of Rooms: 13

**Cuisine**
Country gourmet dining in a casual setting with mountain views. Choose from over 100 bottles of fine wines. Lighter fare available in our sunroom tavern. Full country breakfast included; served while watching birds and maybe even a moose!

**Nearest Airport(s)**
Portland, ME: 60 miles

**Directions**
One half mile south of Conway Village off Rte.16, turn on to Bald Hill Road. Go up the hill one mile, and turn right onto Chase Hill Rd. Proceed one mile to inn.

# The Manor on Golden Pond

www.manorongoldenpond.com
Box T, Rt. 3, 31 Manor Drive, Holderness, NH 03245
**800-545-2141 Reservations** • 603-968-3348 • Fax 603-968-2116
info@manorongoldenpond.com

*Member Since 1995*

*New Hampshire*

*Holderness*

> *"The Manor is elegant and serene and as guests you feel like royalty & comfy at the same time. They offer the epitome of what customer service is all about."*

Innkeepers/Owners
**Brian and Mary Ellen Shields**

It was the sheer romantic beauty of its mountain and lake view setting that inspired the building of The Manor on Golden Pond. And while the view still inspires, so does the hotel's cuisine and leisure facilities. The romantic story behind the resort began in 1904, when a wealthy Englishman fell in love with the mountain and lake view setting and built the Manor for his bride. In many senses, the idyll continues, inspiring the Oscar-winning Hepburn and Fonda film 'On Golden Pond'. Enjoy tea and dreamy end-of-day reveries in the library or alternatively retreat to the excellent restaurant. Guests awaken to our delectable Gourmet breakfasts each morning. The cuisine is the finest in the region, complemented by a celebrated cellar. *Seasons Spa* offers New Hampshire indigenous spa treatments to relax and soothe the most seasoned spa goers. However, despite the excellent golf, skiing, lawn games and water sports, perhaps the best way to enjoy The Manor On Golden Pond is fireside after dinner, with a large Port and entertaining company. Fodor's 2008 Choice Hotel Andrew Harper's "Hideaway Report" recommended. AAA Four Diamond rated.

**Rates**
24 Rooms $210/$475 B&B for two people per night. Open year-round. Carriage house and cottages open seasonally.
Number of Rooms: 24

**Cuisine**
Full Gourmet Breakfast. Afternoon Tea. Van Horn Dining Room offering Fine Dining setting w/New American Cuisine. Ala Carte & daily Chef Tasting menus. "M" Bistro w/Organic French Bistro Cuisine with local organic products. Casual Dining atmosphere in a comfortable setting.

**Nearest Airport(s)**
Manchester, NH (1 hour drive)

**Directions**
I-93, exit 24, E on Rte. 3, proceed for 4.7 mi., turn R at our sign (Less than two hours from Boston.)

# The Glynn House Inn

www.glynnhouse.com
59 Highland Street, Ashland, NH 03217
**866-686-4362** • 603-968-3775
theglynnhouseinn@yahoo.com

*Member Since 2005*

*New Hampshire*

*Ashland*

*For more information visit our website at www.glynnhouse.com*

Innkeepers
**Pamela, Ingrid and Glenn Heidenreich**

The Glynn House Inn – located in the heart of New Hampshire's Lakes & Mountains – provides the perfect setting for recreation, romance and relaxation. Guests can select from 13 spacious, tastefully decorated guest rooms that include queen size beds, private baths, romantic fireplaces, central air, LCD TV's, DVD players, WiFi, luxurious bathrobes & deluxe amenities. Eight of the rooms are deluxe suites that also offer bubbling double whirlpool spas, separate sitting rooms & iPod radios. A gourmet breakfast with choice of delicious entrees is served at individual tables. Afternoon refreshments are offered daily. Guests enjoy complimentary wine & delicious hors d'oeuvres each evening. The friendly innkeepers will make your visit an experience to remember by providing genuine hospitality, personal service & attention to detail. A DVD library is available. Well-behaved dogs are welcome in designated rooms only.

**Rates**
November thru April: $139 - $269; May thru October: $159 - $289; Peak periods: $169 - $299; Number of Rooms: 13

**Cuisine**
A gourmet breakfast with a choice of scrumptious entrees is served each morning. Afternoon refreshments are provided daily. Guests love our homemade cookies & old-fashioned fudge brownies. In the evening, you can join other guests and the innkeepers for complimentary wine, cheese & delicious hors d'oeuvres.

**Nearest Airport(s)**
Manchester

**Directions**
Take I-93 Exit 24 (Ashland). Take US 3 South after leaving Interstate 93. Highland Street is a left hand turn approx. 2 miles after leaving the Interstate.

# Colby Hill Inn

www.colbyhillinn.com
33 The Oaks, P.O. Box 779, Henniker, NH 03242
**800-531-0330** • 603-428-3281 • Fax 603-428-9218
innkeeper@colbyhillinn.com

*Member Since 1993*

*New Hampshire*

*Henniker*

*"Loved the antiques & attention to detail. So romantic and 'Foodies' will love it."*

Innkeepers/Owners
**Cyndi and Mason Cobb**

Intimate and romantic country inn located in the charming unspoiled village of Henniker. Enjoy romantic touches including down comforters, plush bathrobes, two-person whirlpools, crackling fireplaces and luxurious linens. 14 romantic guest rooms including two intimate suites with period antiques. All guest rooms have private baths, phones and WI-FI access. Award winning candlelight dining nightly overlooking lush gardens, antique barns and gazebo. "Exquisite and Romantic Dining..." says Getaways for Gourmets. Bountiful breakfasts and candlelight dinners. Genuine hospitality and central New England location make this an ideal getaway spot. Enjoy cooking classes and theme weekends including "Chocolate Lovers Weekend" and "WineFest Weekends". Outdoor pool, lawn chess, cross country and downhill skiing, hiking, biking, and tennis all nearby. *Yankee Magazine* Editor's Pick. *Wine Spectator* Award of Excellence. Featured in *The Boston Globe* and *Ski Magazine*. 90 Minutes North of Boston.

**Rates**
$140/$279 depending on season. Some guest rooms have two-person whirlpools/fireplaces. Gourmet breakfast included. Number of Rooms: 14

**Cuisine**
Full gourmet breakfast including specialties like pumpkin pancakes with warm maple cream. Afternoon cookies. Award-winning romantic candlelight dining with full service bar, fine wines & spirits. Dinner available nightly for inn guests & public.

**Nearest Airport(s)**
Manchester

**Directions**
17 Miles W. of Concord, N.H. - 93 N. to 89 N. to Rt. 202/9W (Left exit). Continue on 202/9 (West) & Exit at Rt. 114, Turn L. 1 mile to blinker, turn R, 1/2 mile on Right. 90 min. N. of Boston.

# Chesterfield Inn

www.chesterfieldinn.com

Route 9, Box 155, Chesterfield, NH 03443

**800-365-5515** • 603-256-3211 • Fax 603-256-6131

chstinn@sover.net

*Member Since 1990*

*"What a wonderful weekend we had at the Chesterfield Inn! A warm welcome, beautiful room, delicious breakfast and romantic dinner-just what we needed!"*

Innkeepers/Owners
**Phil and Judy Hueber**

The Chesterfield Inn is a comfortable blend of new and old New Hampshire. The inn rests on a hill overlooking the Vermont Green Mountains and Connecticut River Valley. Originally built in 1787 as a farm, this luxurious country hotel is today a showpiece of elegance, style, and comfort. The inn has opulent guest rooms, stunning dining rooms, and beautifully landscaped grounds. Come and relax awhile at this elegant yet comfortable renovated farmhouse with its cathedral ceilings and rambling views of the Connecticut River Valley. Feel the stress of every day life disappear as you sit in front of the fire in the parlor of this small country hotel. Spend the day reading in one of the Adirondack chairs in the back yard or explore local villages and countryside. Return at dusk to a sumptuous dinner in our candlelit dining room. Privacy, delicious cuisine, and relaxation are yours at one of the most unique and accommodating inns in New England. This is a perfect place for a romantic getaway in the country!

### Rates
15 Rooms, $150/$320 B&B 2 Suites, $250/$275 B&B. Open year-round except Christmas Eve and Christmas Day. Number of Rooms: 15

### Cuisine
Full Country Breakfast cooked to order and served daily. Dinner is served Monday through Saturday in our candlelit dining room with sweeping views of the Green Mountains. Room service is available. Wine list and full bar available.

### Nearest Airport(s)
Hartford, CT is a one and a half hour drive and Boston is a two and a half hour drive.

### Directions
From I-91, take exit 3 to Route 9 E. Continue on Route 9 for 2 miles. Turn L onto Cross Road and R into driveway.

# The Hancock Inn

www.hancockinn.com
33 Main Street, P.O. Box 96, Hancock, NH 03449
**800-525-1789** • 603-525-3318 • Fax 603-525-9301
innkeeper@hancockinn.com

*Member Since 1971*

*"Visiting The Hancock Inn is like taking a step back to a kindler, gentler era."*
*"Awesome pot roast!!"*

Innkeeper/Owner
**Robert Short**

Since 1789, the first year of George Washington's presidency, the **The Hancock Inn~1789~NH's Oldest Inn** has hosted rumrunners and cattle drovers, aristocracy, and even a U.S. President. It's seen elegant balls, Concord Coaches, and the first rider of the railroad. Today, the Inn maintains its historic elegance combined with modern day amenities. The town of Hancock, located in the beautiful Monadnock Region of Southern New Hampshire, is considered by many to be one of the prettiest villages in New England, boasting a church with a Paul Revere Bell that rings in each hour, a friendly local general store and many homes that are listed on the National Historic Register. Year-round regional recreation opportunities include hiking, cross country/downhill skiing, swimming, boating and fishing. Visit in any season and find: spring daffodils and real maple sugaring; summer swimming and fishing at Hancock's town beach or music on the village square; fall colors and covered bridges; winter snow...and relaxing by our raging fireplace with a hot toddy!

**Rates**
14 Rooms. $125/$290. Appointed with antiques, TV, phone, AC. 10 with fireplaces, 4 with whirlpools. Number of Rooms: 14

**Cuisine**
Amidst the glow of candles and a flickering fireplace you will dine in Colonial splendor. The recipe for our signature dish, Shaker Cranberry Potroast, was requested by *Bon Appétit.* Full bar with 350 wine selections and many single malts. *Wine Spectator* Award.

**Nearest Airport(s)**
Manchester Airport

**Directions**
From Boston: I 93N then 101W to Peterborough. R on 202. Turn L onto 123 3 miles to historic Main Street. From NY: I 91 to Brattleboro. Route 9 toward Keene to 123. Turn R to Hancock.

# The Inn at Crotched Mountain

www.innatcrotchedmt.com
534 Mountain Rd., Francestown, NH 03043
**603-588-6840** • Fax 603-588-6623
innkeeper@innatcrotchedmt.com

*Member Since 1981*

*"Thank you so much for providing us with the most memorable holiday, a perfect oasis of tranquliity. You both make The Inn a truely special place."*

Innkeepers/Owners
**John and Rose Perry**

A quaint country Inn, offering 13 guestrooms, 8 with private bath, built in 1822, located on 65 acres, on the side of Crotched Mt. with spectacular views of the Piscatiqoug Valley. During the summer and fall, one may stroll among the vegetable, herb and many flower gardens, sit, relax and enjoy the view by the 30x60 swimming pool, or enjoy a game of tennis on one of the two clay tennis courts. There is a 18 hole golf course within 1 mile from the Inn. For the more adventurous, there are numerous activities in the Monadnock Region, including the professional productions of The Peterborough Players, concerts and cultural events at The Old Meeting House of Francestown, and of course, hiking Mt. Monadnock, or enjoying of the, many Antique shops. During the Winter, one can relax in front of the fireplace in one of the two sitting rooms, there is also a downhill skiing within a mile from the Inn. Enjoy a full country breakfast, while looking over the expansive lawn watching the many varieties of birds gathering at the feeders. Light fare is served in The Winslow Tavern on Saturday nights. There are a wide variety of Restaurants in the area for those evenings the inn does not serve. The Inn is a wonderful place to relax and unwind.

**Rates**
13 Rooms, 3 with fireplaces, $75/$150 B&B. Open year round, except first two weeks in November. Number of Rooms: 13

**Cuisine**
Full breakfast daily. Light fare served in The Winslow Tavern on Saturday. Wine & liquor available.

**Nearest Airport(s)**
Manchester, N.H.

**Directions**
From Boston: I-93N 101W to 114N to Goffstown 13S to New Boston 136 W to Francestown 47N 2.5 mi. L onto Mt. Rd 1 mi. From N.Y.: I-91N to Brattleboro Rt. 9E to 31S outside of Antrim, N.H. Continue on Rt 31S to Bennington, N.H. to Rt. 47. Take Rt.47 4.5 mi. R onto Mt. Rd. 1 mi.

# Inn by the Bandstand

www.innbythebandstand.com
6 Front Street, Exeter, NH  03833
**877-239-3837** • 603-772-6352 • Fax 603-778-0212
info@innbythebandstand.com

*Member Since 2006*

*"Charming and cozy. The staff cheerfully made us feel at home!" "Wonderful inn… perfect location" "The Inn is infused with old New England."*

## James and Victoria Lane

The award-winning Inn by the Bandstand is the premier lodging establishment in Exeter, New Hampshire. This inn is an 1809 historic home located in the heart of downtown Exeter. Only two blocks from the prestigious Phillips Exeter Academy, eight miles to the seacoast and beaches, and 20 minutes from Portsmouth, this charming B&B offers nine antique-furnished guest rooms, all private baths and a delicious full breakfast. The inn is surrounded by quaint shops, fine restaurants and an old fashioned movie theater across the street. You can explore the downtown bookstore, toy store, and our own gift shop plus many fine gift and apparel boutiques. Stroll around the river walk near the Academy boat house. We also have the American Independence Museum, plus historical self-guided tours to broaden your knowledge and interest of this area and its importance in our nation's founding history. Our rooms are spacious, most with fireplaces. Each room has amenities such complimentary port wine, luxurious robes, wireless Internet, and cozy seating areas. Our beds are made with designer linens and we exclusively use plush Ralph Lauren towels.

**Rates**
$139/$259 double occupancy rooms. $219/$269 2-room family suites, up to 4 persons. Some weekends require a two-night minimum. Special academy weekends are priced higher. Number of Rooms: 9

**Cuisine**
Full breakfast

**Nearest Airport(s)**
Manchester-Boston Regional Airport

**Directions**
From Interstate 95: Take exit 2 BEFORE the toll booth, Route 101. Take Route 101 west to exit 11, Route 108. Off the exit ramp turn left for 1 1/2 miles and you will come to a "T" intersection with a light (High Street). Turn right and drive to the center of Exeter. You will see the bandstand on your left with the Inn by the Bandstand on the corner.

# New Jersey

## "The Garden State"

Famous for: Princeton University, Battle of Trenton, Atlantic City, Atlantic Coastline, Industry, Menlo Park.

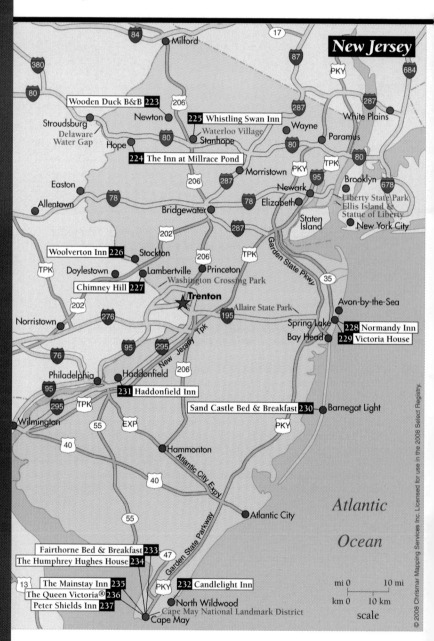

New Jersey

- Wooden Duck B&B **223**
- **225** Whistling Swan Inn
- **224** The Inn at Millrace Pond
- Woolverton Inn **226**
- Chimney Hill **227**
- **228** Normandy Inn
- **229** Victoria House
- **231** Haddonfield Inn
- Sand Castle Bed & Breakfast **230**
- Fairthorne Bed & Breakfast **233**
- The Humphrey Hughes House **234**
- The Mainstay Inn **235**
- The Queen Victoria® **236**
- Peter Shields Inn **237**
- **232** Candlelight Inn

Milford, Stroudsburg, Delaware Water Gap, Newton, Hope, Waterloo Village, Stanhope, Wayne, Paramus, White Plains, Easton, Morristown, Newark, Brooklyn, Liberty State Park, Ellis Island & Statue of Liberty, Allentown, Bridgewater, Elizabeth, Staten Island, New York City, Stockton, Doylestown, Lambertville, Princeton, Washington Crossing Park, Trenton, Allaire State Park, Avon-by-the-Sea, Norristown, Spring Lake, Bay Head, Philadelphia, Haddonfield, Barnegat Light, Wilmington, Hammonton, Atlantic City, North Wildwood, Cape May National Landmark District, Cape May

*Atlantic Ocean*

mi 0     10 mi
km 0     10 km
scale

SelectRegistry.com

# The Wooden Duck B&B

www.woodenduckinn.com
140 Goodale Road, Newton, NJ 07860
**973-300-0395** • Fax 973-300-0395
woodenduckinn@earthlink.net

*Member Since 2003*

*New Jersey • Newton*

> *"We couldn't have asked for a more relaxing, peaceful, enjoyable B&B--the Wooden Duck scored on every point!"*

Innkeepers/Owners
**Beth & Karl Krummel**

An oasis of country pleasures! This mini-estate is nestled on 10 acres adjacent to the 1600-acre Kittatinny Valley State Park, abounding with wildlife and hiking trails. In-ground pool open all summer. All guestrooms have queen bed, private bath, satellite TV/VCR, telephone, clock radio, hair dryers, iron/ironing board, desk, and a comfortable sitting area. Complimentary wireless Internet available throughout. Deluxe rooms have soaking tub for two, two-sided gas fireplace, and private balcony. Guests are welcome to use the game room with double hearth fireplace, bumper pool, board games, and video library. The Guest Pantry with complimentary snacks, homemade chocolate chip cookies, soda, coffee, and tea is available 24/7. Nearby are many antique and craft shops, fine dining, winter and summer sports, NJ Skyhawks Baseball, mineral museums, numerous golf courses, horseback riding, hiking and fishing. The Wooden Duck is the only B&B in Northern New Jersey rated 3 star by Mobile Travel Guide. Less than an hour to the Crossings Outlet Mall in PA and only 55 miles to Times Square in Manhattan. Rural surroundings in a convenient location.

**Rates**
9 rooms, $125/$299 per night/double. Corporate rates Sunday thru Thursday. Open all year. Number of Rooms: 9

**Cuisine**
A full country breakfast featuring a varying menu of homebaked breads or muffins, egg dishes, delicious baked French toast, fruit, juice, tea, coffee and more! Guest pantry features homemade cookies, snacks, trail mix, hot and cold beverages. Fine and casual dining nearby.

**Nearest Airport(s)**
Newark Airport, 45 Miles

**Directions**
I-80 to Exit 25, following Rte 206 N 7.8 mi. to Goodale Rd. Turn right and proceed 1.5 mi. through the Kittatinny Valley State Park to The Wooden Duck's driveway (#140) on the left.

🍽️ 🍽️ 🍽️ 🍷

# The Inn at Millrace Pond

www.innatmillracepond.com
313 Hope Johnsonburg Road, P.O. Box 359, Hope, NJ 07844
**800-746-6467** • 908-459-4884 • Fax 908-459-5276
millrace@epix.net

*Member Since 1988*

*New Jersey*

*Hope*

*"Peaceful, relaxing, wonderful dining."*
*"Unique experience; restful weekend at the Inn."*

Innkeepers/Owners
**Jonathan Teed & William Kirkhuff**

The Inn building located on 23 acres was an operating gristmill from 1769 until the early 1950's. Authentically decorated guestrooms with private baths are located in the Gristmill, Millrace House and Stone Cottage suggesting the quiet elegance of Colonial America. Relax in the ambiance of the parlor. Savor romantic candlelight dinners in the fine dining restaurant. Stroll past the mill's antique water wheel and wine cellar into the tavern offering casual midweek dining beside the walk-in fireplace. An 1830s home from the historic Moravian Village of Hope has been restored into the conference center featuring individual meeting rooms along with library and parlor. Perhaps a game of tennis on the private court or a hike nearby is in order. The Delaware Water Gap Recreation Area (a National Park) is 13 miles west of the Inn. Excellent antiquing, a vineyard, golf, and skiing are nearby. Lunch served daily 11:30am - 5PM  Dinner daily 5 - 8pm Sun - Thurs, Fri & Sat 5 - 10pm

**Rates**
17 Guestrooms $225/$245 Fri-Sat, including holidays ($175/$195 Sun-Thurs) Continental Breakfast included Open year-round. Number of Rooms: 17

**Cuisine**
American

**Nearest Airport(s)**
Lehigh Valley International Airport, Newark International Airport

**Directions**
From South: 31 to 46W to 519N R at blinker follow across stone bridge the Inn at Millrace Pond is directly on your left & parking is just beyond the Gristmill building on the left. From North, East or West: I-80 exit 12 follow signs for Hope,521S to blinker turn left & follow across the stone bridge, the Inn is directly on your left.

# Whistling Swan Inn

www.whistlingswaninn.com
110 Main St., Stanhope, NJ 07874
**888-507-2337** • 973-347-6369 • Fax 973-347-6379
info@whistlingswaninn.com

*Member Since 1992*

*"Every detail has been thought of-wonderful ambiance, friendly hosts, and great food! Perfect! Absolutely the best B&B we've ever visited."*

*New Jersey*

*Stanhope*

Innkeeper
**Liz Armstrong**

One of the Top Ten B&B's in the US says the Inn Traveler magazine. Set amidst a spectacular garden on a quiet, tree-lined street the Whistling Swan Inn exudes romance and warmth. This 1905 Queen Anne Victorian features a gracious wraparound veranda where leisurely breakfasts are served on pleasant mornings. Each room embraces you with comfort and warmth with period antiques and modern conveniences; TV/VCR/DVD, A/C, wireless internet, plus refrigerators, gas fireplaces, and Jacuzzis in our suites. Whatever the season, a myriad of activities awaits you. After a busy day of hiking, biking, shopping or antiquing relax in a hammock or share pleasant conversations with newfound friends. Enjoy fine dining at one of the area gourmet restaurants, some within walking distance. At day's end, snuggle up with your special someone next to a crackling fire. Sink into your queen-sized feather bed and fall asleep to a movie from our video library.

**Rates**
6 Rooms,$99-$149, 3 Suites,$150-$249. Corporate/Gov't rates. All with private bath (some w/jacuzzi and fireplace) Cable TV/VCR/DVD, Wireless Internet, Central AC. Open year round. Romantic packages. Number of Rooms: 9

**Cuisine**
Full country buffet breakfast, 24-hour complimentary guest snack bar.

**Nearest Airport(s)**
Newark - 45 min

**Directions**
Bus & Train via NJ Transit to Netcong. Take Rte 80W to Exit 27B. Take Route 183N until you are at the HESS STATION. Turn left on MAIN ST. Make the left at King St immediately before the Inn - our parking lot is the 2nd driveway on the right. You will see the swan at the end of our driveway.

# Woolverton Inn

www.woolvertoninn.com
6 Woolverton Road, Stockton, NJ 08559
**888-264-6648** • 609-397-0802 • Fax 609-397-0987
sheep@woolvertoninn.com

*Member Since 2002*

*New Jersey*

*Stockton*

*"A luxury getaway like no other...thank you for
a memorable and romantic Honeymoon! Bravo!"*

Innkeepers/Owners
## Carolyn McGavin and Bob Haas

Perched high above the Delaware River, surrounded by 300 acres of rolling farmland and forest, The Woolverton Inn provides the seclusion of a grand country estate, yet the activities of New Hope and Lambertville are just five minutes away. Enjoy the glorious setting and relaxed elegance of this 1792 stone manor, while feeling as comfortable as you would at your own home in the country. All guestrooms are unique and thoughtfully decorated; they feature bucolic views, fireplaces, whirlpool tubs and showers for two, private outdoor sitting areas, stocked refrigerators, and Bose CD Wave radios. Dogs are permitted in the Garden Cottage. As recommended by "1000 Places to See Before You Die in the USA and Canada" and *National Geographic Traveler*, among others.

**Rates**
6 Rooms $145/$315; 2 Suites $275/$345; 5 Cottages $295/$425. Rooms offer featherbeds, fresh flowers, robes, luxury linens, CD Players. Number of Rooms: 13

**Cuisine**
Full gourmet breakfast served in our gardens or in bed. Signature Dishes include: homemade apple-cranberry turkey sausage, lemon-ricotta hotcakes, pina colada scones & fabulous cookies.

**Nearest Airport(s)**
Philadelphia International

**Directions**
Philadelphia: I-95, exit 1 to Rte. 29 N to Stockton. R on 523 for 2/10 mi., L on Woolverton Rd. NY: I-78 W to exit 29 for 287 S, exit for 202 S for Flemington. Exit Rte. 29 N. R on 523, L 2/10 mi.

# Chimney Hill Farm Estate

www.chimneyhillinn.com
207 Goat Hill Road, Lambertville, NJ 08530
**800-211-4667** • 609-397-1516 • Fax 609-397-9353
info@chimneyhillinn.com

*Member Since 1998*

*"We love everything about this lovely Inn! A favorite place with friendly caring Innkeepers and wonderful atmosphere. We will return many times!"*

Owners
**Terry Anne & Richard Anderson**

On a country road high in the hills above the charming historic riverside town of Lambertville, New Jersey, sits Chimney Hill Farm Estate & The Ol' Barn Inn. This gorgeous fieldstone house and barn, built in 1820, are surrounded by beautiful fields and gardens. The perfect spot for romantic getaways or corporate retreats, Chimney Hill is only 1/2 mi from the antique-filled towns of Lambertville and New Hope. Known for great country-style hospitality, Chimney Hill Farm Estate provides its guests with comfort and elegance. Featured as the cover for *Country Inns, New Jersey Country Roads* magazines, it is a connoisseur's choice. Come visit!

**Rates**
Main Estate House M-Th $135/$155. Fri-Sun $189/$255. Ol'Barn Inn Suites M-Th $189/$275. Fri-Sun $289/$395. Number of Rooms: 12

**Cuisine**
Gourmet country breakfast served by candlelight, a guest butler pantry filled with cookies, goodies and sherry. Excellent Resturuants in Lambertville and New Hope.

**Nearest Airport(s)**
Philadelphia 45 miles Newark 42 miles

**Directions**
Phi: I-95N ext1 (Lambertville) to rt. 29N. Travel 7 mi; turn R onto Valley Rd, L on Goat Hill Rd.-1.5 mi on R. NY: I-78W to I-287S to Rt.202S to Rt.179S (Lambertville ex). At traffic light go straight to 2nd L (SWAN St.) Go to 2nd R. (Studdiford St.) to top.

# Normandy Inn

www.normandyinn.com
21 Tuttle Avenue, Spring Lake, NJ 07762
**800-449-1888** • 732-449-7172 • Fax 732-449-1070
normandyinn@optonline.net

*Member Since 1996*

*"Truly a step back in time, this seaside beauty made for the perfect escape!"*

Owners
**The Valori Family**

A romantic 19th Century inn, the Normandy Inn is on the National Register of Historic Places. Fine antique furnishings adorn this tradionally elegant home which is located just steps from the ocean. Upon visiting the inn, your welcome begins in the spacious double parlors decorated in Victorian splendor. Many guest rooms, each of which are unique, boast cozy fireplaces, Jacuzzis, canopy beds and a peek at the ocean. All rooms include private baths, air conditioning, and telephones. Guests' wake up call is the sound of the ocean as a private table awaits you in the gracious dining room. The Normandy offers a hearty country breakfast, tempting afternoon treats, evening cordials, and prides itself on exceptional service. The Normandy, just 1/2 block to the ocean, is centrally located to cultural and outdoor activities. Mobil and AAA rated, the Normandy makes for the perfect getaway. *New York* Magazine calls it "an antique-laden dreamworld," your inn for all seasons.

**Rates**
18 Rooms, high season $149/299; shoulder season $119/229; quiet season $79/129. 2 Suites $309/399. Open year round. Number of Rooms: 20

**Cuisine**
Full gourmet breakfast included and served at your own private table. Sumptuous afternoon treats including seasonal fruits and fresh squeezed juice in the summer, homemeade soups in the quiet season. Evening cordials. Fine dining restaurants located nearby.

**Nearest Airport(s)**
Newark International

**Directions**
Garden State Pkwy to exit 98. Follow Rte 34 S to traffic circle, 3/4 around to Rte 524 E. Take to ocean, turn R onto Ocean Avenue & then first R onto Tuttle. Fifth house on the L.

# Victoria House Bed & Breakfast

www.victoriahouse.net
214 Monmouth Avenue, Spring Lake, NJ 07762-1127
**888-249-6252** • 732-974-1882 • Fax 732-974-2132
info@victoriahouse.net

*Member Since 1998*

*New Jersey*

*Spring Lake*

*"Best B&B experience at the Shore." "Best Breakfast, my compliments to the chef." "My favorite place to stay." "One of the finest B&B's we've stayed in"*

Innkeepers/Owners
**Lynne and Alan Kaplan**

Relax, refresh, renew in our lovingly restored 1882 Queen Anne Victorian B&B; the perfect seaside oasis for romantic getaways and business travelers. Enjoy the sea breeze on the veranda or read a book in front of the parlor fireplace. Escape in the distinctive decor of your accommodations; fireplaces, featherbeds, TV/VCRs/DVDs, refrigerator, Jacuzzis for two; all with private baths, air-conditioning, individual temperature controls. Stroll our beach boardwalk or around the lake; bicycle our tree-lined streets; discover a treasure in one of our charming main street shops. Taste our wonderful gourmet breakfasts. Timeless hospitality awaits you. Enjoy our Victorian splendor with modern amenities. A romantic B&B Inn for all seasons. Recently renovated and restored with care. Open all year.

**Rates**
8 beautifully appointed guests rooms: Jacuzzis, Fireplaces, TV/VCR's/DVD's. High Season $199/$399; Low Season $99/$299. Number of Rooms: 8

**Cuisine**
Gourmet-served breakfast with house specialties on the veranda or at tables for two in our dining room. Enjoy afternoon tea & treats and evening cordials & chocolates.

**Nearest Airport(s)**
Newark, Philadelphia

**Directions**
From NY, CT, North NJ: GS Pkwy S to ex. 98, to 138E to Rte 35S, 3rd light L Warren Ave. Through next light, turn R on 3rd Ave (Church on L) L on Monmouth Ave. From DC/DE/PA: Rte I-95N/NJ TPKE to 195E to 138E, then follow above dir. NYC/AC 60, Phil 70 miles.

# Sand Castle Bed & Breakfast

www.sandcastlelbi.com
710 Bayview Avenue, Box 607, Barnegat Light, Long Beach Island, NJ  08006
**800-253-0353** • 609-494-6555
info@sandcastlelbi.com

*Member Since 2003*

New Jersey

Long Beach Island

*"We've stayed at numerous B&B's over the years but the Sand Castle by far stands above the rest; magnificent breakfasts, immaculate, 5 stars in our book!"*

Innkeeper/Owner
**Nancy Gallimore**

A truly incomparable experience on Long Beach Island! Spacious suites and luxurious rooms with beautiful bay views, all with seasonal fireplace, private entrance, private bath (some with jacuzzi), A/C, cable TV/DVD/CD player, in-room phone/voicemail, current DVD movie library, wireless internet, complimentary snacks, 24 hour coffee/tea, soft drinks. Start your day with Nancy Gallimore's sumptuous breakfast and relaxed hospitality. Enjoy the heated outdoor pool, jacuzzi and exercise room. Take a bike ride or spend a day at our beach, which has been rated one of the top 20 in the USA! The inn provides the bikes and beach gear. Climb the Barnegat Lighthouse and visit the museum. Hike the dunes and beach trails. Watersports, fishing, golf, theater, shopping, birdwatching...we have it all nearby. Then celebrate a spectacular sunset on the rooftop deck at the end of a relaxing, fun-filled day. This mini-resort is the perfect romantic escape for couples and singles looking for the ultimate in relaxation and fun. Voted top ten "Best Breakfast in the Northeast" by *Inn Traveler* magazine.  We would love to have you visit us!

## Rates
5 Rooms $165/$295, depending on season and 2 suites $255/$425. Open April through Thanksgiving  Number of Rooms: 7

## Cuisine
Full sumptuous breakfast included. Complimentary coffee, tea, snacks, soft drinks available 24 hours. Restaurants next door and within a short walk or drive.

## Nearest Airport(s)
Atlantic City, Phila, Newark

## Directions
Garden State Parkway Exit 63. Take Route 72 East to end. Left onto Long Beach Blvd. Follow 8 mi. to Barnegat Light. At 2nd traffic light (blinking yellow off season) make Left onto 10th St. Turn Right onto Bayview Ave. Sand Castle is 2 blocks on Right.

# Haddonfield Inn

www.haddonfieldinn.com
44 West End Avenue, Haddonfield, NJ 08033
**800-269-0014** • 856-428-2195 • Fax 856-354-1273
innkeeper@haddonfieldinn.com

*Member Since 2005*

*New Jersey*

*Haddonfield*

> *"What a wonderful place to set up visiting dignitaries!"*
> *"Keeping up the best of B&B traditions."*

Innkeepers/Owners
**Nancy and Fred Chorpita**

This intimate, elegant hotel in historic Haddonfield is just minutes from Philadelphia and the Cooper and Delaware Rivers. The historic village of Haddonfield offers over 200 unique shops and restaurants. The surrounding areas include countless attractions from aquariums to zoos, museums, the Battleship New Jersey, art, concerts, history, sports and theatre in-between! Each of our lovely guest rooms has a private bath (many have whirlpools), fireplace, TV, phone with free local calls and voicemail, and wireless Internet access. Enjoy a full, gourmet breakfast served on individual tables adorned with candles and fine linens in our firelit dining room. In the warmer months, enjoy breakfast on the large, wrap-around porch in our beautiful residental neighborhood. Packages and extras include tickets for major sporting events in nearby Philadelphia, and fine dining. We specialize in business conferences and retreats with special rates for the business traveler.

**Rates**
9 Rooms. $179/$349, depending on room and day of week.
Number of Rooms: 9

**Cuisine**
Full, gourmet breakfast.

**Nearest Airport(s)**
Philadelphia International

**Directions**
From N: NJ turnpike to exit 4. Rt. 73N to 295S. Take exit 30 and follow Warwick Rd to Kings Hwy. L at next light and then R onto West End. From S: 95N to Walt Whitman Bridge. Exit 168(Audubon). L onto Kings Hwy and L onto West End. From W: I-76 to I-676 to Ben Franklin Bridge. Rt. 70E to Cuthbert Blvd (turn R). L onto Park Blvd which becomes West End Ave.

# Candlelight Inn

www.candlelight-inn.com
2310 Central Avenue, North Wildwood, NJ 08260
**800-992-2632** • 609-522-6200 • Fax 609-522-6125
info@candlelight-inn.com

*Member Since 2001*

*New Jersey*

*North Wildwood*

*"If you only have one vacation to take, spend it at the Candlelight".*

Innkeepers/Owners
**Bill and Nancy Moncrief and Eileen Burchsted**

Come visit a unique part of Wildwoods. Enjoy the quiet elegance reminiscent of another era. The Candlelight Inn is a beautifully restored 1905 Queen Anne Victorian home, offering rooms and suites with private baths, some w/double whirlpool tubs and/or fireplaces. Sit on our veranda where cool ocean breezes delight you, relax anytime of the year in our outdoor hot tub or warm yourself by a roaring fire in our inglenook. Minutes away are spacious beaches, water sports, lighthouses, antiquing, fine dining, nature activities, golfing, shopping, history, and a fun-filled boardwalk...something for everyone. Cape May County has islands with great Atlantic Ocean beaches and a Naval Air Station Museum, Historic Cold Spring Village, one of the top ten small zoos in the country, and Leaming's Gardens, the country's largest garden of 'annuals.' The Candlelight is our small piece of the New Jersey Coast that we would like to share with you and your special someone.

**Rates**
7 Rooms, $100/$199; 3 Suites, $170/$260. Some units have double whirlpool tubs. All rooms have either queen or king beds & all have private baths, air conditioned, gas or electric fire places. Open year-round. Number of Rooms: 10

**Cuisine**
A 3-course, sit-down breakfast with a choice of entrees and afternoon refreshments.

**Nearest Airport(s)**
Atlantic City (ACY)

**Directions**
S-bound: G.S. Pkwy to exit 6; Rte. 147 E; L on 2nd Ave.; R on Central Ave.; go to 24th Ave.; Inn is on R. N-bound: G.S. Pkwy to exit 4 into Wildwood. After bridge, L at 6th light (Atlantic Ave.). L at 24th for 1 block.

# The Fairthorne

www.fairthorne.com
111 - 115 Ocean Street, Cape May, NJ  08204
**800-438-8742** • 609-884-8791 • Fax 609-898-6129
fairthornebnb@aol.com

*Member Since 2001*

*"I will savor the memory of your hospitality for years to come.
Thanks so much!"*

**New Jersey**

**Cape May**

### Innkeepers/Owners
**Ed and Diane Hutchinson**

Innkeepers Diane and Ed Hutchinson warmly welcome you to their romantic old whaling captain's home. This 1892 Colonial Revival-style Inn features a gracious wraparound veranda where sumptious breakfasts are served on pleasant mornings and stress-relieving rockers offer afternoon relaxation. The Fairthorne is beautifully decorated in period style without being too frilly or formal. Guestrooms are appointed with a seamless blend of fine antiques and contemporary comforts, including air conditioning, mini-fridges and TV/VCR,CD players plus gas log and electric fireplaces and whirlpool tubs in some rooms. Each day Diane and Ed invite you to gather for tasty snacks and fresh-baked cookies.

**Rates**
9 Rooms, $145/$280, Antique furnishings, lace curtains, king or queen beds, TVs/VCR,CD player private baths, some fireplaces and whirlpool baths. Open year-round. Closed only Thanksgiving Eve and Day, Christmas Eve and Day.  Number of Rooms: 9

**Cuisine**
Full breakfast & afternoon hot tea & coffee on cool days or iced tea & lemonade on summer days. Complimentary sherry. Excellent restaurants a short walk.

**Nearest Airport(s)**
Philadelphia & Atlantic City

**Directions**
Garden State Pkwy S to end; continue straight over bridges, becomes Lafayette St. 2nd light, turn L onto Ocean St. 3rd. block on L?111 Ocean Street.

# The Humphrey Hughes House

www.humphreyhugheshouse.com
29 Ocean Street, Cape May, NJ 08204
**800-582-3634** • 609-884-4428
TheHumphreyHughes@comcast.net

*Member Since 1999*

*New Jersey*

*Cape May*

*"The Inn is so clean and the food is delicious. We will be back soon."*

Innkeepers/Owners
**Lorraine & Terry Schmidt**

Nestled in the heart of Cape May's primary historic district, The Humphrey Hughes is one of the most spacious and gracious Inns. Expansive common rooms are filled with beautiful antiques. Relax on the large wraparound veranda filled with rockers and enjoy the ocean view and colorful gardens. Our large, comfortable guest rooms offer pleasant, clean accommodations. All rooms are air-conditioned with cable TV. Our location offers the visitor the opportunity to walk to the beach, restaurants, shops, theatre, concerts, nature trails. A full breakfast is served to all guests at 9:00 a.m. each day.

**Rates**
$140/$350 per night, Dbl. Weekday discounts Fall and Spring. All rooms and suites with queen or king beds, TV, Air conditioning. Number of Rooms: 10

**Cuisine**
Delicious and beautifully presented Hot Breakfast (served on the front veranda when weather permits).

**Nearest Airport(s)**
Atlantic City International

**Directions**
Take Garden State Parkway S to end. Follow Lafayette Street S. Turn L at second stop light; Ocean Street. The inn is on your Left, the corner of Ocean & Columbia Streets - only one block from the Ocean.

SelectRegistry.com

# The Mainstay Inn

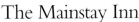

www.mainstayinn.com
635 Columbia Ave., Cape May, NJ 08204
**609-884-8690** • Fax 609-884-1498
mainstayinn@comcast.net

*Member Since 1976*

*New Jersey*

*Cape May*

*"I want you to know how much I enjoyed my time at The Mainstay Inn.
Service, hospitality, and lovely accommodations were far above my expectations!"*

Proprietors
**David & Susan Macrae**

Once an exclusive gambling club, The Mainstay is now an elegant Victorian inn furnished in splendid antiques. Within a lovely garden setting, the Inn and adjacent Cottage feature wide rocker-lined verandas, and large, high-ceilinged rooms which are lavishly but comfortably furnished. The Mainstay is a landmark within a National Historic Landmark town, and is but a short walk to restaurants, shops, theater, concerts, nature trails and beaches.

**Rates**
9 Rooms, $165/360 B&B 3 Suites, $195/$350 B&B. Open year-round; Fridays and Saturdays only from January to April. Number of Rooms: 12

**Cuisine**
Breakfast and elegant afternoon tea. Excellent restaurants a short walk away. No liquor license.

**Nearest Airport(s)**
Atlantic City International 45 minutes away

**Directions**
Take Garden State Pkwy. (S). In Cape May, Pkwy. becomes Lafayette St. Take L. at light onto Madison Ave. Go 3 blocks, R. at Columbia. Inn on R.

# The Queen Victoria®
www.queenvictoria.com
102 Ocean Street, Cape May, NJ 08204-2320
**609-884-8702**
reservations@queenvictoria.com

*Member Since 1992*

*"The Queen Victoria is a dream come true! Your hospitality is genuine."*
*"Our two days at The Queen Victoria were the best two days of my life."*

Innkeepers/Owners
**Doug and Anna Marie McMain**

A Cape May tradition since 1980, The Queen Victoria is one of America's most renowned bed & breakfast inns. Four impeccably restored 1880s homes are filled with fine antiques, handmade quilts, and many thoughtful extras. The hospitality is warm and the atmosphere is social. Choose from thirty-two inviting and spacious rooms and suites, all with private bath, AC, mini-refrigerator, and TV with DVD. Pamper yourself with a whirlpool tub or gas-log fireplace. For your Victorian enjoyment, rocking chairs fill porches and gardens. Wicker swings carry you back to a quieter time. Bicycles are provided free of charge, as are beach chairs and beach towels. The Queen Victoria is open all year and is located in the heart of the historic district, one block from the Atlantic Ocean, tours, shopping, and fine restaurants. Victorian Cape May offers tours, special events, and activities all year including the Spring Music Festival, the Jazz Festival, Victorian Week, and the Food & Wine Festival.

**Rates**
23 Rooms: $105/$260. 9 Suites: $150/$495. Weekday discounts Fall, Winter & Spring. Always open. Thanksgiving and Christmas packages. Number of Rooms: 32

**Cuisine**
Rates include generous buffet breakfast & afternoon tea with sweets and savories. Complimentary juices, soft drinks, bottled water, coffee and teas. Fresh fruit always available. Fine dining nearby.

**Nearest Airport(s)**
Atlantic City (ACY), Philadelphia (PHL)

**Directions**
Garden State Parkway to S end; continue straight over bridges, becomes Lafayette St. 2nd light turn L onto Ocean St. 3 blocks turn R onto Columbia Ave. Loading areas for check-in on R.

# Peter Shields Inn

www.petershieldsinn.com
1301 Beach Drive, Cape May, NJ 08204
**800-355-6565** • 609-884-9090
petershieldsinn@comcast.net

*Member Since 2008*

*New Jersey*

*Cape May*

*"First class rooms,attentive and courteous staff; breathtaking ocean views and a fabulous 5 star restaurant! Can we extend our stay?"*

Proprietors
**David & Susan Macrae**

This 1907 Georgian revival mansion is an architectural masterpiece, directly across from the Atlantic Ocean in Cape May, New Jersey. The Inn has 9 well appointed guest rooms all with private baths, most of which have Jacuzzis and fireplaces. Awake each morning to a homemade breakfast and enjoy watching the dolphin play. Fill your days with the sun, and sand or go exploring through town in America's first national historic city. Cape May has something for everyone. In the late afternoon you can unwind while enjoying complimentary hors d'oeuvres & refreshments. You will not have to travel far to enjoy fine dining. The Peter Shields Inn is host to one of South New Jersey's most desirable restaurants with a Zagat Rating of 26/27/25. Enjoy the classic elegance in one of the five distinctive dining rooms all with ocean views.May we suggest the Lobster Crab Cake or the South African Lobster Tail from our Chefs New American cuisine? The Inn also specializes in both casual and elegant ocean front weddings, receptions and special dinners. Our knowledgeable staff will guide you through all of the planning.Come enjoy the best the Jersey Shore has to offer with golfing, fishing & Atlantic City all within reach.

**Rates**
135.00-395.00  Number of Rooms: 9

**Cuisine**
The Peter Shields offers five distinctive dining rooms, an outside porch, two fireplaces, a Cappuccino bar and spectacular views of the Atlantic Ocean.Enjoy gourmet dining at it's finest!

**Nearest Airport(s)**
Atlantic City or Philadelphia International

**Directions**
Follow the Garden State Parkway to Exit 0. Once in town turn left at Sidney Street, left again at Washington Street, and right at the traffic island. Follow Pittsburgh Avenue to Beach Drive and turn right. The Peter Shields is located at the corner of Beach & Trenton Aves.Make a right to turn into our parking lot for check in.

# *New Mexico*

## "The Land of Enchantment"

Famous for: Taos, Santa Fe, Pueblos, Adobe, Cliff Dwellings, Carlsbad Caverns (the largest in the world), White Sands, National Monument, Ghost Ranch, Ship Rock, Pecos National Historical Park, Pancho Villa State Park.

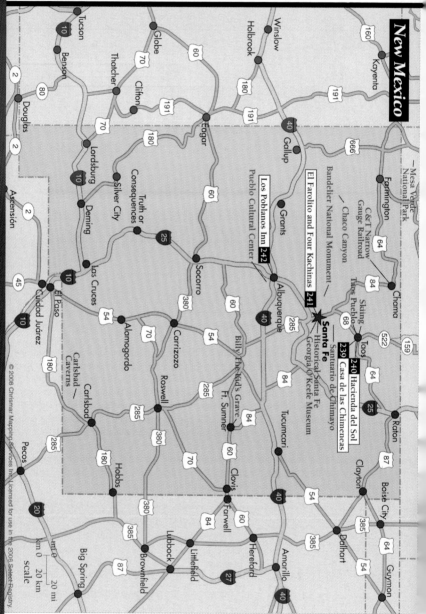

Los Poblanos Inn **242**

El Farolito and Four Kachinas **241**

Santa Fe

Historical Santa Fe
Georgia O'Keefe Museum
Santuario de Chimayo
Casa de las Chimeneas **240**
Hacienda del Sol **239**

Pueblo Cultural Center

Bandelier National Monument

Chaco Canyon

C&T Narrow Gauge Railroad

Taos Pueblo Skiing

Mesa Verde National Park

km 0    20 km

20 mi

scale

# Casa de las Chimeneas

www.VisitTaos.com
405 Cordoba Road, 5303 NDCBU, Taos, NM 87571
**877-758-4777** • 575-758-4777 • Fax 575-758-3976
casa@newmex.com

*Member Since 1998*

*New Mexico*

*Taos*

> *"This, quite possibly, was the most wonderful travel experience we've had. Everything - we do mean everything - was fabulous! Great value for the price."*

Four Diamond Award

Innkeeper
**Susan Vernon**

Guests to this AAA Four Diamond inn delight in offerings not often found at small properties. The Wellness Spa, complete with workout room, massage and spa treatment room, sauna and hot tub, entices guests to unwind. A dedicated concierge sees to every guest's need from a menu of possibilities as rich as Taos' multi-cultural history. Special seasonal activities bookable through the inn include hot air ballooning over and into the Rio Grande Gorge, white water rafting, golf, fly fishing, llama trekking, horseback riding, skiing and snowmobiling. A talented kitchen staff prepares two hearty and delicious meals a day. With three scenic byways in Taos County, guests often spend a day enjoying the same views that inspire the many artists that make Taos their home with a lunch packed in a custom backpack. Southwest gardens, to-die-for accommodations and a perfect location near the Historic Plaza complete the picture. The result: delighted guests who leave with refreshed and renewed spirits, eager to return to Taos' *House of Chimneys*.

**Rates**
6 Rooms, $180/$290 MAP 2 Suites, $325/$615 MAP Open year-round. Number of Rooms: 8

**Cuisine**
Hearty breakfast with hot entree, evening buffet supper, complimentary in-room bars with juices, sodas, mineral waters and hot beverages. Optional custom picnics.

**Nearest Airport(s)**
Albuquerque International Sunport

**Directions**
From Santa Fe (Hwy. 68): turn R onto Los Pandos, go 1 block & turn R on Cordoba at the four-way stop. The inn is the first L off Cordoba. From Colorado (Hwy 522): turn L on Kit Carson Rd., go 1 block & turn R on Montoya. At the four-way stop, go straight. The inn is the first L.

# Hacienda del Sol

www.taoshaciendadelsol.com
P.O. Box 177, 109 Mabel Dodge Lane, Taos, NM 87571
**866-333-4459** • 575-758-0287 • Fax 575-758-5895
sunhouse@newmex.com

*Member Since 2003*

*New Mexico*

*Taos*

---

*"One of the ten most romantic inn in the US"* USA Today

---

Innkeeper/Owner
**Gerd and Luellen Hertel**

Taos Mountain provides a magnificent backdrop to our Hacienda which borders thousands of acres of panoramic and peaceful Indian Pueblo land. Enjoy a serene and beautiful view from the tranquil gardens or steaming jacuzzi as you stargaze in the stillness of our many clear nights. Consisting of four buildings, the original 1804 adobe once belonged to legendary art patroness Mabel Dodge Luhan. This historic Inn has hosted guests such as D.H. Lawrence, Georgia O'Keefe, Frank Waters and Ansel Adams. Southwestern rooms enchant our guests with kiva fireplaces, viga and latilla ceilings, thick adobe walls and handcrafted furniture. In the heat of summer, Taos elevation combined with the shade of towering cottonwoods, elms, willows and blue spruce on the property provide blissful conditions. Experience the culinary talents of award winning chef/owner Gerd Hertel when we introduce cooking lessons, theme dinners for holidays and special occasions, custom backpack lunches and fun barbecue evenings. Weddings overlooking Taos sacred mountain as well as full package meeting retreats and group functions are welcome.

**Rates**
7 Rooms, $135/$325 B&B.4 Suites, $190/$540 B&B. Open year round.   Number of Rooms: 11

**Cuisine**
2-course breakfast w/hot entree. Gourmet Coffees and tea & hot cocoa available all day. Afternoon homemade snacks & sweets are available in the Dining room. Breakfast served on the patio overlooking Taos Mountain in summer or by the open kiva fireplace in winter.

**Nearest Airport(s)**
Santa Fe and Albuquerque Airport

**Directions**
From Santa Fe on Hwy 68: 1 mi. N of the Taos Plaza, turn R 100 yards past the Laughing Horse Inn

# El Farolito and Four Kachinas Inn

www.farolito.com
514 Galisteo Street, Santa Fe, NM 87501
**888-634-8782** • 505-988-1631 • Fax 505-989-1323
innkeeper@farolito.com

*Member Since 2001*

*New Mexico*

*Santa Fe*

*"Quintessential Santa Fe! You create an ambiance
that promotes rest and restoration."*

Innkeepers/Owners
**Walt Wyss and Wayne Mainus**

Surround yourself with the richness of Santa Fe's art, culture and history in two beautiful downtown properties - **El Farolito Bed and Breakfast Inn** (ELF) and the **Four Kachinas Inn** (4K). These inns, under the same ownership and management, offer you award-winning accommodations, showcasing exquisite original Southwestern art and handcrafted furnishings. The rooms are decorated in styles relevant to Santa Fe's rich cultural heritage of native American, Spanish and Anglo inhabitants. Modern amenities also abound including fine linens, rich fabrics, AC, private entrances, TVs, telephones and free Internet access. The two inns are conveniently located in the downtown historic district, a short pleasant walk to numerous galleries, shops, museums, world-class fine dining, and the central Plaza. In the warm sunshine, savor a leisurely breakfast on the back portal and relax on your garden patio. At ELF, enjoy a fireside breakfast in the brightly decorated dining room and the coziness of a fireplace in your room. At the 4K Inn, enjoy access to the cozy lounge and relax on one of our many garden patios. Warm personal and knowledgeable service awaits you.

**Rates**
12 Rooms, $120/$230; 1 Suite, $200/$265 . Features: TV, phones, fine linens, AC, patios. Fireplaces at ELF. Number of Rooms: 13

**Cuisine**
Complete healthy breakfast w/quality home-baked goods, hot entre, fresh fruit, yogurts, & ample accompaniment. Compli-mentary afternoon light refreshments.

**Nearest Airport(s)**
Santa Fe & Albuquerque

**Directions**
From Albq. I-25 N, exit 282. St. Francis N to Cerrillos, R on Cerrillos, R at Paseo de Peralta, To ELF: L at Galisteo to 514. To 4K: R at Webber to 512. From Taos: S on U.S. 84/285, exit to downtown, L on Paseo de Peralta. (See above.)

# Los Poblanos Inn

www.lospoblanos.com
4803 Rio Grande Blvd. NW, Albuquerque, NM 87107
**866-344-9297** • 505-344-9297 • Fax 505-342-1302
info@lospoblanos.com

*Member Since 2005*

*New Mexico*

*Albuquerque*

*"Rough-hewn ceiling beams, Saltillo tiles, and traditional kiva fireplaces give Los Poblanos a cozy, comfortable charm."* - Bon Appetit Magazine

Innkeepers/Owners
**The Rembe Family**

Set among 25 acres of lavender fields and lush formal gardens, Los Poblanos Inn is one of the most prestigious historic properties in the Southwest. The Inn was designed by the region's foremost architect, John Gaw Meem, the "Father of Santa Fe Style," and is listed on both the New Mexico and National Registers of Historic Places. Guest rooms are in a classic New Mexican style with kiva fireplaces, carved ceiling beams, hardwood floors, and antique New Mexican furnishings. Guests can relax around the Spanish hacienda-style courtyard or spend hours exploring the property's extensive gardens and organic farm. The buildings feature significant artwork commissioned during the WPA period by some of New Mexico's most prominent artists, including a fresco by Peter Hurd and carvings by Gustave Baumann. Detailed tours highlighting the property's cultural, political, agricultural and architectural history are available to every guest. "One could spend a lifetime at Los Poblanos and never fall out of love." - *Su Casa* Magazine

**Rates**
3 Guest Rooms, 4 Suites, $145/$250. Fireplaces, spa services upon request, wireless internet. Open year-round. Number of Rooms: 7

**Cuisine**
Complimentary gourmet breakfast buffet w/ fresh organic produce & ingredients from our farm.

**Nearest Airport(s)**
Albuquerque International Sunport

**Directions**
From Airport: I-25 N to I-40 W (Gallup Exit 226B). Continue W 3 mi. to Rio Grande Ex. 157A. Turn R and go N 3.3 mi. to 4803 Rio Grande Blvd. From Santa Fe/Taos: I-25 S to Alameda Ex. 233. W on Alameda for 3.2 mi. L on S. Rio Grande Blvd. for 3.8 mi. to property on R.

# New York

## "The Empire State"

Famous for: Statue of Liberty, Ellis Island, Empire State Building, Times Square, Metropolitan Museum of Art, Central Park, Madison Square Garden, Madison Avenue, Wall Street, Brooklyn Bridge, Catskill Forest, Adirondack Mountains.

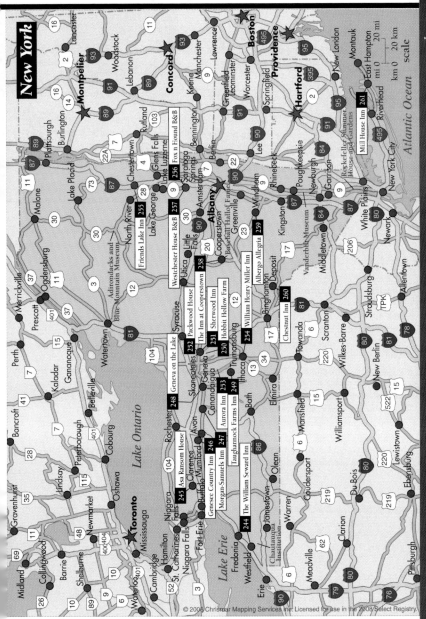

# The William Seward Inn

www.williamsewardinn.com
6645 South Portage Rd., Westfield, NY 14787-9603
**800-338-4151** • 716-326-4151 • Fax 716-326-4163
williamsewardinn@fairpoint.net

*Member Since 1992*

*New York*

*Westfield*

*"Charming and romantic -- gracious hosts and spectacular food"*

Innkeepers/Owners
**Charles & Jane Linton Breeding**

Built in 1821, the majestic William Seward Inn offers luxurious accommodations, exceptional pampering, and the outstanding genteel service of a by-gone era. Centrally located, guests at the inn can explore the famous Chautauqua Institution, the Chautauqua Lake Erie Wine Trail featuring award-winning New York wines, water sports, bird watching, golfing, hiking and so much more. After an invigorating bicycle ride through the local vineyards, take pleasure in one of the inn's delectable wicker basket lunches resplendent with gourmet delights! Return to the inn to peruse the extensive library, enjoying a glass of wine and an afternoon nap. Later, savor a romantic candlelit dinner accompanied by an extensive wine list and delicious homemade desserts before retiring to the cozy stylishly appoinnted rooms, many of which feature fireplaces, soaking tubs, whirlpool baths, and some with balconies. Sense the luxury of an in-room massage paired with our signature bedtime snack or champagne cocktail. Your stay at the inn will be an experience not soon to forget!

**Rates**
10 rooms with king or queen, some with whirlpools or fireplaces $145/$235. 2 rooms with double beds $115/$135. OPEN ALL YEAR. Number of Rooms: 12

**Cuisine**
Dinner available Wed.-Sun., by advance reservation with guests pre-select their appetizer and main entree from our seasonal menu at least one day in advance of dining. Fine wines and champagnes are available.

**Nearest Airport(s)**
Jamestown, NY - 30 minutes; Erie, PA - 40 minutes.

**Directions**
4 mi. S on Rte 394 from I-90, exit 60. 2.5 hrs. NE of Cleveland, OH; 2.5 hrs. N of Pittsburg, PA; 1.5 hrs. SW of Buffalo, NY; 3 hrs. SW of Toronto, Canada.

# Asa Ransom House

www.asaransom.com
10529 Main St. Rt. 5, Clarence, NY 14031
**800-841-2340** • 716-759-2315 • Fax 716-759-2791
innfo@asaransom.com

*Member Since 1976*

🍽️ 🍽️ 🍽️ 🍷

*"Our favorite place to stay whenever we travel."*

Three
Diamond Award

### Innkeepers/Owners
**Robert Lenz and Abigail Lenz**

On the site of the first gristmill built in Erie County (1803), where guests are romanced in the winter by the glowing fireplaces and spacious grounds full of herbs and flowers in the summer. Many rooms have porches or balconies to view the grounds or just relax. Experience world-class cuisine and full country breakfasts with delicious regional accents. Voted best food, service, hospitality, romantic setting and historical charm in Buffalo News readers survey. Often upon arrival you will find the aroma of fresh pies and breads lingering in the air! Clarence is known throughout the east for its antiques and treasures, along with unusual shops full of gifts, art and crafts. Explore the bike trails or visit the nearby Opera House, Erie Canal Cruises, Albright-Knox Art Gallery and Frank Lloyd Wright's Martin House Complex. Also Niagara wineries, Fort Niagara, Letchworth State Park and much more. Only 28 miles from Niagara Falls.

**Rates**
10 Rooms, $110/$185 B&B; $165/$325 MAP. Full breakfast included. Number of Rooms: 10

**Cuisine**
Fine country dining with regional specialties. Fully licensed - NYS Wine award. "Best Place to Take Out-of-Town Guests" award.

**Nearest Airport(s)**
Buffalo/Niagara - 9 miles

**Directions**
Traveling E: I-90, exit 49, L on Rte. 78 for 1 mi. to R on Rte. 5 for 5.3 mi. Traveling W: I-90 exit 48A & R on Rte. 77 for 1 mi. to R on Rte. 5 for 10 mi. to Inn.

# Genesee Country Inn Bed and Breakfast

www.geneseecountryinn.com
948 George Street, Mumford-Rochester, NY 14511
**800-697-8297** • 585-538-2500 • Fax 585-538-9867
stay@geneseecountryinn.com

*Member Since 1988*

*"We so enjoyed our stay! Lovely surroundings, dreamy room, restful sleep, excellent breakfast, and gracious hospitality. Who could ask for more?"*

Innkeepers/Owners
**Deborah & Richard Stankevich**

Step back to an era of simple elegance, fine hospitality and natural beauty. This historic Bed and Breakfast/Country Inn is situated on Spring Creek with mill ponds and a waterfall to enthrall any traveler. The Inn has wireless Internet, fax and conference facilities. Hike the grounds, the MacKay Wildlife Preserve or the Genesee Country Village & Museum Nature Center. Enjoy the art of fly-fishing on our private Spring Creek, fish the famed Oatka Creek and visit the historic NYS Fish Hatchery. The Inn, an 1833 plaster-paper mill, is situated on eight acres of natural setting, perfect for bird watching! The Inn's idyllic country ambience is perfect for a secluded, romantic getaway, yet it is close enough to the arts, entertainment, Finger Lakes wineries, antique shops and over 70 golf courses. The Inn is a wonderful location for family reunions, corporate events, bridal or baby showers, and intimate weddings. Romance, spa and fly-fishing packages are available! Check our web site for additional special packages and getaway weekends.

**Rates**
Six Old Mill Rooms-$120/$155; Three Garden Rooms-$150/$180; and One King Suite-$175/$195  Number of Rooms: 10

**Cuisine**
Full Country Breakfast daily. Refreshments available all day.

**Nearest Airport(s)**
Rochester International Airport

**Directions**
I-90 to Exit 47 to Rte. 19S. Follow "Genesee Country Village & Museum" green signs. Turn left onto North Road. At stop sign, turn right onto Rte 36S. Follow Rte 36S to flashing light. Turn right onto George St. The Inn is 2 blocks up on the right at 948 George St. From I-390, take exit 10. Follow Rte 5W to 36N. Turn left at the flashing light onto George St.

# Morgan-Samuels Inn

www.morgansamuelsinn.com
2920 Smith Rd., Canandaigua, NY 14424
**585-394-9232** • 585-721-3383 • Fax 585-394-8044
MorSamBBC@aol.com

*Member Since 1992*

*New York*

*"We award you two more diamonds making this
New York's only 6 Diamond Inn."*

*Canandaigua*

Innkeepers/Owners
**Julie & John Sullivan – Brad & Connie Smith**

Travel the 2,000 foot tree-lined drive to the secluded 1810 English style mansion and sense the difference between ordinary and legendary. The Inn sits like a plantation on a rise surrounded by 46 acres. Four patios, trickling waterfall, tennis court, acres of lawn and gardens canopied by 250 noble trees. Three rooms with French doors and balconies, 7 fireplaces. Tea room with stone wall and 16-foot glass windows, pot-bellied stove. Library, common room, large enclosed porch/dining room, four Jacuzzis, outside hot springs spa Jacuzzi, museum quality furniture, oil paintings. Recognized as one of the "12 Most Romantic Hideaways in the East" by *Discerning Traveler* Magazine.

**Rates**
5 Rooms, $119/$249 B&B; 1 Suite, $219/$295 B&B;
3 Lake Villas $225/$395 B&B. Number of Rooms: 6

**Cuisine**
Memorable, extended, candlelit full gourmet breakfast; dinner prix fixe by reservation, special request for eight or more. On day of arrival we serve hot appetizers, fruit, cheeses, and soft beverages served on the Victorian Porch.

**Nearest Airport(s)**
Rochester International

**Directions**
I-90 from exit 43 R on 21 to 488; L 1st R on East Ave. to stop. Continue 3/4 mi. to Inn on R. The Inn is located two minutes from Canandaigua Lake.

# Geneva On The Lake

www.genevaonthelake.com
1001 Lochland Road, Route 14, Geneva, NY 14456
**800-3-GENEVA** • 315-789-7190 • Fax 315-789-0322
info@genevaonthelake.com

*Member Since 2003*

*New York*

*Geneva*

*"Heavenly!! Thank you (and your wonderful staff) for the grandest stay we've ever had!!"*

General Manager
**William J. Schickel**

Experience European elegance and friendly hospitality in the heart of Finger Lakes Wine Country. Amidst an ambiance of Italian Renaissance architecture, classical sculptures, luxurious suites and Stickley furnishings guests from around the world enjoy vacation getaways, family gatherings, weddings and conferences. Rest, relax and surrender yourself to gracious service and breathtaking surroundings. Candlelight dining with live music. A complimentary bottle of wine and basket of fruit are in your suite on arrival and *The New York Times* is at your door each morning. Complimentary high-speed wireless Internet is available. Glorious formal gardens for lawn games, a 70' outdoor pool, and a boat-house with dock and moorings. Adjacent are Geneva's charming Historic District and the campus of Hobart and William Smith Colleges, both replete with architectural gems. Enjoy magnificent scenic beauty on the Seneca Lake Wine Trail. Golf is nearby. "The food is extraordinarily good." – *Bon Appetit*. "One of the 10 most romantic inns in the United States." - *American Historic Inns*.

**Rates**
29 Guest Suites (10 w/ 2 bedrooms). Open year-round. Many 4-Season Vacation Packages offered for a romantic getaway, honeymoon, gala New Year's & more. $217/$1245 per night. Number of Rooms: 29

**Cuisine**
Gourmet cuisine is served with a smile in the warmth of candlelight and live music. Breakfast daily and Sunday Brunch. Lunch On The Terrace in summer.

**Nearest Airport(s)**
Rochester International

**Directions**
From the North: NY State Thruway Exit #42 then Rt 14 South 7 mi. From the South or NY City: I-86 to Exit #52 then Rt 14 N to Geneva. 1 hour from Rochester, Syracuse or Ithaca Airports.

SelectRegistry.com

# Taughannock Farms Inn

www.t-farms.com

2030 Gorge Road, Trumansburg, NY  14886

**888-387-7711** • 607-387-7711 • Fax 607-387-7721

*Member Since 2002*

*New York*

*Trumansburg*

*"This place is magical! The inn, the falls, the lake, the wine!
I wish I could live here!"*

Innkeepers/Owners
**Susan and Tom Sheridan**

Relax and enjoy a bygone era at this Victorian country inn. Majestically situated above Cayuga's waters, the inn offers commanding views of the lake. This Finger Lake's wine region landmark, built in 1873, is known for its gracious hospitality, abundant American cuisine, and charming accomodations. In addition to the five rooms in the Main inn that are furnished with antiques, we also have four guesthouses for a total of 23 rooms. Edgewood, the newest of the four, opened in 2004. All 10 rooms with covered balconies/patios have outstanding views of Cayuga Lake. Four king units feature Jacuzzis. Savor a romantic dinner in the 150-seat fine dining restaurant overlooking the lake. The four-course meal features American cuisine and is complimented by wonderful Finger Lakes wine.

**Rates**
Main Inn rooms $80/$185. 3 guesthouses $150/$210 per room. Full cottage $150/$475. Seasonal rates for all accommodations.   Number of Rooms: 23

**Cuisine**
Expanded Continental breakfast of juice, coffee, fruit, breakfast pastries and at least one hot item. Dinner includes appetizer, salad or sorbet, entree, and dessert. Banquets available.

**Nearest Airport(s)**
Tompkins County Airport

**Directions**
From Ithaca: Take Rte. 89 N for 9 mi. to Gorge Rd. Turn L; Inn is on R. From NY State Thruway: Exit 41; Take 318-E to Rte. 5 & 20. Go 1/4 mi.; turn R on Rte. 89, S for 34 mi. Inn on R.

# Hobbit Hollow Farm

www.hobbithollow.com
3061 West Lake Road, Skaneateles, NY 13152
**800-374-3796** • 315-685-2791 • Fax 315-685-3426
innkeeper@hobbithollow.com

*Member Since 1998*

*"From the moment you pass through the stone pillars, you will feel everyday cares lift away."*

Proprietor
**William B. Eberhardt**

Hobbit Hollow Farm has been carefully restored inside and out to recreate the casual comfort of an elegant country farmhouse. Hobbit Hollow serves a full, farm breakfast as part of the room price. Overlooking Skaneateles Lake, Hobbit Hollow Farm is situated on 320 acres of farmland with trails and ponds as well as private equestrian stables. Spend time contemplating the lake on our east verandah. Enjoy afternoon tea or coffee and watch the light play on the water in the soft wash of dusk. Rediscover what it means to be truly relaxed in a setting of tranquility. This is the perfect spot for a quiet, romantic getaway.

**Rates**
5 Rooms, $100/$270, elegantly decorated with master-crafted period furniture and antiques. 3 rooms include four-poster beds. Master Suite $250/$270; Lake View $200/$230; Chanticleer $175/$200; Meadow View $150/$170; Twin $100/$120. Open year-round. Number of Rooms: 5

**Cuisine**
Full gourmet country breakfast. Find excellent dinner and lunches at the Sherwood Inn, Blue Water Grill, and Kabuki.

**Nearest Airport(s)**
Syracuse (Hancock International)

**Directions**
Located on the west side of Skaneateles Lake on 41A. Rte 20 (Genesee St.) to 41A South. In less than 2 miles, the stone entrance to Hobbit Hollow Farm will be on the right.

SelectRegistry.com

# The Sherwood Inn

www.thesherwoodinn.com

26 West Genesee Street, Skaneateles, NY 13152

**800-374-3796** • 315-685-3405 • Fax 315-685-8983

info@thesherwoodinn.com

*Member Since 1979*

*New York*

*Skaneateles*

*"The Sherwood has it all…the rooms, the food, the lobby, the village setting…a perfect getaway for leisure or business!"*

Wine Spectator
AWARD OF EXCELLENCE

Owner

**William B. Eberhardt**

Built as a stagecoach stop in 1807, The Sherwood Inn has always been a favorite resting place for travelers. The handsome lobby with fireplace, gift shop, antiques and orientals offers a warm reception. Each room has been restored to the beauty of a bygone era to create a relaxing harmony away from everyday cares. Our newly renovated dining and banquet rooms are able to accommodate groups of all sizes. In addition to our dining rooms, many of our 24 guest rooms overlook beautiful Skaneateles Lake. Casual lakeside dining and The Sherwood are synonymous, and we have been recognized by the *New York Times, Bon Appetit, Country Living, Harper's Bazaar* and *New Yorker* magazines. Our extensive menu offers American cooking with a continental touch, accompanied by an impressive wine list which received the Wine Spectator "Award of Excellence".

**Rates**
15 Suites and 10 Rooms, $130/$225. Suites have fireplaces/whirlpool baths. All have private baths, telephones & televisions. We are open year-round. Number of Rooms: 25

**Cuisine**
Our Tavern serves traditional American fare in a relaxed atmosphere. Our Dining Room offers candlelight dining in a lovely setting overlooking Skaneateles Lake. Serving Daily.

**Nearest Airport(s)**
Syracuse (Hancock International)

**Directions**
From New York Thruway: Exit Weedsport (exit 40) Rte. 34 S to Auburn. E on Rte. 20, 7 miles to Skaneateles. From the South: 81 N to Cortland, Rte. 41 N to Skaneateles Lake, L (west) on Rte. 20 for 1 mi.

# Packwood House

www.packwoodhouse.com
14 West Genesee Street, Skaneateles, NY 13152
**877-225-9663** • 315-217-8100 • Fax 315-685-8983
info@packwoodhouse.com

*Member Since 2005*

*"...comfort and amenities for business or pleasure!"*

Proprietor - **Michael P. Falcone**
Property Manager - **Julia Bergan**

The Packwood House is located in the center of the quaint historic village of Skaneateles on the north shore of Skaneateles Lake, the easternmost of the Finger Lakes. Many of the Packwood's guest suites provide picturesque views of the lake and the village; several feature oversized balconies where guests may sit back and enjoy the view from a unique perspective. The Packwood House is designed to provide all the comforts of home while enjoying the luxury of "getting away." There are many things to see and do, including a scenic boat cruise around the lake, lakeside concerts on summer weekends, and downhill or cross country skiing at nearby trails during the fall and winter months. There is no shortage of activity for guests looking for adventure, and no better place to just sit back, relax and enjoy the scenery.

**Rates**
19 guest suites. $135/$230 Suites feature a sitting area, desk, cable television, hi-speed internet access, and a kitchenette with microwave, refrigerator and coffee-maker. Number of Rooms: 19

**Cuisine**
Continental breakfast included. Find excellent dinner and lunches at the Sherwood Inn, Blue Water Grill, and Kabuki.

**Nearest Airport(s)**
Syracuse (Hancock International)

**Directions**
From New York Thruway: Exit Weedsport (exit 40) Route 34 S to Auburn. E on Route 20, 7 miles to Skaneateles. From the South: 81N to Cortland, Route 41 N to Skaneateles Lake, L (west) on Rte. 20 for 1 mile.

SelectRegistry.com

# Aurora Inn/E.B. Morgan Inn

**IOI IOI IOI** ♀

www.aurora-inn.com
391 Main Street/State Route 90, Aurora, NY 13026
**866-364-8808** • 315-364-8888 • Fax 315-364-8887
info@Aurora-Inn.com

*Member Since 2005*

*New York*

*Aurora*

*"The Inn is exceptionally well restored, beautifully decorated and staying there was a most gracious experience and of great comfort after a long work day."*

Innkeeper
**Sue Edinger**

In the heart of Finger Lakes wine country on the shores of Cayuga Lake, the Aurora Inn awaits. Steeped in history and restored to luxury, the inn is a beautiful setting for fine dining, comfortable lodging and special events. Elegant decor, fine art and antiques, fireplaces and gracious porches offer a warm welcome. Its ten luxurious guest rooms are decorated with designer fabrics and furnishings that place an emphasis on comfort. All have well-appointed marble bathrooms with thick towels and terrycloth robes, high-speed Internet access, flat-panel televisions, DVD players and Bose stereos. Most rooms have spacious balconies overlooking the lake or village, and some have inviting fireplaces, deep whirlpool baths with skylights. The Aurora Inn's restaurant, featuring refined American cuisine, is one of the few places in the Finger Lakes to dine outdoors with views of the lake and its spectacular sunsets. During your visit, explore the lake on a kayak or canoe, visit famed pottery maker Mackenzie-Childs, tour the area's unique wineries and spectacular waterfalls or simply relax by the fire. AAA Four Diamond Award winner.

**Rates**
8 Rooms, 2 Suites. $225/$375 in-season (June - October), $175/$275 off-season (November - May). Number of Rooms: 10

**Cuisine**
The Inn serves refined American fare, using the freshest of regional produce Guests enjoy lakeside indoor or outdoor dining for breakfast, brunch, lunch or dinner.Full breakfast is included in your stay.

**Nearest Airport(s)**
Syracuse's Hancock International Airport, 60 miles

**Directions**
Situated on the east shore of Cayuga Lake on State Route 90, the Aurora Inn is located approx. 30 minutes south of the NY State Thruway (exit 40 or 41). Call for specific directions.

# William Henry Miller Inn

www.MillerInn.com
303 North Aurora Street, Ithaca, NY 14850
**877-256-4553** • 607-256-4553 • Fax 607-256-0092
millerinn@aol.com

*Member Since 2003*

*Karen Brown's Guide says "...fortunate is the traveler to snare one of the inn's nine rooms."*

Innkeepers/Owners
**Lynnette Scofield & David Dier**

So centrally located...two blocks to The Ithaca Commons...eight blocks to Cornell...a short drive to Ithaca College...enjoy your morning coffee at a nearby waterfall...homemade English Muffins...an award winning example of 1880 architecture with all the modern amenities...evening homemade dessert buffet...Baked Fudge...great for business travel...parking on site...ADA accessible room...Triple Chocolate Cake...WiFi...comfy throws that just beckon you to curl up and nap...amazing stained glass...cookies warm from the oven...come in the door and smell the aroma of baking bread...sleep in the top of the turret...have breakfast on the front porch and watch the world go by...Kiplinger's says that The Miller Inn is what they love about Ithaca...pick a book from the shelf and read in front of a fireplace...poached pears with marscapone cream...walking distance to theaters...Apple Crisp Stuffed French Toast...two blocks to the world famous Moosewood...Ithaca Farmers' Market...and more... we'd love to have you stay with us!

**Rates**
$155/$250. King/Queen beds. Three rooms with two beds. Private baths; some Jacuzzis and fireplaces. Wireless Internet. Closed Christmas and New Year's Number of Rooms: 9

**Cuisine**
Breakfast with choice of two main dishes served during a two hour period. Homemade evening dessert and always available coffee and tea. Wonderful restaurants nearby including the world famous Moosewood.

**Nearest Airport(s)**
Tompkins County (Ithaca) Airport is just ten minutes away. Syracuse, an hour and fifteen minutes.

**Directions**
2 blocks from The Commons on the NE corner of Aurora & Buffalo Streets. 8 blocks from Cornell U. - 1 mi. from Ithaca College.

SelectRegistry.com

# Friends Lake Inn

www.friendslake.com
963 Friends Lake Road, Chestertown, NY 12817
**518-494-4751** • Fax 518-494-4616
friends@friendslake.com

*Member Since 1998*

*Ultimate Distinction Award - Wine Enthusiast Magazine - DiRoNA dining Award; Wine Spectator Grand Award.*

Innkeepers/Owners
**John and Trudy Phillips**

Experience the comfort and intimate ambiance of this elegantly restored inn, surrounded by the natural beauty of the Adirondacks. Guest rooms feature antiques, fine fabrics, and featherbeds, most with lake views, Jacuzzis, steam showersand/or fireplaces. Nationally acclaimed cuisine is served daily in the candlelit Nineteenth Century dining room, complemented by gracious service and a *Wine Spectator* Grand Award-winning wine list for the tenth year. Swim in the lake or the pool, canoe, kayak or fish on Friends Lake. Ski, snowshoe or hike on 32 kilometers of trails. Many activities close by. DiRoNA award of dining excellence.

**Rates**
17 Sumptuous guest rooms, all with private baths and lake or mountain views. Rooms with Jacuzzis or Adirondack Rooms with fireplaces available. Rooms range from $329/$479/couple. (MAP) Number of Rooms: 17

**Cuisine**
Full country breakfast & candlelight dinner served daily, lunch served on weekends; inquire about conferences, rehearsal dinners, and weddings. Lighter Wine Bar Menu available. Extensive wine collection.

**Nearest Airport(s)**
Albany

**Directions**
I-87 (The Northway) to exit 25, follow Rte. 8W for 3.5 miles, turn L at Friends Lake Rd. Bear R at fork, continue for one mile, then turn R. 8/10ths of a mile to Inn, on the R.

# Fox 'n' Hound B&B

www.foxnhoundbandb.com
142 Lake Ave., Saratoga Springs, NY 12866
**518-584-5959** • Fax 518-584-5959
Innkeeper@FoxnHoundBandB.com

*Member Since 2004*

*New York*

*Saratoga Springs*

*"A truly special B&B thanks to your warm hospitality. I will enjoy writing about the Fox 'n' Hound- a place I can totally recommend." Katherine Dyson*

Innkeeper/Owner
**Marlena Sacca**

Visit the historic Saratoga Springs, New York Fox 'n Hound Bed and Breakfast. Conveniently located within walking distance from downtown Saratoga shopping, dining, Saratoga Race Course, Skidmore College and Museums. A restored Victorian Mansion with colonial and Queen Ann architectural detail, that offers comfortable elegance with a cosmopolitan flair, European hospitality with the warmth of home, attention to detail found in the finest resorts, and the convenience of in-town location.

MARLENA'S FRITATTA (for complete ingredients, visit www.FoxnHoundBandB. com): Beat 2 eggs per person; add 2 tbsp. sour cream, 1 to 2 tbsp. grated Jarlsburg cheese. You can also add minced fresh basil, parsley if desired. Pour into oven-proof skillet coated with remaining 1/4 cup olive oil, and place on low burner to brown just a bit. Top with some salsa and bake in a 350 degree oven on middle shelf. The Frittata is done when the center is firm (approximately 15 minutes depending on the amount of eggs used). Cut into wedges and top with a dollop of sour cream and minced fresh basil if desired.

**Rates**
5 Rooms $157/$245 Racing Season $295/$400  Number of Rooms: 5

**Cuisine**
Guests can expect to find seasonal fresh fruit, ethnic entrees, fresh fruit cobblers, fresh baked scones, strudels, muffins, fresh-brewed coffee, an assortment of specially blended teas, afternoon refreshment. Menu changes daily.

**Nearest Airport(s)**
Albany International Airport

**Directions**
I87 take Exit 14 and bear R into Rte 29 to Saratoga Springs. 1st traffic light take a R onto Henning Ave-Rt. 29. Go approx 1 mi. At the light turn L onto Lake Ave (29W). We are at the corner of Lake Ave & Marion Place. Parking lot behind the house.

# Westchester House

www.westchesterhousebandb.com
102 Lincoln Ave., P.O. Box 944, Saratoga Springs, NY  12866
**800-579-8368** • 518-587-7613 • Fax 518-583-9562
innkeeper@westchesterhousebandb.com

*Member Since 1996*

*New York*

*Saratoga Springs*

*"A little gem that made us feel immediately welcomed.
The B&B was immaculate!"*

Owners/Innkeepers
**Bob & Stephanie Melvin**

Welcome to **Westchester House Bed & Breakfast** - Saratoga's hidden jewel. Nestled in a residential neighborhood of tree-lined streets and surrounded by exuberant gardens this enticing Victorian confection combines gracious hospitality, old-world ambiance and up-to-date comforts. Lace curtains, oriental carpets, high ceilings, the rich luster of natural woods, king-or queen-sized beds, tiled baths and luxury linens provide elegance and comfort. The charm and excitement of Saratoga is at our doorstep. After a busy day sampling the delights of Saratoga, relax on the wraparound porch, in the gardens, or in the parlour, and enjoy a refreshing glass of lemonade. Walk to thoroughbred race track, historic districts, downtown shopping, dining and entertainment, Spa State Park/SPAC. National Museums of Dance and Racing as well as Saratoga Automobile Museum and Skidmore College are less than a mile away. A short ride in the country to historic Saratoga Battlefield.

**Rates**
Queen and King beds. Customary $140/$250, Special Events $195/$295, Racing Season $285/$475. B&B Closed December and January. Number of Rooms: 7

**Cuisine**
Full cold breakfast includes fruit salad, platter of cold meat and cheeses, muffins and scones. A variety of excellent restaurants within easy walk of the Inn.

**Nearest Airport(s)**
Albany (commercial)

**Directions**
From South: 30 mi. N of Albany, I-87 to exit 13N. 4 mi. N to 6th traffic light. R (E) on Lincoln to 102. From North: I-87 to exit 14. R on Union Ave .4 mi. to 3rd traffic light. L (S) on Nelson 1 block to Lincoln. R (W) on Lincoln to 102.

# The Inn at Cooperstown

www.innatcooperstown.com
16 Chestnut Street, Cooperstown, NY 13326
**607-547-5756** • Fax 607-547-8779
info@innatcooperstown.com

*Member Since 1998*

*New York*

*Cooperstown*

*"Beautiful historic inn, meticulously maintained. Friendly, welcoming staff. We would come back at the proverbial drop of a hat."*

Innkeepers/Owners
**Marc and Sherrie Kingsley**

A stay at The Inn at Cooperstown is a special treat. This award-winning historic hotel is ideally situated to enjoy all that Cooperstown offers. The Inn was built in 1874, fully restored in 1985 and is thoughtfully improved upon every year. Spotless rooms are individually decorated with many charming touches. A relaxing atmosphere enables guests to escape the hectic pace of the modern world. After exploring the lovely village of Cooperstown, visitors unwind in rockers on The Inn's sweeping veranda or enjoy the fireplace in a cozy sitting room. Nearby streets are lined with historic buildings, interesting shops and restaurants. The National Baseball Hall of Fame is just two blocks from The Inn. It is a brief trolley ride to experience another century at The Farmers' Museum, where exhibits, a recreated village and costumed staff depict life over 150 years ago. Nearby, the Fenimore Art Museum displays a premier collection of Native American Indian art, American paintings and folk art. The Glimmerglass Opera, beautiful Otsego Lake and many other treasures are located just beyond the village.

**Rates**
Guest rooms have private bath, A/C, CD/clock radio, hair dryer, iron, wireless internet. Televisions in sitting rooms and suites. Standard: $105/$206, Premium: $131/$256, Suites: $178/$308, $350/$525. Open year-round. Number of Rooms: 18

**Cuisine**
Expanded continental breakfast, afternoon refreshments, and fine restaurants within walking distance.

**Nearest Airport(s)**
Albany, NY or Syracuse, NY.

**Directions**
Cooperstown is 70 mi. W of Albany. From the S, I-88 to exit 17 to Rte 28N, to 16 Chestnut St. From the W I-90 to exit 30 to Rte 28S, to The Inn. From the SE, I-87 to exit 21 to Rte 23W to Rte 145 to Rte 20W to Rte 80W to The Inn.

# Albergo Allegria

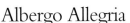

www.AlbergoUSA.com
43 Route 296, P.O. Box 267, Windham, NY 12496-0267
**518-734-5560** • Fax 518-734-5570
mail@AlbergoUSA.com

*Member Since 2001*

*New York*

*Windham*

*"This truly is the Inn of Happiness."*

Innkeepers/Owners
**Vito and Lenore Radelich**

Italian for the 'Inn of Happiness,' Albergo Allegria is an 1892 Inn set in the Northern Catskill Mountains. Situated on manicured lawns and country gardens, guests can relax under the 100 year old Oak tree or by the creek that is home to natural wildlife. The Inn's guestrooms offer beauty and history, while the Millenium, Master and Carriage House suites are gracious and inviting with whirlpool and fireplace. A full gourmet breakfast consisting of various frittatas, filled omelettes, Belgian waffles, stuffed French toast, and specialty pancakes are served hot from the kitchen. In addition, a marble side board filled with fresh fruit, homemade muffins, scones, granola and a variety of breads, cereals and juices are offered. Voted '2000 Inn of the Year' by author Pamela Lanier. AAA Four Diamond for 11 consecutive years.

**Rates**
14 Rooms, $83/$189 B&B; 8 Suites, $169/$299 B&B. Guestrooms have down comforters, modern amenities. Number of Rooms: 22

**Cuisine**
Hearty, full gourmet breakfast served each morning. 24-hour guest pantry with complimentary soft drinks, hot beverages and sweets. Afternoon tea served on Saturdays. Video Library with over 400 complimentary videos, Dinner restaurants nearby.

**Nearest Airport(s)**
Albany International Airport 50 miles North.

**Directions**
I-87 Exit 21 (Catskill). Take Rte. 23 W for 24 miles. L onto Rte. 296. 1/10 mile on L.

# Chestnut Inn

www.chestnutinn.com

498 Oquaga Lake Road, Deposit, NY 13754

**607-467-2500** • Fax 607-467-5911

chestnutinn@chestnutinn.com

*Member Since 2007*

*New York*

*Deposit*

*"We absolutely enjoyed ourselves! The atmosphere, people and food was above and beyond our expectations! We will be back!"*

General Manager
**James Briggs**

Situated on the calm waters of Oquaga Lake in the picturesque foothills of the Catskill Mountains, the Chestnut Inn offers guests the traditional charm of yesterday and the modern luxury of today. Built in 1928, the Inn's recent renovations provide guests with elegant accommodations and gourmet dining. The lobby is adorned with beautiful antique furniture around our signature massive stone fireplace. Original chestnut wood trims doorways throughout the Inn reminding guests of the Chestnut's long history. The Inn offers five deluxe rooms and 12 suites, each with luxury linens, private baths, plush bathrobes and slippers. Suites include two-person whirlpools. Three to five bedroom guest cottages are available to rent on property. Enjoy dinner in our enclosed Sun Room overlooking the lake, or head to the Waterside Tavern for cocktails and more casual fare. Tour Oquaga Lake by boat in one of our canoes or paddle boats, or settle in on the dock with a good book. Stop in the gift shop, or visit the Children's Playroom for a variety of crafts and games. Located just a short drive from area golf courses, AA baseball, historic & local museums, wineries, theater and more! Conference and Wedding facilities available.

**Rates**
5 Rooms, 12 Suites, $169/$279. All with private bath (suites w/ Jacuzzi), Cable TV, Wireless Internet, BOSE Radio, Heat, A/C. Open Year Round. Guest Cottages on property for rental. Non-smoking property. No pets, please. Number of Rooms: 17

**Cuisine**
Fine Dining Restaurant and Waterside Tavern. Continental Breakfast included. Dinner served seven days a week. Lunch served seasonally.

**Nearest Airport(s)**
Binghamton Regional Airport

**Directions**
Rt.17 to Exit 82 McClure/Sanford. If traveling E turn right off the exit ramp. If traveling W, turn L off the exit ramp. Make a L and continue for 1/2 mile. Take the first R on to Oquaga Lake Rd. and travel 2 1/2 miles up. Follow the signs. Chestnut Inn is on the L. Valet Parking at bottom of driveway.

# Mill House Inn

www.millhouseinn.com
31 North Main Street, East Hampton, NY 11937
**631-324-9766** • Fax 631-324-9793
innkeeper@millhouseinn.com

*Member Since 2002*

New York

East Hampton

*"Finally a place in The Hamptons where I can be truly comfortable. Gary is an amazing chef... Plain breakfast will no longer do. And a good dog fix, too!"*

Proprietors
**Sylvia & Gary Muller, Lee Ellis**

Our historic inn, named one of America's Top 50 Small Hotels in the Zagat 2008 Hotel Suvey, is located in the heart of East Hampton, 'America's most beautiful village.' Surrounded by spectacular ocean beaches, pristine bays, ospreys nesting over sparkling estuaries and quiet country roads, the East End of Long Island is a fisherman's playground, a vintner's paradise and an artist's inspiration. Enjoy foggy mornings, lazy days, blazing sunsets and starry nights. Walk to world-class restaurants, shops, galleries and theatres. Take a scenic drive to all that the Hamptons have to offer - Montauk's fishing boats, Sag Harbor's quaint antique shops, Bridgehampton's wineries and Southampton's magnificent mansions! Curl up on cozy leather sofas, relax in amazingly comfortable Adirondack chairs on our front porch overlooking the Old Hook Windmill, or sneak away for a bit of solitude in our lush gardens. Spacious dog-friendly suites, luxurious baths, fine linens, lofty featherbeds, down quilts and pillows, gas fireplaces, a leisurely breakfast our guests proclaim 'simply the best' and our old-fashioned hospitality assure you a memorable stay.

**Rates**
Rooms $225/$750. Suites $450/$1195. Queen or King bed, private bath, gas fireplace. Number of Rooms: 10

**Cuisine**
Our guests call Gary's menu "THE breakfast" & there are over 20 reasons why! Among them: crayfish & andouille etouffee, house-cured salmon & goat cheese pizza, chicken sausage & wild mushroom hash, "uncle shorty's breakfast" & "the bb&t sandwich."

**Nearest Airport(s)**
MacArthur (ISP) 50 miles

**Directions**
Rte 495 E to Exit 70. Right on Rte 111 S to end. Left on Rte 27 E. Go approx 30 miles into East Hampton Village. Just past Newtown Lane bear left onto North Main St. We are on the left directly across from the windmill.

# *North Carolina*

## "The Tar Heel State"

Famous for: Blue Ridge Mountains, Smoky Mountains, Outer Banks, Roanoke Island, Cape Hatteras, Kitty Hawk, Tobacco, Textiles, Furniture.

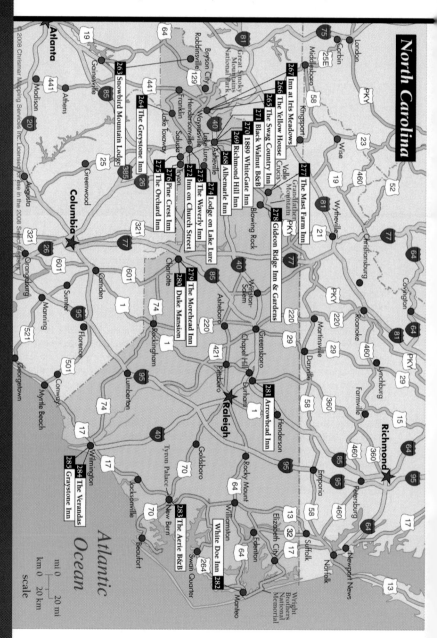

263 Snowbird Mountain Lodge
264 The Greystone Inn
265 The Yellow House
266 Inn at Iris Meadows
267 Inn at Iris Meadows
268 Richmond Hill Inn
269 1889 WhiteGate Inn
270 1889 WhiteGate Inn
271 Black Walnut B&B
272 Inn on Church Street
273 The Waverly Inn
274 Lodge on Lake Lure
275 Pine Crest Inn
276 The Orchard Inn
277 The Mast Farm Inn
278 Gideon Ridge Inn & Gardens
279 The Morehead Inn
280 Duke Mansion
281 Arrowhead Inn
282 White Doe Inn
283 The Aerie B&B
284 The Verandas
285 Graystone Inn

## Atlantic Ocean

scale

mi 0    20 mi
km 0    20 km

SelectRegistry.com

# Snowbird Mountain Lodge

www.snowbirdlodge.com
4633 Santeetlah Rd., Robbinsville, NC 28771
**800-941-9290** • 828-479-3433 • Fax 828-479-3473
innkeeper@snowbirdlodge.com

*Member Since 1973*

*North Carolina*

*Robbinsville*

*"...an unspoiled, hidden vacation oasis tucked away in the Southern Appalachians."*

Innkeepers/Owners
**Karen & Robert Rankin**

High up in Santeetlah Gap, on the Southern border of the Great Smoky Mountains National Park, lies this secluded, rustic yet elegant, historic lodge built of stone and huge chestnut logs. Offering the finest in modern convenience and traditional comfort, Snowbird is the perfect retreat from the pressures of a busy world. The view from the lovely mountaintop terrace is one of the best in the Smokies. An excellent library, huge stone fireplaces, tennis courts and hiking trails on 100 acres of forest with numerous "quiet getaway" spots, offer guests a rare chance to relax. Award-winning gourmet cuisine and a lovely fireside bar with an exceptionally well-stocked wine cellar will have you looking forward to your next meal. Whether it's fly-fishing, hiking, biking, or just relaxing in front of the fire, we can make your next trip to the mountains picture-perfect. It's no wonder that guests have been coming to Snowbird to relax and renew themselves for over 60 years.

**Rates**
23 Rooms, $180-$365 FAP. In-room fireplaces, air conditioning, whirlpool tubs, steam showers and private hot tubs available. Number of Rooms: 23

**Cuisine**
Full gourmet breakfast, packed picnic lunch and four course gourmet dinner.

**Nearest Airport(s)**
Knoxville, Atlanta

**Directions**
From Robbinsville take Highway 143 W. 10.5 miles to the Snowbird Mountain Lodge.

# The Greystone Inn

www.greystoneinn.com
Greystone Lane, Lake Toxaway, NC  28747
**800-587-5351** • 828-966-4700 • Fax 828-862-5689
info@greystoneinn.com

*Member Since 1991*

*North Carolina*

*Lake Toxaway*

---

*Rated one of the best hotels/resorts in the world by both Travel + Leisure and
Condé Nast Traveler magazines.  AAA Four-Diamond rated.*

---

Owner
**Reg Heinitsh, Jr.**

All of the intimacies of a AAA Four Diamond, historic (National Register) inn with the luxurious amenities of a full service resort are combined on North Carolina's largest private mountain lake. Exceptionally romantic, highlights include a pampering spa, championship golf (complimentary certain times of the year) including a Tom Fazio designed golf learning center, guided hikes and full lake activities. Included in your rate are afternoon tea and cakes on the sun porch just before our signature evening champagne lake cruise on our 26-passenger mahogany launch "Miss Lucy." Also included is a sumptuous 7-course gourmet evening meal and complete high-country breakfast. Clay tennis courts and fully equipped health and fitness center complement the nearby mountain resort experiences. Each guestroom is unique with amenities that include gas and wood fireplaces, private porches, oversized Jacuzzi tubs, wet bars and more. Wireless high-speed internet available throughout the campus. Personal guest recognition and exceptional service are our hallmark.

---

**Rates**
30 Rooms, $290/$560 MAP; 3 Suites, $440/$640 MAP;
Includes boats & most recreational activities. Open year-round,
except week days Dec./Mar.  Number of Rooms: 33

**Cuisine**
Includes full breakfast, bottled water and soft drinks, afternoon tea, hors d' oeuvres, & gourmet dinner. Great wine list; liquor available.

**Nearest Airport(s)**
Asheville Regional

**Directions**
*From I-40 in Asheville, I-26E, 9mi, Rte 280S 20mi to Brevard, US-64W 20mi to Lake Toxaway Country Club/Greystone Inn sign. Right turn at entrance & gatehouse, proceed 3.5mi to Inn. Specific directions from other locations available on website.

# The Swag Country Inn

www.theswag.com
2300 Swag Road, Waynesville, NC  28785
**800-789-7672** • 828-926-0430 • Fax 828-926-2036
swaginnkeeper@earthlink.net

*Member Since 1991*

*"The Swag is an experience maker. How can you improve upon The Swag?!?"*

Innkeeper/Owner
**Deener and Dan Matthews**

Where stress disappears ... has an address ... 30 miles west of Asheville. The Swag Country Inn is an intimate hideaway that invites you to discover the wonders of nature just steps from your bedroom. The Swag is where our favorite amenity, nature, meets the luxury resort. The Great Smoky Mountains National Park shares an old split rail fence boundary with our inn that stretches more than a mile. The spectacular beauty of our Appalachian high country is captured architecturally in the historic hand-hewn logs and local field stone design. Our construction was inspired by the past while built for the future. Our hidden and secluded mountain top setting opens to you treasures the crowds have yet to find. It all starts to unfold at the bottom of our mountain where the pavement stops, our gate opens, and your romantic adventure begins. The Swag -- a small luxury resort as the Appalachians used to be.

**Rates**
12 Rooms $430/$645; 3 Cabins/Suites $650/$750; AP. Open late April through mid-November.  Number of Rooms: 15

**Cuisine**
A not-to-be-missed hors d'oeuvre hour precedes superb cuisine nightly. All 3 meals are included for two people in the room rate. We are in a dry county. Guests are welcome to bring their own spirits.

**Nearest Airport(s)**
Asheville, NC, Knoxville, TN and Greenville, SC

**Directions**
Via Interstate 40: North Carolina on I-40. Exit #20 onto Hwy. 276 for 2.8 mi. R on Grindstone Rd. At stop sign turn R onto Hemphill Rd. Four miles up blacktopped road, L on Swag Road. 2.5 miles up our gravel road to the inn at 5,000 feet.

*North Carolina*

*Waynesville*

# The Yellow House on Plott Creek Road

www.theyellowhouse.com
89 Oakview Drive, Waynesville, NC  28786
**800-563-1236** • 828-452-0991 • Fax 828-452-1140
info@theyellowhouse.com

*Member Since 1998*

*"Our first visit was like a fairy tale. This visit was like a dream come true."*

Innkeepers/Owners
**Susan Cerise and Don Cerise**

A European-style inn of casual elegance, the 19th century Yellow House accents fine service in a romantic, intimate setting. Located a mile from the lovely mountain community of Waynesville, NC, the inn sits atop a knoll 3,000 feet above sea level. Five beautifully landscaped acres of lawns and gardens feature two ponds, a waterfall, a footbridge and a deck. The Inn offers three rooms and seven suites, each with luxury linens, private bath, gas fireplace, coffee service, refrigerator and bathrobes; suites also have wet bar and 2-person jetted tub. Most accommodations include private balcony or patio. The Yellow House offers a quiet rural setting with exceptional views, soothing music, and complimentary wireless internet service for guests. Minutes from the Blue Ridge Parkway, Great Smoky Mountains National Park, Pisgah National Forest, Cherokee Indian Reservation, Cataloochee horseback riding and ski area, and Maggie Valley. Close to four mountain golf courses, Asheville and the spectacular Biltmore Estate.

**Rates**
3 Rooms, 7 Suites, $175-$275. Seasonal Rates and Packages Available.  Number of Rooms: 10

**Cuisine**
Gourmet breakfast each morning served en suite, on private balcony, verandah or dining room depending on accommodation; appetizers each evening.Picnics available by request.

**Nearest Airport(s)**
Asheville (AVL) Greenville/Spartanburg (GSP)

**Directions**
From the S, take exit 100 (Hazelwood Ave) off US 23/74. Proceed to the L for 1 1/2 mi. on Plott Creek Rd. From the N, exit 100 (Hazelwood Ave) from US 23/74, turn R on Eagles Nest Rd, L on Will Hyatt, R on Plott Creek Rd.

# Inn at Iris Meadows

www.irismeadows.com
304 Love Lane, Waynesville, NC 28786
**888-466-4747** • 828-456-3877 • Fax 828-456-3847
info@irismeadows.com

*Member Since 2006*

*"We came for a few days and wanted to spend the rest of our lives."*

Innkeepers/Owners
**George and Becky Fain**

Nestled high upon over 5 acres of rolling meadows and iris gardens with commanding views of the picturesque town of Waynesville and the surrounding mountains, this stately inn is the perfect destination for romantic getaways, honeymoons, celebrations, and relaxing escapes. Seven lavishly appointed guest rooms, all with fireplaces, private designer baths, large jetted tubs, heavenly king/queen beds, fluffy robes, TV/VCR/DVDs, phones, high speed wireless Internet, air conditioning, and intriguing antiques. A meticulously restored turn-of-the-century Greek Revival mansion in Waynesville's historic Love Lane neighborhood, Iris Meadows has spacious gathering areas including a library, music room, grand halls with leaded glass doors throughout, intricate wood work, carved mantels, and wraparound porches. Chosen as "one of our new favorites" by the Atlanta Journal Constitution's 2006 "Go Guide" of southern retreats and one of the Palm Beach Daily Post's "Seven Southern Spots to Sit a Spell." Walking distance of 1/2 mile to area shops, galleries, and fine restaurants; just minutes to the Blue Ridge Parkway; a half hour to Asheville.

**Rates**
$225/$275 weeknights; $250/$300 weekends, holidays, & October. Number of Rooms: 7

**Cuisine**
A bountiful breakfast is included in room rates. Complimentary beverages, cookies in guest kitchen which includes coffee service, guest refrigerator, microwave.

**Nearest Airport(s)**
Asheville Greenville SC

**Directions**
From Asheville I-40W to Exit 27 to US 23/74; 5 miles to Exit 102 to Russ Ave. R at 2nd light to Dellwood Rd; R on Love Lane. From Atlanta, 441 N from Clayton to Dillsboro, NC; US 23/74 to Exit 102, etc. From Knoxville hwy 40 E 75 mi to Exit 20/US 276 to hwy 19; L 4 mi, R on 276/Russ Ave, etc.

# Albemarle Inn
www.albemarleinn.com
86 Edgemont Road, Asheville, NC 28801-1544
**800-621-7435** • 828-255-0027 • Fax 828-236-3397
info@albemarleinn.com

*Member Since 2002*

*North Carolina*

*Asheville*

> *"Can't imagine a more perfect stay...snuggly robes, dreamy mattresses & mouthwatering menus. Takes breakfast to an entirely new dimension."*

Innkeepers/Owners
**Cathy and Larry Sklar**

A classic turn-of-the-century Southern mansion on the National Register, the Albemarle Inn offers elegance in a warm and inviting atmosphere. Guests are greeted in the main parlor which glows with recently restored oak wainscoting. An intricately carved staircase leads to period guest rooms, appointed with antiques, fresh flowers, and cozy robes. Morning begins with coffee or tea by the Arts & Crafts style marble fireplace, followed by a gourmet breakfast on the enclosed, plant-filled sunporch. Late afternoon offers the opportunity to relax on the massive stone veranda overlooking lush gardens while enjoying refreshments and conversation. Near downtown and the Biltmore Estate.

**Rates**
$130/$375, B&B. Elegantly appointed period rooms w/claw-foot tubs, fine linens, fresh flowers & turndown service w/chocolates. Rooms w/whirlpool tub, fireplace or private balcony available. Open year round. Number of Rooms: 11

**Cuisine**
Full gourmet breakfast at private tables, late afternoon refreshments on the veranda, complimentary beverages.

**Nearest Airport(s)**
Asheville/Hendersonvillle Airport (AVL)

**Directions**
From I-26 or I-40: to I-240, Exit 5-B (Charlotte St.). Travel 1 mi. N on Charlotte St. to Edgemont Rd. Turn R on Edgemont & proceed to the end of the street to the inn.

# Richmond Hill Inn

www.richmondhillinn.com
87 Richmond Hill Dr., Asheville, NC 28806
**888-742-4550** • 828-252-7313 • Fax 828-252-8726
reservations@richmondhillinn.com

*Member Since 1991*

*Voted Top 3 Country Inns by Southern Living*

Wine Spectator AWARD OF EXCELLENCE

AAA *Four Diamond Award*

Innkeepers
**Susie Zimmerman and Sara Hodgdon**

Romance is encouraged every moment. The 1889 mansion is perched on a hillside, and each room is uniquely decorated and furnished with antiques. Charming cottages surround a croquet court and feature fireplaces and porch rockers. Each of the spacious rooms in the Garden Pavilion offers beautiful views of the Parterre Garden, waterfall, and mansion. Stroll through gardens by the cascading brook. Relax at afternoon tea in the stately Oak Hall. Savor an exquisite dinner in Gabrielle's, our AAA Four Diamond restaurant, featuring an extensive wine list.

**Rates**
33 Rooms, 2 family cottages and 4 Suites, $205/$615.
Number of Rooms: 39

**Cuisine**
Full breakfast and afternoon tea included. Gabrielle's fine dining in the historic mansion. The Ambassador's Grille and Gabrielle's available for groups, Weddings and private functions. Extensive award-winning wine list.

**Nearest Airport(s)**
Asheville Regional Airport

**Directions**
Take Highway 251 exit on US Highway 19/23, three miles NW from downtown. Follow signs.

# 1889 WhiteGate Inn and Cottage

www.whitegate.net
173 East Chestnut Street, Asheville, NC 28801
**800-485-3045** • 828-253-2553 • Fax 828-281-1883
innkeeper@whitegate.net

*Member Since 2005*

*"It's like waking up to a beautiful dream every morning. A healing place for the mind, body, and soul. The gardens are breathtaking."*

Innkeepers/Owners
**Ralph Coffey and Frank Salvo**

Romance, elegance and tranquility describe the ambiance at the 1889 WhiteGate Inn and Cottage. The Inn is listed on the National Register of Historic Places, and is minutes from the Biltmore Estate and nestled in The Blue Ridge Mountains. Enjoy a special place for your special moments. Sumptuous breakfasts begin your day. Luxurious spa suites with two-person Jacuzzi tubs and fireplaces set the tone for romance. Wander the stunning award winning gardens or stroll to shops and restaurants in Asheville, less than a five-minute walk. Enjoy the ultimate in luxurious accommodations in our new Carriage House. Rooms include a complete handicapped accessible suite. All rooms will have King beds, two person whirlpools, seperate showers and stone fireplaces.A new spa room will have workout equipment, a dry sauna, and room for couples massages.

**Rates**
$125/$369. Separate cottage with full kitchen, on site orchid greenhouse, gym and dry sauna. Closest Inn to downtown.
Number of Rooms: 9

**Cuisine**
Full 3 Course Gourmet Breakfast, Late afternoon refreshments, Complimentary Beverages and Snacks

**Nearest Airport(s)**
Asheville

**Directions**
From I-40 or I-26 to I-240 Exit 5B (Charlotte Street) Proceed north on Charlotte; turn LEFT on E. Chestnut Go one block. Turn LEFT onto Central. Turn into the first driveway on the right. Parking is behind the greenhouse in the lower lot.

SelectRegistry.com

# Black Walnut Bed & Breakfast

www.blackwalnut.com
288 Montford Avenue, Asheville, NC 28801
**800-381-3878** • 828-254-3878 • Fax 828-254-3875
info@blackwalnut.com

*Member Since 2007*

*North Carolina*

*Asheville*

*"This is better than the Relais et Chateau we stayed in Europe! You out-do yourselves with food and wine and we loved the stories! We will be back..."*

Innkeepers/Owners
**Peter and Lori White**

The perfect in-town location in the heart of the Historic District of Montford. Within walking distance to the shops, restaurants and galleries of the city. Surrounded by manicured gardens and waterfall Koi ponds. Relax in the rockers on the porch, or the terrace when the weather is fair, or enjoy a fire in one of the 11 fireplaces. All guest rooms are complete with private bath en-suite and King or Queen luxury kingsdown mattresses, most with working fireplaces and Jacuzzis. Fresh flowers, chocolates and luxury bedding compliment the antiques. Indulge in a gourmet 3-course breakfast with homemade pastries, fruit and hot entree. Your innkeepers have more than 50 years of experience as professional bakers and chefs! In the late afternoon, relax with complimentary fine wines and hors'douvres with your hosts. We are always happy to help with suggestions, recommendations and reservations!

**Rates**
6 rooms in the main house, 1 pet-friendly suite located in the carriage house. $170/$280. Full breakfast, complimentary beverages, Wi-Fi, computer station, afternoon tea included. Off season rates available. Open all Year. Number of Rooms: 7

**Cuisine**
Decadent 3 course breakfasts. Afternoon tea with selection of fine wines and hot and cold hors'douvres, homemade pastries. 24 hour complimentary beverages.

**Nearest Airport(s)**
Asheville (AVL)

**Directions**
From I-40 or I-26 to 240 to Asheville, exit 4C off 240, R on Haywood and R on Montford. 1/2 mile on L, #288. Off street parking in rear.

# Inn on Church Street

www.innonchurch.com
201 3rd Ave West, Hendersonville, NC 28739
**800-330-3836** • 828-693-3258 • Fax 828-693-7263
inncarolina@innonchurch.com

*Member Since 2003*

*North Carolina*

*Hendersonville*

---

*"We have traveled & dined around the world and Inn On Church Street's beautiful decor, fabulous food & award-winning wine list make it a must visit!"*

Innkeepers/Owners
**Brenda and Steve Merrefield**

A beautiful mountain inn of distinction, located in the heart of historic downtown Hendersonville, walking distance to all shops and events, and just moments away from mountain adventures. Listed on the National Register of Historic Places. Our 1921 three story brick inn has guest rooms graciously decorated in a European Boutique style. Relax in the rocking chairs on our wrap around porch and enjoy dinner in our excellent restaurant in cozy dining rooms or on the porch. Celebrate the next morning with the Chef's country breakfast. The perfect getaway for vacationers and business travelers alike. Relax as our knowledgeable staff show you their Southern hospitality for a memorable experience.

**Gold Medal Winner, Select Registry's "Inn-credible Breakfast Cook-off" in 2007.**

**Rates**
19 guest rooms beginning at $99 off-season. In-season rates range from $129-$179, 2 suites -$250, and adjacent 2 bedroom Juniper House at $275($1400 per week). All rates include a full breakfast. Number of Rooms: 23

**Cuisine**
Experience our culinary team's award-winning cuisine where we marry natural products and techniques w/locally harvested organics. Choose from the Inn's list of over 70 global wines. Consistent winner of Wine Spectator Award.

**Nearest Airport(s)**
Asheville, NC

**Directions**
Hwy 26 exit 49 to downtown Hendersonville. L on Church St. to the corner of Church & 3rd Ave.

SelectRegistry.com

# The Waverly Inn

www.waverlyinn.com
783 North Main Street, Hendersonville, NC 28792
**800-537-8195** • 828-693-9193 • Fax 828-692-1010
register@waverlyinn.com

*Member Since 1991*

*North Carolina*

*Hendersonville*

*"Everything from the delicious full breakfast to the comfortable bed was perfect!
We come back every year because of John, Diane, and Darla's hospitality."*

Innkeepers
**John & Diane Sheiry,
Darla Olmstead & Debbie Jones**

Located in the beautiful Blue Ridge Mountains of Western North Carolina, the Inn is a short drive from the Biltmore Estate, Blue Ridge Parkway, Dupont State Forest, Chimney Rock Park, and the Flat Rock Playhouse. Cited in national publications such as *The New York Times* and *Southern Living*, we received high praise in *Vogue* Magazine for our "southern breakfast" with your choice of fresh fruit, omelets, french toast, pancakes with real maple syrup, grits, meats, farm fresh eggs and egg substitutes. Special touches like luxury sheets and towels, Shelbourne mattress pillowtops, robes, free wireless Internet, DVD players, and cable TV make our $189-$285 rates a real value. The Inn is within walking distance of the Mast General Store, several fine restaurants, exceptional shopping, and antiquing. Two porches with rocking chairs await you. *The New York Times* suggests that you "arrive early enough to sit outside and enjoy the descending darkness." "Come experience hospitality as it was meant to be."

**Rates**
13 Rooms, $189/$219 B&B; Suite, $245/$285 B&B. Seasonal & promotional specials appear regularly on our web site at www.waverlyinn.com. Number of Rooms: 14

**Cuisine**
Full breakfast each morning. A wide variety of beverages are available 24 hours a day. Darla's freshly baked delectables each afternoon. Evening social hour 5-6 p.m. Guests are welcome to bring their own spirits.

**Nearest Airport(s)**
Asheville (AVL)
Greenville-Spartanburg, SC (GSP)

**Directions**
From I-26, take NC Exit 49B, then U.S. 64W for 2 miles into Hendersonville. Bear Right onto Route 25N for 500 yards. Inn is on Left.

# Lodge on Lake Lure

www.lodgeonlakelure.com
P.O. Box 519, 361 Charlotte Drive, Lake Lure, NC 28746
**800-733-2785** • 828-625-2789 • Fax 828-625-2421
info@lodgeonlakelure.com

*Member Since 2003*

*"Exquisite rooms, dining and service have made this our favorite place in the mountains! Lovely surroundings. Stay was super. Very helpful and friendly."*

Innkeeper/Owner
**Giselle Hopke**

Along the shores of majestic Lake Lure in the Blue Ridge Mountains, you can golf, hike, boat, fish, ride horses, or just lounge and be spoiled at this elegant seventeen-room getaway with fabulous views, stone fireplace, terraces and distinctive dining. A wonderful combination of an elegant country inn and a casual bed and breakfast, the Lodge is situated on the hillside to afford a sweeping view of the lake and mountains. All guest rooms have beautiful private bathrooms and have been individually decorated with antiques. Many rooms have terraces or balconies overlooking the lake. During the warmer months, swim, boat and fish from our beautiful lakeside dock. North Carolina Our State Magazine named us one of the 21 perfect places to stay.

**Rates**
17 Guest Rooms. $160/289, based on single or double occupancy. Rate increases during peak weekends.   Number of Rooms: 17

**Cuisine**
Price includes a full breakfast, afternoon coffee, tea and pastries, and evening wine and hors d'oeuvres.

**Nearest Airport(s)**
Asheville Regional, Greenville-Spartanburg, Charlotte

**Directions**
The Lodge is located on Lake Lure, just off of Highway 64/74A in scenic Hickory Nut Gorge, 30 miles SE of Asheville.

# The Orchard Inn

www.orchardinn.com
Highway 176, P.O. Box 128, Saluda, NC 28773-0128
**800-581-3800** • 828-749-5471 • Fax 828-749-9805
innkeeper@orchardinn.com

*Member Since 1985*

*North Carolina*

*Saluda*

*"I feel like I'm letting folks in on a special secret when I tell them about this Inn."*

Innkeepers/Owners
**Kathy & Bob Thompson**

No matter where you start, The Orchard Inn is a perfect destination. Situated on a 20-acre mountaintop with stunning views, this national historic structure has long been a favorite retreat with its wraparound porches and large, inviting living room with stone fireplace. Guest quarters are furnished with period pieces and antiques. Private cottages feature fireplaces, whirlpools and private decks. Enjoy award-winning cuisine while overlooking the gardens, vineyard and mountains. Walk to waterfalls; hike nearby trails; watch the birds; visit Biltmore Estate, Carl Sandburg's home or local craft galleries; then, experience the peace and tranquility of this gracious retreat. Wedding and Group packages available.

**Rates**
9 Rooms, $125/$195 B&B; 5 Cottages, $175/$425 B&B. All rooms have private baths, some with whirlpool and steam shower. Open year-round. Number of Rooms: 14

**Cuisine**
A full breakfast is included in room rate. Award-winning cuisine served by reservation Thurs-Sat evenings. Fine wines and beer available. Listed as a "Food Find" by *Southern Living*.

**Nearest Airport(s)**
Asheville, NC

**Directions**
Airports Asheville and Charlotte NC and Greenville/Sptnbg SC to I-26. From I-26, take Exit 59 (Old Exit 28)/Saluda NC. Head WEST up hill 1 mile to Hwy 176. Turn LEFT on Hwy 176, and the Inn will be 1/2 mile on right.

🍴 🍴 🍴 🍷

# 1906 Pine Crest Inn & Restaurant

www.pinecrestinn.com
85 Pine Crest Lane, Tryon, NC 28782
**800-633-3001** • 828-859-9135 • Fax 828-859-9136
select@pinecrestinn.com

*Member Since 1991*

*North Carolina*

*Tryon*

*"We loved the idyllic mountain solitude & beautiful flower gardens, but the impeccable Southern hospitality made our stay!" "Comfort for your soul!"*

Innkeeper/Owner
**Carl Caudle**

Imagine a 245-year old romantic cabin so captivating that it inspired the writings of literary greats F. Scott Fitzgerald & Ernest Hemingway. Picture sunlight flowing through the vaulted ceiling skylight in your intimate cottage that was once the studio for a renowned portrait artist in the 1920s. Envision a relaxing evening on our verandas sipping tea or your favorite scotch from our collection of over 30 single-malts & watching the sun sink behind the beautiful Blue Ridge Mountains. Championship golf, superb art & antique shopping, waterfall hikes & winery tours, intimate couples massage... these experiences & more can be found at an inviting, distinctive retreat nestled in Historic Tryon just south of Asheville. Recognized in Southern Living, Fodor's, Our State Magazine, & listed on the National Historic Registry with 13 consecutive 4-Diamond awards, the hospitality of the "Hidden Gem of Tryon" embraces our guests as they create memories that will last a lifetime. Even with all the abundance of natural beauty, your eyes will still envy your taste buds! Renowned for our "Best Breakfast in the Southeast," exceptional fine dining, wine tastings & celebrity wine dinners. Our cellar has received the coveted Wine Spectator Best of Award of Excellence. Inquire about our romance packages, destination weddings, reunions, or executive retreats & planning sessions in our modern conference center.

**Rates**
20 Rooms $99/219; 8 Suites $179/279; 4 Cottages $179/599.
Open year-round. Seasonal specials & packages on website.
Number of Rooms: 32

**Cuisine**
Sumptuous, made-to-order 3-course breakfast that can be served in bed. Distinctive a la carte dinner menu with regional accents, organic ingredients & fresh herbs from our gardens. Afternoon tea, award-winning wine list, & evening port & sherry. Candlelight room service.

**Nearest Airport(s)**
Greenville (GSP), Asheville (AVL), Charlotte (CLT)

**Directions**
From CLT & ATL, I-85 to I-26 W. From AVL I-26 E. Exit 67 off I-26 in Columbus. Follow Hwy 108 4 mi. to Tryon. Turn L onto New Market Rd. 1/8 mi. & turn L onto Pine Crest Ln.

SelectRegistry.com

# The Mast Farm Inn

www.MastFarmInn.com
2543 Broadstone Road, P.O. Box 704, Valle Crucis, NC 28691
**888-963-5857** • 828-963-5857 • Fax 828-963-6404
stay@mastfarminn.com

*Member Since 1988*

*North Carolina*

*Valle Crucis*

*"...genuine warmth and hospitality...a unique inn
that is wonderfully regional...delightful"*

Innkeepers/Owners
**Sandra Siano Danielle Deschamps**

The Mast Farm Inn is more than a bed and breakfast, with inn rooms, private getaway cottages, fine dining and great wines, organic gardens, and unique gifts completing our historic country appeal. The key to the Inn's success, however, lies in the exceptionally friendly and caring service offered to lodging and dinner guests alike. With inspired restoration and continuing care, the Inn continues to welcome guests, as it did over 100 years ago. Choose from eight guest rooms in our 1880s farmhouse and seven cottages, some restored from original farm buildings. Cottages range in size from cozy ones suitable for a couple to large ones for up to six guests. All are unique spaces. The inn's restaurant is celebrated, enjoyed by lodging guests and locals. The service is attentive, yet relaxed and friendly. Enjoy fireside or terrace dining, depending on the season. The current innkeepers place special emphasis on the environment, creating a "green" inn where recycling, reducing waste, and buying organic produce locally are taken seriously.

**Rates**
8 guest rooms: $145/$250. 7 private cottages: $225/$450.
Number of Rooms: 15

**Cuisine**
Full 2-course gourmet breakfast included with lodging. Dinner features fresh, organic delightfully creative cuisine. Dining schedule varies seasonally. Fine wines & beer available. Private parties.

**Nearest Airport(s)**
Greensboro (GSO) or Charlotte (CLT)

**Directions**
Boone/Blowing Rock/Banner Elk area. From E & S: turn at V.C. sign on 105 betw Boone & Linville. Inn is 2.5 mi from 105 on Broadstone Rd. From W & N: take 194 from 321/421 west of Boone. In V.C., continue STRAIGHT on Broadstone Rd. to the Inn, 1/4 mile on the right.

# Gideon Ridge Inn

www.gideonridge.com
202 Gideon Ridge Rd., P.O. Box 1929, Blowing Rock, NC 28605
**888-889-4036** • 828-295-3644 • Fax 828-295-4586
Innkeeper@gideonridge.com

*Member Since 1990*

*North Carolina*

*Blowing Rock*

> *"I always find magical moments at Gideon Ridge Inn... Such elegance and intimacy... The views of the mountains are truly spectacular."*

Innkeepers/Owners
**Cindy & Cobb Milner**

Gideon Ridge Inn is ten delightful guest rooms with mountain breezes, French doors and stone terraces. Ceiling fans and wicker chairs. Antiques and good books. Bedrooms with warm fireplaces and comfortable sitting areas. Crisp cotton bed linens and well-appointed bathrooms. Suites with whirlpool tubs and king beds.

Fine breakfasts to linger over. Afternoon tea with fresh-baked shortbread to savor. Evening dining at Restaurant G, where traditional European cuisine meets the classic American steak house.

And in the library, a piano with a breathtaking view of the mountains. Really...

Guests enjoy hiking and walking the Blue Ridge Parkway. Golf at nearby clubs. Shopping and dining at Blowing Rock Village shops & restaurants. Biking in summer and skiing in winter.

**Rates**
10 Rooms, including 3 Deluxe Suites, and 3 Terrace Rooms.
9 rooms have fireplaces. 4 have whirlpools. All rooms B&B.
$155/$315. Open year-round. Number of Rooms: 10

**Cuisine**
Full breakfast included, featuring cornmeal pancakes,
blueberry-stuffed French Toast or other signature entrees.
Afternoon tea with fresh-made shortbread cookies or scones.
Dinner served Tu.-Sat.. Cocktails & full wine list.

**Nearest Airport(s)**
Charlotte; Greensboro

**Directions**
US 321, 1.5 mi. S of Village of Blowing Rock, turn on Rock Rd.
across from Green Park Inn. 1st L on Gideon Ridge Rd. Go to
top of the ridge.Only 2 miles from the Blue Ridge Parkway.

# The Morehead Inn

www.moreheadinn.com
1122 East Morehead Street, Charlotte, NC  28204
**888-MOREHEAD** • 704-376-3357 • Fax 704-335-1110
reservation@moreheadinn.com

*Member Since 2002*

*"Everything was perfect--the room, the breakfast and, most of all, the staff! The Morehead Inn is the only place I'll stay when I'm in the Carolinas."*

Innkeeper/Owner - **Billy Maddalon**
Guest Service Manager - **Linda Kiss**

Located in Charlotte's oldest neighborhood, known as Dilworth, the inn is one mile from the center of the uptown business district. The historic home was built in 1917, by a businessman who required a wonderful place in which to entertain. Today, the inn stands as Charlotte's finest example of Southern hospitality. The Morehead Inn offers six suites and six guest rooms, each with luxurious private baths, color cable TV, and period antiques. All guest rooms have hi-speed and wireless internet access. The inn's public areas feature intimate fireplaces and grand twelve-foot ceilings. Guests may walk or jog the quiet, stately streets of our affluent community, or walk to an array of wonderful dining. Our guests are also afforded complimentary access to the fitness center and pool of the YMCA, which is located five blocks from the inn. A full Southern breakfast is served each morning and your shoes will be shined each evening. You will discover why Charlotteans refer to The Morehead Inn as 'Charlotte's most unique southern estate.'

**Rates**
6 Rooms $130/$160 6 Suites $179/$219. All rooms are elegantly appointed w/ period antiques & private baths. Open year-round.  Number of Rooms: 12

**Cuisine**
Full breakfast consists of fresh-baked breads and pastries, waffles, eggs & fresh fruits. Full bar is service available with a substantial wine list.

**Nearest Airport(s)**
Charlotte-Douglas Int'l

**Directions**
From I-77 S: Exit at Morehead St. Take L onto Morehead St., Inn is on R, one and one half miles. From I-77 N: take I-277, Exit Kenilworth Ave. Take R onto Kenilworth. Take R onto Morehead St. Inn will be on L, 200 yards. From I-85: Take I-77 S.

# The Duke Mansion
www.dukemansion.com
400 Hermitage Road, Charlotte, NC 28207
**888-202-1009** • 704-714-4400 • Fax 704-714-4435
frontdesk@tlwf.org

*"We truly felt like we were guests in an elegant Southern home."*

General Manager
**Tim Miron**

The Duke Mansion, built in 1915 and listed on the National Register of Historic Places, offers 20 unique guest rooms in true Southern splendor with a full breakfast. The rooms are residential in their d?cor, and appointed with beautiful artwork and furnishings, giving you a breathtaking image of what it was like to be a member of the prestigious Duke family who made The Mansion their home. All rooms have queen or king sized beds, private baths, exquisite linens, luxurious robes, and a gourmet goodnight treat. The Mansion is an integral part of Charlotte's most prestigious and beautiful neighborhood, and is situated on four and a half acres of beautiful grounds. Its professional culinary staff and beautiful public rooms can accommodate family or business celebrations of 10-300 guests. When you select The Duke Mansion, you are supporting a nonprofit where all of the proceeds are used to preserve and protect it.

**Rates**
20 Rooms. $179/$279, including breakfast, plus tax. Special seasonal rates also available. Number of Rooms: 20

**Cuisine**
Full-time onsite professional culinary staff featuring New South cuisine.

**Nearest Airport(s)**
Charlotte-Douglas International Airport, 20 minutes

**Directions**
From Brookshire Freeway, take 3rd Street exit, turn left. 3rd turns into Providence. Follow Providence to Hermitage Road, turn R. Take second entrance into The Mansion is on the left.

# Arrowhead Inn

www.arrowheadinn.com
106 Mason Road, Durham, NC 27712
**800-528-2207** • 919-477-8430 • Fax 919-471-9538
info@arrowheadinn.com

*Member Since 2003*

*North Carolina*

*Durham*

*"Everything was superb-from the furnishings and service to the gourmet food...
compliments to you on the right blend of class & warm hospitality!"*

Innkeepers/Owners
**Gloria and Phil Teber**

Relax in the quiet comfort of our 18th Century plantation home. The Arrowhead Inn rests on six acres of gardens and lawns amid venerable magnolia and pecan trees. Each of our elegant guest rooms, Carolina Log Cabin, and Garden Cottage provide a serene respite with the amenities of a fine hotel. The Arrowhead Inn, built circa 1775, has been carefully renovated retaining original moldings, mantelpieces, and heart-of-pine floors. Watch hummingbirds flutter on flowering hibiscus while relaxing with friends on our sun-warmed patio. Drift off for an afternoon nap next to your cozy fireplace. Unwind in your private whirlpool while enjoying fine wine and savory delicacies. Slip into your luxurious soft terry robe after refreshing yourself in a soothing steam shower. Awake to the delight of our abundant breakfast. Savour the cuisine of our fine dining, along with that of Durham's nationally famous chefs and restaurants. The Arrowhead Inn welcomes you for peaceful and romantic getaways, family gatherings, seminars, and business retreats. Our Tiffany Gazebo provides a lovely setting for small weddings. AAA Four Diamond property.

**Rates**
Rooms & Suites in Manor House, Garden Cottage & Log Cabin $150/$350. Whirlpools, steam showers & fireplaces. Wireless Internet access. Corporate & mid-week rates available.   Number of Rooms: 9

**Cuisine**
Delicious homemade breakfasts: puffed soufflés, blueberry french toast, fresh herbed frittatas, glazed scones, & baked fruits. Chef/owner prepares mouth-watering 6-course tasting dinners served in romantic settings or in the privacy of your suite.

**Nearest Airport(s)**
Raleigh/Durham

**Directions**
Take I-85 to Exit 176B and turn Right. Travel 7 mi. on Rt.501 N to Mason Rd and turn Left.

# White Doe Inn

www.whitedoeinn.com

319 Sir Walter Raleigh Street, Post Office Box 1029, Manteo, NC 27954

**800-473-6091** • 252-473-9851 • Fax 252-473-4708

whitedoe@whitedoeinn.com

*Member Since 2005*

*"This is a place of what the Italians call laniappe, the extra touch, the exquisite detail, they know what you need before you do..."*

## Bebe & Robert Woody

As one of the most photographed historic homes on Roanoke Island, The White Doe Inn Bed & Breakfast has been welcoming guests since the turn-of-the-century. For years, visitors have admired its beautiful architectural details and old world charm. Now guests come from near and far to experience gracious hospitality in this lovely old home. Located in the heart of the Outer Banks, just minutes from the Atlantic Ocean and its beautiful beaches. The White Doe Inn is listed on the National Register of Historic Places and is noted for its historic and architectural significance. The Inn has been awarded the AAA Three Diamond Rating, and we are also members of the North Carolina Bed & Breakfast Inns and the Professional Association of Innkeepers International.

**Rates**
Off $175/$265 Mid $195/$280 In$225/325  Number of Rooms: 8

**Cuisine**
The White Doe Inn is pleased to provide outstanding service and a delicious full four-course seated and served breakfast that will delight your palate and be pleasing to the eye. Afternoon tea and pastries are set out daily as is evening sherry.

**Nearest Airport(s)**
Norfolk International Airport, VA

**Directions**
Go S on VA-168 to the NC border. Once in NC, US-168 merges into US-158 E. Stay on this road. Follow US-158 E to the Outer Banks. At Mile Post 16 turn W on US-64/264 crossing the George Washington Baum Bridge to Roanoke Island and Manteo.

# The Aerie Bed & Breakfast

www.aeriebedandbreakfast.com
509 Pollock Street, New Bern, NC 28562
**800-849-5553** • 252-636-5553 • Fax 252-514-2157
info@aeriebedandbreakfast.com

*Member Since 2008*

*"You seem to have hit a perfect balance of friendly hospitality & respect for privacy.
I've stayed in quite a few B&Bs, and Marty & Michael have a winner."*

Innkeepers/Owners
**Michael and Marty Gunhus**

This delightful circa 1882 Late Victorian property is the favorite year-round luxury accommodation for enjoying Eastern North Carolina and to truly understand that "North
Carolina Begins Here". Experience the warmth and charm of historic New Bern by day
and relax in comfort and elegance at night in The Aerie. An inviting welcome pervades the
inn at every turn as the staff surrounds you with detailed service, striking the perfect balance
between personal attention and individual freedom. Recognized in "Our State" magazine, The Washington Post and featured on PBS, The Aerie has enjoyed many distinctive
awards and acclamations including repeatedly being voted as "Simply The Best B&B" by
the Sun Journal. A gourmet breakfast features a menu that changes daily and each guest
may choose between three different hot-entree selections. Seven delightfully distinctive
guest rooms are ready to pamper with luxurious linens, exquisite beds and modern amenities. Suites offer whirlpool baths and king or queen beds—several with canopy beds, and all
feature period antiques as well as modern convieniences such as TV/DVD/CD and Wifi
Internet.

**Rates**
7 Rooms including 3 Suites with whirlpools. All have access
to the courtyard, rear deck or front covered balcony. All are elegantly appointed with period antiques & reproductions. Rooms
$119-$159. Suites $159-$169. Number of Rooms: 7

**Cuisine**
Full breakfast included with a distinctive menu that changes
each day. Starter course and choice of 3 entrees. Evening
wine & hors d'oeuvres. Coffee, tea and various cold beverages
available 24 hours.

**Nearest Airport(s)**
New Bern (EWN), Raleigh (RDU)

**Directions**
From NC-70 exit #416 and follow signs to Tryon Palace.
From US-17 exit Historic New Bern to Tryon Palace. The inn
is 1 block.

# The Verandas

www.verandas.com
202 Nun Street, Wilmington, NC 28401
**910-251-2212** • Fax 910-251-8932
verandas4@aol.com

*Member Since 2001*

*"Visit number forty-nine was as wonderful as our first.
Thanks Chuck and Dennis! We love you guys."*

Owners
## Dennis Madsen and Chuck Pennington

Towering above a quiet tree-lined street in the historic district stands this grand antebellum mansion. Built in 1854, the 11 year award-winning Inn is a blend of history, luxury, charm and hospitality. Guest space abounds with wonderful colors, original art, French and English antiques. Four verandas, garden terrace and cupola offer hideaways. Professionally decorated guestrooms have sitting areas, telephone, cable TV, PC jacks. Hand-ironed linens dress comfortable beds. Baths have soaking tubs, showers, marble floors, luxury amenities and robes. French pressed coffee with a gourmet breakfast. Complimentary beverages and snacks and social wine hour. Walking distance to the Riverwalk and restaurants and shopping. High speed wireless internet. Enjoy The Verandas - "An Inn Second to Nun!"

**Rates**
8 Corner Rooms $169/$269. Two-nights required on weekends. Closed first two weeks of Jan. Number of Rooms: 8

**Cuisine**
Included with the room rate is a full gourmet breakfast with French pressed coffee served in our beautiful dining room. Complimentary beverages and snacks are available and white wine is served in the evening.

**Nearest Airport(s)**
Wilmington International

**Directions**
I-40 to I-140 W to 421 S. Go 2.2 mi. S.on 421, cross drawbridge, straight 10 blocks on 3rd, R on Nun. Next block on L. N on 74/76, go over drawbridge, make 2nd R Front Street N, go 3 blocks, make R on Nun. "Second to Nun"

SelectRegistry.com

# Graystone Inn

www.graystoneinn.com
100 South 3rd Street, Wilmington, NC 28401
**888-763-4773** • 910-763-2000 • Fax 910-763-5555

*Member Since 2005*

*North Carolina*

*Wilmington*

*"Fabulous room, fabulous hosts, fabulous time!"*

Innkeepers/Owners
**Rich & Marcia Moore**

The Graystone Inn, one of the most elegant historical structures in Wilmington, is located in the heart of the historic district and just three blocks from shopping, fine dining and the River Walk. The Graystone, originally the "Bridgers Mansion", was built as a private residence in 1905 by Elizabeth Haywood Bridgers and is an excellent representation of the neo-classical revival style. Each elegantly decorated bedroom has its own private bath, telephones with voice mail and data port, WiFi and cable TV. All rooms contain period furnishings, exquisite draperies and fine pima cotton linens, towels and robes. Intricately carved fireplaces grace seven of the nine bedrooms. The Graystone has frequently been used as a set for motion pictures and television and lists many notable personalities among its guests.

**Rates**
6 rooms $159/$269. 3 Jr. suites $209/$369. Two night weekends. Open year round. Number of Rooms: 9

**Cuisine**
Full gourmet breakfast prepared by chef-owner. Early morning coffee bar. Complimentary beverages. Evening wine.

**Nearest Airport(s)**
Wilmington International

**Directions**
I-40E to 74W to downtown Wilmington. Corner of Third and Dock Streets.

Famous for: Cincinnati Zoo, Cincinnati Union Terminal, Taft Museum,
Neil Armstrong Air and Space Museum, Put-in-Bay Village and Perry Memorial
(largest Doric column in the world), Rolling Hills, Farmlands, Burial Mounds.

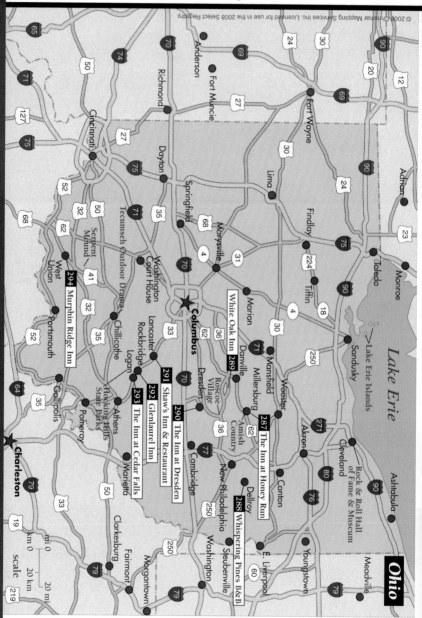

© 2008 Christian Mapping Services Inc. Licensed for use in the 2008 Select Registry.

294 Murphin Ridge Inn

White Oak Inn 289

291 Shaw's Inn & Restaurant

292 Glenlaurel Inn

293 The Inn at Cedar Falls

290 The Inn at Dresden

287 The Inn at Honey Run

288 Whispering Pines B&B

Lake Erie

Lake Erie Islands

Rock & Roll Hall of Fame & Museum

Ohio

# The Inn and Spa at Honey Run

www.innathoneyrun.com
6920 County Road 203, Millersburg, OH 44654
**800-468-6639** • 330-674-0011 • Fax 330-674-2623
info@innathoneyrun.com

*Member Since 1984*

*"WOW! The world and all the stress disappeared the instant I turned into your drive." "Very peaceful, great atmosphere, delicious food, awesome spa!"*

Innkeeper/Owner
**Phillip T. Jenkins**

An award-winning contemporary inn located in the world's largest Amish community of Holmes County. The Inn and Spa at Honey Run provides a chance to recharge batteries and refresh souls. Located on 70-acres of woods and pasture, the Inn offers privacy and serenity in various accomodations. 24 uniquely decorated rooms in its Main Lodge; 12 earth-sheltered Honeycombs with stone fireplaces, patios and shower/whirlpool tubs; 2 Guest Cottages each with two bedrooms and a honeymoon/anniversary cottage with jacuzzi tub. Three VIP Suites at the Monarch House are perfect for private getaways or couple retreats. Visit our Day Spa for massage therapy, body and facial treatments, breema, or meditative guidance. Watch birds and nature from picture windows, read by blazing fireplaces, and explore the sights, sounds and backroads of Scenic Byways. Visit the Inn's Gallery Gift Shop or shop for furniture, quilts, cheese and local artisan wares in nearby villages. Enjoy seasonal educational symposiums, Sunday evening fireside presentations, hike private trails or enjoy cocktails in the Pheasant's Nest Lounge. Full Service Executive Conference Center.

### Rates
$119/$349 Full Service including 3 Guest Cottages and Monarch House VIP Suites. Deluxe Continental Breakfast. Room amenities include TV, VCR and/or DVD, CD/Clock Radio, Hairdryer, Iron.  Number of Rooms: 43

### Cuisine
Breakfast served daily. Lunch and dinner reservations required. Fine wines, beers and spirits served in the lounge and dining room.

### Nearest Airport(s)
Local airport (15 minutes) in Millersburg. International Airport 1 1/2 hours.

### Directions
From Millersburg: (3.5 mi.) Rts 62/39 (E) for 2 blocks, L on SR 241 N for 1.9 mi. R (E) on CR 203 for 1.5 mi. From Berlin: (5.5 mi.) Rts 62/39 (W) R on CR 201, L on CR 203 for 2.7 mi.

# Whispering Pines Bed & Breakfast

www.atwoodlake.com

1268 Magnolia Road, P.O. Box 340, Dellroy, OH 44620

**866-4LAKEVU (452-5388)** • 330-735-2824 • Fax 330-735-7006

whisperingpines@atwoodlake.com

*Member Since 2006*

*"You have spoiled us so much...we will return. You set yourself apart in so many ways beginning with your warmth on the phone and throughout our stay."*

Innkeepers/Owners
**Bill & Linda Horn**

Whispering Pines is located in the gently rolling hills of Carroll County and sits on a hill overlooking beautiful Atwood Lake and its picturesque lush landscape. The lake views will take your breath away and the surroundings are indescribably tranquil. Enjoy a quiet conversation mesmerized by the birds singing and the pines whispering and gather around the warmth of the firepit in the evening. Nine guest rooms with 2-person whirlpool tubs, wonderful views, Bose music system and exquisite authentic victorian antiques. Most rooms have a fireplace and private balcony. Breakfast is served on the enclosed porch overlooking the lake or in the dining room. We offer additional services such as an in-room massage, other gift and seasonal packages for boating and golf. We can also accommodate small weddings. You will discover several first class restaurants in the area for dining. Endless activities with 28 miles of shoreline - a walk/hike in the park, boating, day and night golf, top-notch museums, wineries and the Amish area. Whispering Pines - the perfect place for celebrating a special occasion or brief getaway.

## Rates
9 guestrooms with 2-person whirlpool tub, scenic views, and comfortable reading chairs. Most have fireplace and private balcony. $185/$235. Number of Rooms: 9

## Cuisine
A delicious breakfast of seasonal fruit or warm cobblers, freshly baked breakfast cakes, and a variety of warm entrees served between 9 - 10:30 a.m., earlier upon request. Morning coffee delivered to your room. Afternoon cookies, and organic tea and coffee.

## Nearest Airport(s)
Akron/Canton

## Directions
I-77 S to exit #103. 800 S, left on 183, right on 542-8 miles to the Inn. I-77 N to exit #81. 39 E to 542 N, 2 miles to the Inn. 90 m from Cleveland/Pittsburgh.

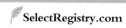

# The White Oak Inn

www.whiteoakinn.com
29683 Walhonding Rd (SR715), Danville, OH 43014
**877-908-5923** • 740-599-6107
info@whiteoakinn.com

*Member Since 1989*

*Ohio*

*Danville*

*"We loved the peaceful country setting and charm of the inn. The meals were delicious."*

**Innkeepers/Owners**
**Yvonne & Ian Martin**

We invite you to visit our turn-of-the-century farmhouse in a quiet wooded country setting. The inn has ten comfortable, antique-filled guest rooms and two luxury log-cabin cottages. You can enjoy a candlelit dinner in the inn's dining room, or a romantic dinner basket delivered to your room. Tour local wineries or experience a private wine tasting at the inn. Visit Ohio's Amish area, Roscoe Village, or Longaberger baskets. Hike the local trails, go golfing or canoeing or simply spend your time soaking up the peace and quiet. Let us entertain you at a Murder Mystery, Wine Tasting, Nature weekend or Cooking Class. Perhaps you'd prefer a pampering weekend with in-room massages and room service. We'll be happy to arrange a guided tour of Amish Country for you. Our gazebo is perfect for elopements, weddings and vow renewals. We offer girlfriend getaway and family reunion packages. The inn has received three major awards from *Inn Traveler* Magazine, including "Best Weekend Escape" for 2004 and was featured in *Ohio Magazine* in 2006 for Best Romantic Getaways. Come join us soon. The cookie jar is always full

**Rates**
10 Rooms and 2 cottages, $120/$215 B&B. Fireplaces and whirlpool tubs in some rooms. Seasonal packages that include dinners available. Number of Rooms: 12

**Cuisine**
Generous country breakfast daily. Dinners or romantic dinner baskets by advance reservation. Private wine tastings and wine pairing dinners can be arranged. BYOB.

**Nearest Airport(s)**
Columbus - 55 miles

**Directions**
From I71: Rte 36E or Rte 13S to Mount Vernon. Then Rte 36E 13 Mi to Rte 715. The inn is 3 miles East on SR715. From I-77: Rte 36W 35 mi to Rte 206N. 2 mi to Rte 715. The inn is 4 miles W on SR715.

# The Inn at Dresden

www.theinnatdresden.com
209 Ames Drive, Dresden, OH 43821
**800-373-7336** • 740-754-1122 • Fax 740-754-9856
info@theinnatdresden.com

*Member Since 2000*

*Ohio*

*Dresden*

> *"This is our ninth visit. We thank you for all the beautiful hospitality, the wonderful food, and the bluebirds."*

Innkeeper/Owner
**Verona, William & Burke Madigan**

Tucked away among the rolling hills of southeastern Ohio, The Inn at Dresden provides the perfect setting for a relaxing getaway with family and friends, or a quiet weekend with someone special. Originally built by Dave Longaberger, founder of Longaberger Baskets, this elegant Tudor home offers guests a panoramic view of Dresden and the surrounding countryside. Guests at the Inn enjoy an evening social hour and a full buffet breakfast. Individually decorated rooms feature VCRs, CD players and special ammenities such as wraparound private decks, two person Jacuzzi tubs and gas-log fireplaces.

**Rates**
10 Rooms $105/$190 per night. Each room is individually decorated to depict the area. Many rooms have fireplaces, decks and Jacuzzi tubs. Number of Rooms: 10

**Cuisine**
The Inn provides a full breakfast; an evening social hour of wine and cheese, followed by optional evening fine dining, by reservation for guest and their guests only.

**Nearest Airport(s)**
Columbus Airport Akron/Canton

**Directions**
The Inn may be reached by SR 60N or Northpointe Dr. from Zanesville, or SR 16 from Newark or Coshocton.

# Shaw's Restaurant & Inn

www.shawsinn.com
123 North Broad St., Lancaster, OH 43130
**800-654-2477** • 740-654-1842 • Fax 740-654-7032
shaws@greenapple.com

*Member Since 2005*

*"...a uniquely pleasant experience...rooms are a delight...staff attentive."*
*"..fresh and creative menu." "..relaxed environment, yet elegant."*

Wine Spectator
AWARD OF EXCELLENCE

**Innkeepers/Owners**
**Bruce & Nancy Cork, Susie Cork**

Located on a tree-shaded square in historic downtown Lancaster, Shaw's has been described as "a unique blend of country freshness and well traveled sophistication." Just minutes from Hocking Hills, Shaw's Inn offers nine individually decorated theme rooms with large in-room whirlpool tubs, including the Napa Valley, the Pearl, the Caribbean, and Louis XIV. Full breakfast in the restaurant is included with all rooms. Shaw's Restaurant has a reputation for New York Strip, Filet Mignon, Prime Rib, and Fresh Seafood. The Chef creates a daily changing menu with seasonal items—Spring Lamb, Soft Shell Crab, Fresh Walleye, 4-pound Lobster, and many others. Add to your Holiday Festivities with four weeks of Christmas Dinners. There are Cooking Classes every Saturday. Cork's Bar, serving every day (Sunday after 1:00), has a warm setting of dark wood and brass. Free High-Speed Wireless Internet access throughout. Nearby attractions include: the Sherman House, the Decorative Arts Center of Ohio, the Georgian, and the Ohio Glass Museum.

**Rates**
Whirlpool Rooms $152/$218 Deluxe Rooms $125/$145 Corporate Rooms $86/$96 Double Occupancy Full Breakfast is Included in the Restaurant. Number of Rooms: 25

**Cuisine**
Known for Steaks, Prime Rib, and Seafood. Pasta, Small Plates. Changing Seasonal Menu—Holiday Dinners. Wine Spectator Award of Excellence.

**Nearest Airport(s)**
Port Columbus Airport

**Directions**
From Columbus: Rt. 33 East to Lancaster. Left on Main. Two blocks, Left on Broad. From Hocking Hills: Rt. 33 West to Lancaster. Right on Main, Left on Broad.

# Glenlaurel, Scottish Inn & Cottages

‖O‖ ‖O‖ ‖O‖ ♀

www.glenlaurel.com
14940 Mt. Olive Road, Hocking Hills, OH 43149-9736
**800-809-REST** • 740-385-4070 • Fax 740-385-9669
Info@glenlaurel.com

*Member Since 1998*

*"When we arrive in heaven, it will be similar to the royal treatment that we received during our stay at Glenlaurel."*

Innkeepers/Owners
**Greg & Kelley Leonard**

Sometimes at dinner, the story is told of how Glenlaurel was first imagined-300 years ago in the heart of the Scottish Highlands. Today, the heavily wooded 140-acre estate has the look of the old world, a veil of romance, and a pace of times gone by. Whether in the stately Manor House, the nearby Carriage House, or one of the crofts or cottages, Glenlaurel defines pampering as lazy kidless afternoons, sumptuous fine dining for two, hot tub frolics, intimate fireside secrets, sleeping past 7, hearty breakfast choices, & morning walks through our own Camusfearna Gorge ~ with ne'er a soul in sight! As a Scottish Inn with wooded cottages, we offer the finest amenities for the sophisticated leisure or business traveler who expects unpretentious elegance in both lodging and fine dining. The old-world elegance of the Inn and the secluded, peaceful setting are ideal for romantic nights for two, peaceful getaways for one, weddings, and business conferences. Our Anniversary Club honors a successful marriage, year after year. Please visit our web site to learn more about our anniversary club, our luxurious spa, and our property.

**Rates**
3 Rooms $149/$219, 3 Suites $209/$259, 7 Crofts $239/$289, 6 Cottages $289/$339. Midweek specials & corporate rates, open year-round. Number of Rooms: 19

**Cuisine**
Dinner is "a private invitation to dine at an estate house in the country" with social time, greetings from your host, and a candlelit culinary adventure-in the European tradition.

**Nearest Airport(s)**
Columbus, 55 mins & onsite helipad.

**Directions**
From N, take Rt 33 around Lancaster 12 mi to 180 exit, R onto 180, 4.8 mi, L at sign for .5 mi. From W, take 180 thru Laurelville 10 mi. From S, take Rt 33 around Athens 30 mi to 180 exit, L onto 180, 4.8 mi. From E, use Rt 33.

# Inn & Spa At Cedar Falls

www.innatcedarfalls.com
21190 State Route 374, Logan, OH 43138
**800-653-2557** • 740-385-7489 • Fax 740-385-0820
info@innatcedarfalls.com

*Member Since 1989*

*Ohio*

*Logan*

*"Could there be any better place to recharge and reconnect?" "The Inn made magic happen." "Meals were delicious and artistically served."*

Innkeepers/Owners
**Ellen Grinsfelder and Terry Lingo**

The restored and comfortably rustic 1840 log houses are an open kitchen-dining room, serving the most refined of American cuisine. Antique appointed guest rooms in a barn-like structure have rockers and writing desks and offer sweeping views of meadows, woods and wildlife. We have quaint cottages ideal for two, or secluded, fully-equipped 19th century log cabins accommodating up to four. Casual fine dining for lunch and dinner is served on the patio or the 1840's log cabins. Discover a new degree of relaxation as you escape into a sanctuary of natural beauty and personal discovery at the Spa At Cedar Falls. We offer renewing experiences with lasting effects. The rugged and beautiful Hocking Hills State Parks with glorious caves and waterfalls flanks the Inn's 75 acres on three sides. Casual and avid hikers will enjoy Old Man's Cave, Cedar Falls, Ash Cave and Conkle's Hollow. A variety of cooking classes, wine tastings, and hikes are scheduled year round. Call for a calendar of events, off season rates and specials.

**Rates**
9 Rooms, $119/$159 B&B; 12 Cottages, $169/$229 B&B; 5 Cabins, $179/$279 B&B  Number of Rooms: 26

**Cuisine**
Watch meals being created in the open kichen. Hearty country breakfasts, delectable lunches, sumptuous dinners by candlelight. Patio dining in the warm months. Enjoy an early beverage at Kindred Spirits, our tavern.

**Nearest Airport(s)**
Columbus which is 50 miles.

**Directions**
From Columbus, U.S. Rte. 33S to Logan-Bremen Exit 664S, R on 664, 9.5 miles, L on St Rte. 374, Inn is 1 mile on L. From Cincy, 71N to Washington CH, take 35E to 22E. In Circleville, access 56E to St. Rte. 374, turn L, Inn is 2 1/2 miles on R.

# Murphin Ridge Inn

www.murphinridgeinn.com
750 Murphin Ridge Rd., West Union, OH 45693
**877-687-7446** • 937-544-2263 • Fax 937-544-8151
murphinn@bright.net

*Member Since 1992*

*"R&R for the soul! Great hosts, accommodations, food,
and trails worthy of frequent visits."*

Innkeepers/Owners
**Sherry & Darryl McKenney**

Selected by *National Geographic Traveler* as one of the top 54 Inns in the U.S. and achieving
a prestegious spot on the National Geographic Geotourism MapGuide this prize-winning
Inn welcomes you to 142 acres of four-season beauty. The Inn showcases the Guest House
with ten spacious rooms, some with fireplaces or porches, and nine romantic cabins, each
with fireplace, two person whirlpool, two person shower and porch. All are decorated with
David T. Smith Early American and Shaker reproduction furniture. The 1828 farmhouse
features four dining rooms with original fireplaces, and gift shop. Enjoy award winning
regional cuisine, in season, gathered from the Inn's gardens and dine outside at The High
Grill. View the Appalachian foothills, enjoy the night sky by the bonfire, and visit local
Amish Shops, the Edge of Appalachia Preserve, and the Serpent Mound State Memorial.
Then schedule an Inn Room massage. The Inn has an outdoor pool, hiking, bird-watch-
ing, tennis, lawn games and more. Golf is nearby. With Wi-Fi available, Murphin Rdige
Inn is perfect for retreats, reunions, and conferences.

**Rates**
19 rooms and cabins $125/$260  Number of Rooms: 19

**Nearest Airport(s)**
Cincinnati/Northern Kentucky International

**Cuisine**
Award-winning country inn fine dining. Full breakfast. The chef
and staff make dining a charming experience that brings guests
back time and again. Selected fine wine premium beer and
spirits available in the Dining House. Inn Guests Dine Nightly.

**Directions**
FROM CINCINNATI: SR 32E., Right on Unity Rd. 2-1/2 mi. to
Stop Sign turn Left on Wheat Ridge Rd. 2-7/10 mi. to Left on
Murphin Ridge Rd. FROM COLUMBUS: SR 23 to 32W. Left
on 41S to Right on Wheat Ridge Road at Dunkinsville. 1-1/2
mi. to Right on Murphin Ridge.

# Oklahoma

## "The Sooner State"

Famous for: Will Rogers Memorial, Alabaster Caverns, State Park, National Cowboy Hall of Fame, Pioneer Woman Statue, Cattle Ranching, Oral Roberts University, Oil, Plastics, Rubber, Cotton.

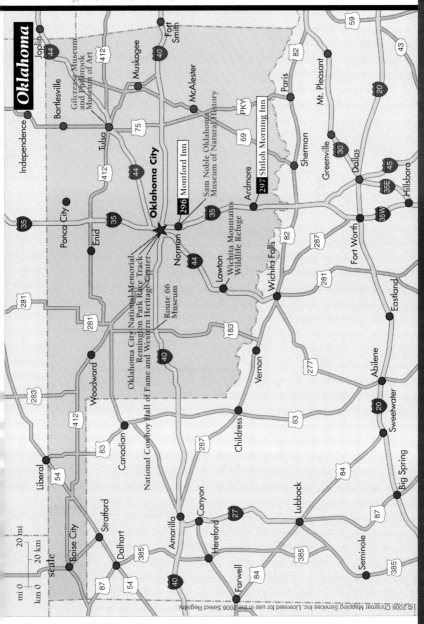

**Oklahoma**

296 Montford Inn

297 Shiloh Morning Inn

Gilcrease Museum and Philbrook Museum of Art

Sam Noble Oklahoma Museum of Natural History

Oklahoma City National Memorial
Remington Park Race Track
Route 66 Museum
National Cowboy Hall of Fame and Western Heritage Center

Wichita Mountains Wildlife Refuge

© 2006 Chrismar Mapping Services Inc. Licensed for use in the 2008 Select Registry

# Montford Inn & Cottages

www.montfordinn.com
322 W. Tonhawa, Norman, OK 73069
**800-321-8969** • 405-321-2200 • Fax 405-321-8347
innkeeper@montfordinn.com

*Member Since 1997*

*Oklahoma*

*Norman*

*"Thank you so much for your warm hospitality. Our experience at Montford Inn rivals any five-star hotel we've stayed in. You have created a gem."*

Innkeepers/Owners
**Phyllis & Ron Murray, William & Ginger Murray**

Celebrating their 13th year of operation, the Murrays welcome you to the award-winning Montford Inn and Cottages. With its ten uniquely decorated rooms in the main house, and six incredible cottage suites, the Montford Inn has everything the discriminating inngoer is looking for in lodging. Located in the heart of Norman's Historic District, this Prairie-style inn envelops travelers in a relaxing atmosphere. Antiques, family heirlooms and Native American art accent the individually decorated guest rooms and suites. Awaken to rich coffees and a gourmet country breakfast served in the beautifully appointed dining room or in the more intimate setting of the suites. Relax in private hot tubs. Escape in luxurious whirlpool bathtubs. Unwind in elegant cottage suites. Stroll through beautiful gardens. Find your heart...at the Montford Inn and Cottages! Featured in *Southern Living, Country, Holiday,* Fodor's, and *Oklahoma Today.*

**Rates**
10 Rooms, $95/$169 B&B; 6 Cottage Suites, $199/$229 B&B. Open year-round, main inn closed Christmas Eve & Christmas Day. Cottage suites open all year. Number of Rooms: 16

**Cuisine**
Gourmet Breakfast served in cottages and dining room. Complimentary wine and refreshments early evening.

**Nearest Airport(s)**
Will Rogers World Airport in Oklahoma City

**Directions**
20 minutes S of Oklahoma City. From I-35, take Main St., Downtown exit 109. Turn L on University (about 2.2 miles from I-35). Go 2 blocks, turn R 1/2 block on Tonhawa.

# Shiloh Morning Inn & Cottages

www.shilohmorning.com
2179 Ponderosa Road, Ardmore, OK 73401
**888-554-7674** • 580-223-9500 • Fax 580-223-9615
innkeepers@shilohmorning.com

*Member Since 2004*

Ardmore

*"Shiloh Morning Inn is the Gold Standard for what a B&B should be."*

**Innkeepers/Owners**
## Bob & Linda Humphrey

When life becomes too hectic, the peace and quiet of southern Oklahoma's rolling hills hold the answer. Shiloh Morning Inn is located on 73 beautifully wooded acres, just minutes off I-35, yet a world away. Uniquely designed suites and cottages offer large luxurious baths, king beds, fireplaces, TV/VCR/DVD, private hot tubs or jetted tubs for two, and a private balcony, patio, or deck. Guests choose from an extensive library of movies and books. Walking trails are dotted with hammocks and park benches. Wildlife abounds. Privacy is a number one priority. Two of the cottages take luxury to a new level. Roadrunner Hideaway is so secluded, its occupants are furnished with a personal golf cart. Enjoy watching deer, or soaking in a hot tub on a deck cantilevered into the trees. The Villa at Shiloh is a two story cottage for the ultimate quixotic experience including an upstairs jetted tub for two, a spa shower, and a downstairs outdoor room with hot tub. The perfect romantic getaway for couples seeking the quiet seclusion of a rural countryside, Shiloh Morning Inn is truly a "Place of Peace & Rest".

### Rates
5 luxurious suites and 4 very private cottages. $159/$299. Two night minimum on weekends. Some holidays three night minimum. Closed Thanksgiving & Christmas. Number of Rooms: 9

### Cuisine
Three course gourmet breakfast at tables for two in the dining room is included. Dinner by advance reservation available for intimate in-room dining Fri-Sat. Light Dinner Trays available, by reservation, any evening.

### Nearest Airport(s)
Dallas (DFW)Oklahoma City (OKC)

### Directions
Map sent with reservation confirmation. Gated Entry.

*297*

# Oregon

## "The Beaver State"

Famous for: The Oregon Trail, Mount Hood, Flowers, Lumber, Wineries, Rose Festival, Crater Lake, Painted Hills National Monument, Columbia River, Gorge, Coast Range, Cascade Range, Redwoods.

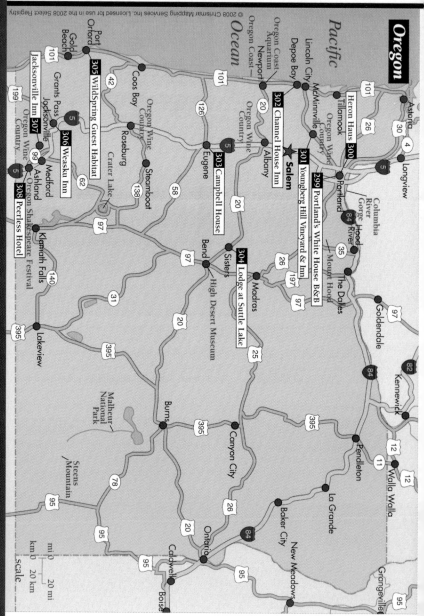

**Oregon**

Pacific

Ocean

★ **Salem**

Astoria

Longview

Gold Beach

Port Orford

Coos Bay

Jacksonville

Grants Pass

Ashland

Medford

Roseburg

Steamboat

Klamath Falls

Lakeview

Eugene

Albany

Bend

Sisters

Madras

Portland

The Dalles

Mount Hood

Goldendale

Kennewick

Walla Walla

Pendleton

La Grande

Baker City

New Meadows

Grangeville

Burns

Canyon City

Ontario

Caldwell

Boise

Tillamook

Newport

Depoe Bay

Lincoln City

McMinnville

Crater Lake

High Desert Museum

Oregon Coast Aquarium

Columbia River Gorge

Malheur National Park

Steens Mountain

Oregon Wine Country

Oregon Wine Country

Oregon Wine Country

Oregon Wine Country

Oregon Coast —

**305** WildSpring Guest Habitat

**306** Weasku Inn

**307** Jacksonville Inn

**308** Peerless Hotel

**302** Channel House Inn

**301** Youngberg Hill Vineyard & Inn

**299** Portland's White House B&B

**303** Campbell House

**304** Lodge at Suttle Lake

**300** Heron Haus

Oregon Shakespeare Festival

101  26  30  4  5

101  199  101  42  126  20

5  5  305  306  307  99  62  138  58  97  20  26  197  97  35  84

307  308  140  31  97  395  20  395  25  95  78  26  20  84  82  12  11  12  84  97  395  395

mi 0  20 mi

km 0  20 km

scale

# Portland's White House B&B

www.portlandswhitehouse.com
1914 NE 22nd Ave., Portland, OR 97212
**800-272-7131** • 503-287-7131 • Fax 503-249-1641
pdxwhi@portlandswhitehouse.com

*Member Since 2004*

*"Be prepared to get spoiled rotten. Everything about this place is decadent, from the breakfast to the big beds to the bath amentities."*

Innkeeper/Owner
**Lanning Blanks**

Situated in Portland's North East Historic Irvington District, Portland's White House was built as a summer home in 1911 by Robert Lytle, a wealthy lumber baron. The house was billed as the most expensive home built in the district for the period. This Greek Revival Mansion boasts a lifestyle of past years with 14 massive columns, circular drive and fountain to greet you. Summer days show impressive hanging baskets and wonderful flowers to warm your senses. Restored to its original splendor by Lanning and Steve with sparkling European Chandeliers, formal linened Dining Room, Large Parlor, grand staircase, magnificent leaded glass windows, gilt-gold ceilings, Trompe loiel and Grande Ballroom. Extensive collections of European and Continental Porcelains, 18th and 19th Century oil paintings. Guest rooms are appointed with period antiques, paintings, king or queen feather beds and exquisite linens. Fresh local Breakfast, utilizing SLOW FOODS, is served in the Main Dining room by candle light. "Top 10 City Inns" - *Sunset* Magazine.

**Rates**
$135/$235. Molton Brown amenities is all rooms. Wired and wireless complimentary, Flat screens. Spa suites include Champagne, Moonstruck Chocolate gift box and DVD flat screen televisions. Number of Rooms: 8

**Cuisine**
Candlelight breakfast. Always vegetarian, meats offered on the side. Bread Pudding French Toast, Crab Cakes Eggs Benedict, Oregon Blueberry Muffins, Pear Ginger Scones. Full Espresso bar

**Nearest Airport(s)**
Portland International Airport, within 20 minutes.

**Directions**
From I-5 take Weidler to 22nd, N to NE Hancock. Hgwy 84 to Lloyd Center, R at light, R on Multnomah to 22nd, N to NE Hancock.

*Oregon*

*Portland*

# Heron Haus
www.heronhaus.com
2545 NW Westover Road, Portland, OR  97210
**503-274-1846** • Fax 503-248-4055
info@heronhaus.com

*Member Since 1994*

*Oregon*

*Portland*

*"An inviting sitting garden provides a quiet
and relaxing getaway for the weary visitor."*

Owner
**Julie Beacon Keppeler**

This elegant three-story turn-of-the-century tudor sits high in the hills, offering accommodations for both the business traveler and romantic getaways for couples.  Each room has sitting areas, work areas, phones with computer hook-ups, and TVs; all have fireplaces.  All have queen or king-sized beds.  The baths offer special extras—one has a spa on a windowed porch; another has a shower with seven shower heads.  Off-street parking is provided.  Two and one half blocks down the hill is the Nob Hill area with boutiques, specialty shops, and some of the best eating places in Portland.

**Rates**
6 Rooms, all with fireplaces, TV, sitting areas, phones, wireless/DSL hook-up, work areas, parking, AC: $95/$185 Single; $135/$350 Double. Open year-round.  Number of Rooms:

**Cuisine**
Continental breakfast.

**Nearest Airport(s)**
Portland Airport - 20 minute drivelite-rail access

**Directions**
On website.

# Youngberg Hill Vineyards & Inn

www.youngberghill.com
10660 SW Youngberg Hill Road, McMinnville, OR 97128
**888-657-8668** • 503-472-2727 • Fax 503-472-1313
info@youngberghill.com

*Member Since 2008*

*Wine Spectator - "2004 & 05 Pinot Noir is a top choice at a rating of 91.
Taste the Wine, Savor the View!"*

Innkeeper
**Nicolette Bailey**

Oregon's premier wine country inn and one of Wine Spectator's favorite locations; Youngberg Hill Inn sits atop a mountain with commanding views over the valleys below. Located on 50 acres and surrounded by 17 acres of award-winning Pinot Noir, the Inn provides guests the opportunity to explore the 20 year old organic vineyard and to begin tasting Oregon's amazing wines. We are located 20 minutes from over 80 premier Oregon wineries. Accommodations are luxurious and guests discover well appointed common rooms including a library and an expansive veranda surrounding the house. Youngberg Hill will take your breath away with the most beautiful views, warm luxurious Inn, and exceptional estate wines. Youngberg Hill is the highest rated Inn in the valley and provides the perfect location for those seeking a quiet, romantic getaway, events, as well as a great base for those wishing to tour the Oregon wine country.

**Rates**
$180-$290 Number of Rooms: 7

**Cuisine**
A full gourmet breakfast is served using fresh local ingredients.

**Nearest Airport(s)**
Portland International (PDX)

**Directions**
From PDX, exit the airport onto I-205 S, to I-5.Exit onto I-5 North to the FIRST exit Tualatin-Sherwood Road and proceed L (west) to Highway 99W. Turn L (south) at Highway 99W through Newberg and Dundee to the Hwy 18 bypass (toward coast/flashing yellow light) drive approx. 9 mi. Once past McMinnville, turn R on Masonville Road and follow the blue signs 2 miles to Youngberg Hill Road, turn R for 1/2 mile.

# Channel House Inn

www.channelhouse.com
35 Ellingson Street, P.O. Box 56, Depoe Bay, OR 97341
**800-447-2140** • 541-765-2140 • Fax 541-765-2191
cfinseth@channelhouse.com

*Member Since 1997*

*Oregon*

*Depoe Bay*

*"Too many accolades to count. Relax & enjoy the peace and tranquility, listen to the sound of the ocean and enjoy a truly unforgettable experience."*

Owners
**Carl & Vicki Finseth**

Nestled in the Oregon Coast's magnificent scenery, Channel House combines the comforts of a first-class hotel with the congeniality of a small country Inn. Imagine fresh ocean breezes, sweeping panoramic views, powerful surf, truly unbelievable sunsets and whales within a stone's throw. Perched on an oceanfront bluff, guestrooms have an understated natural elegance and contemporary decor, including whirlpools on oceanfront decks and gas fireplaces. The friendly staff will attend to your every need. One of the West Coast's most renowned and romantic inns, it has been listed by Harry Shattuck among "a baker's dozen of world's (sic) most delectible hotels" and by *Sunset Magazine* as one of the 20 best Seaside Getaways on the West Coast.

**Rates**
3 Oceanfront Rooms $230/$265; 9 Oceanfront Suites, $245/$330. Number of Rooms: 14

**Cuisine**
Buffet-style breakfast featuring fresh-baked goods is served in our oceanfront dining room. Enjoy a morning repast while having one of the best views on the coast. We have a significant wine selection available and there are many fine restaurants nearby. The friendly staff will attend to your every need.

**Nearest Airport(s)**
Portland International (PDX) - 2.5 Hours

**Directions**
Just off Hwy 101, one block South of Depoe Bay's only Bridge. Turn West onto Ellingson Street, 100 feet to our parking lot.

# Campbell House, A City Inn

www.campbellhouse.com
252 Pearl Street, Eugene, OR 97401
**800-264-2519** • 541-343-1119 • Fax 541-343-2258
campbellhouse@campbellhouse.com

*Member Since 2003*

*Oregon*

*Eugene*

*"A change in pace, place and a break in routine for the weary business traveler."*

Proprietor
**Myra Plant**

Built in 1892 and restored in the tradition of a fine European hotel, the Campbell House is surrounded by beautiful gardens. It is located in the historic district, within walking distance of downtown, restaurants and the theater. Hike Skinner's Butte or use over ten miles of riverside jogging and bicycle paths. Elegant guest rooms have private bathrooms, hidden TV with VCR/DVD, telephones and luxury amenities. Luxury rooms feature gas fireplaces, four-poster beds and Jacuzzi tubs. Enjoy complimentary wine in the evening and a full breakfast with newspaper in the morning. The Dining Room serves dinner seven nights a week, with a full wine list and bar. "Top 25 Inns in the nation," *American Historic Inns.* Weddings, receptions, meetings.

**Rates**
12 Rooms $169/$259; 5 Luxury FP/Jacuzzi $249/$359; 2 two-room Luxury Suites FP/Jacuzzi $349/$399; 1 Guest Cottage $289/$429. Number of Rooms: 20

**Cuisine**
The Dining Room offers an ever-changing dinner menu utilizing the freshest local ingredients. Complimentary full breakfast. Summer outdoor patio. Dinners from $16/$55. Room Service available.

**Nearest Airport(s)**
Mahlon Suite/Eugene Airport

**Directions**
From Airport: Hwy. 99 becomes 7th Ave, L on High, L on 5th, R on Pearl. From I-5, take I-105 to Eugene (exit 194B), to Coburg Rd (exit 2), stay L, merge onto Coburg Road, cross over River, take the second R (6th Ave), R on Pearl.

🍽️ 🍽️ 🍽️ 🍷

# Lodge at Suttle Lake

www.thelodgeatsuttlelake.com
13300 Hwy 20, Sisters, OR 97759
**541-595-2628** • Fax 541-595-2267
gm@thelodgeatsuttlelake.com

*Member Since 2008*

*Oregon*

*Sisters*

*"A Gem in the Wilderness." "An amazing honeymoon and a great getaway." "We come here once a month to renew."*

Innkeeper/Owner
**Ronda Sneva**

We are nestled in the heart of the Deschutes National Forest amid soaring pines, meandering mountain rivers and the snow capped Cascades. We believe in sustainability and wellness while offering a unique experience alongside our glacial lake. We invite you to enjoy everything from outdoor adventure and activity, to more leisurely and reflective pursuits through a variety of active weekends. We host a murder mystery weekend, wellness retreat weekends, holiday packages and concert BBQs. We promote fly fishing, bird watching, kite surfing, kayaks, sailing, hiking, eco tours, and meditation. We offer all the elements: a fully equipped spa, dramatic views, well-appointed accommodations, spectacular meeting and event space, impeccable cuisine, personal service and thoughtful attention to every detail. Our Boathouse Restaurant serves home-style breakfasts, pub style lunch and fine dining dinners along with some of the best Northwest wines. We buy local organic food when available, and grow our own summer herbs to compliment our chef driven daily features. We believe in the details of comfort and the quality of memories. Come see us soon!

### Rates
11 lodge guest rooms $140/$250 per night, 3 historic waterfront cabins $200/$575 per night, 4 luxury cabins $250/$350 per night, 6 rustic cabins $99/$150 per night. Some accomodations are pet friendly, no children under 14 in lodge at night. Number of Rooms: 24

### Cuisine
Comp Breafast and Wine Social for lodge guests,Lunch is pub style $5-$15,Dinner is NW Cuisine fine dining $22-$36,Full Bar,36-50 Wines

### Nearest Airport(s)
Redmond Airport (27 miles), Sisters Airstrip (13 miles), Portland Airport (153 miles),

### Directions
From West Santiam Pass out of Salem 5m past Hoodoo. From East Highway 20 out of Bend, 13m past Sister

# WildSpring Guest Habitat

www.wildspring.com
92978 Cemetery Loop, PO Box R, Port Orford, OR 97465
**866-333-WILD** • 541-332-0977 • Fax 775-542-1447
michelle@wildspring.com

*Member Since 2006*

*Oregon*

*Best Places of the Northwest - highest rating/Editors Choice. "For a dose of eco-luxury, snuggle into WildSpring." Sunset Magazine, April 2008*

*Port Orford*

Innkeepers/Owners
**Dean & Michelle Duarte**

The great outdoors now comes with an equally great indoors. A small ecofriendly resort overlooking the ocean on the spectacular south Oregon coast, WildSpring Guest Habitat? is the perfect escape from your daily life. On five acres of old Native American grounds, it offers luxurious accommodations and facilities in a naturally beautiful setting. Stay in elegant cabin suites filled with art and antiques in a secluded forest. Relax in the Guest Hall, help yourself to hot chocolate, play a game or just gaze at the ocean on its expansive deck. Immerse in the open-air slate hot tub/spa and enjoy whale-watching by day or the Milky Way at night. Wander the walking labyrinth, find a hammock or secluded alcove and take a nap. Indulge in an incabin massage. Make yourself popcorn, choose a movie and retire to your cabin. Sleep to the sound of wind through the trees and wake up to deer outside your window. A short walk to an uncrowded beach for agates and driftwood, in a lovely small town with art galleries, hiking trails, birdwatching, historical sites and the most westerly lighthouse in the 48 states. Think of it as nature with 4 stars.

**Rates**
$198/$275 double; $35/additional adult; $25 for children under 16. Open all year. Number of Rooms: 5

**Cuisine**
An opulent extended continental breakfast buffet. Each day we ask our guests what they would enjoy the following morning. Organic fruits. Dairy- and wheat-free available. On Sat. nights, indulge in our signature homemade hot fudge sundae bar.

**Nearest Airport(s)**
United or Alaska Air connect into Crescent City, CA, 1 hour S and North Bend OR, 1 hour N. Hertz at both. Or fly into Eugene or Medford - 3-hour drives; or Portland, 4.5 hours.

**Directions**
Take Cemetery Loop off Hwy 101 in Port Orford, 60 mi. N of California.

# Weasku Inn

www.weasku.com
5560 Rogue River Hwy., Grants Pass, OR 97527
**800-493-2758** • 541-471-8000 • Fax 541-471-7038
reservations@weasku.com

*Member Since 2001*

*Oregon*

*Grants Pass*

## Top 25 Great American Lodges - Travel + Leisure
## County Living - Inn of the Month

Owner - **Vintage Hotels**
Front Desk Manager - **Erik R. Johnson**

The Weasku Inn was recently named as 'One of the Country's Greatest Inns' by Travel + Leisure, and "Inn of the Month" by Country Living Magazine. The resort rests on the banks of the famous Rogue River, in southern Oregon. This secluded fishing lodge was a favorite vacation spot of Clark Gable during the 1920s and '30s. A complete remodeling took place in 1998, restoring the Inn to its former glory. The warm log exterior, surrounded by towering trees and 10 private acres, provides a tranquil setting ideal for an intimate getaway or corporate retreat. The lodge houses five guestrooms, and there are an additional 12 riverside cabins. A wine and cheese reception and deluxe continental breakfast are served each day.

**Rates**
5 Lodge Rooms, $195/$295; Jacuzzi Suites, $325; 12 River Cabins with fireplaces, $220. Open year-round. Number of Rooms: 17

**Cuisine**
Complimentary wine and cheese reception and continental breakfast are provided each day. BBQ on lodge deck for minimum fee, weekends May-September. Several restaurants are within minutes.

**Nearest Airport(s)**
Medford Airport

**Directions**
Located 51 miles north of the California and Oregon border. Take I-5, exit 48. Turn W, go across the bridge to the stop sign. Rogue River Hwy. Turn R. Go 3 miles. The Inn is on your Right.

# Jacksonville Inn

www.jacksonvilleinn.com
P.O. Box 359, Jacksonville, OR  97530
**800-321-9344** • 541-899-1900 • Fax 541-899-1373
jvinn@mind.net

*Member Since 2003*

*"A destination for relaxing and pampering."*

Innkeepers/Owners
**Jerry and Linda Evans**

The Inn offers its guests luxury and opulence, and its honeymoon cottages cater to romance and privacy of special occasions. Each has a king-sized canopy bed, whirlpool tub, steam shower, entertainment center, wet bar, fireplace, sitting room, computer with high-speed internet accessibility, and private patio with lovely surrounding gardens and waterfall--perfect for intimate weddings, receptions, and private parties. Nestled in a National Historic Landmark town, the Inn was featured on CNN and the Learning Channel's "Great Country Inns." Its restaurant is one of Oregon's most award-winning restaurants and features a connoisseurs' Wine Cellar and private catering. Five-star Diamond Academy Award of the Restaurant Industry. Recipient of "Readers' Choice Award--Best Restaurant" by Medford's MAIL TRIBUNE newspaper five consecutive years. Two of the last three U. S. Presidents have dined at The Inn.

**Rates**
8 Rooms, $159/$199 B&B; 4 Honeymoon Cottages, $270/$465 B&B.  Number of Rooms: 12

**Cuisine**
Restaurant with International Cuisine; Both formal and Bistro dining; Sunday Brunch; Patio Dining; Catering--on and off premises; Wine and Gift Shop featuring over 2,000 wines.

**Nearest Airport(s)**
Medford Airport (5 miles)

**Directions**
From I-5 N - Exit 30: follow signs to Jacksonville. L on California Street. From I-5 S - Exit 30: follow signs to Jacksonville. L on California Street.

# The Peerless Hotel & Restaurant

www.peerlesshotel.com
243 Fourth Street, Ashland, OR 97520
**800-460-8758** • 541-488-1082 • Fax 541-488-5508
innkeeper@peerlesshotel.com

Member Since 2003

*Oregon*

*Ashland*

*"We could not have chosen a more perfect place to stay in Ashland!"*

Innkeeper/Owner
**Crissy Barnett**

Welcome to Ashland's Peerless Experience! Built in 1900, The Peerless Hotel has been lovingly restored and is now included in the National Register of Historic Places. The hotel is located in Ashland's Historic Railroad and Gallery District, just three blocks from downtown and six blocks from the "Tony" award-winning Oregon Shakespeare Festival. Whimsically and elegantly decorated with hand-painted murals, fine art, and an eclectic mixture of antique furnishings gathered from New Orleans to Hawaii. Guests are pampered with Italian bed linens, English silk and cotton towels, AVEDA bath products, spa tubs, and a sumptuous complimentary breakfast. Enjoy the serene surroundings of our beautiful gardens, as well as a staff that prides itself on personalized service. Next door discover an oasis of inspired cuisine at The Peerless Restaurant & Bar. Offering an array of small plates, as well as steaks, chops and fresh seafood that are truly Peerless! *Wine Spectator's* Award of Excellence. Featured in "1,000 Places To See Before You Die."

**Rates**
4 Guest Rooms & 2 Suites, $79/$264 (rates vary seasonally). Gourmet breakfast, locally roasted organic coffee and tea service, morning newspaper, turn down service, homemade cookies, Lobby port wine service. WiFi access. Number of Rooms: 6

**Cuisine**
The Peerless Restaurant & Bar specializes in seasonal Pacific Northwest Cuisine. Full Bar/Lounge. Wine Spectator Award of Excellence. Banquet & Wedding Facilities. Room Service.

**Nearest Airport(s)**
Rogue Valley International-Medford Airport

**Directions**
Ashland's Historic Railroad District.

# Pennsylvania

## "The Keystone State"

Famous for: Liberty Bell, Declaration of Independence, Articles of Confederation, Constitution, Gettysburg Address, Valley Forge National Historical Park, Poconos, Hershey Chocolate World, Amish Homestead, Steel, Pumpkins, Glass.

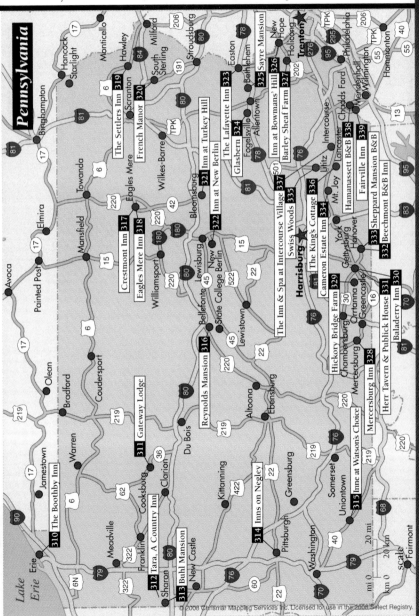

310 The Boothby Inn
311 Gateway Lodge
312 Tara, A Country Inn
313 Buhl Mansion
314 Inns on Negley
315 Inne at Watson's Choice
316 Reynolds Mansion
317 Crestmont Inn
318 Eagles Mere Inn
319 The Settlers Inn
320 French Manor
321 Inn at Turkey Hill
322 Inn at New Berlin
323 The Lafayette Inn
324 Glasbern
325 Sayre Mansion
326 Inn at Bowmans' Hill
327 Barley Sheaf Farm
328 Mercersburg Inn
329 Hickory Bridge Farm
330 Baladerry Inn
331 Herr Tavern & Publick House
332 Beechmont B&B Inn
333 Sheppard Mansion B&B
334 Cameron Estate Inn
335 Swiss Woods
336 The King's Cottage
337 The Inn & Spa at Intercourse Village
338 Hamanassett B&B
339 Fairville Inn

© 2008 Christmar Mapping Services Inc. Licensed for use in the 2008 Select Registry.

# The Boothby Inn

www.theboothbyinn.com
311 West Sixth Street, Erie, PA 16507
**866-266-8429** • 814-456-1888 • Fax 814-456-1887
info@theboothbyinn.com

*Member Since 2005*

*Pennsylvania    Erie*

*"Details! Details! Details! Your attention to the needs of the guests is extraordinary...A lovely, well-appointed and comfortable home. Bravo!"*

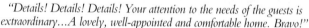

Innkeepers/Owners
**Wally and Gloria Knox**

Swing open the door of this Victorian era home and thrill to the rich oak paneled hallway with its impressive stairway. Notice the three stained glass windows that grab the sunlight and shine on the portrait of Gloria Boothby, namesake of the Inn. Settle down in the living room awash with natural light and pale yellow walls, or sit in front of a fireplace in the adjoining library filled with old and treasured family books. Enjoy the large dollhouse built as an exact replica of a family home in Springfield, Illinois, or curl up with a book in the Shakespeare room, so called because of the tiles around the fireplace of different Shakespeare plays. Outside on warm mornings, you may have breakfast served to you in the garden patio with a fountain's quiet soothing sounds, or stroll through the perennial garden. You may also sit on the comfortable front porch and watch the world go by! The rooms are luxurious, restful and quiet. This is a sanctuary for the vacationer and business traveler. New this year we are offering the Inn for small intimate weddings of 25 or less. AAA Three Diamond, Mobil Three Star rated.

**Rates**
$120/$170 with Midweek and corporate discounts of $20 per room and AAA 10% discounts on the full rates. Some rooms have a gas-log fireplace or a Jacuzzi tub. Number of Rooms: 4

**Cuisine**
A full gourmet breakfast is included. A guest galley at the end of the hall is stocked with refreshments and snacks all free to guests.

**Nearest Airport(s)**
Erie International Airport is only 20 minutes away.

**Directions**
Easily accessible from I-79 or I-90 and located on W. 6th Street (Alt. Rte #5). Detailed directions available on the website or from the Innkeepers.

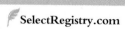

# Gateway Lodge – Country Inn

www.gatewaylodge.com
14870 Route 36, P.O. Box 125, Cooksburg, PA 16217
**800-843-6862** • 814-744-8017 • Fax 814-744-8017
info@gatewaylodge.com

*Member Since 1983*

*"The in 'INN' if you're looking for a way to escape from stress and pressure of everyday life." "To say that guests are pampered is an understatement."*

Innkeeper
**Deb Adams**

Pennsylvania's 2004 Innkeepers of the Year. Amid some of the most magnificent forest scenery east of the Mississippi, this rustic log cabin inn has been awarded one of the top 10 best inns in the U.S. is also *Money* Magazine's Top Travel Pick. The Inn features two large stone fireplaces, fine dining by candlelight, wireless internet, billiards room, afternoon tea, nightly turn-down, AC. 22 Suites with king size beds, each with a two-person fireside jacuzzi tub. Customized small weddings, retreats and meetings. Conference complex. Spa services available. Gateway buildings are non-smoking.

**Rates**
Suites, $199-$250 includes full gourmet breakfast. Mid-week and weekend packages. Closed Christmas day. Number of Rooms: 39

**Cuisine**
Regional Fine DIning. Dinner served daily 5-9 p.m. Menu is sourced locally and changes often, see website. Gourmet Breakfast served daily form 7:30-11 a.m.

**Nearest Airport(s)**
DuBois Regional, Pittsburgh International

**Directions**
I-80 E: Exit 78 (Brookville) R on Rte. 36 N, 17 miles. Lodge on R. I-80 W: Exit 62 (Clarion) L on Rte. 68, go thru 4 stop lights to Main St. continue 10 mi. to Rte 36 At stop sign turn R, go S 4 miles cross river Go 1/2 mile farther, Lodge is on L.

# Tara - A Country Inn

www.tara-inn.com
2844 Lake Road, Clark, PA 16113
**800-782-2803** • 724-962-3535 • Fax 724-962-3250
info@tara-inn.com

*"The owners have succeeded in capturing the essence of the grand mansion that was the cynosure of Gone With The Wind."* Dallas Morning News.

Proprietors
**Donna & Jim Winner**

Inspired by the greatest movie of our time, Gone With the Wind, Tara recreated is in a real sense an embodiment of the Old South. Tara, although located in the "North", offers you a lasting impression of Southern Hospitality and a chance to enjoy the luxuries of days gone by. Tara is a virtual museum of Civil War and Gone With the Wind memorabilia and antiques. Indulge in our magnificent guest rooms complete with fireplaces and Jacuzzis and enjoy the finest in gourmet or casual dining. Tara offers an extensive wine list and an expertly stocked lounge. Afternoon Tea is a daily opportunity for houseguests to mingle and enjoy. Take a leisurely swim in either our indoor or outdoor heated pools, or stroll through formal gardens overlooking the beautiful 450-acre Shenango Lake. Celebrating 22 years of award-winning dining and overnight accommodations, Tara is the ultimate in World Class Country Inns, devoted to guests who expect the exceptional and appreciate the best. Jim and Donna Winner were named Pennsylvania's Innkeepers of the Year in 2007.

**Rates**
Gone With The Wind Getaway Packages (MAP) $250/$425.
B&B $195/$350. Corporate and Off-Season Rates Available.
Number of Rooms: 27

**Cuisine**
Ashley's Gourmet Dining Room offers the finest in 7-course white-glove and candlelight service while Stonewall's Tavern boasts a casual atmosphere with a wide array of hearty dinner selections.

**Nearest Airport(s)**
Pittsburgh, PA Cleveland, OH

**Directions**
From I-80 take Exit 4-B to Sharon/Hermitage Follow Rt. 18 North and drive 7 miles to exit PA 258.

# Buhl Mansion Guesthouse & Spa

www.buhlmansion.com
422 East State Street, Sharon, PA 16146
**866-345-2845** • 724-346-3046 • Fax 724-346-1702
info@buhlmansion.com

*Member Since 2002*

*Pennsylvania*

*Sharon*

*"Here in the westernmost part of Pennsylvania sits one of the most elegant, romantic properties in the United States." - The Washington Post*

Proprietors
**Jim and Donna Winner**

Buhl Mansion Guesthouse & Spa, rated one of America's Top 10 Most Romantic Inns, offers the ultimate in luxury, pampering & unsurpassed hospitality. Listed on the National Register of Historic Places, this 1890 Romanesque castle is steeped in history & romance. After years of neglect & abuse, the opulent home of Steel Baron Frank Buhl is now lovingly restored & offers grand memories of a lifetime as guests experience the life of America's royalty in our lavishly appointed guestrooms with fireplaces and Jacuzzis. The full-service spa offers the epitome of indulgence with over 100 options of services from which to choose. The Spa Romance Package is the most popular, offering couples massages, facials, manicures, lunch and a bottle of champagne. Guests have complimentary access to the spa's sauna, steam room & monsoon showers. Indulge each morning with breakfast in bed or dine in the picturesque breakfast room. Perfect for romantic getaways, indulgent spa escapes, exclusive executive retreats & castle weddings. Buhl Mansion was featured on the cover of Inns Magazine. Jim and Donna Winner were named PA Innkeepers of the Year in 2007.

**Rates**
Castle Escape Packages: $350 King and Queen Rooms; $450 Royal Grand Rooms; Spa Packages, 2nd night discounts and off-season rates available. Castle for a Day Package offers exclusive use. Number of Rooms: 10

**Cuisine**
Champagne & Welcome Tray await in each room. Afternoon Tea served daily, Champagne Reception served Fri & Sat. Rates include 25% discount at Ashley's Gourmet Dining Room or Stonewall's Tavern both at nearby Tara-A Country Inn (Limo provided on weekends).

**Nearest Airport(s)**
Pittsburgh, PA Cleveland, OH

**Directions**
From I-80: Exit 4-B to Sharon/Hermitage; N on Rt.18 for 3 mi.; L on E. State St. for 3 mi. Buhl is on L.

# The Inn on Negley
www.theinnonnegley.com
703 South Negley, Pittsburgh, PA 15232
**412-661-0631** • Fax 412-661-7525
info@theinnonnegly.com

*Member Since 2006*

*Pennsylvania*

*Pittsburgh*

*"During my visit to the university, The Inn on Negley met my every need.
The rooms are sensational and the food is even better!"*

Proprietor
**Elizabeth Sullivan**

The Inn on Negley is a beautifully restored period home located in the heart of Pittsburgh's charming and historic Shadyside area. Each of our eight guest rooms are custom designed with period furnishings, exquisite linens, Lady Primrose amenities, and a careful attention to detail. The Inn is just one block from Walnut Street and Ellsworth Avenue, which offers the finest and most unique shopping, dining, and entertainment experiences in Pittsburgh. Guests can linger and enjoy the tranquil atmosphere over refreshments while the innkeepers assist with plans to enjoy Pittsburgh. Additionally, our lovely Fernwood Tea room accepts appointments for English High Tea service offered each afternoon. Whether guests plan a full day of activities, business meetings, or an afternoon enjoying a splendid high tea service, The Inn on Negley can accomodate every guest preference.

**Rates**
King Suites: $195/$235. Queen Suites: $170/$190. Suites are beautifully appointed with private baths, luxurious linens, fireplaces, jacuzzi tubs, personal robes, high speed Internet, cable television and private phones with voicemail. Complimentary on site parking is also included. Number of Rooms: 8

**Cuisine**
Room rate includes gourmet breakfast for two. Breakfast: onsite chef prepared baked goods, hot, sweet & savory gourmet entrees, fresh fruit, yogurt, homemade cereals & granola.

**Nearest Airport(s)**
Pittsburgh Intl (20 miles)

**Directions**
Three miles from Downtown Pittsburgh. Call or visit website for directions.

# Inne at Watson's Choice

www.watsonschoice.com
234 Balsinger Road, Uniontown, PA 15401
**724-437-4999** • Fax 724.437.4999
innkeeper@watsonschoice.com

*Member Since 2007*

*"Beautiful place, great breakfast and loved the grounds."*

Innkeepers
**Nancy and Bill Ross**

Situated in the beautiful Laurel Highlands of Southwestern, PA and only thirty minutes from Fallingwater and House on Kentuck Knob, a property comprising two Frank Lloyd Wright masterpieces, **the Inne at Watson's Choice and Harvest House B&B** is located on 42 acres. It offers casual elegance in a warm country setting. The quaint circa-1800 brick farmhouse features seven charming and well-appointed guestrooms with private baths and a Great Room where a full country breakfast is served each morning. The Harvest House, across the courtyard from the Inne, has four guestrooms and one suite. All guestrooms are climate-controlled and include private baths and other amenities. The Inne's restored stable provides a unique and ideal setting for reunions, intimate weddings and other special occasions for ninety guests. The Inne at Watson's Choice is only 50 miles south of Pittsburgh and 25 minutes from Morgantown, WV.

**Rates**
$130.00 - $225.00 Open weekends only in Jan/Feb. Open full time in March thru December. Smoking permitted outdoors. No pets  Number of Rooms: 12

**Cuisine**
Full Country Breafast. Continental breakfast served to guests for an  in-depth tour at Fallingwater. Guests are welcome to bring their own spirits.

**Nearest Airport(s)**
Pittsburgh International 1 1/2hrs

**Directions**
RT 40E to Uniontown.RT 119S Bypass to McClellandtown Rd Exit. Turn left at light -Go 3mi on RT21W. Turn right on S&T Rd. Go to T - Turn left. RT40W to RT 119N to McClellandtown Rd Exit. Same as above. RT 51S to Uniontown. Take 119S Bypass. Same as above.

# Reynolds Mansion
www.reynoldsmansion.com
101 West Linn Sreet, Bellefonte, PA 16823
**800-899-3929** • 814-353-8407 • Fax 814-353-1530
innkeeper@reynoldsmansion.com

*Member Since 2001*

*Pennsylvania*

*Bellefonte*

*"A night or two at The Reynolds Mansion is a week's worth of vacation relaxation."*

Innkeepers/Owners
## Charlotte and Joseph Heidt, Jr.

Escape to the Reynolds Mansion and enter a romantic atmosphere of Victorian elegance and luxurious comfort. Enjoy a game of pool in the billiard room or curl up by the fire in the snuggery with your favorite book. Relax in four common rooms, each with a unique wood-carved and tiled fireplace. Built in 1885, the mansion is a blend of the Gothic, Italianate and Queen Anne styles. Interior details include a marble vestibule, classic mirrors, Eastlake woodwork, stained glass windows and inlaid parquet floors. Come and experience the architectural wonders of Bellefonte's Victorian days. Flyfish in "Class A" trout streams, attend top-notch concerts and legendary sporting events. Go antiquing or golfing. If you are looking for a romantic getaway, or a retreat from the stress of daily life, come visit us. A warm welcome awaits you. The Reynolds Mansion has been featured on the cover of "County Victorian" and voted "Best in the US near a University." Penn State is only 10 miles away.

**Rates**
6 Suites, $135/$325. Spacious rooms feature private baths with showers, fireplaces, Jacuzzi or steam shower, air conditioning, TV/VCR/DVD. Open year-round. Number of Rooms: 6

**Cuisine**
Full breakfast included. Walk to fine dining at the Wine Spectator award winning Gamble Mill Tavern. Complimentary Brandy.

**Nearest Airport(s)**
University Park (SCE)

**Directions**
I-80 exit 161. Take Rte. 220 S. toward Bellefonte to 550. Go right at bottom of ramp and follow 550 into town. At 3rd light, turn right onto Allegheny St. At 2nd light turn left on Linn. Enter through iron gates on right.

# Crestmont Inn

www.crestmont-inn.com
Crestmont Dr, Eagles Mere, PA 17731
**800-522-8767** • 570-525-3519 • Fax 570-525-3534
crestmnt@epix.net

*Member Since 1989*

*"Your hospitality made us feel like treasured friends visiting in your home."*

Innkeepers/Owners
**Elna & Fred Mulford**

The Crestmont Inn is nestled in the woods on the highest point in Eagles Mere, a quiet historic mountaintop town surrounded by a pristine lake, State Parks and State Forests. Our Restaurant is well known for delicious cuisine, romantic fireplaces, original art and warm hospitality. Our suites include king or queen beds, large private baths with clawfoot tubs, whirlpool tubs, spacious sitting areas with cable TV/HBO, fireplaces and refrigerators. Our family suites can accomodate 4 to 6 people. Enjoy nature walks, hiking, biking, tennis, lake activities, cross country skiing, ice skating, antiquing, shopping or simply relax. Crestmont Inn "Romance and Nature at its Best"!

*Pennsylvania*

*Eagles Mere*

**Rates**
$110/$240 per night Bed & Breakfast. MAP Rates are available. Economy Rooms, Suites, Whirlpool Suites, and Family Suites each with private bath, Cable TV/HBO and telephone. Number of Rooms: 15

**Cuisine**
Traditional country breakfast included. Fine dining and casual dinners available weekends in off season and 6 nights per week in season. Cocktail lounge with fine selection of spirits, wine and beer.

**Nearest Airport(s)**
Williamsport, PA

**Directions**
From Interstate 80, exit 232 to 42(N) for 33 miles to Eagles Mere Village. Turn left onto Lakewood Ave, then first right onto Crestmont Drive.

# Eagles Mere Inn

www.eaglesmereinn.com

Box #356 Corner of Mary & Sullivan Avenues, Eagles Mere, PA 17731
**800-426-3273** • 570-525-3273 • Fax 570-525-3904
relax@eaglesmereinn.com

*Member Since 1993*

*Pennsylvania*

*Eagles Mere*

*"Wonderful Food; Accomodating Staff; Ultimate Relaxation;*
*A Nature Photographer's Dream"*

Innkeepers
## Matthew Gale and Barbie Gale

Eagles Mere, 'the last unspoiled resort,' sits on a mountain with a pristine lake surrounded by giant hemlock, rhododendron, and mountain laurel. Restored in 2000, we are the last full service Historic Inn remaining from the 1800s. Incredible waterfalls, sunsets, hiking trails, birding, covered bridges, fishing, golf, tennis and swimming. Featured by numerous travel writers. Guests enjoy genuine hospitality and personal attention. We loan our bikes, xc skis and canoe. If you want a quiet, relaxing place to spend time together while enjoying warm hospitality and gourmet meals, visit our web site or call for reservations. "The LAST UNSPOILED RESORT" now waits for you!

**Rates**
16 rooms/3 suites $169/$279 includes five course Gourmet Dinner & Breakfast for two. Number of Rooms: 19

**Cuisine**
Selected as a "Top Ten" Pennsylvania Inn, our experience is in 3-and 4-star restaurants. Meals included in rates. We have the area's best reputation for excellent 5-course candlelit gourmet dinners. Wine List. Enjoy cocktails, beer & wine in our Pub. We serve ample full Country breakfasts.

**Nearest Airport(s)**
Williamsport Regional Airport (IPT)

**Directions**
Print directions from our website. I-80 to Exit #232 to Rt# 42N. I-99/15 take Rt. 220 east to Rt. 42N. From Rt 6 go south on 220 to 42S. In Eagles Mere turn on Mary Avenue.

SelectRegistry.com

# The Settlers Inn at Bingham Park

www.thesettlersinn.com
4 Main Ave., Hawley, PA 18428
**800-833-8527** • 570-226-2993 • Fax 570-226-1874
settler@thesettlersinn.com

*Member Since 1992*

*Visit this Inn's website at www.thesettlersinn.com*

Innkeepers/Owners
**Jeanne and Grant Genzlinger**

The Settlers Inn is a place to gather. Relax, play & rejuvenate at this artfully restored arts & crafts inn. Stroll the extensive grounds & discover colorful flower & herb gardens, a quiet reflecting pond, or sit along the banks of the meandering Lackawaxen River. Guestrooms are thoughtfully appointed with your comfort in mind. Luxurious European linens, featherbeds, whirlpool tubs and fireplaces invite travelers to pamper themselves. High speed wireless Internet, available at no additional cost, provides the flexibility to stay connected with friends, family or business associates. The cornerstone of the inn is the chef-owned farm-to-table restaurant highlighting artisan breads & menus influenced by the season. The Dining Room & Chestnut Tavern reflect the style of William Morris carried through-out the building. After a day of hiking or cross-country skiing, bask in the warmth of the bluestone fireplace. Summer offers dining alfresco on the terrace overlooking the grounds as well as The Potting Shed, a gift shop in the garden.

**Rates**
21 Rooms and Suites, $140/$250 B&B. Open year-round.
Number of Rooms: 21

**Cuisine**
The seasons and cultural history of the area shape both our ever-changing menu and the preparation of each dish which highlight products of local farmers and producers. In addition to the dining room, the Chestnut Tavern is the perfect place for conversation and a flavorful microbrew. In season, alfresco dining is available on our Terrace overlooking the gardens.

**Nearest Airport(s)**
Scranton (AVP) Allentown (ABE)

**Directions**
I-84 West to Exit 26. Route 390 N to Rt. 507 N. At light, turn left onto Rt. 6 West. 2 1/2 miles to the Inn.

# The French Manor

www.thefrenchmanor.com
P.O. Box 39, 50 Huntingdon Drive, South Sterling, PA 18460
**877-720-6090** • 570-676-3244 • Fax 570-676-8573
info@thefrenchmanor.com

*Member Since 1991*

*Pennsylvania*

*South Sterling*

*"A lovely getaway comprised of elegance, serenity, European architecture, warm customer service values & French cuisine that raises the bar in fine dining."*

Innkeepers/Owners
**The Logan Family**

An enchanting storybook stone chateau, the French Manor is nestled on 45 acres overlooking the beautiful Pocono Mountains. Old world charm and elegant furnishings are seamlessly joined with all the modern conveniences. Guests can enjoy luxurious suites with fireplace, Jacuzzi, and private balconies. Every guest is welcomed with complimentary sherry, cheese and fruit plate, and pampered with turndown service with Godiva chocolates. Our fine French restaurant features authentic and Nouvelle French cuisine served in our "Great Hall" where a wonderful vaulted ceiling and magnificent twin fireplaces create a romantic setting. Travelers can also enjoy our midweek 'Enchanted Evening' package or a special weekend throughout the year. Enjoy miles of trails for hiking, mountain biking, picnicking, snowshoeing, and cross-country skiing. Opening soon - the French Manor Spa including soothing spa services, indoor pool, whirlpool, fitness room, couples massage suite with fireplace, and five luxurious suites, all with Fireplace, Jacuzzi, & balcony views. This new facility will be eco-friendly using energy efficient equipment and green materials.

**Rates**
6 Rooms, $165/$255 B&B; 9 Suites, $240/$340 B&B. 8 Suites w/ fireplace & Jacuzzi. Rates are per couple. Number of Rooms: 15

**Cuisine**
Gourmet breakfast. Room service available. Nouvelle & authentic French cuisine for dinner, semi-formal attire. An extensive wine list is available & top-shelf liquors.

**Nearest Airport(s)**
Scranton/Wilkes-Barre & Lehigh Valley International

**Directions**
From NY & NJ: I-80 W to PA exit 307. Follow 191 N 28 miles, to South Sterling, turn L on Huckleberry Rd; From PA tpke (NE Extension): take exit #95, 80E to 380N to Exit #8 for Route 423 N for 8 mi to Route 191 N, 2 miles and turn L on Huckleberry Rd.

# The Inn at Turkey Hill

www.innatturkeyhill.com
991 Central Road, Bloomsburg, PA 17815
**570-387-1500** • Fax 570-784-3718
info@innatturkeyhill.com

*Member Since 2002*

*"How nice to find an enclave of good taste and class."* - Philadelphia Inquirer
*"Exquisite flavors seem to be the trademark."* - Times Leader

Innkeeper/Owner
**Andrew B. Pruden**

From romantic couples looking for a weekend diversion, corporate travelers seeking a tranquil place to rest, to visiting celebrities and dignitaries seeking quiet anonymity, the Inn is a casually elegant and comfortably appointed escape of charm and class. Among the rolling hills and farmlands of rural Pennsylvania, The Inn at Turkey Hill is considered "an oasis along the interstate." Just a moment off Interstate 80 and minutes from downtown Bloomsburg, guests are treated to a hospitable atmosphere of towering trees and friendly ducks waddling about the courtyard. Rejuvenate yourself in one of our guest rooms attractively furnished with reproduction pieces or give in to the alure of a whirlpool bath and fireplace or take advantage of some of our amenties such as complimentary high speed Internet and DVD/CD players. An award winning restaurant is located on the property featuring creative, world class cuisine and a critically acclaimed wine list along with a friendly and accommodating staff. A warm welcome awaits you.

**Rates**
14 Traditional rooms $121/$135; 2 Inn rooms $126/$140 5 Stable Rooms $159/$193; Deluxe King $175/$215; King Supreme $182/$235. Number of Rooms: 23

**Cuisine**
Complimentary continental breakfast including hot entree. Afternoon refreshments. American-Continental cuisine featured nightly. Full service tavern.

**Nearest Airport(s)**
Wilkes-Barre

**Directions**
Convenient at Exit 236 of I-80. Traveling W on I-80, take Exit 236A. At 1st traffic light, turn L, & the Inn will be on your L. Traveling E on I-80, take Exit 236. Turn L at off-ramp stop sign. Turn L at 1st light. The Inn is on the L.

# The Inn at New Berlin

www.innatnewberlin.com
321 Market Street, P.O. Box 390, New Berlin, PA 17855
**800-797-2350** • 570-966-0321 • Fax 570-966-9557
stay@innatnewberlin.com

*Member Since 1997*

*Pennsylvania • New Berlin*

*"A feast for the soul. Your chef is a treasure and your gift shop is dangerous.
An uptown experience in a rural setting!"*

Innkeepers/Owners
**Nancy and Robert Schanck**

Wine Spectator
AWARD OF EXCELLENCE

The *Philadelphia Inquirer* purports, "A luxurious base for indulging in a clutch of quiet pleasures." A visit to central Pennsylvania wouldn't be complete without a stay at The Inn at New Berlin. In the heart of the pastoral Susquehanna Valley, this romantic getaway offers an abundance of life's gentle pursuits. Bike country roads and covered bridges less traveled; explore charming downtowns and mountain hiking trails; shop antique coops, and artist's galleries. Meanwhile, back at The Inn, Innkeepers Nancy and Robert Schanck invite guests to relax on The Inn's front porch, savor an exquisite meal and a glass of fine wine, and rediscover the nourishing aspects of simple joys and time together. The Inn offers gracious accommodations in two restored historic homes, fine dining at Gabriel's Restaurant, lighter fare at the Salutation Tavern, Swedish massages in our Carriage House Spa, and a treasure trove for shopping at Gabriel's Gifts. Wednesday evenings, all bottled wines are half price. Friday evenings enjoy live piano music. Guests relay they depart feeling nurtured, relaxed, and most of all inspired.

**Rates**
11 rooms in 2 historic buildings, $149/$219 B&B. Whirlpool, fireplace & suite rooms available. Number of Rooms: 11

**Cuisine**
Gabriel's Restaurant & Salutation Tavern: dinner Wed. through Sun., lunch Sat., brunch Sun. Contemporary American cuisine. *Wine Spectator* Award of Excellence.

**Nearest Airport(s)**
Harrisburg

**Directions**
In central PA, exit 210A (Lewisburg) off I-80. Rt 15 south 11 miles to Rt 304W 8 miles to New Berlin. (OR) Rt 15 north from Harrisburg to Selinsgrove exit Rt 35. In Selinsgrove, R on Market St and L on Rt 522. R on Rt 204W 9 miles to New Berlin. The Inn is a stone's throw from the intersection of Rts 204 & 304.

# The Lafayette Inn

www.lafayetteinn.com
525 W. Monroe St., Easton, PA 18042
**800-509-6990** • 610-253-4500 • Fax 610-253-4635
info@lafayetteinn.com

*Member Since 2000*

*Pennsylvania*

*Easton*

*"We loved your inn. So many special touches and the staff so sweet & helpful.
Loved the hot tub, the entire breakfast layout, and overall coziness!"*

Innkeepers/Owners
**Paul and Laura Di Liello**

Our elegant mansion, built in 1895, is situated in a beautiful historic neighborhood near Lafayette College. Eighteen antique filled guest rooms welcome travelers visiting the Lehigh Valley's many attractions. The suites feature fireplaces and whirlpool tubs for that special getaway. The inviting parlor, wrap-around porch and tiered patio call out to those longing to relax with a cup of coffee and a good book. A bountiful breakfast is served at individual tables in our bright sunroom or on the porch. Complementary soft drinks, coffee, fresh baked goods and fruit are available all day. The entire inn has wireless high-speed internet access and a loaner laptop is available. Whether visiting the colors of the Crayola Factory with the kids, riding the historic, mule-drawn canal boats, hot air ballooning above the countryside, exploring underwater diving excitement, visiting area colleges or just lounging and rejuvenating, The Lafayette Inn makes a great base for your getaway. Welcome to our inn!

**Rates**
18 Rooms/Suites $125/$250. Antique-filled rooms, private baths, TV/DVD, phones. Premier rooms and suites with gas fireplaces, whirlpool or soaking tubs, balcony. The entire inn is high-speed wireless. Open year-round. Number of Rooms: 18

**Cuisine**
Full breakfast daily, complimentary soft drinks, coffee, fruit, and pastries available all day. Excellent restaurants within walking distance. No liquor license.

**Nearest Airport(s)**
Lehigh Valley International, Newark, Philadelphia

**Directions**
I-78, Easton exit North to Third St. toward Lafayette College. Up hill to corner of Cattell and Monroe Streets.

# Glasbern

www.glasbern.com
2141 Pack House Road, Fogelsville, PA 18051
**610-285-4723** • Fax 610-285-2862
innkeeper@glasbern.com

*Pennsylvania*

*Fogelsville*

*"Unbeatable-so relaxing and warm-we'll be back."*

Owner
**Al Granger**

At the edge of Pennsylvania Dutch Country, a 21st Century Country Inn has evolved from a 19th Century family farm. Our grounds include many pastures & gardens that flourish amidst 100 acres of paths, streams, & ponds; all of which are available for our guests to explore. Inside, whirlpools and fireplaces enhance most guest rooms. All have private baths, phones, high-speed Internet access, TVs and DVDs. Some luxury suites include wet bars, Jacuzzi shower systems and CD music systems. Canine-friendly suites are available with limitations for our four-legged friends. For the physically ambitious guest, an outdoor pool, bicycles, hiking trails and an indoor fitness center are available. Contemporary American Cuisine is offered under the Barn's timbered cathedral ceiling. Much of the food comes from the gardens and pastures of the Inn. Rated one of the country's **TOP 10 ROMANTIC INNS** by American Historic Inns & iloveinns.com, Glasbern provides a romantic glimpse of the past, with an invitation to enjoy the pleasures of today.

### Rates
Ten rooms, $140/$250. Eleven whirlpool/fireplace rooms, $175/$325. Nine whirlpool/fireplace suites, $225/375. Five deluxe suites and one whirlpool/fireplace cottage, $275/$475. Number of Rooms: 36

### Cuisine
A full country breakfast, including a continental buffet, is served daily. Contemporary American Cuisine is offered in the Dining Room nightly. Four-course dinner service with a pre-fixe menu is held Saturday evenings.

### Nearest Airport(s)
Lehigh Valley International - 15 miles

### Directions
From I-78 take Rt. 100 (N) for .2 mi.; L. at light for .3 mi. to R. on Church St. (N) for .6 mi.; R. on Pack House Rd. for .8 mi. to our driveway.

# Sayre Mansion

www.sayremansion.com
250 Wyandotte Street, Bethlehem, PA 18015
**877-345-9019** • 610-882-2100 • Fax 610-882-1223
innkeeper@sayremansion.com

*Member Since 2003*

*Pennsylvania*

*Bethlehem*

*"Your Inn provided a delightful respite from a busy life! Your service and friendliness were exceptional. We shall return!"*

Proprietors
## Jeanne and Grant Genzlinger and Carrie Ohlandt

Timeless Elegance in a Distinguished Gothic Revival Mansion. The Inn offers luxury and comfort in eighteen guest rooms each preserving the architectural details of the Main House. In addition to the Main House, our classically restored Carriage House offers guests a home away from home atmosphere in their choice of three suites. Each suite provides a separate living room and bedroom allowing guests ultimate privacy. Amenities include: fine linens, private baths, high-speed wireless internet access, featherbeds, jacuzzi bathtubs, and flat screen TV's. Robert Sayre's Wine Cellar offers guests an opportunity to sample a selection of wine. Personal Service is the cornerstone of the guest experience. The Asa Packer Room, our unique conference center, is ideal for business meetings. Gatherings and special events are held in a pair of elegant parlors, each with its own fireplace. Century old trees adorn the two acres of picturesque grounds which provide a beautiful setting for weddings or large gatherings under our 30' x 60' tent.

**Rates**
21 rooms and suites, $160/$325 B&B Open Year-Round.
Number of Rooms: 21

**Cuisine**
Breakfast highlights homemade artisan breads, pastries, house specialties including french pudding, stratas and quiche, omelets. Excellent restaurants serving lunch and dinner are located within one mile of the Inn.

**Nearest Airport(s)**
Lehigh Valley International Airport is a five minute drive.

**Directions**
Located within blocks of Lehigh University, St. Lukes Hospital and Historic Bethlehem. See the website for door-to-door driving directions.

# The Inn at Bowman's Hill

www.theinnatbowmanshill.com
518 Lurgan Road, New Hope, PA 18938
**215-862-8090** • Fax 215-862-9362
info@theinnatbowmanshill.com

*"World class elegance." "An amazing retreat." "How do you go elsewhere after this experience?"*

Owner/Innkeeper
**Mike Amery**

Award-winning luxury, romance and privacy on a manicured 5-acre estate adjacent to Bowman's Hill Wildflower Preserve ... and yet just minutes from the "action" in downtown New Hope. AAA Four-Diamond and Condé Nast recommended. Selected in 2006 as one of the "Top 10 Most Romantic" Inns in the nation in 2006, this exclusive retreat offers just two suites and four rooms, all with king-size featherbeds, DVD players, high-speed Internet and flatscreen TVs. Beautifully appointed bathrooms feature heated whirlpools for two, separate showers and heated towel racks. Our two-person Manor Suite shower has 11 jets ... enter at your own risk! The dramatic Tower Suite features cathedral ceilings, master bedroom, bathroom, sitting room and private entrance. Other amenities include outdoor hot tub and heated swimming pool (seasonal). Romance packages and engagement packages are available as well as in-room massage by certified therapists. Our beautiful, fully-equipped boardroom offers a unique working environment for creative brainstorming, strategic planning or high-level client interactions. Corporate jet access is just 15 minutes away.

**Rates**
4 rooms $295/$415. Suites $404/$555. 2-night minimum most weekends. Seasonal rates may vary. Rooms feature king-size featherbeds, whirlpools, fireplaces and robes ... some rooms with verandas. Number of Rooms: 6

**Cuisine**
3-course gourmet breakfast included. Full-English breakfast or gourmet choices. Selections cooked to order. Seasonally appropriate afternoon snacks. 24-hour tea & coffee service.

**Nearest Airport(s)**
Trenton Mercer or Philadelphia Int'l

**Directions**
Exit 51 on I-95 toward New Hope. 7 miles TL onto River Rd. 2 miles TL onto Lurgan Rd. Inn is 1/4 mile on left. From New Hope 2 1/2 miles S on River Rd. TR onto Lurgan Rd. See above.

# Barley Sheaf Farm Estate & Spa

🍽️ 🍽️

www.barleysheaf.com
5281 Old York Road (Rte 202), Holicong, Bucks County, PA 18928
**215-794-5104** • Fax 215-794-5332
info@barleysheaf.com

*Member Since 1982*

*Pennsylvania*

*Holicong*

*"A living masterpiece...Barley Sheaf Farm Estate & Spa."*

Innkeeper/Owner - **Christine Soderman**
General Manager/Owner - **Lola E. Liebert**

An exclusive destination estate spa in historic Bucks County, once the home of Pulitzer-prize winning playwright George S. Kaufman, is surrounded by 100-acres of pasture and woodland views. Sixteen luxurious suites in the 1740 manor house, the guest cottage, and 19th Century barn feature whirlpool tubs, fireplaces, feather beds, full body steam showers, sunrooms,wet bars private balconies and terraces. The spa offers exceptional all-natural custom blended products and services in private in-suite treatment rooms. The elegant estate has trellis gardens, an antique French gazebo, pond, a junior Olympic-size pool and fitness center. A gourmet brunch is presented in the conservatory and on the terrace. Wine and cheese are offered in your suite upon arrival, a fully stocked courtesy wet bar, flat-screen TV and Bose CD. Centrally located near New Hope and Peddler's Village shops, antiquing, museums, fine restaurants and outdoor activities. Available for conferences and weddings with event planners on staff. French, German and Swedish spoken.

**Rates**
16 luxurious suites, $250/$750 Open year round. Activities: Spa, New Hope shops, antiquing, museums, art galleries, Delaware River outdoor activities. Number of Rooms: 16

**Cuisine**
Full gourmet brunch, afternoon snack, dinners Friday and Saturday evenings, other nights by request. Wine and cheese on arrival.

**Nearest Airport(s)**
Philadelphia Airport (PA) and Newark Airport (NJ)

**Directions**
On Rte 202/263 between New Hope and Doylestown, 0.5 mi SW of Lahaska, 4 miles south of New Hope.

# Mercersburg Inn

www.mercersburginn.com
405 South Main St., Mercersburg, PA 17236
**717-328-5231** • 866-MBURG-01 • Fax 717-328-3403
Lisa@mercersburginn.com

*Member Since 1998*

*"Absolutely Wonderful! Great food, great service! The Inn and our room was so elegant. We felt so at home. Thank you for a beautiful and relaxing stay."*

Innkeepers/Owners
**Lisa and Jim McCoy**

In 1909, Ione and Harry Byron had a magnificent dream, to build a home that brought comfort and entertainment to those that entered. From that dream, the 24,000 sq. ft Prospect, with 11 ft ceilings throughout, was born. The mahogany-paneled dining room and the sun-filled enclosed porch invite our guests to a culinary experience that will not be soon forgotten. Large enough to ensure your privacy but still able maintain the intimacy and service of a country inn. The double-curving staircases lead you to our luxuriously appointed guest rooms. Draw yourself a nice warm bath in one of our antique soaking tubs, dry off with the softest of towels, slip on a fine robe, and drift away to sleep on your featherbed. Awake in the morning to the smell of fresh baked morning goods, and our delicious 3-course breakfast. If the season permits, stroll through the flower and herb gardens that appoint the 5.5 acre property. If golfing, hiking, fly-fishing, or skiing are on your to-do-list, let our staff make the arrangements for you. All these activities and more are only a few minutes from the Inn. We look forward to having you in our home

### Rates
$140/$395 B&B. 3 w/fireplaces, 1 w/clawfoot whirlpool tub, 2 w/Jacuzzi & TV, 3 w/antique baths. Kings and Queens. Open year round except Christmas Eve & Christmas Day. Number of Rooms: 17

### Cuisine
Full gourmet breakfast. Fine dining and wines at Byron's, our fine dining restaurant. Seating from 5:30 till 8:30 p.m. Thurs. Fri. and Sat. and 5:00 till 8:00 p.m. on Sunday. Reservations are recommended. Full bar service

### Nearest Airport(s)
BWI, Dulles

### Directions
From I-81, PA exit 5 (Greencastle), West on Route 16; twelve miles to historic Mercersburg. Located at junction of 16 and 7

# Hickory Bridge Farm

www.hickorybridgefarm.com
96 Hickory Bridge Road, Orrtanna, PA 17353
**717-642-5261** • Fax 717-642-6419
hickory@pa.net

*Member Since 1976*

*Pennsylvania*

*Orrtanna*

*"What a special retreat from life's demands! Thank you."*

Innkeepers/Owners
**Robert and Mary Lynn Martin**

A quaint country retreat offering 5-bedroom farmhouse (circa 1750's) accommodations (some with whirlpool baths), and four private cottages with wood burning fireplaces along a mountain stream. Dinner is served in a beautiful restored Pennsylvania barn decorated with hundreds of antiques. All meals are farm-fresh & bountiful. Full breakfast is offered to overnight guests at the farmhouse and is taken to their room on Sunday morning. The farm is located 9 miles west of Gettysburg, Pennsylvania, on 75 beautiful acres-a wonderful place to relax while visiting Gettysburg or antiquing in the nearby area. Featured in *Taste of Home* magazine. Serving guests since 1977.

**Rates**
9 Rooms, Cottages and Farmhouse, $95/$165 B&B. Open year-round. Number of Rooms: 7

**Cuisine**
Fine country dining in a beautiful restored Pennsylvania barn? Friday, Saturday, and Sunday. banquets and parties served daily. No spirits are served; you may bring your own.

**Nearest Airport(s)**
Harrisburg

**Directions**
Gettysburg, Rte 116 W to Fairfield and R 3 mi N to Orrtanna. Or Rte 997 to Rte 30 E for 9 mi turn S at Cashtown for 3 mi.

# Baladerry Inn at Gettysburg

www.baladerryinn.com
40 Hospital Road, Gettysburg, PA 17325
**800-220-0025** • 717-337-1342
innkeeper@baladerryinn.com

*Member Since 1998*

*Pennsylvania*

*Gettysburg*

> *"Beautiful site and accomodations. Great breakfast. We love it.*
> *A warm place like home."*

Innkeeper/Owner
**Suzanne Lonky**

Baladerry Inn is located five minutes from downtown Gettysburg on four acres at the edge of the Gettysburg Battlefield. Walk or bike to Little Round Top, site of the second days battle. This brick Federal-style home (circa 1830), served as a field hospital during the battle at Gettysburg. A large two-storied great room dominated by a massive brick fireplace is both a dining and gathering area. A brick terrace provides an outdoor area for breakfasting and for socializing. A garden gazebo offers tranquil privacy. Enjoy a game of tennis on our court. Private and spacious, the Inn is an excellent choice for history buffs, leisure travelers, bicyclists, small business meetings, weddings and reunions.

### Rates
10 Rooms, $135/$250 B&B; $20 extra person in room. Open year-round. Smoking permitted outdoors only. No pets. Number of Rooms: 10

### Cuisine
A full served breakfast, delicious baked snacks. Guests are welcome to bring their own spirits.

### Nearest Airport(s)
Harrisburg

### Directions
From U.S. 15, exit at Taneytown Road. N 1 mile, R at Blacksmith Shop Road, R onto Hospital Road.

# Inn at Herr Ridge

www.herrtavern.com
900 Chambersburg Rd., Gettysburg, PA 17325
**800-362-9849** • 717-334-4332 • Fax 717-334-3332
info@herrtavern.com

🍽️ 🍽️ 🍽️ 🍷

*Member Since 2004*

*Pennsylvania*

*Gettysburg*

> *"We can't say enough to truly explain how happy we are with the beautiful room and excellent staff" "Dinner last night was exquisite"*

Wine Spectator
AWARD OF EXCELLENCE

Innkeeper/Owner
**Steven Wolf**

The enchanting atmosphere of the Inn at Herr Ridge is unforgettable. Built in 1815 and nestled between the historic battlefields of Gettysburg and one of Pennsylvania's wooded treasures, Caledonia State Park on historic Rt 30. The Inn offers a rare experience to every guest who crosses the threshold, and is only minutes from town. Tastefully decorated, charmingly unique rooms await. Enjoy an evening in your room by the fireplace, or step into your private Jacuzzi bath. Hungry? Experience the alluring setting of our private dining room. And don't forget the wine. We offer an extensive Wine Spectator award winning wine list. Many of which are stored in our exquisite, windowed wine cellar. Our full-service bar also offers premium spirits. The main house of the Inn, became the first Confederate hospital during the battle of Gettysburg. It is beautifully restored and listed in the National Register of Historic Places. If you are searching for a relaxing and romantic getaway, look no further. The fireplace is glowing, and the wine is chilled. Come visit us!

**Rates**
16 rooms $159/$359. Open year-round.   Number of Rooms: 16

**Cuisine**
Fabulous innovative and seasonal influenced menu. Private Dining and Banquet facilities.

**Nearest Airport(s)**
Harrisburg (MDT), Baltimore (BWI)

**Directions**
From Gettysburg square, Proceed on Route 30 west, 1.7 miles. Inn is on left at Herr's Ridge Road intersection.

# The Beechmont Bed & Breakfast Inn

www.thebeechmont.com
315 Broadway, Hanover, PA 17331
**800-553-7009** • 717-632-3013 • Fax 717-632-2769
innkeeper@thebeechmont.com

*Pennsylvania*

*Hanover*

*"We definitely made the right choice when we came here!" "The breakfasts were fantastic...you have the best coffee ever!" "...a fun spot to enjoy."*

Innkeepers/Owners
**Kathryn and Thomas White**

Located on a tree-lined street of stately historic homes, The Beechmont has welcomed business and leisure travelers since 1986 with exceptional hospitality and thoughtful extras designed to meet your needs. Strolling through the garden guests are awed by its center-piece, a 145-year-old Magnolia tree. A well-stocked library and parlor offer a backdrop for relaxed conversation, while well-appointed, spacious guest rooms assure a comfortable stay. High speed wireless internet access is available, or use our guest internet station. Guests often explore President Eisenhower's home and farm and the National Military Park in Gettysburg (just 14 miles west of Hanover). A marker in front of the house proclaims the spot where General Jeb Stuart met union troops and was forced north, delaying his arrival in Gettysburg. Guests love our numerous antique malls and gift shops, enjoy golfing on championship courses, touring wineries throughout the county, and discovering vibrant fall colors in the hills of southern Pennsylvania. The innkeeper's sincerest wish is for The Beechmont to be a memory that lingers joyously long after your visit has ended.

**Rates**
$169 - 104. Corporate rates Mon-Thur. All rooms have A/C, WIFI, cable TV & telephones. Some w/ fireplaces & whirlpools. Open year round. Number of Rooms: 7

**Cuisine**
Sumptuous breakfast. Help yourself cookie jar. Complimentary soft drinks and bottled water. Excellent restaurants nearby.

**Nearest Airport(s)**
Baltimore Washington Int'l (BWI)

**Directions**
From Baltimore: I-695 to I-795 to MD 30/PA 94. Turn R at the square on Broadway (PA 194). Inn is 3.5 blocks from square on the R; guest parking in the rear of the inn. From DC: I-495 to I-270 to Rt. 15 N to Rt. 116 E.

# The Sheppard Mansion

www.sheppardmansion.com
117 Frederick St., Hanover, PA 17331
**877-762-6746** • 717-633-8075 • Fax 717-633-8074
reservations@sheppardmansion.com

*Member Since 2002*

*Pennsylvania*

*Hanover*

*"Sinking into the cloud-like beds provided our best night's sleep ever!"*

Innkeeper/Owner - **Kathryn Sheppard-Hoar**
General Manager - **Timothy Bobb**

Nestled in the heart of Hanover's Historic District stands a grand 3-story brick and marble Mansion surrounded by lush gardens. Built in 1913 by Mr. and Mrs. H.D. Sheppard, co-founder of The Hanover Shoe, the Mansion now operates as an elegant full service Inn and event facility. Featuring the original furnishings and restored with modern amenities, the Mansion features numerous parlors, bedrooms and suites with oversized soaking tubs in the private marble baths--all for our guests' enjoyment. Days can be spent exploring nearby Gettysburg, antique hunting or touring Lancaster, Baltimore, Washington, DC or Hershey. Want to relax instead? Have a massage and lounge around the house. Complete your pampered experience with an exquisite meal in our Dining Room, serving French-inspired cuisine Wednesday through Saturday nights. Check our website for lodging and dining packages.

**Rates**
9 rooms and suites, King, Queen and Twin Beds, $140/$350 per night. 2 BR Guest Cottage on property available weekly. Corporate rates available. All rooms have private baths, A/C, Data Port, TV, Telephones and in-room coffee.   Number of Rooms: 9

**Cuisine**
Full gourmet breakfast included. Fine dining offered Wed. thru Sat. nights featuring a seasonal menu of French-inspired cuisine.

**Nearest Airport(s)**
BWI 1hr, MDT 1hr

**Directions**
1 block S of Center Square in Hanover, @ intersection of Frederick St. (Rt 194) & High St. (Rt 116). Minutes from US Rt 15, I-83, I-270, I-795 & PA Turnpike.

# Cameron Estate Inn & Restaurant

www.cameronestateinn.com
1855 Mansion Lane, Mount Joy, PA 17552
**888-422-6376** • 717-492-0111 • Fax 717-653-8596
info@cameronestateinn.com

*Member Since 2005*

*Pennsylvania*

*Mount Joy*

*"What a treasure! Lovely house, beautiful guest rooms, charming hosts! The restaurant rivals any in New York or Philly. Highly recommended!"*

Innkeepers/Owners
**Randy Wagner**
**John Jarboe**

The Cameron Estate Inn is the former summer estate of Secretaries of War to Lincoln and Grant. It is the largest historic Inn in the Pennsylvania Dutch and Hershey regions of the Susquehanna Valley. This grand 1805 Federal style mansion is secluded on 15 acres of lawn and woodland with two trout streams and provides the perfect venue to relax and unwind in an unspoiled country setting. Step back in time and let us pamper you with our historic, yet sumptuous guest accommodations featuring authentic European antiques and Ralph Lauren linens. Allow us to tantalize you with our refined culinary expertise, a full liquor license and our extensive wine list. For brides, grooms and their families, the Inn provides an elegant outdoor wedding venue. Well-situated out-of-the-way location ideal for exploring Lancaster, Hershey, Harrisburg, York, day trips to Gettysburg or Longwood Gardens, and all major tourist activities that include Amish/Pennsylvania Dutch, Lancaster, Hershey Park and Spa, golfing, theaters, fine dining, museums, antiquing, hiking and biking. Physically located midway between Hershey and Lancaster, but truly located....A WORLD AWAY! Visit us on the web at www.cameronestateinn.com.

**Rates**
16 guest rooms & suites and a 2 bedroom cottage, some w/fireplaces & Jacuzzi tubs. Private baths, A/C. $119/$249. Open year round. Corporate Rates. Number of Rooms: 18

**Cuisine**
Complimentary daily served breakfast. Fine Dining Wed-Sun. Contemporary American Cuisine w/ full liquor license.

**Nearest Airport(s)**
Harrisburg (MDT) Philadelphia (PHL) Baltimore (BWI)

**Directions**
Midway between Harrisburg & Lancaster, Hershey & York. Detailed directions online at http://www.cameronestateinn.com/directions.htm

 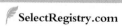

# Swiss Woods

www.swisswoods.com
500 Blantz Road, Lititz, PA 17543
**800-594-8018** • 717-627-3358
innkeeper@swisswoods.com

*Member Since 1993*

*Pennsylvania*

*Lititz*

*"Truly a haven of rest"... "Spectacular--I didn't want to leave!"... "beautiful grounds!"*

Innkeepers/Owners
**Werner and Debrah Mosimann**

Surrounded by meadows and gardens, Swiss Woods is a quiet retreat on 30 acres in Lancaster's Amish country. All rooms feature patios or balconies, some with lake views, and are decorated with the natural wood furnishings typical of Switzerland. Fabulous breakfasts, complemented by our own blend of coffee, are served in a sunlit common room. Convenient to Lancaster's famous farmers markets and wide variety of activities, Hershey is also just a short drive. After a day of antiquing, shopping or visiting quilt shops, enjoy the views of extraordinary gardens, landscaped with a wide variety of annuals and perennials. Take a relaxing hike through the woods, watch the birds, or enjoy a drink on the garden swing with a good book and a sweet treat from our kitchen. In winter settle in to read next to the inn's handsome sandstone fireplace. We offer a quiet, restful place for you to reconnect and refresh. German spoken.

**Rates**
6 Rooms (2 with Jacuzzi), all with patios and balconies.
$135/$190. 1 suite $170/$190. Number of Rooms: 7

**Cuisine**
Inn breakfast specialties may include garden fritatta, freshly-baked breads from old world recipes, honey apple french toast, or a potato quiche. The afternoon boasts sweets on the sideboard. Don't miss the biscotti!

**Nearest Airport(s)**
Harrisburg & Philadelphia

**Directions**
From Lancaster: 11 miles N on 501 thru Lititz. L on Brubaker Valley Rd 1 mi to lake. R on Blantz Rd. Inn is on the L. From NYC: Rt 78/22 West to exit 13-Bethel. S on Rt 501 1 mile beyond Brickerville. R on Brubaker Valley Rd. 1 mi to lake.

# The King's Cottage

www.kingscottagebb.com
1049 East King Street, Lancaster, PA 17602-3231
**800-747-8717** • 717-397-1017 • Fax 717-397-3447
info@kingscottagebb.com

*Member Since 1995*

*Pennsylvania*

*Lancaster*

*"We loved the King's Cottage. We stayed in the Majestic Chambre. The room was beautiful, innkeepers friendly & breakfast excellent. Rose petal bath is great!"*

Innkeepers/Owners
**Janis Kutterer and Ann Willets**

**The King's Cottage, A Bed & Breakfast Inn** is a beautifully restored 1913 mansion with modern amenities in the heart of Lancaster County. Close to historic Lancaster and scenic Amish country, it is the perfect place for touring farmland, farmers markets and Amish shops, or visit Lancaster's thriving arts community. Or use us as a hub for visits to PA colleges. Guests enjoy original crystal chandeliers, polished hardwood floors, fireplaces and free WIFI in a casually elegant atmosphere. Luxurious rooms with King or Queen beds, antique armoires, private baths, some fireplaces, antique soaking tubs or whirlpools. After a gourmet breakfast, visit scenic Amish farmlands, tour historic sites, shop for hand-made quilts, crafts & antiques, or day trip to Hershey, Gettysburg, Winterthur & Longwood Gardens. Onsite massage available. During afternoon refreshments we assist with dinner or next day's itinerary. Dinner in Amish home arranged in advance. On National Register. Awarded 'Top 10 Most Romantic Inn' by American Historic Inns. For business travelers: WIFI, fax, full or early continental breakfast to fit schedule, late check in, same day cancel by noon & corporate rates.

**Rates**
7 rooms, 1 Honeymoon Cottage: $150/$300 Fireplaces, Whirlpools, Hot Tub, DVD, WIFI, Business rates available. Holiday rates higher. Number of Rooms: 8

**Nearest Airport(s)**
Harrisburg (MDT) 35 minutes
Philadelphia (PHL) 65 minutes
Baltimore (BWI) 95 minutes

**Cuisine**
Gourmet breakfast, afternoon refreshments. Dietary restrictions accomodated with advance notice. Close to casual & fine dining. 24 hr. guest kitchen w/ice, bottled water, snacks, hot beverages.

**Directions**
Rt 30 to Walnut St exit. At 2nd light turn L on Ranck. At 2nd stop sign turn L. Go 1 block & turn R onto Cottage Ave. Inn is last house on R. Parking: turn R at our white wall.

# The Inn & Spa at Intercourse Village

www.amishcountryinns.com
3542 Old Philadelphia Pike  -  Box 598, Intercourse, PA  17534
**800-664-0949** • 717-768-2626
innkeeper@inn-spa.com

*Member Since 2005*

*"Perfect Honeymoon Setting. Most Elegant & Delicious Breakfast. Staff is very
Friendly.  Highest Recommendations."*

**Innkeepers/Owners**
## Ruthann & Elmer H. Thomas, CHA

Surround yourself in luxury, comfort and pleasures for the body and spirit at our inn and
spa. Enjoy elegance in a quiet village setting that entreats you to a place of peace, beauty
and comfort. Travel through time as you enter the 1909 Victorian Inn filled with period
furnishings and antique treasures. Its refinement and sophistication deliver high-class ac-
coutrements for those of discerning tastes. If upscale country is more your style, then reserve
one of our Country Homestead suites with private entrance and over 400 sq. ft. of space
to relax in and forget the world around you. Our suites include ensuite bath, jetted tub,
steam shower, sitting area with love seat, fireplace, wet bar and many other special treats
which await you. For the ultimate escape in luxury, for divine romance and relaxation, find
yourself engulfed in sumptuous grandeur in our Grand Suites complete with Jacuzzi, King
Bed and Fireplace. Arise to a full five course gourmet candlelit breakfast and then indulge
yourself in a delightful diversion at our on site Spa. AAA Four Diamond Award Bed &
Breakfast

### Rates
All suites have king/queen beds, ensuite bath, gas log
fireplace, loveseat, microwave, refrigerator, coffee maker, CTV,
VCR/DVD player, phone, data port, Wi-Fi, & AC. Grand Suites
$299/$399 Homestead Suites $169/$239 Victorian Rooms
$159/$199.   Number of Rooms: 9 Suites

### Cuisine
5 course gourmet candlelit breakfast, prepared by our chef &
served on fine English china in our formal dining room.

### Nearest Airport(s)
Harrisburg 1 hr, Philadelphia 1 1/2 hrs, Baltimore 1 1/2 hrs.

### Directions
Located on Pa Rte 340 in the Historic Village of Intercourse. 11
mi. E of Lancaster, Pa. More Directions on our web site.

# Hamanassett Bed & Breakfast

www.hamanassett.com
725 Darlington Road, P.O. Box 366, Chadds Ford, PA 19017
**877-836-8212** • 610-459-3000
stay@hamanassett.com

*Member Since 2005*

*Pennsylvania*

*Chadds Ford*

*"The elaborate breakfasts are a highlight."* - NY Times.
*"Southern hospitality at its finest"* - Pennsylvania magazine.

Innkeepers/Owners
**Ashley and Glenn Mon**

Located in the Brandywine Valley, home to Longwood Gardens, Hamanassett is a grand 1856 English country house where Southern hospitality and personal service is emphasized. The main house has six spacious bedrooms and suites, each individually decorated and featuring en suite baths, original hardwood floors, antique furniture, queen or king beds, TV/VCR with free film library, free wireless internet access, robes, and gorgeous views of the wooded grounds. Some of the rooms have fire places. Enjoy the billiards room, sip a glass of sherry or port in the elegant living room or light-filled solarium, or enjoy a quiet moment on the terrace or beside the koi pond with waterfall. Charming two story 2 bedroom 2 1/2 bath carriage house for those traveling with small children or dogs or for those who just want a little extra privacy. Although quietly elegant, there are no formalities. Near all attractions such as Winterthur, Wyeth Museum, Barnes museum, Nemours, and Philadelphia -- but a world away.Also recommended by *The New York Times*, Time Out New York, Frommers, Fodors, and Philadelphia, Pennsylvania, and Baltimore magazines.

**Rates**
Rooms and Suites: $155/$250. Carriage House: $350/$500.
Weekly/monthly rates available.  Number of Rooms: 7

**Cuisine**
Full gourmet breakfast. Special diets accommodated if notified in advance. Guest pantry stocked with complimentary soft drinks and snacks, microwave oven, ice maker, refrigerator and home baked cookies.

**Nearest Airport(s)**
Philadelphia International, Baltimore Washington International

**Directions**
From Route 1, turn onto Darlington Road, left onto Indian Springs Drive. Bed and Breakfast is at the top of the hill on the right. See web site for detailed directions.

SelectRegistry.com

# Fairville Inn

www.fairvilleinn.com
506 Kennett Pike (Rte. 52), Chadds Ford, PA  19317
**877-285-7772** • 610-388-5900 • Fax 610-388-5902
info@fairvilleinn.com

*Member Since 1995*

*"We found the accommodations spotless and the service exceptional. Our room was by far the most spacious and comfortable B&B room we have ever stayed in."*

**Innkeepers/Owners**
**Rick and Laura Carro**

Located in the heart of the Brandywine Valley, the Fairville Inn, listed on the National Register of Historic Places, echoes the pastoral scenes of Wyeth Family paintings. The allure of the Brandywine Valley, which reaches in all directions from Chadds Ford, comes from the enchanting landscape. Longwood Gardens and distinguished museums, such as Winterthur, Hagley, and the Brandywine River Museum, are minutes away. Leisurely travel the Brandywine Valley Wine Trail and sample the latest vintages of local wineries. Accented with barn wood, beams, and the occasional cathedral ceiling, the Inn is the embodiment of elegant comfort. Most rooms feature decks overlooking the gardens or acres of meadow rolling toward a serene pond. Each room in the Main House (ca. 1837), Carriage House, and Springhouse has a private bath, satellite TV, telephone (complimentary local & long-distance service), wireless Internet and individually controlled heating/air conditioning. Most rooms have a canopy bed and many have fireplaces in season. Fresh flowers gracefully welcome you to your room, which has all the comforts of a country inn. Tea served daily.

**Rates**
13 Rooms, $160/$245 and 2 Suites, $275/$295. B&B Open year-round. Number of Rooms: 15

**Cuisine**
Full breakfast (Mon-Fri 7-9 a.m.; weekends and holidays 8-10 a.m.) of refreshing beverages, cereal, fruit, yogurt, homemade baked goods and a choice of three hot entrees. Tea served daily from 4-6 p.m. with cheese, crackers, and homemade baked goods. Guests are welcome to bring their own wine or spirits. Special diets upon request.

**Nearest Airport(s)**
Philadelphia International airport, 28 miles.

**Directions**
Located on Rte. 52, 8 miles N of I-95 (exit 7 Wilmington DE.), 1.5 mi. S of US Rt. 1 (Mendenhall/Longwood Gardens area), PA.

# Rhode Island

## "Little Rhody"

Famous for: Jazz Festivals, Seaside Victorian Mansions, "Mile of History."
Cliff Walks, Beaches, Sailing.

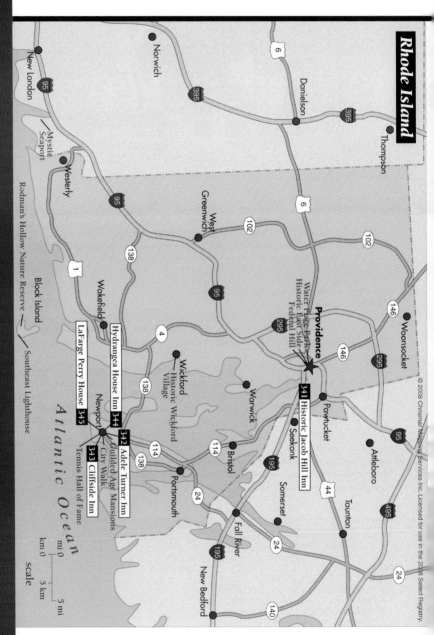

**Rhode Island**

New London
Norwich
Danielson
Thompson
Mystic Seaport
Westerly
West Greenwich
Woonsocket
Rodman's Hollow Nature Reserve
Block Island
Wakefield
Providence
Water Place Park
Historic East Side
Federal Hill
Pawtucket
Attleboro
Southeast Lighthouse
Wickford
Historic Wickford Village
Warwick
Seekonk
Taunton
LaFarge Perry House **345**
Hydrangea House Inn **344**
Newport
**342** Adele Turner Inn
Gilded Age Mansions
City Walk
**343** Cliffside Inn
Tennis Hall of Fame
**341** Historic Jacob Hill Inn
Bristol
Somerset
Fall River
Portsmouth
New Bedford

*Atlantic Ocean*

scale
mi 0
km 0
5 km
5 mi

SelectRegistry.co

# Historic Jacob Hill Inn

www.Jacobhill.com
P.O. Box 41326, Providence, RI  02940
**508-336-9165** • 888-336-9165
host@jacobhill.com

*Member Since 2000*

> *"Attention to every detail, exceptional service, delicious breakfast and elegant decor."*

**Innkeepers/Owners**
**Bill and Eleonora Rezek**

Located on a peaceful country estate, just a ten-minute drive from downtown Providence, the Rhode Island Convention Center, Brown University and the Historic East Side. Built in 1722, Jacob Hill has a long history of hosting America's most prominent families, including the Vanderbilts. Recently updated rooms are spacious, all with private bathrooms; most have Jacuzzi tubs. King-and queen-sized canopied beds blend with hand-picked antiques, period wall coverings and Oriental rugs. The gleaming wood floors mirror the romantic flames from the original fireplaces. The elegant surroundings are complemented by the genuine warm hospitality that will make you feel at home. Central to several major day trip attractions: Newport, Boston, Plymouth, Cape Cod, and Mystic.  Awarded "Top 10 Most Romantic Inns", ZAGAT "2008 Top U.S. Hotels, Resorts & Spas", TripAdvisor. com "Travelers' Choice Award", *Inn Traveler* "Best Guest accommodations," "Ten best Urban Inns" Forbes.com, "Room of the Year" *North American Inns* Magazine. AAA Four Diamond Award. Featured by the *New York Times, USA Today* and many others.

**Rates**
12 unique guestrooms, w/private bathrooms $199/$459 Phones, TV, AC, Internet Access. Open year-round. Pool, tennis, ping pong, billiard room w/large plasma TV, meeting room, & gazebo to view the beautiful sunsets. Spa services. Number of Rooms: 12

**Cuisine**
Award-winning breakfast, complimentary beverages, chocolate chip cookies and cheese plate. Many fine restaurants nearby for lunch and dinner

**Nearest Airport(s)**
Providence T F Green

**Directions**
From I-95 North: exit 19 Rte. 195 E Mass. exit 1 Seekonk Rte 114A. Turn L follow to Flashing light, stay R to Rte 44 E. Turn R follow 1 mi. Turn L on Jacob St.120 Jacob St. Seekonk, MA.

# Adele Turner Inn

www.adeleturnerinn.com
93 Pelham Street, Newport, RI 02840
**401-847-1811** • 800-845-1811 • Fax 401-848-5850
reservations@legendaryinnsofnewport.com

*Member Since 2002*

*"Sumptuous Tea And Wine Tasting," Frommer's. "Affordable Luxury," Smarter-Travel.Com Top Newport Pick. Top 10 Most Romantic Inn, American Historic Inns.*

Proprietor
**Winthrop Baker**

Named one of America's "Top 10 Most Romantic Bed and Breakfast Inns," Adele Turner sits quietly tucked away in one of Newport's most historic in-town neighborhoods, amid 2 and 3-century-old homes. Framed by 27 distinctive round-top windows, this elegant Victorian was built in 1855 on the first gas-lit street in America, and is on the National Historic Register. Thirteen finely appointed guest quarters all feature fireplaces, grand beds with fine linens, antiques, and artwork. Luxury suites also feature whirlpools or steam bath, and one showcases its own private roof deck and hot tub, with panoramic views of Newport Harbor. Multi-course breakfast and a renowned afternoon tea get things started. But the Inn's unique wine and food tasting events are a daily delight unlike any other in Newport, featuring the best wines from southern New England's flourishing wine country, enjoyed in the Victorian parlor or outside tables during warmer months. Adele Turner is centrally located just two blocks from Newport's picturesque harbor and downtown restaurants, shops, and famous mansions. In the middle of the action, but a world away.

**Rates**
13 Guest Quarters on 3 Floors: 7 State Rooms & Luxury Suites, 6 Classic Rooms. $125/$575 Number of Rooms: 13

**Cuisine**
Multi-course breakfast. Afternoon tea service. Daily wine & food events pairing flights of regional wine with New England cheeses & other fine foods. Dining & wine tasting in the Victorian parlor or on the veranda & outside tables.

**Nearest Airport(s)**
TF Green Providence. Logan Airport Boston.

**Directions**
NY: 95N to Rte. 138E, first exit off Newport Bridge to America's Cup, 3rd light L on Memorial, 2nd light L on Bellevue, 1 block L on Pelham. Boston: 95S to Rte. 24S to 138S to Memorial.

# Cliffside Inn

www.cliffsideinn.com
2 Seaview Avenue, Newport, RI  02840
**800-845-1811** • 401-847-1811 • Fax 401-848-5850
reservations@legendaryinnsofnewport.com

*Member Since 1997*

*Rhode Island*

*Newport*

*Top U.S. "Ritzy Weekend Retreat," Forbes. Top 10 Classic New England Inn, Travel+Leisure Magazine. Top 5 New England Getaway, Fortune.*

Proprietor
**Winthrop Baker**

The celebrated Cliffside Inn, former home of legendary artist Beatrice Turner, has earned a worldwide reputation as one of New England's most distinguished Bed and Breakfast luxury Inns. Known for seamlessly blending today's finest deluxe amenities -- whirlpools, steam baths, fireplaces, grand beds, fine Italian linens, iPod sound systems -- with Victorian elegance and antiques, refined design, and stunning artwork from the Turner collection, Cliffside is a magical hideaway.  The grand Victorian Manor House and Seaview Cottage are peacefully perched above the Atlantic Ocean and Newport's dramatic Cliff Walk. Also nearby are Newport's largest beach, and the other well known Gilded Age mansions of Newport. Relaxing escape or romantic getaway, guests enjoy warm hospitality and attentive service with a number of Cliffside special touches and epicurean delights -- including an internationally acclaimed high tea, named one of the 20 best in America. The regional wine bar features the best of the nearby vineyards, and signature in-room spa service has been designed exclusively for Cliffside by organic spa guru Brenda Brock.

**Rates**
4 Deluxe Suites $300/$650; 5 State Rooms & Suites $225/$510; 7 Classic Rooms $150/$395.  Number of Rooms: 16

**Cuisine**
In-room morning coffee service. Multi-course breakfast. Legendary Newport Afternoon tea (named one of America's 20 best) features seasonal menu of tea sandwiches, scones, Devon Cream & curds, tarts, other sweets & savories. Artisan chocolates.

**Nearest Airport(s)**
Providence, Boston

**Directions**
From NY: 95 N to RI exit 3 to Rte. 138, follow into Newport. America's Cup Blvd to Memorial Blvd. R on Cliff Ave. L on Seaview Ave. From Boston: 93 S to Rt. 24 S to 114 S to 214 S to Newport. L on Cliff Ave. L on Seaview.

# Hydrangea House Inn

www.hydrangeahouse.com
16 Bellevue Avenue, Newport, RI 02840
**800-945-4667** • 401-846-4435 • Fax 401-846-6602
hydrangeahouseinn@cox.net

*Rhode Island*

*Newport*

*"I have never felt warmer hospitality like I experienced at this inn. Kudos!"*
*"Quiet sophistication in the 'City by the Sea'."*

**Innkeepers/Owners**
**Grant Edmondson & Dennis Blair**

The *Boston Globe* writes, "In a city renowned for its lodging, Hydrangea House is not to be missed!" Enter a world of grace, elegance and style where the intimate charm of Hydrangea House is complemented by its prestigious Bellevue Avenue address where once lived the Vanderbilt's, the Astors and the Dukes. Its proximity to the magical gilded mansions, recreational harbor, historic sites, fine dining, and extraordinary shopping means you can walk to almost everything right from our front door. All nine rooms and suites are individually decorated with a dramatic use of color, sumptuous fabrics and trims and elegant furnishings. Suites have the added luxury of a two-person spa tub, marble shower and steam bath and flat screen "mirror" television. All rooms offer plush robes, triple sheeting, complimentary high speed Internet, long distance and local calling, CD players and iPod hook-ups. Complimentary wine and cheese is served daily in the parlor or one of Hydrangea House's expansive porches, and don't miss a home-made cookie to make the night complete. AAA Four diamond award. Named "Top 10 Most Romantic Inn" in 2008 by American Historic Inns and ILoveInns.com. Winner of *Yankee* Magazine "Editors Choice" 2006 award.

**Rates**
$265/$475 year round. Year round packages available.
Number of Rooms: 10

**Cuisine**
Expect to find more than the usual continental breakfast. We will serve you our own special blend of fresh ground House Coffee, home-baked breads & granola--as well as our incredible raspberry pancakes perhaps or seasoned scrambled eggs in puff pastry. Be assured, a Hydrangea House breakfast will last the day & energize you for your Newport experience.

**Nearest Airport(s)**
Providence Airport (PVD) 30 minutes.

**Directions**
From the S: 95N to 138E to Newport. From the N: 95S to 4S to 138E to Newport.

# La Farge Perry House

www.lafargeperry.com
24 Kay Street, Newport, RI  02840
**877-736-1100** • 401-847-2223 • Fax 401-847-1967
mknerr@lafargeperry.com

*Member Since 2006*

*Rhode Island*

*Newport*

*"Midge was WONDERFUL-the inn was beautiful-is a completely relaxing place for a weekend. It's our 3rd stay and it only gets better-we can't wait to return."*

Innkeeper-Midge Knerr
**Jeanie Shufelt-Owner**

La Farge Perry House is a Victorian-era Luxury Inn-located on a quiet street within walking distance to all of the major attractions in Newport. Named after the famed stained glass artist John La Farge and his wife Margaret Perry La Farge. The rambling inn has six rooms honoring the family, each with its own panache and Jacuzzi baths. All rooms have fresh flowers and sparkling wine available for special occasions. New additions are king-sized beds to our handsome Commander Oliver Hazard Perry room and stunning Master Suite-both with fireplaces and in room spa massage services which can be booked on-line. A formal living room, French Provencal kitchen with separate sitting room and a large fireplace, secluded balcony on the third floor, a porch that extends across the front of the house with white wicker furniture and adirondack chairs in our backyard gardens comprise the common areas.  The dining room is exquisite with panoramic murals of Newport. A recent guest stated, "The table looks like a scene from 'Lives of the Rich and Famous.'" A former chef and local food reporter she can advise on the restaurants best suited for you!

**Rates**
$265/$465 mid-week; $325/$565 weekends-in season
$145/$295 mid-week; $175/$325 weekends-off season
Number of Rooms: 6

**Cuisine**
Breakfast is served at the grand table in the main room. All breakfasts are cooked to order by our innkeeper with many choices-especially Eggs Benedict on Sundays. The table is set with homemade jams and pastries, juices and fresh fruit. Seasonal refreshments are offered in the afternoon with coconut macaroons.

**Nearest Airport(s)**
TF Green Providence, RI

**Directions**
Available on line on our website.

# South Carolina

"The Palmetto State"

Famous for: Congaree Swamp National Monument, Hilton Head Island, Myrtle Beach, Plantations, Charleston, Blue Ridge Mountains, Fort Sumter, Tobacco, Corn, Peaches, Cotton, Textiles.

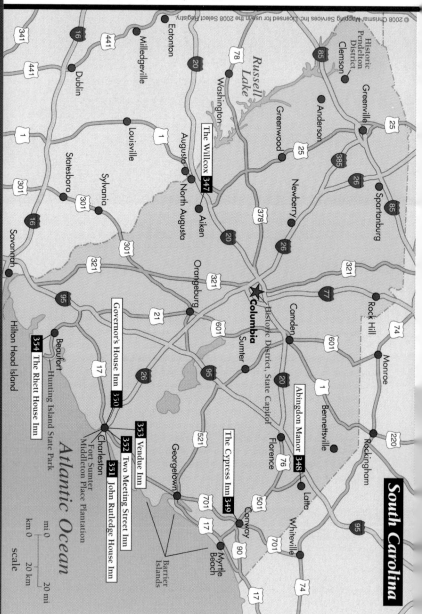

© 2008 Christar Mapping Services Inc. Licensed for use in the 2008 Select Registry.

The Willcox 347

Governor's House Inn 350

354 The Rhett House Inn

353 Vendue Inn

352 Two Meeting Street Inn

351 John Rutledge House Inn

The Cypress Inn 349

Abingdon Manor 348

Atlantic Ocean

Hilton Head Island

scale

mi 0     20 mi
km 0     20 km

SelectRegistry.com

# The Willcox

www.thewillcox.com
100 Colleton Avenue SW, Aiken, SC  29801
**877-648-2200** • 803-648-1898 • Fax 803-648-6664
info@thewillcox.com

*Member Since 2007*

*South Carolina*

*Aiken*

*"The South's finest hospitality awaits you at The Willcox."*

Owners
## David & Christie Garrett

Walk the shady, oak-vaulted streets past clapboard cottages and rambling mansions, and you'll come upon The Willcox. An old-fashioned Southern hotel, a grand white-pillared glory. As lovely and genteel as a rose on a lapel. Every winter, the well-heeled of the Gilded Age came to Aiken seeking horse racing, fox hunting, and high society. The Willcox was the most stately of the hotels that sprang up to serve them. Today, as grand and graceful as ever, the Willcox's quiet, sumptuous bedrooms, high ceilings, fireplaces, cream-papered walls and dark wood invite repose. Every room is unique and all have sitting areas with restful, generous beds, blanketed in cool, clean linen. They are elegantly appointed with period antiques, high ceilings with crown moldings, luxurious featherbeds and pillows, and serviced by housekeeping each day. The Willcox is romantic, warm, extraordinarily comfortable and filled with a sense of history that takes you back to simpler times. Gracious, genteel, understated, yet sophisticated and hospitable, The Willcox is the quintessential Southern experience.

**Rates**
15 rooms,7 suites: $185/$525. Suites and most guest rooms have fireplaces. Bathrooms are chapels to water, soap and lotion, with deep soaking tubs, double sinks, stacks of thick towels and plush robes.  Number of Rooms: 22

**Cuisine**
We offer a full buffet breakfast and wine or cocktails in the evening.

**Nearest Airport(s)**
Augusta Airport

**Directions**
From Augusta Airport: At airport exit, turn R onto Barnard Pkwy. toward Augusta. Go 5 miles to U.S. Hwy #1. Turn R & follow U.S.#1 to downtown Aiken. Turn R on Chesterfield St. (Regions Bank on corner). Go 2 blocks to Colleton Ave. Turn R and you will be directly in front of the Inn.

# Abingdon Manor

www.abingdonmanor.com
307 Church Street, Latta, SC 29565
**888-752-5090** • 843-752-5090
abingdon@bellsouth.net

*Member Since 2005*

*"There isn't a better place to stay anywhere on the East Coast."*
*Alexander Ix, Croquet News*

**Innkeepers/Owners**
**Michael & Patty Griffey**

The only establishment offering luxury accommodations and fine dining in the Carolinas and Georgia close to I-95, Abingdon Manor is the overnight destination for travelers on the East Coast. Halfway between New York and Palm Beach, the Inn offers superior lodging, extraordinary cuisine and impeccable service. One of only a select few properties in South Carolina to be awarded a AAA 4-diamond rating annually for both the Inn and Restaurant, Abingdon Manor offers the amenities of a small luxury hotel in an opulent National Register mansion. Located in a historic neighborhood in a quaint turn of the century village, the Inn features three acres of landscaped grounds. For destination travelers, the Inn offers a variety of activities including cooking school weekends, historic touring, antiquing, nature-based activities and private country club golf. Food writers and critics consistently rank the restaurant as one of the best in the Carolinas. Abingdon Manor offers a refined, yet comfortable, atmosphere for the discriminating traveler. Abingdon Manor is a AAA Four Diamond and Mobil Three Star Inn and Restaurant.

**Rates**
$170/$205. All rooms offer cable TV, working fireplaces, individual temperature controls. Number of Rooms: 7

**Cuisine**
The award winning restaurant offers exceptional dining nightly. The one seating,six course meal, crafted daily using the freshest ingredients available begins with cocktails at 7:00. A full breakfast is offered from 7:45 to 9:00 am. Premium liquor and wine service available.

**Nearest Airport(s)**
Florence, Myrtle Beach

**Directions**
I-95 exit 181A, 1 mi. E to Rte. 917 turn L and go 5 mi. to 1st light (Marion St.), L for 2 blocks and R onto Church St. Abingdon is at the end on the L.

# The Cypress Inn

www.acypressinn.com
16 Elm Street, Conway, SC 29526
**800-575-5307** • 843-248-8199 • Fax 843-248-0329
info@acypressinn.com

*Member Since 2001*

*South Carolina*

*Conway*

*"The Carolina Coast at its Best."*

Innkeepers/Owners
**Hugh & Carol Archer and George & Anne Bullock**

Overlooking the Waccamaw River, tucked away in the historic town of Conway, this luxury Inn is near, but distinctly apart from the golf mecca of Myrtle Beach. Located 2 blocks from the downtown area of Conway, the Inn is within walking distance of charming shops, restaurants, art galleries and stately live oak trees. Eleven unique guestrooms offer comforts such as en-suite private baths with Jacuzzis, plush robes, individual heat/air, high speed internet (Wi-Fi). We also have an on-site massage therapist. The Inn offers the privacy of a hotel with the personal service of a bed and breakfast. Enjoy the pristine beaches of the South Carolina coast or the peacefulness of an ancient river; an outstanding sculpture garden, or live theater shows. Many extras such as fresh flowers, chocolates & strawberries and a selection of fine wines are available. In addition to being a charming destination, the Inn is great for those traveling north or south along the east coast and for the business traveler seeking a relaxing atmosphere. Meeting and banquet facilities are also available.

**Rates**
$130/$225 B&B. Open year-round. Corporate Rates. Number of Rooms: 11

**Cuisine**
A wonderful hot breakfast is served each morning. There are fine restaurants within walking distance. A small guest refrigerator is stocked with lemonade, sodas, bottled water. Complimentary wine and beer, cookies and other treats.

**Nearest Airport(s)**
Myrtle Beach

**Directions**
From Hwy. 501: Take Bus. 501. W on 3rd Ave. L on Elm St. Inn is on L. From Charleston, SC: Use Hwy 701. R on Elm St. Inn is on L. From Wilmington, NC: Use Hwy. 90 R on Bus. 501. L on 3rd Ave. L on Elm St. Inn is on L.

# Governor's House Inn

www.governorshouse.com
117 Broad Street, Charleston, SC 29401
**800-720-9812** • 843-720-2070 • Fax n/a
governorshouse@aol.com

*Member Since 2000*

*"I'm not easily impressed, but I was overwhelmed with your glorious Inn."*
*"A magical, mystical place."*

General Manager
**Mary Kittrell**

Governor's House is a magnificent National Historic Landmark (circa 1760) reflecting the Old South's civility and grandeur. Praised by one national publication as "Charleston's most glamorous and sophisticated inn," the former Governor's mansion is the perfect blend of historic splendor and romantic elegance. The mansion's original living rooms, dining room, nine fireplaces, Irish crystal chandeliers, and sweeping southern porches delight guests from around the globe. Harmonize these aristocratic pleasures with luxuries like whirlpool baths, wetbars, high speed Internet and individually controlled room environments, and the result is refined gentility. During the American Revolution, Governor's House was the home of Edward Rutledge, youngest signer of the Declaration of Independence. Today, the Inn has been acclaimed as "a flawless urban hideaway" by *Southern Living*.

Visit us online at: *www.governorshouse.com*

### Rates
Governor's House offers 11 elegant guest rooms and suites. Rates are $280-$585 in season. Rates include gracious Southern breakfast, afternoon tea, wine and cheese, bicycles, private parking and WI-FI internet access. Number of Rooms: 11

### Cuisine
Southern breakfast, Low country afternoon tea. Premier restaurants nearby.

### Nearest Airport(s)
Charleston

### Directions
From I-26 or Hwy 17 S take Meeting St. 2.0 miles S to Broad. Turn right. Inn is on left 1 block past King St. From Hwy 17 N or James Is., cross Ashley River, then go right on Lockwood Blvd. S until it becomes Broad (sharp left curve). Inn is on the right, past third light.

# John Rutledge House Inn

www.johnrutledgehouseinn.com
116 Broad Street, Charleston, SC 29401
**800-476-9741** • 843-723-7999 • Fax 843-720-2615
kleslie@charminginns.com

*Member Since 1992*

*2004 Gold List - "World's Best Places to Stay" - Condé Nast Traveler*

*South Carolina*

*Charleston*

Owner
**Richard Widman**

Built in 1763 by John Rutledge, a signer of the U.S. Constitution, this antebellum home is now an elegant B&B Inn. Located in the heart of the Historic District, the Inn is a reminder of a more gracious time. Guests enjoy afternoon tea, wine and sherry in the ballroom where patriots, statesmen and presidents have met, evening turn-down service with chocolates at bedside and pastries delivered to the room each morning. A charter member of Historic Hotels of America, designated a National Historic Landmark.

**Rates**
16 Rooms, $190/$315 B&B 3 Suites, $330/$385 B&B.
Open year-round. Number of Rooms: 19

**Cuisine**
Continental breakfast included, full breakfast available.
Afternoon tea with refreshments.

**Nearest Airport(s)**
Charleston International

**Directions**
From Charleston Visitor's Ctr.: (R) on John St., then (L) on King St., 1 mile then (R) on Broad St. The John Rutledge House Inn is 4th house on right.

# Two Meeting Street Inn

2 Meeting Street, Charleston, SC 29401
**843-723-7322**
innkeeper2meetst@bellsouth.net

*Member Since 1992*

*South Carolina*

*Charleston*

*People's choice for the City's Best Bed and Breakfast in Charleston City Paper - Seventh Year. Featured in Southern Living Magazine, October 2004.*

Innkeepers/Owners
**Pete and Jean Spell, Karen Spell Shaw**

Two Meeting Street Inn is the city's oldest inn welcoming guests for over half a century located in the heart of the historic district. The Queen Anne Mansion was given as a wedding gift by a bride's loving father in 1890. Elegant from head to toe, the inn features a carved English oak stairwell and Tiffany windows, as well as the Spell's collection of antiques and silver. The softly curved, two tiered verandahs overlook the manicured landscaped garden and Charleston's harbour. Guests enjoy a Southern continental breakfast and gracious afternoon tea in the dining room or on the piazza. "Never have we stayed in a place so beautiful or so lovingly cared for, nor have we ever felt as pampered. Thank you for making our stay both comfortable and memorable."

**Rates**
9 Guest Rooms, $219/$485 B&B; Victorian Rooms with 12' ceilings, canopy beds, and private baths. Closed 3 days for Christmas. Number of Rooms: 9

**Cuisine**
A gracious continental breakfast; afternoon tea; evening sherry. No bar in the Inn.

**Nearest Airport(s)**
Charleston International Airport 12 miles from downtown.

**Directions**
From I-26, exit Meeting Street/Visitor Center. A left-hand exit. When Meeting Street dead ends into the park, we are the last house on the Left.

# Vendue Inn

🍽️ 🍽️ 🍽️ 🍷

www.vendueinn.com
19 Vendue Range, Charleston, SC 29401
**800-845-7900** • 843-577-7970 • Fax 843-577-2913
info@vendueinn.com

*Member Since 2002*

*USA Today named Vendue Inn as the Best Place in America
to "rekindle connubial passion"*

General Manager
**Susie Ridder**

Imagine a place where the genteel comfort of a bygone era has been perfectly preserved.
Where the style is more sophisticated, the service, more gracious. A place that offers
every convenience in an intimate setting that exceeds every expectation. You've found
someplace very special at Charleston's Vendue Inn where comfort, cobblestone streets
and genteel Southern hospitality await. Charleston, South Carolina is known for its warm
hospitality, gracious living, vibrant history, and Southern charm. Experience it all at The
Vendue Inn. In the heart of Charleston's Historic District, one block from the harbor and
Waterfront Park, the Vendue Inn is nestled in what is known as the French Quarter. Guests
consistently remark on the attentive personal service they receive; our staff's hospitality is
warm even by Southern standards! The Vendue Inn, a luxury historic small hotel. Our
friendly, caring, and experienced staff awaits your arrival.

**Rates**
50 Rooms, $129/$379; 15 Suites, $259/$699. Forty-eight
beautifully appointed guest rooms and suites, many with
canopy and four poster beds, working fireplaces and whirlpool
tubs. Number of Rooms: 65

**Cuisine**
Complimentary Southern Family Breakfast. The Rooftop Bar
and Restaurant serves lunch and dinner 7 days and features
nightly live entertainment. The Library Restaurant is open
Tuesday through Saturday from 5:00 PM until 10:00 PM.

**Nearest Airport(s)**
Charleston

**Directions**
I-26 E to East Bay Exit. Continue S on East Bay approximately
3 miles. L onto Vendue Range. Check-in is halfway down the
block on R at 19 Vendue Range.

# The Rhett House Inn

www.rhetthouseinn.com
1009 Craven Street, Beaufort, SC 29902
**888-480-9530** • 843-524-9030 • Fax 843-524-1310
info@rhetthouseinn.com

*Member Since 1991*

*South Carolina*

*Beaufort*

*"Beautiful rooms, lovely grounds, exquisite desserts - what an enchanting place."*

Owners
**Steve & Marianne Harrison**

Located in historic Beaufort. The Rhett House Inn is a beautifully restored 1820s plantation house, furnished with English and American antiques, oriental rugs, fresh orchids, fireplaces and spacious verandahs. Lush gardens provide the perfect setting for weddings and parties. Our town was the film site for "Forrest Gump," "Prince of Tides," "The Big Chill" and "White Squal." History-laden Beaufort, Charleston and Savannah offer rich exploring.

**Rates**
17 Rooms $175/$315, 8 with fireplaces and whirlpool baths. Open year-round.  Number of Rooms: 17

**Cuisine**
Breakfast, afternoon tea, evening hors d'oeuvres, picnic baskets, desserts.

**Nearest Airport(s)**
Savannah/Hilton Head International Airport

**Directions**
From the North, take I-95 to Exit 33, then follow the signs to Beaufort. From the South, take I-95 to exit 8 and follow the signs.

# Tennessee

## "The Volunteer State"

Famous for: Cumberland Gap National Historic Park, Cumberland Caverns, Fall Creek Falls, Grand Ole Opry House, Great Smokey Mountains, Graceland, Guinness World Research Museum, Country Music Hall of Fame, Tennessee Valley.

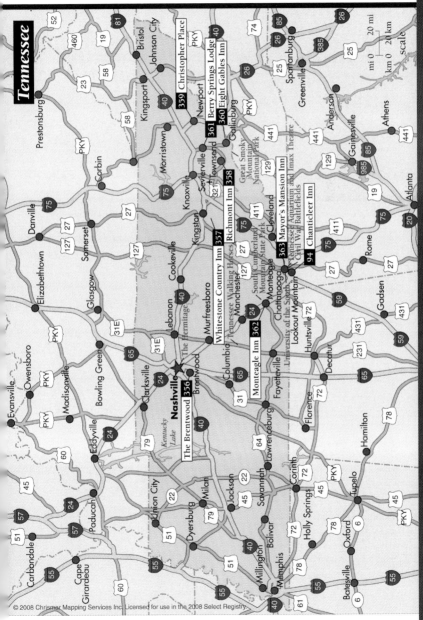

# The Brentwood, A Bed & Breakfast

www.brentwoodbandb.com
6304 Murray Lane, Brentwood, TN 37027-6210
**800-332-4640** • 615-373-4627 • Fax 615-221-9666
info@brentwoodbandb.com

*Member Since 2003*

*Tennessee*

*Brentwood*

## Where Classic Hospitality Lives!

Innkeeper/Owner
**Ly Anne & Dick Thorman**

The luxurious Brentwood estate is located in one of the finest sections of greater Nashville. The drive over the stream, through the trees and up to the white columns welcomes you to our "Classic Hospitality." The casual elegance of the interior and eclectic combination of traditional furnishings, family and European antiques and objects d'arte creates an atmosphere of quiet relaxation. Private decks overlook the rolling hillside and fireplaces warm the cool evenings. Tours of Civil War sites, Grand Ole Opry, Country Music Hall of Fame, The Ryman, The Hermitage and Antebellum mansions can be arranged. Close to fine dining, country music spots, shopping and downtown Nashville. Only 10 minutes to historic Franklin, golf courses, hiking and nature trails.

**Rates**
Rooms $145/$175, Suites $199/$250. All suites have custom Jacuzzi tubs, some with fireplace and decks. Data ports, DSL, TV, phone, VCR library, terry robes. Number of Rooms: 6

**Cuisine**
Full breakfast & afternoon refreshments. Special dietary menus w/ notice. Minutes from fine dining & the historic attractions of Nashville, Belle Meade & Franklin.

**Nearest Airport(s)**
Nashville Int'l - 20 Minutes

**Directions**
From Nashville take I-65 S to Exit 71 (Concord) & turn R. At Franklin Road (Dead End) turn R. At Murray Lane turn L & proceed 1 mi. past Granny White Pike. The Brentwood Sign is on your R.

# Whitestone Country Inn

**iOi iOi iOi**

www.whitestoneinn.com
1200 Paint Rock Rd., Kingston, TN 37763
**888-247-2464** • 865-376-0113 • Fax 865-376-4454
moreinfo@whitestoneinn.com

*Member Since 2000*

*"Just a brief note to say that at Whitestone we found a true 'Sanctuary of the Soul.' Your hospitality has demonstrated extraordinary grace."*

**Innkeepers/Owners**
**Paul Cowell and Jean Cowell**

A spectacular 360 acre Country Estate with views of the Smoky Mountains provides you with a serene combination of natural woods and landscaped gardens. Whitestone's rolling hillsides and peaceful surroundings are guaranteed to soothe your soul and calm your spirit. We serve three lavish meals a day and you can nibble on home baked cookies and other delectable treats anytime. Many of our rooms are equipped with the sensuous delight of waterfall-spa showers and private decks. You will be surrounded by 5,400 acres of wildlife-waterfowl refuge and 39,000 acre Watts Bar Lake with opportunities for birding, fishing, kayaking, canoeing, paddle-boating or just rocking on our many porches and swinging in our hammocks. This is the perfect place for vacations, retreats, meetings, weddings or honeymoons. Whitestone Country Inn is one of only six AAA, four-diamond inns in Tennessee, and was named one of the '10 Most Romantic Inns in America!' Find a Sanctuary for your Soul.

**Rates**
21 Rooms/Suites, $150/$280 per night. Each room and suite has fireplace, king bed, spa tub, TV/DVD, and refrigerator. Number of Rooms: 21

**Cuisine**
The very best classic cuisine. Enjoy elegant meals in one of our three dining rooms, two overlooking the lake. For between-meal snacks, sample from the cookie jars in our kitchen.

**Nearest Airport(s)**
Knoxville, Mcghee/Tyson airport

**Directions**
From I-75, exit 72. Turn W on Hwy 72, go 9 mi. R on Paint Rock Rd., just after Hwy. 322 jct. Entrance is 4 mi. on R.
- From I-40, exit 352. S on Hwy 58. Go 6 mi. to L on Hwy 72E, then 5 mi. to L on Paint Rock Rd. 4 mi.

# Richmont Inn

www.richmontinn.com
220 Winterberry Lane, Townsend, TN 37882
**866-267-7086** • 865-448-6751 • Fax 865-448-6480
richmontinn@aol.com

*Member Since 1997*

*Selected by National Geographic Traveler Magazine as
"one of the top 25 authentic hotels across the United States."*

Innkeeper
**Nancy Schimmick**

Escape to the Great Smoky Mountains and refresh your body and soul. Relax in our historic Appalachian cantilever barn, elegantly furnished with 18th Century English antiques and French paintings. Breathtaking views, private balconies, spa tubs and woodburning fireplaces. Ten minutes to the Great Smoky Mountains National Park. Activities: hiking, biking, fishing, picnicking, wildflower walks, and the Heritage Museum. Announcing the Walker Lodge, a unique, relaxing, productive atmosphere for business meetings and socials. Chapel-in-the-Woods and wedding services for small groups, private and memorable. Rated "Top Inn" by *Country Inns* and awarded grand prize by *Gourmet Magazine* for our signature dessert. "...may be the most romantic place in the Smokies" –*Southern Living*. "A wonderful place to recharge your batteries" –*Country Magazine* "Romantic getaway" –*HGTV* Richmont Inn, "A Gracious Plenty™," rich in luxury and heritage, located "On the Peaceful Side of the Smokies."

**Rates**
9 Rooms, $160/$185, 5 Luxury Suites $205/$275 King beds/ spa tubs/fireplace/balconies/fridge   Number of Rooms: 14

**Cuisine**
Full French and Swiss style breakfasts. Also complimentary gourmet desserts and flavored coffees by candlelight. Evening dinners by reservation - classic four course Swiss fondue. Fine wines and imported beers.

**Nearest Airport(s)**
Only 30 mins. from McGhee Tyson (Metro Knoxville) airport.

**Directions**
Enter Townsend (near mile marker 26), from Maryville on US 321 N. 1st R on Old Tuckaleechee Rd., R on next paved road (Laurel Valley), 0.8 miles thru stone gate, crest hill, turn left at sign.

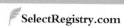

# Christopher Place

www.christopherplace.com
1500 Pinnacles Way, Newport, TN 37821
**800-595-9441** • 423-623-6555 • Fax 423-613-4771
stay@christopherplace.com

*Member Since 2000*

*Tennessee*

*Newport*

*"Thanks for providing a place for people to experience life
the way they wish it was."*

Innkeeper/Owner
**Marston Price**

Secluded in the scenic Smoky Mountains on a 200-acre private estate, **Christopher Place, An Intimate Resort,** is the ideal inn for a romantic, relaxing getaway. An elegant setting is coupled with friendly, unpretentious service and unspoiled, panoramic views. The hosts know your name and greet you with a warm smile. You can fill your days with activities, or with none at all, as the inn is centrally located to most of the sights and attractions of the Smokies and offers many resort amenities of its own. Rooms and Suites are spacious and romantically appointed. Casual fine dining with an extensive wine list completes your romantic retreat. Special requests are encouraged. Voted the area's Best B&B. Named one of the 10 most romantic inns in America and one of the 12 best locations for a fantasy B&B wedding.

### Rates
4 Rooms, $175; 4 Suites, $275/$330. Most have double whirlpools, woodburning fireplaces and/or scenic views. Number of Rooms: 9

### Cuisine
Hearty mountain breakfast served at your leisure. Picnics. Intimate 4-course candlelit dinners by reservation at tables set for two in our exquisite dining room overlooking the mountains. Some seats available to non-inn guests. Light afternoon snacks available.

### Nearest Airport(s)
Knoxville

### Directions
I-40 to exit 435. Go S 2 mi. on Hwy 32. Turn R on English Mountain Rd. Go 2 mi. Turn R on Pinnacles Way. Follow to the top.

# Eight Gables Inn
www.eightgables.com
219 North Mountain Trail, Gatlinburg, TN 37738
**800-279-5716** • 865-430-3344 • Fax 865-430-8767
inquiries@eightgables.com

*Member Since 2002*

*Tennessee*

*Gatlinburg*

*"An excellent getaway from the everyday world!*
*Your Inn has nourished both body and soul!"*

Owners
**The Binning Family**

Eight Gables Inn, The Smoky Mountains' Premier Country Inn, offers 19 luxurious rooms and suites. All rooms have private baths, cable TV, feather top beds, plush bathrobes, telephones, personal amenities and several feature the warmth of fireplaces and whirlpool tubs. Our rates include a full served breakfast, afternoon tea and evening dessert. Conveniently located on the drive between Gatlinburg and Pigeon Forge, our peaceful setting lends itself to a casual elegance and relaxing charm. Eight Gables is easily accessible to all the area attractions and Knoxville is just 30 miles away. AAA Four Diamond rated.

**Rates**
10 Rooms $140/$230; 9 Suites $210/270. Luxurious rooms, TV/VCR/CD, some with King beds, fireplaces, Jacuzzis.
Number of Rooms: 19

**Cuisine**
Full sit down breakfast, afternoon tea and evening dessert.

**Nearest Airport(s)**
Knoxville TN

**Directions**
From Hwy. 441, one mi. N of Gatlinburg, turn on Little Smoky Road. Go to stop sign, road turns into North Mountain Trail (sign posted). First drive on L.

# Berry Springs Lodge

www.berrysprings.com
2149 Seaton Springs Road, Sevierville, TN 37862
**888-760-8297** • 865-908-7935
stay@berrysprings.com

*Member Since 2005*

*Tennessee*

*"Berry Springs Lodge is one of our new favorite places! We needed a few days away from the world and this was the perfect answer."*

*Sevierville*

Innkeepers/Owners
**Patrick & Sue Eisert**

Perched on a 33 acre secluded scenic ridge top in the Great Smoky Mountains, this lodge offers the perfect picture of solitude and romance. Take a leisurely walk down to the bass or catfish ponds and try your luck. Ride bikes, play horseshoes, relax in a hammock or just sit back and enjoy the beautiful views of the Smoky Mountains from your rocking chair on the main deck of the lodge. With this remote setting, one would not guess the lodge is within a 15-minute drive of most area destinations, including Gatlinburg, Pigeon Forge, Sevierville and the "Great Smoky Mountain National Park" Awards and Accolades 2007 Trip Advisor: "Top-Rated B&B in TN" 2006 USA Today: "10 great places to settle into for fall viewing" 2005 Blue Ridge Country: "Tennessee's Berry Springs Lodge Gives the Gift of Trees" 2004 Arrington's Inn Traveler: "Best Scenic Mount View" 2003 Arrington's Inn Traveler: "Best Inn for Rest and Relaxation" 2001 Better Bed and Breakfasts: "Enjoy the Best of Both Worlds at Berry Springs Lodge" AAA Three Diamond rated.

## Rates
9 rooms. $169/$229, 2 Suites $229/$269. Includes breakfast and evening desserts. King Beds, Fireplace, Hot Tubs, Whirlpool Tubs TV/VCR/CD. Open year-round. Number of Rooms: 11

## Cuisine
Country gourmet breakfast. Lunch & dinner picnic baskets are available upon advanced request. Local restaurants within 15 minutes. Nightly signature desserts.

## Nearest Airport(s)
Knoxville

## Directions
I-40 exit #407 Go 8 mi. turn L (North) on Route 411. Go 1.8 mi. and turn R at Veterans Blvd. Go 4 mi. and turn L on Jay Ell Road. Go 1.6 mi. turn R on McCarter Hollow. Go 1/4 mi. turn L on Seaton Springs.

# Monteagle Inn

www.monteagleinn.com
204 West Main Street, P.O. Box 39, Monteagle, TN 37356
**888-480-3245** • 931-924-3869 • Fax 931-924-3867
suites@monteagleinn.com

*Member Since 2006*

*"An exceptional gathering place for the remarkable individual celebrating a special moment in time."*

Innkeeper/Owner
**Jim Harmon**

Monteagle Inn is located atop the Cumberland Plateau just minutes away from The University of the South, hiking trails, antique shops and superb restaurants. You are greeted by warm Mediterranean colors and soft music as you enter the foyer. The Living areas are outfitted with overstuffed furnishings washed by accent lighting and graced with special antiques, which invite you to relax and experience the mountaintop in all of its seasons. The Inn's large living room with 4 distinct sitting areas encourages you to curl up on one of the oversized sofas with a good book. A welcoming fire in the cool months adds to the total relaxation you will enjoy. Picturesque balconies, a spacious front porch and garden courtyards provide private outdoor relaxation hide-a-ways. Crisp white linens welcome you to relax and enjoy your bedroom as hot cookies & flavored teas reward your visit. The spacious dining room is filled with light and color from windows on 3 sides while Provencal linens grace the windows & tables. Brightly-patterned Italian urns, bowls & dishes serve as a backdrop for your gourmet breakfast specialties. Monteagle Inn is the perfect place for your getaway and business retreats, family reunions & wedding functions.

### Rates
All of the rooms have spacious private baths and are furnished with luxurious white bed & bath linens including coverlets; fluffy towels, the most comfortable pillows. Wireless DSL is available throughout the Inn. $160/$265. Number of Rooms: 13

### Cuisine
Extensive herb & vegetable gardens help create acclaimed "mountain gourmet" breakfast. New Orleans Praline French Toast, Mays Eggs Béarnaise, Garden Fresh Frittatas & Herb Roasted Sweet Potato Fries are just a few bountiful items prepared each morning.

### Nearest Airport(s)
Chattanooga-45 miles
Nashville-85 miles

### Directions
Conveniently located less than 1/2 mile from I-24 between Nashville & Chattanooga at exit 134.

SelectRegistry.com

# Mayor's Mansion Inn

www.mayorsmansioninn.com
801 Vine Street, Chattanooga, TN 37403
**888-446-6569** • 423-265-5000 • Fax 423-265-5555
info@mayorsmansioninn.com

*Member Since 1996*

*Tennessee*

*Chattanooga*

*"Thank you for your grand southern hospitality. Grounds are immaculate and the service is outstanding. This is the finest B&B in which we have ever stayed."*

Owners
**Gene & Carmen Fenn Drake**

Entering the Fort Wood neighborhood, Chattanooga's premier historic district, you are immediately greeted by a magnificent mansion, built in 1889 by the city's Mayor. Picture majestic oaks sheltering this massive stone Victorian treasure that carries a prestigious award for historical preservation from The National Trust. Find yourself exploring lazy porches, 16-foot ceilings, carved pocket doors, hand-painted murals, as well as breathtaking mountain views. Hidden among the treasures of yesteryear, you suddenly discover subtle modern conveniences of 300-gallon soaking tubs, televisions, VCRs, and modem connections. Most importantly, you will rest easy always knowing our dedicated hospitality team eagerly awaits every opportunity to make your stay as unforgettable as your surroundings.

**Rates**
4 Suites, $175/$295; 7 Rooms, $130/$190. Open all year.
Number of Rooms: 11

**Cuisine**
Full breakfast, dinner served on Friday and Saturday evenings by reservation. Many fine restaurants a short distance away.

**Nearest Airport(s)**
Chattanooga Metro Airport

**Directions**
From Atlanta or Knoxville I-75 to I-24W. 27N to exit 1C. 1 mile straight. R on Palmetto St. L on Vine St. Immediate L into parking lot. From Nashville I-24E to 27N, then same.

# *Texas*

## "The Lone Star State"

Famous for: The Alamo, San Antonio Missions National Historic Park, Enchanted Rock, Big Bend National Park, Padre Island National Seashore, Marfa Lights, Guadalupe Mountains National Park, Lyndon B. Johnson Space Center.

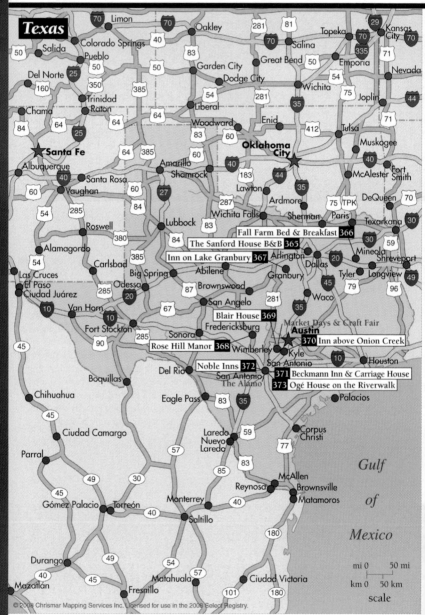

# The Sanford House Inn & Spa

🍽 🍽 🍽 ❡

www.thesanfordhouse.com
506 N. Center St., Arlington, TX 76011
**817-861-2129** • 817-861-3624 • Fax 817-861-2030
info@thesanfordhouse.com

*Member Since 2003*

*Texas*

*"...the accomodations were superb. The staff was attentive
and the dining incredible. I'll be back again."*

*Arlington*

General Manager
**McBerg, Inc.**

The Sanford House Inn and Spa is located in the heart of the Dallas Fort Worth metroplex. There are 7 luxurious rooms and 4 secluded cottages with private baths and whirlpool tubs. The Grand Courtyard is ideal for events up to 200 people. The event coordinator and executive chef will take care of all the details for weddings, executive retreats, and receptions for small or large groups. The Sanford House Inn & Spa is only a short drive away from the museums and other attractions of Dallas and Fort Worth.

**Rates**
7 Rooms, 4 Private Cottages. Rates from $125/$250. Number of Rooms: 11

**Cuisine**
The Sanford House Signature Breakfast is included with your stay. Lunch is served daily from 11:30-2:30 pm Monday - Friday and is open to the public. Fine dining is available for small or large groups with reservations.

**Nearest Airport(s)**
DFW Airport

**Directions**
From Dallas: I-30 W to Cooper St. Go S on Cooper to Sanford St. Turn L and go E to Center St.From Fort Worth: I-30 E to Cooper St. Go S on Cooper to Sanford St. Turn L on Sanford St. and go E to Center St. Located on the corner of Center and Sanford.

# Fall Farm, A Fine Country Inn

www.fallfarm.com
2027 F.M. 779, Mineola, TX  75773-3287
**877-886-7696** • 903-768-2449 • Fax 903-768-2079
info@fallfarm.com

*Member Since 2000*

*Texas*

*Mineola*

*"Every room and view is a warm profusion of color and pattern."*

Innkeepers/Owners
**Mike and Carol Fall**

Escape to this tranquil, ten-acre retreat in the scenic piney woods of East Texas and be drawn into a luxurious country farmhouse with unique personality, reflecting Mike and Carol's history and welcoming spirit. The inviting atmosphere conveys a familiar feeling of home, yet transforms you with beautifully decorated rooms filled with color and whimsical details. Enjoy the sparkling pool in the afternoon, as well as stargazing in the soothing spa after dark. Professional massages are available in the spa room, a perfect way to end the day. A bountiful breakfast assures that no one leaves hungry. Quiet moments and total relaxation are inevitable...our hospitality awaits!

## Rates
2 Rooms/3 Suites $135/$185. Cottages $200/$275. Guest House $600. Conference Ctr. $200. Elegantly appointed rooms with comfortable sitting areas, fine linens and lovely views. Open year-round.   Number of Rooms: 9

## Cuisine
Full gourmet breakfast, afternoon refreshments, fresh fruit, cold drinks. Complimentary evening wine. Fine and casual dining in and around Mineola.

## Nearest Airport(s)
Tyler, Dallas, Shreveport

## Directions
Mineola is approx. 90 mi. from both Dallas and Shreveport. From I-20, take Hwy 69 N to Mineola. When Hwy 69 forks, take Hwy 37 N for 6 mi. and turn L on FM 779. Fall Farm is 2 mi. on L.

# Inn on Lake Granbury

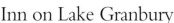

www.innonlakegranbury.com
205 West Doyle Street, Granbury, TX 76048
**877-573-0046** • 817-573-0046
info@innonlakegranbury.com

*Member Since 2006*

*"Thank you for everything! We love it here, and are leaving
feeling relaxed and refreshed."*

Innkeepers/Owners
**Cathy Casey and Jim Leitch**

The Inn has eight upscale guestrooms on almost two acres directly on Lake Granbury.
Each room has a oversized king bed, fabulous guest robes, private shower (some with steam
showers), some with jetted tubs, some with lake views, and all with wireless Internet access.
Experience our flagstone encased pool with tanning ledge and waterfall or sit on the swing
under 200 year old oak trees for a spectacular view of the lake. Walk less than three blocks
to the historic square for shopping and fine dining. Complimentary appetizers and beverages
are served every afternoon along with a full breakfast each morning.

**Rates**
$195/$245 Sunday-Thursday and $215/$295 Friday and
Saturday. Number of Rooms: 8

**Cuisine**
Rates include a full gourmet breakfast and appetizers and
beverages each afternoon. Lunch and dinner for groups upon
request.

**Nearest Airport(s)**
Dallas Fort Worth Airport

**Directions**
From Dallas or Ft. Worth take I-20W to Hgwy 377 exit to
Granbury. Go approx. 35 mi. Take Business 377 to Historic
District. At downtown square, continue one block past square.
Take L on Lambert Street. Go to end of Lambert - Inn at the
corner of Lambert and Doyle.

# Rose Hill Manor

www.rose-hill.com
2614 Upper Albert Road, Near Fredericksburg, TX 78671
**877-767-3445** • 830-644-2247
rosehill@ktc.com

*Member Since 2006*

Texas

Fredericksburg

*"A perfect retreat from a hectic world. A memorable meal, a beautifully comfortable cottage and delicious breakfast - all provided over by wonderful hosts and staff."*

Innkeepers/Owners - **Robert & Patricia VanderLyn**
Innkeepers - **Jan MacAllister & Bill Bayha**

Rose Hill Manor will enchant you with it's peaceful setting high on a hill, with panoramic views of the Texas hill country from every guest room. As the only AAA Four Diamond lodging in the Fredericksburg, Texas area, our graciously appointed and spacious accomodations offer all the amenities required by this prestigious standard. Enjoy the celebrated cuisine of the on-site gourmet restaurant, where great meals are creatively prepared and wines are poured from a thoughtfully chosen cellar highlighted by fine vintages from around the world and premium liquor. Nestled in the heart of the Texas wine country, Rose Hill is located only fifteen minutes from the historical town of Fredericksburg, Texas and serves as an excellent base for exploring the region's best wineries, historical architecture, shopping and museums. Rose Hill has received critical acclaim for both the lodging and restaurant in *Gourmet* Magazine, *Wine Spectator*, *The Dallas Morning News*, and *Texas Highways*. Come escape to an oasis of tranquility, Texas hill country style!

### Rates
2 Queen Suites, $155/$249. 2 King Suites, $155/$249. 8 King Cottages, $155/$249.  Number of Rooms: 12

### Cuisine
Complimentary multiple-course breakfast to overnite guests at private tables. On-Site upscale gourmet restaurant with outstanding wine list, each Wednesday through Sunday night - open to both our guests and the general public. Most popular is our five course, prix-fixe dinner, but we also offer a very limited a la carte menu.

### Nearest Airport(s)
Either the San Antonio or Austin airport are approx. one hour away. Airport for small planes in Fredericksburg - 15 minutes.

### Directions
See website at www.rose-hill.com or call us at 1-877-rosehil.

# Blair House

www.blairhouseinn.com
100 W. Spoke Hill Drive, Wimberley, TX 78676
**877-549-5450** • 512-847-1111
info@blairhouseinn.com

*Member Since 1998*

*Texas*

*Wimberley*

> *"We have spent just 48 hours with you. We thank you now for a lifetime of wonderful memories."*

Innkeepers/Owners
**Mike and Vickie Schneider**

Conveniently located just minutes from the Wimberley Square, Blair House Inn is situated on 22 peaceful acres featuring breathtaking hill country vistas. Meticulous service, warm hospitality, delectable food and luxury amenities provide the ultimate in comfort. This inviting inn is light and airy and features one of the best art galleries in Wimberley. A pool and whirlpool spa set in the hillside allows for spectacular views while relaxing. Blair House also provides spacious and attractive common areas including a living room with a fireplace, a television/game room, a library, plus a front porch with beautiful sunset views and a patio by the herb garden. Guests can enjoy a massage, use the sauna, hike the grounds, venture out on one of the bicycles or just nap in a hammock. Rated third nationwide as "Best Evening Cuisine" and "Best B&B for Relaxing and Unwinding," by *Inn Traveler* Magazine and the "Best Breakfast in Texas" - *Southern Living.*

**Rates**
3 rooms, main house, $150/$170. 8 rooms or executive suites, $185/$285. All uniquely decorated guest rooms have luxurious linens, lovely views, satellite TV/VCR/CD/some DVD, wireless Internet and private baths, most with whirlpool tubs. Open year-round  Number of Rooms: 11

**Cuisine**
Full breakfast, evening dessert, 5-course, fixed menu gourmet dinner on Saturday evenings. Complimentary beverages.

**Nearest Airport(s)**
Austin/San Antonio

**Directions**
From Austin take I-35 S to Kyle Exit 213; continue W to Wimberley; 1.6 miles S of Wimberley Square on E side of Ranch Road 12.

# The Inn Above Onion Creek

www.innaboveonioncreek.com
4444 W. FM 150, Kyle, TX 78640
**800-579-7686** • 512-268-1617 • Fax 512-268-1090
info@innaboveonioncreek.com

*Member Since 2003*

*Texas*

*Kyle*

*"...beautiful sunrises and sunsets, rolling hills, flowers, butterflies, wildlife... excellent food and service...simply magnificent!"*

Owners
**John and Janie Orr**

The Inn Above Onion Creek is a replica of a late 1800's homestead set on a 100-acre hill country plot with panoramic views. The Inn's buildings were built to remember the past with all of the present day amenities, each of the twelve rooms feature classic antique pieces, comfortable furnishings, feather beds, wireless internet, and entertainment centers with satellite television. Included in each night's stay is a three-course dinner and full hot breakfast, prepared using the freshest seasonal ingredients. During your stay you can explore the miles of hiking and biking trails on the property, take a dip in our pool or just enjoy the view from one of our many porches! The Inn is close to many of the Hill Country attractions, including Wimberley, Fredericksburg, and many of the Hill Country wineries. Providing a tranquil setting and a comfortable atmosphere, The Inn Above Onion Creek makes it easy to unwind and appreciate the surrounding beauty. And now, with our spa, you will be more relaxed than ever. The Spa offers carefully selected body and skin treatments to expand your senses, quiet the mind, and enrich your appearance.

**Rates**
12 rooms, incl. 2 suites, 3 cottages: $230/$495. All w/fireplace & porch, 6 w/whirlpool bath. Breakfast & dinner included in room rate. 10% discount Sun.-Thur. Number of Rooms: 12

**Cuisine**
3-course dinner served at 6:00 each evening. Full hot breakfast served from 8:30-10:00 each morning.Complimentary coffee, tea, cold drinks, homemade cookies and fruit.

**Nearest Airport(s)**
Austin Bergstrom

**Directions**
25 mi. SW of Austin. Exit 213 off I-35 and head W. on Center St. thru Kyle 10 blocks to 3-way stop. Turn R on W. FM 150 to Driftwood 5.3 mi.

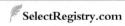

# A Beckmann Inn & Carriage House

www.beckmanninn.com
222 E. Guenther Street, San Antonio, TX 78204
**800-945-1449** • 210-229-1449 • Fax 210-229-1061
InnJoy@beckmanninn.com

*Member Since 1997*

*Texas*

*"Warm and personal hospitality, gourmet breakfast,
artistically served, best location!"*

*San Antonio*

Innkeepers/Owners
**Paula & Charles Stallcup**

Experience gracious *Texas* hospitality at its very best in a beautiful Victorian home built in 1886. Located in the picturesque King William Historic District, rooted in German heritage, the Beckmann Inn is the perfect downtown location for business or leisure travel accommodations. This **"hidden treasure"** of San Antonio is one block from the beautifully landscaped Riverwalk, minutes to the Alamo and Convention Center via trolley streetcar, and walking distance to outstanding restaurants, great shops and unique galleries.

The wonderful wraparound porch welcomes guests to spacious antique filled rooms, ornately carved queen size Victorian style beds, private bathrooms, terry robes, cable TVs, phones, wireless internet access, mini-refrigerators, hairdryers, and irons/ironing boards. A gourmet breakfast including a hot breakfast entree with fresh seasonal fruit, coffee/tea/juice and a breakfast dessert is personally prepared and delightfully served in our dining room.

**Rates**
5 rooms $109-$179; Open year-round. Number of Rooms: 5

**Cuisine**
Full gourmet breakfast, with a breakfast dessert.

**Nearest Airport(s)**
San Antonio International

**Directions**
From airport, take 281 South to 37 South, exit Right on Durango, Left on South St. Mary's St., then immediately take Right on King William St., Left on E. Guenther Street.

# Noble Inns

www.nobleinns.com
107 Madison Street, San Antonio, TX 78204
**800-221-4045** • 210-225-4045 • Fax 210-227-0877
stay@nobleinns.com

*Member Since 2001*

*Texas*

*San Antonio*

> *"Your inn is gorgeous! Our room cozy, spacious bath,
> delightful spa, delicious breakfast!"*

Owners
**Liesl and Don Noble**

Don and Liesl Noble, sixth-generation San Antonians, invite guests to experience the rich history and ambiance of San Antonio. Noble Inns comprise The Jackson House (JH) and Aaron Pancoast Carriage House (PCH), two 1890s-era historic landmarks, located four houses apart in the King William Historic District. Both provide Victorian elegance with modern luxuries and superior amenities for the discerning business or leisure traveler, and are just off the Riverwalk near all downtown sites, including the Alamo, convention center and Alamodome. All rooms include private marble bath, gas fireplace with antique mantel, antique furnishings and elegant fabrics, complimentary high-speed internet (wired and/or wireless), color cable TV w/HBO, private phone w/ voice mail, custom guest robes, and central air conditioning. Gardens feature two pools and heated spa. Two-person whirlpool tub in bath, canopy bed, DVD player w/ complimentary DVD library are available in certain suites and rooms. Complete your experience by booking transportation in our classic 1960 Rolls Royce Silver Cloud II. The Jackson House is rated AAA 4-diamond.

**Rates**
7 Rooms, $159/259; 2 Suites, $209/299. Inquire about special weekday & corporate rates in low season. Number of Rooms: 9

**Cuisine**
The Jackson House features a delicious full breakfast, afternoon refreshments, evening sherry & port. Aaron Pancoast Carriage House features an expanded continental breakfast and full kitchens en suite.

**Nearest Airport(s)**
San Antonio International

**Directions**
From airport to Jackson House: US 281 S to Durango/Alamodome exit downtown. Rt on Durango. Lft on S. St. Mary's. Rt on Madison to #107. To PCH: same as above, then continue Rt on Turner. Lft on Washington. Enter gates at 202 Washington.

SelectRegistry.com

# The Ogé Inn on the Riverwalk

www.nobleinns.com
209 Washington St, San Antonio, TX 78204
**800-242-2770** • 210-223-2353 • Fax 210-226-5812
stay@nobleinns.com

*Member Since 1994*

*"Wonderful location, excellent and warm staff. Fabulous Breakfasts.
4 stars, in my opinion."*

Owners
**Liesl and Don Noble**

Boasting 1.5 landscaped acres directly on the famous River Walk in the King William
Historic District, this 1857 Antebellum Mansion is one of Texas' historic architectural gems.
With its grand verandas and spacious rooms, it is known for its elegance, quiet comfort
and luxury. Furnished in European and American antiques, all rooms have been recently
redecorated and feature a king or queen bed w/ down featherbed, private bath w/ tub &
shower, flat-panel TV w/ cable and DVD player, DVD library access, phone, custom robes
and guest refrigerator. Delicious full breakfast served at private tables in the dining room
or on front veranda. Some rooms have fireplace and/or porch. All suites feature luxurious granite baths with double Jacuzzi tub and separate shower, multi-room stereo system
w/ CD player, fireplace and porch (one w/private Riverwalk balcony). Conveniently
located downtown near the Alamo, convention center, Alamodome, shopping, dining and
entertainment. Amenities for business travelers include complimentary high-speed Internet,
in-room desk, and flexible breakfast options. Board meetings, retreats & small functions that
include lodging can be accommodated.

**Rates**
7 Rooms & 3 Suites on 3 floors, $189/$399. Inquire about
special corporate & weekday rates in low season. Number of
Rooms: 10

**Cuisine**
Delicious full breakfast, afternoon refreshments, evening
sherry & port.

**Nearest Airport(s)**
San Antonio International - 9 mi./13 min. via expressway to
downtown.

**Directions**
From airport: US 281 South (IH 37) to Durango/ Alamodome
exit downtown. Rt on Durango & go thru 3 stoplights. Left
onto Pancoast St. and angle right onto Washington St. Inn
is 1st house on Right. Historic marker and address plaques
(#209) in front.

*Texas*

*San Antonio*

# Vermont

## "The Green Mountain State"

Famous for: Maple Syrup, Dairies, Lakes, Forests, Mountains, and Skiing.

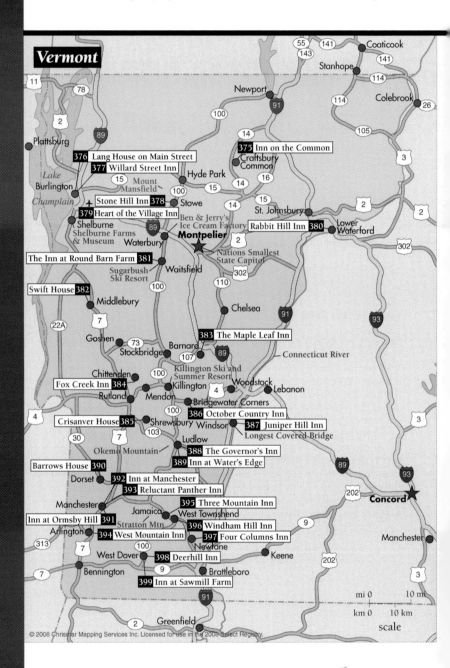

Vermont

- 376 Lang House on Main Street
- 377 Willard Street Inn
- 375 Inn on the Common
- 378 Stone Hill Inn
- 379 Heart of the Village Inn
- 380 Rabbit Hill Inn
- 381 The Inn at Round Barn Farm
- 382 Swift House
- 383 The Maple Leaf Inn
- 384 Fox Creek Inn
- 385 Crisanver House
- 386 October Country Inn
- 387 Juniper Hill Inn
- 388 The Governor's Inn
- 389 Inn at Water's Edge
- 390 Barrows House
- 391 Inn at Ormsby Hill
- 392 Inn at Manchester
- 393 Reluctant Panther Inn
- 394 West Mountain Inn
- 395 Three Mountain Inn
- 396 Windham Hill Inn
- 397 Four Columns Inn
- 398 Deerhill Inn
- 399 Inn at Sawmill Farm

Ben & Jerry's Ice Cream Factory

Montpelier — Nations Smallest State Capitol

Shelburne Farms & Museum

Sugarbush Ski Resort

Killington Ski and Summer Resort

Okemo Mountain

Stratton Mtn.

Longest Covered Bridge

Connecticut River

© 2008 Christmas Mapping Services Inc. Licensed for use in the 2008 Select Registry.

# Inn on the Common

www.innonthecommon.com
P.O. Box 75, 1162 N. Craftsbury Road, Craftsbury Common, VT 05827
**800-521-2233** • 802-586-9619 • Fax 802-586-2249
info@innonthecommon.com

*Member Since 1976*

*Vermont*

*Craftsbury Common*

*"After an incredible scenic drive, we pulled into the Inn and it was just...
'wow.' It feels like how life is supposed to be...beautiful, tranquil, inspiring."*

Innkeepers/Owners
**Jim and Judi Lamberti**
**Vermont Innkeeper of the Year 1994**

Dreaming of a classic Vermont country inn experience? Visit Inn on the Common in scenic Craftsbury Common, one of the state's most photographed hill towns. Profiled on NBC's famous *Today Show*, the Inn has been showcased in many national and international publications. Nestled in the Northeast Kingdom's pristine countryside, this jewel of an inn offers a quiet, sophisticated retreat from today's hectic lifestyle. Surrounded by manicured gardens and the legendary Green Mountains, the Inn's lovely campus is home to three meticulously restored Federal houses. Guestrooms feature private baths, hand-stitched quilts, beautiful artwork and heirloom antiques. This is THE vacation getaway that you'll be telling all your friends and family about! Come stay a while, enjoy our gracious hospitality and superb customer service, and take home a wealth of warm, happy memories! Skiiers: Our area offers some of the best cross-country skiing in the East. Corporate, groups and weddings welcome. Check our website for specials. Gift Certificates available.

**Rates**
16 Rooms. $145/$295 B&B (for one or two people per night including refreshments and full breakfast). Rates adjusted seasonally. Rooms available with wood-burning fireplaces and/or whirlpool tub. Number of Rooms: 16

**Cuisine**
On-site Trellis Restaurant offers classic country cuisine to Inn guests only Sun. - Thurs. at The Innkeeper's Table, a limited pre-selected entree menu. During the summer months Trellis is closed on Monday. A full fine dining menu is available on Fri. & Sat. evenings with advance reservations.

**Nearest Airport(s)**
Burlington, VT

**Directions**
Call or visit www.innonthecommon.com.

# Lang House on Main Street

www.langhouse.com
360 Main Street, Burlington, VT 05401
**877-919-9799** • 802-652-2500 • Fax 802-651-8717
innkeeper@langhouse.com

*Member Since 2003*

*Vermont*

*Burlington*

*"We are two very harried professionals who greatly appreciated the relaxing comfort of your inn. Your staff treated us like family: warm and familiar."*

Innkeeper/Owner
**Kim Borsavage**

Built as a private residence in 1881, the Lang House was converted in 2000 to an 11-room bed and breakfast inn. The renovation preserved the house's historic nature and added a number of contemporary amenities. The Lang House features qualities guests expect in a 19th century Victorian home; antiques, soaring ceilings, stunning woodwork, stained glass windows, and the rosette pattern repeated throughout the house. The inn is situated in Burlington's Hill Section, which is known for its remarkable residential architecture and proximity to the University of Vermont and Burlington's restaurants, shopping, waterfront, and cultural venues. Fresh, locally procured ingredients -- including eggs, herbs from our garden, smoked breakfast meats, berries and vegetables, Challah French Toast, and Organic Vermont maple syrup -- are used in our expertly prepared breakfast fare. Wind down from the day with locally crafted wine or beer and a Vermont cheese plate in our comfortable sun porch or elegant sitting room. The Lang House innkeepers and staff provide genuine hospitality and personalized attention to leisure and business traveler.

**Rates**
Rates are seasonal from $145-$245 plus tax  Number of Rooms: 11

**Cuisine**
Gourmet Breakfast

**Nearest Airport(s)**
Burlington International (BTV)

**Directions**
On Main Street (Rte 2) approx. 1.5 mi. from I-89, just E of Rt 7. From I-89, exit 14W, Rt 2, which turns into Main St. As you come down the hill into Burlington, Lang House is on your R, just before the light. Coming from across the Lake via the Lake Champlain ferry, take a L at the 1st light onto Battery St. At the 1st light, take a R & head up Main St (or Rt 2 E). We are located approx. 1/2 mi. up Main, on the L side of the street.

# Willard Street Inn

www.willardstreetinn.com
349 South Willard Street, Burlington, VT 05401
**800-577-8712** • 802-651-8710 • Fax 802-651-8714
info@willardstreetinn.com

*Member Since 2002*

*"...all of the charms of a country getaway, yet with an urban setting."* Vermont
*Magazine. "Burlington's most charming bed-and-breakfast."* The Boston Globe

*Vermont*

*Burlington*

Innkeepers/Owners
**Katie and Larry Davis**

Built in 1881, this 3-story Georgian/Queen Anne revival style mansion is located in Burlington's picturesque hill district with sweeping views of Lake Champlain and the Adirondack Mountains. This historic inn offers 14 elegant rooms, each individually appointed, and all with private baths. Tall double front doors with antique brass handles invite guests into the beautiful cherry paneled foyer with its high ceilings and grand staircase. Start the day in our sunny marble floored solarium, enjoying gourmet breakfasts featuring Vermont products, seasonal items fresh from the gardens, and a delightful dash of the unexpected. In the spring and summer, enjoy the English gardens from colorful Adirondack chairs, and come winter, cozy up fireside with a good book.

Centrally located, this certified Green Hotel is within walking distance to the shops and restaurants of the Church Street Marketplace, Lake Champlain's Waterfront, and area colleges- University of Vermont and Champlain College. Whether for a weekend escape or simple relaxation, the Inn is the perfect getaway for all seasons providing 19th century charm with 21st century service.

## Rates
14 Rooms including 2 suites, $140/$230. Private baths, AC, LCD TV w/cable, free high-speed wireless Internet, antiques, lake views and gardens. Open year-round. Number of Rooms: 14

## Cuisine
Full breakfast featuring Vermont products served from 7:30-10:00 AM. 3 different choices daily: egg entree, sweet entree, or our homemade granola. Daily in-room snack plate with: cookies, Lake Champlain Chocolates & dried fruit.

## Nearest Airport(s)
Burlington

## Directions
From I-89 take Exit 14 W. Follow Rte. 2 West for 1.5 mi. Turn left onto South Willard St. (also Rte. 7 South). We are 1/4 mi. down on the right at the corner of Spruce St.

# Stone Hill Inn

www.stonehillinn.com
89 Houston Farm Road, Stowe, VT 05672
**802-253-6282** • Fax 802-253-7415
stay@stonehillinn.com

*Member Since 2002*

*Vermont*

*Stowe*

*"...every detail speaks to a level of comfort and perfection not ordinarily experienced" - Travel & Leisure Golf*

Innkeeper/Owner
**Amy Jordan**

Newly built in 1998, the Inn was created to be a peaceful, romantic, one-of-a-kind getaway. Relax in your bubbling, fireside Jacuzzi for two--every room has one--along with many other thoughtful touches and indulgent amenities. Schedule a massage by the fireplace in the privacy of your room, or outside in our spectacular summer perennial gardens. In winter, glide down the hill on the toboggan, or borrow some snowshoes to explore our wooded trail. Stowe has long been known as the 'Ski Capital of the East,' but this scenic mountain village offers so much to do year-round. After dinner at one of 40 local restaurants, return to the Inn for billards, games, and puzzles by the huge stone fireplace, or select a movie from the movie library (popcorn provided!). This is truly a place for couples who treasure their time together. Chosen one of the Twelve Best B&Bs in North America, Forbes.com. Recommended by the *New York Times, Boston Globe, Montreal Gazette, Washington Post,* and *USA Today.*

**Rates**
All rooms offer a king bed and fireside Jacuzzi for two. LCD TV & DVD/VCR. $295 to $425 B&B, depending on season. Number of Rooms: 9

**Cuisine**
A memorable, full country breakfast is served from 7:30 to 10:00 AM in the sunny, window-walled breakfast room with tables set for two. An evening hors d'oeuvre and 24-hour soft drinks included. BYOB if you wish.

**Nearest Airport(s)**
Burlington, VT.

**Directions**
From I-89, take exit 10. Follow Rte 100 North for 10 miles to Stowe. At the 3-way stop, turn left on Rte 108. Go 3 miles. Turn right on Houston Farm Rd. It's the first driveway on the left.

# Heart of the Village Inn

www.heartofthevillage.com
5347 Shelburne Road, Shelburne, VT 05482
**877-808-1834** • 802-985-2800 • Fax 802-985-2870
innkeeper@heartofthevillage.com

*Member Since 2002*

*"We enjoyed the hospitality and the breakfast was the best I have experienced in many Inn stays over the years - delicious but not fussy."*

Innkeepers/Owners
**Geoff and Maureen Conrad**

Located in the heart of Shelburne Village, this 1886 historic inn welcomes guests with elegance and warmth. The Inn has retained its prominence as one of the centerpieces of the Village, and is listed on the National Register of Historic Places. There are five Inn rooms and four Carriage Barn rooms - each elegantly decorated with a mix of period furnishings - armoires, comfortable beds, plus linens and a sunny view of Shelburne Village. Each room has a private bath, air conditioning, phone service, cable television, Free Wireless Internet and a cozy reading chair. The Inn's large living room, library and wrap around porch provide comfortable rocking chairs to relax in and enjoy morning coffee, afternoon tea, or a glass of wine. Spectacular hydrangeas, peonies and perennial gardens make for an ideal setting for your leisure gatherings. Walk to Shelburne Museum, fine dining and shopping. Shelburne Farms, Vermont Teddy Bear, downtown Burlington, and the airport are close by.

**Rates**
4 king/twins $190/$220; 3 queens $175/$205; 1 queen suite $250/$270; 1 queen $150/$170. TV, telephone, Free WiFi, AC, private baths, 3 w/clawfoot tub, Whirlpool Tub in Suite. Two King rooms are accessible. Number of Rooms: 9

**Cuisine**
Early AM coffee & tea. Full Vermont breakfast featuring home made granola, yogurt, fresh fruit, baked goods & freshly prepared hot entree each day. Fresh baked cookies. Beer & Wine available.

**Nearest Airport(s)**
Burlington VT

**Directions**
From I-89 N, exit 13,I-189 to Rt 7 S; 4.7 mi. to the Inn. From I-87 N, exit 20; Rt 9 to Rt 149 to Ft Ann, NY; Rt 4 to Rt 22A N to Vergennes, VT; Rt 7 N to Shelburne.

*Vermont*

*Shelburne*

# Rabbit Hill Inn

**{o{** **{o{** ♀

www.rabbithillinn.com
48 Lower Waterford Rd., Lower Waterford, VT 05848
**800-76-BUNNY** • 802-748-5168 • Fax 802-748-8342
info@rabbithillinn.com

*Member Since 1990*

*Vermont*

*Lower Waterford*

> *"...accommodations are incredible, meals are amazing... this just might be the most romantic place on the planet." Zagat's*

Innkeepers/Owners
**Brian & Leslie Mulcahy**

Even time could not change this 1795 Country Inn classic ~ an enchanting, romantic and luxurious hideaway in a tiny hamlet set between a river and the mountains. With elegant and uniquely styled guest rooms, most with fireplaces, many with double whirlpool tubs and private porches, Rabbit Hill Inn is recognized for award-winning candlelit dining, pampering service, attention to detail, and warm hospitality unlike you have ever experienced from staff and ever-present innkeepers. With the inn as your base, explore a myriad of exciting activies and attractions such as downhill and XC skiing, snowshoeing, golfing, hiking, antiquing and much more in both Vermont's Northeast Kingdom and New Hampshire's North Country. In-Room massage service is also available. Rabbit Hill has been repeatedly voted one of America's Best Inns by writers, guidebooks, and magazines and has earned a perfect score in Select Registry's quality inspection. Come experience for yourself why Rabbit Hill is "a paradise for the senses, vacation for the soul."

**Rates**
Classic Rooms: $199/$239B&B / Superior Rooms w/fireplace: $259/$299 B&B / Luxury Rooms w/whirlpool & fireplace: $339/$399 B&B. All offer queen or king beds, plush robes, CD players and many fine amenities. Number of Rooms: 19

**Cuisine**
Full country breakfast and afternoon tea & pastries included. Enjoy a multi-course gourmet candlelit dinner in our romantic dining room. Beer, wine, and spirits available in our Snooty Fox Pub.

**Nearest Airport(s)**
Manchester, NH/Burlington, VT

**Directions**
From I-91 (N or S), exit 19 to I-93 S. Exit 1 R. on Rte. 18 S 7 mi. to Inn. From I-93 N, exit 44, L on Rte. 18 N, 2 mi. to Inn.

# The Inn at Round Barn Farm

www.theroundbarn.com

1661 East Warren Road, Waitsfield, VT 05673

**802-496-2276** • Fax 802-496-2276

lodging@theroundbarn.com

*Member Since 2000*

*"The Round Barn Farm is the most peaceful and nourishing place on earth!
Friendly and helpful Innkeepers make this Inn memorable."*

Innkeepers/Owners
## AnneMarie DeFreest & Tim L. Piper

We invite you to our elegant, romantic Bed & Breakfast Inn, located admidst 245 acres of lush green hills, flower-covered meadows, graceful ponds, and extensive perennial gardens in Vermont's Green Mountains. This four season retreat in the Sugarbush/Mad River Valley has offered an escape for lovers of the arts, history, and the outdoors since 1987. The interior of the Inn is memorable; the restoration impeccable. Each of the Inns 12 guest rooms is individually decorated while maintaining refurbished wide-board pine floors covered in oriental rugs, beautiful wallpapers in a palette of rich tones, decorative accents and attention to the details that matter. In winter, our meadows and woodlands are covered in a blanket of white. Snowshoe trails and snowshoes are available for our guests to experience the magic of our Vermont winter wonderland. In the summer enjoy concerts, theater, and a variety of outdoor activities. Our Innkeepers (and freshly baked cookies) await your arrival at the Inn at the Round Barn Farm.

**Rates**
Rates $165/$325. Tempur-Pedic beds, down comforters, whirlpool tubs, steamshowers, Neutrogena products, gas fireplaces, individual heat and A/C. Number of Rooms: 12

**Cuisine**
As founding members of the Vermont Fresh Network and having our own certified organic garden, our breakfasts and hors d'oeuvres are prepared with seasonal/local ingredients. Dinner is enjoyed at one of 15 area restaura

**Nearest Airport(s)**
Burlington Airport (BTV)

**Directions**
I-89 S exit 10, Rte. 100 S 14 mi. L on Bridge St., through covered bridge, R at fork up 1 mile. I-89 N exit 9, Rte. 100B 14 mi. L on Bridge St., through covered bridge, R at fork, up 1 mile.

*Vermont*

*Waitsfield*

# Swift House Inn

www.swifthouseinn.com
25 Stewart Lane, Middlebury, VT 05753
**866-388-9925** • 802-388-9925 • Fax 802-388-9927
info@swifthouseinn.com

*Member Since 2005*

*"Exceptional food, wonderful service..."*

Innkeepers/Owners
**Dan & Michele Brown**

Life's most memorable moments are spent with loved ones in exceptional places. The Swift House Inn is just such a place. This historic 20-room former governor's mansion is Middlebury's only in-town AAA Three Diamond Country Inn, and offers the essence of New England warmth. Inside, candlelit dinners await you. Large, comfortable rooms offer modern amenities in period decor. Relax. Sip a glass of wine by the fireplace, or ponder your favorite book while the kids explore the garden or sled on a nearby hill. Every window frames a picture of country tranquility, yet shops, museums, and Middlebury College are a short walk away. The Inn's three buildings are on five acres with extensive lawns and gardens. Enjoy hiking just out the back door or in the nearby Green Mountains. Bike the Champlain Valley, fly fish our numerous rivers and creeks or participate in water activities on nearby Lake Champlain or Lake Dunmore. Several downhill or cross country ski areas are just a short drive. Bring you bike, golf clubs, fly rod or just come to relax. The Inn is the perfect place to stay when visiting Middlebury College.

**Rates**
20 Rooms in three buildings $115/$285. Many with fireplaces and two person whirlpool tubs. All with telephone, individually controlled AC/heat, and satelliteTV. On site sauna, steam shower, and conference room. Number of Rooms: 20

**Cuisine**
Full Breakfast. Dinner served 4 nights a week winter/spring and 5 nights summer/fall; changing menu prepared with many local Vermont products. Full bar service and extensive wine list, *Wine Spectator* Award.

**Nearest Airport(s)**
Burlington International Airport, 35 miles

**Directions**
The Inn is located on Stewart Lane just off of Route 7, 2 blocks N of the village green.

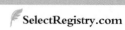

# The Maple Leaf Inn

www.mapleleafinn.com
PO Box 273, 5890 Vermont Route 12, Barnard, VT 05031
**800-516-2753** • 802-234-5342 • Fax 802-234-6456
innkeeper@mapleleafinn.com

*Member Since 2002*

*Vermont*

*Barnard*

> *"When couples stay at the Maple Leaf Inn, they fall in love again . . . what guests leave behind are tales of romance." The Boston Globe*

**Innkeepers/Owners**
**Nancy and Mike Boyle**

We welcome you to refresh your spirit and restore your soul in this pastoral corner of Vermont. Nestled snugly within sixteen acres of maple and birch trees. Enjoy hiking, biking, cross-country skiing, and snow-shoeing on the trails nearby. Our Victorian-style farmhouse was lovingly designed and built by the innkeepers. Each spacious guest room has its own personality and charm with delicate stenciling, stitchery, and handmade quilts. Individually controlled central heating/air-conditioning, heated bathroom tile floors and a pillow library all add to your personal comfort. Woodburning fireplaces are set daily for your convenience and a collection of romantic videos awaits your viewing. Snacks, sodas and bottled water are available at any time and room service, including delectable treats, beer and wine, may be ordered as well. "Nook and Cranny Gift Shelf". Memorable gourmet breakfasts are prepared fresh each morning and served at individual candlelit tables for two. Dinners are available upon request. Our Inn has been awarded the AAA Four Diamond award for 11 years in a row. Come share our dream. Open all year.

**Rates**
$160/$290 B&B. Spacious guest rooms with king beds, luxurious private baths w/whirlpools, TV/VCR w/premium satellite service, wi-fi, telephones, woodburning fireplaces, spa robes, hair dryers, air-conditioning. Number of Rooms: 7

**Cuisine**
A gourmet three-course breakfast is served at individual candlelit tables for two, and light afternoon refreshments are served in the parlor at check-in. Dinners available upon request. Beer and wine available.

**Nearest Airport(s)**
Burlington, VT

**Directions**
From Woodstock, VT: 9 miles N on Rte. 12. Inn sits back in woods on R, just before school.

# Fox Creek Inn

www.foxcreekinn.com
49 Dam Road, Chittenden, VT  05737
**800-707-0017** • 802-483-6213 • Fax 802-483-2623
innkeeper@foxcreekinn.com

*Member Since 1998*

*"Terry and I loved staying at Fox Creek.
We felt like we were guests in your home."*

Innkeepers/Owners
**Jim and Sandy Robertson**

Just the way you have always pictured a Country Inn. Here is the Vermont you have been searching. There are a myriad of activities: hiking, biking and water sports in summer and downhill alpine and cross country skiing in winter. Relaxing in front of a fireplace or sitting on the front porch with a glass of wine, these are the times when memories are made. Once the home of William Barstow, you can easily imagine the family entertaining their friends, the Fords, Firestones, and his partner, Thomas Edison. We strive to keep the tradition of entertaining alive.Fox Creek is an inn full of charm and casual elegance and with a gentle pace that permits you to relax enjoy the moment.

**Rates**
8 Rooms, all with private baths most rooms have fireplaces and jacuzzi tubs  Rates are $195/$295 B&B; $225/$400 MAP. Number of Rooms: 8

**Cuisine**
Enjoy a full Vermont country breakfast and a candlelit 4-course dinner. Enjoy our ever-changing menu, featuring the freshest ingredients. Select a wine from our extensive wine menu with many older vintages. Sample the hors d'oeuvres with a single malt scotch or a martini in our delightful little pub.

**Nearest Airport(s)**
Rutland and Burlington

**Directions**
Chittenden is 10 miles NE of Rutland, VT. From Rutland take Rt. 7N or Rt. 4E and follow the state hospitality signs.

# Crisanver House

www.crisanver.com
1434 Crown Point Road, Shrewsbury, VT 05738
**800-492-8089** • 802-492-3589 • Fax 802-492-3480
info@crisanver.com

🍴 🍴 🍴 ♀

*Member Since 2005*

*Vermont*

*Shrewsbury*

*"Beautiful setting, gracious service and delicious artful food."*

**Innkeepers/Owners**
**Carol & B. Michael Calotta**

A BEAUTIFUL INN WHERE CONTENTMENT REIGNS...
Escape to a cherished experience full of gracious hospitality, marvelous accommodations, great food, wonderful service, magnificent views and blissful surroundings. Feel relaxed, revived, refreshed and rekindled in spirit - that's some of what our guests say.

On a country road minutes from the highway, at 2000 feet amid a 120-acre preserve, Crisanver is surrounded by a panoramic tapestry of the Green Mountains and brilliant sunsets. This historic grand home is totally renovated and decorated in upscale classic chic. A beautiful and romantic destination, perfect for every occasion with its classic antiques, original artworks, and warm decor, creating comfort and charming elegance.

Recreation for all seasons - a heated swimming pool, tennis court, hiking trails, snowshoeing, yoga, and birdwatching are on site. Shopping, museums, art galleries, live music and historical sites are only a short drive. Weddings of distinction. Listed in "1000 Places to See Before You Die" (2007).

**Rates**
4 Deluxe Rooms Main House $155-$230, 2 Suites Main House $230-370, 2 Cottage Deluxe Rooms $220-330. Rates are B&B. Number of Rooms: 8

**Cuisine**
Epicurean cuisine featuring the freshest of local offerings and our garden harvest. Complimentary served bountiful country breakfast. Prix fixe candlelight dinner by reservation. Fine European wines. Many restaurants nearby.

**Nearest Airport(s)**
Rutland Regional - 10 min  Burlington Int'l - 2 hr

**Directions**
89 North or South > 4 West > 7 South > 103 South > Left to Lincoln Hill Road, to Crown Point Road (dirt road), second house on the Left

# October Country Inn

www.vermontinns.net

P.O. Box 66, 362 Upper Road, Bridgewater Corners, VT 05035

**800-648-8421** • 802-672-3412 • Fax 802-672-1163

innkeeper@octobercountryinn.com

*Member Since 1992*

*"What a wonderful place! We love the laid back atmoshpere, delicious food, and cozy feel. A great place to come 'home' to on a cold Vermont night."*

Innkeepers/Owners
**Edie and Chuck Janisse**

Loved for its hospitality and relaxed atmosphere, Chuck and Edie's converted nineteenth century farmhouse between Woodstock and Killington offers warmth and intimacy in the finest innkeeping tradition. The scents of baking muffins, fresh herbs and homemade desserts fill the inn as Chuck works magic in French Country, Mexican, Italian, Greek, and even American cuisines. Swim in the pool, bicycle, hike, ski, shop, sight-see or simply relax by the fire-then dine by candlelight. Away from the crowds, yet close to Killington, Okemo, Woodstock, Weston, and Dartmouth. Bridgewater Corners and October Country Inn are always just around the corner.

**Rates**
$150/$180 Dbl. B&B. Dinner, $30.00 per person. Number of Rooms: 10

**Cuisine**
Full country breakfast. Internationally-themed dinners cooked to gourmet standards and served family-style. Beer and wine license.

**Nearest Airport(s)**
Manchester, NH

**Directions**
From Woodstock, follow Rte. 4 westward about 8 miles. Go 1/10 mile past Country Store at junction of Rte. 100A, turn right on Bridgewater Center Rd., and right again on Upper Rd. From Rutland, follow Rte. 4 eastward about 20 miles. Just before the Long Trail Brewery, turn left on Bridgewater Center Rd., and right on Upper Rd.

# Juniper Hill Inn

www.juniperhillinn.com
153 Pembroke Road, Windsor, VT  05089
**800-359-2541** • 802-674-5273 • Fax 802-674-2041
innkeeper@juniperhillinn.com

🍽️ 🍽️ 🍽️ 🍷

*Member Since 2002*

*Vermont*

*Windsor*

*"Perfection relized!" "Attention to detail and charming innkeepers." "We travel all over the world and give JHI Five Stars!" "Spectacular! We'll be back"*

Owner - **Ari Nikki**
General Manager - **Robert Dean**

Ascend a winding driveway canopied by ancient pines to a restored Colonial Revival mansion surrounded by acres of lawns and gardens. Experience incomparable views of Lake Runnemede and Ascutney Mountain from our new spectacular 1,800 sq. ft. terrace surrounded by lush gardens and flanked by our crystal clear pool! History and elegance abound creating a peaceful retreat for you to enjoy. Finely appointed guest rooms feature antiques, decanters of sherry, chocolates, robes, hair dryers, CD players. Many guest rooms also include fireplaces, private balconies or porches. Attention to detail and the fine, but comfortable, dining are additional reasons Juniper Hill is awarded a Romantic Hideaway destination by *The Discerning Traveler* and featured in the *Boston Globe*, Newsday, and many others. Near popular Vermont/New Hampshire locations including Woodstock, Quechee, Dartmouth College. Enjoy golfing, skiing, canoeing, horse or sleigh rides, bicycling, croquet, shopping, historic sites or simply relax, restore, revive, rekindle!

### Rates
$105/$285 B&B. Many rooms w/fireplaces, porches or balconies, queen beds, antiques, woods, garden or mountain views, all individually air conditioned. Number of Rooms: 16

### Cuisine
Full country breakfast menu plus daily special, afternoon refreshment from 3-5 PM. Single 7PM seating for 4-course dinner, advance reservation only, Tues-Sat. Self-serve warm beverages 7-10 PM.

### Nearest Airport(s)
Manchester, NH

### Directions
From I-91 North: Exit 9. R (L from I-91 S) onto Rte. 5 S. Proceed 2.7 mi., R onto Juniper Hill Rd, stay L at fork. Driveway on R at crest of hill.

# The Governor's Inn

www.thegovernorsinn.com
86 Main Street, Ludlow, VT 05149
**800-468-3766** • 802-228-8830
innkeeper@thegovernorsinn.com

*Member Since 1987*

*Vermont*
*Ludlow*

*"Everything about the inn says 'relax and enjoy'...and we did!*
*Incredible gourmet breakfast!"*

Innkeepers/Owners
**Jim and Cathy Kubec**

From the moment you step into this late Victorian country home, you are surrounded by the gracious elegance and warm hospitality befitting its first owner, Vermont Governor William Stickney. Enjoy afternoon tea, sweets, and tea sandwiches served in the parlor with its extraordinary slate fireplace, polished woodwork, and oriental rugs. Retire to your cozy bed chamber, warmed by a gas fireplace in cooler weather or air conditioned during warmer months. Read or watch TV, relax in the whirlpool. Awake to a bountiful breakfast – perhaps gingerbread pancakes or our Potato Cheese Torte - served on antique china, w/ silver and crystal. Culinary Magic Cooking Seminars are held on premises. Walk to village restaurants, shops, and galleries. Near Okemo Mountain, downhill and cross-country skiing, maple houses, cheese factory, golf, hiking, antiquing, summer theater, bicycling, Weston Priory. Take along one of Cathy's Vermont Country picnics as you relax and explore Vermont. Wireless internet access, and computer available for guest use. Mobil Three Star.

**Rates**
7 Rooms, $149/$249, B&B; 1 Suite, $249/$299 B&B. Ski, Golf, Hiking, Picnic Packages. Fully air conditioned. Wireless internet. Open year-round, except 2 wks in Apr., 2 wks in Nov, and Dec. 22-Dec. 25. Number of Rooms: 8

**Cuisine**
Full, hot breakfast, afternoon tea and sweets. Extensive tea menu. Prix fixe dinner by reservation for 6 or more. Beer/wine available. Vermont Country Picnics by request.

**Nearest Airport(s)**
Burlington 114 miles; Hartford 125 miles; Boston 144 miles.

**Directions**
Ludlow is located at intersection of VT Rte. 100 & VT Rte. 103. Inn is south on Main St. (Rte 103), just off village green.

# Inn at Water's Edge

www.innatwatersedge.com
45 Kingdom Road, Ludlow, VT 05149
**888-706-9736** • 802-228-8143 • Fax 802-228-8443
innatwatersedge@mail.tds.net

*Member Since 2003*

*Vermont*

*Ludlow*

*"The 4-course dinner is not to be missed. A real Gem, don't change a thing!"*

Innkeepers/Owners
**Bruce & Tina Verdrager**

Situated on Echo Lake and the Black River, this 150 year old Victorian estate has been thoroughly restored and now boasts all the charm and ambiance of a truly unique Victorian Inn. The Inn exudes the endless enthusiasm of the innkeepers to create the feeling of a bygone era along with the warmth and comfort of being home. Located minutes from skiing and golfing at Okemo and Killington mountains, the Inn is only a short drive to the attractions of Manchester, Weston and Woodstock. Our library, gathering room and English pub all have fireplaces and comfortable seating for guests to enjoy. Each of our 11 guest rooms has a private bath, most with Jacuzzi bathtubs and fireplaces. Whether relaxing in our outdoor hot tub, swimming off our private beach, canoeing or biking, the Inn offers year-round activities. The Inn is also completely air-conditioned and handicapped accessible.

**Rates**
$125/$250 B&B. $175/$300 MAP. Golf and Spa packages from $150/ppdo includes golf or spa, lodging, breakfast & 4-course dinner. Ski packages from $100/ppdo include adult lift ticket at Okemo Mt., lodging, breakfast & 4-course dinner. Reservations 60 days in advance. Number of Rooms: 11

**Cuisine**
Full country breakfast. Afternoon refreshments. 4-course candlelit Dinner. Beer, wine & spirits available in Doc's English Pub & in the Dining Room.

**Nearest Airport(s)**
Bradley International (Hartford)

**Directions**
4 mi. N of Ludlow Village on Rte 100 at Echo Lake between Okemo & Killington Resorts.

# Barrows House

www.barrowshouse.com
3156 Route 30, P.O. Box 98, Dorset, VT 05251-0098
**800-639-1620** • 802-867-4455 • Fax 802-867-0132
innkeepers@barrowshouse.com

*Member Since 1974*

*Vermont*

*Dorset*

*"Soft beds, wonderful food, beautiful place, best hosts-I wish
I could come here every day!"*

Innkeepers/Owners
**Linda & Jim McGinnis**

Barrows House is a collection of nine white clapboard buildings on 12 groomed acres in the heart of the picture-book Vermont village of Dorset. Guests have a choice of 28 rooms and suites in nine different buildings, each with a history and style of its own. All rooms and suites have as a minimum their own private bath, king or queen bed, expanded cable TV, air conditioning and private telephones. Nine also have fireplaces and two have whirlpool tubs. Dining at Barrows House is an informal and delicious adventure in American regional cuisine in our three dining rooms. Whether with iced tea in the gazebo or English garden or mulled cider in front of a warm fire and historic stenciling, Barrows House extends its welcome. Weddings and family reunions are done with a very personal touch.

**Rates**
$120/$260 B&B double occupancy for 18 double sized rooms and 10 suites, nine with fireplaces and two with whirlpool tubs. Number of Rooms: 28

**Cuisine**
Dining is relaxing and informal. The menu is Regional American in style with Continental influence. The quality of your meal will impress especially in a village of less than 1,000 people. A speciality of the Inn is Maine Crab Cakes, Chesapeake Style.

**Nearest Airport(s)**
Albany, NY

**Directions**
Boston: 3 hours New York: 4 hours Montreal: 4 hours

# The Inn at Ormsby Hill

www.ormsbyhill.com
1842 Main Street, Historic Route 7A, Manchester, VT 05255
**800-670-2841** • 802-362-1163 • Fax 802-362-5176
stay@ormsbyhill.com

*Member Since 1996*

*Vermont*

*"...a romantic bed-and-breakfast of the highest caliber."*
*Andrew Harper's Hideaway Report*

*Manchester*

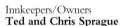

**Four Diamond Award**

Innkeepers/Owners
**Ted and Chris Sprague**

Experience the romance of the past, in the luxury of the present. Steal away to a magical bed and breakfast, rich with history (c. 1764), and nestled in the Green Mountains. "...arguably one of the most welcoming inns in all of New England." *Lonely Planet.* Renowned for comfort, heartfelt hospitality and profound attention to detail. Be pampered in bed chambers with canopies, fireplaces, air-conditioning, and digital flat-screen televisions. Luxurious bathrooms with Jacuzzis for two and some with two-person steam saunas. Indulge in "...the attention to detail, the romantic ambiance..." *Colonial Homes.* If our luxurious rooms aren't enough to take your breath away, our mountain views will. Recipients of the AAA Four Diamond Award for the past nine years - a Manchester inn exclusive. One enchanting night with us and you'll understand why.

**Rates**
8 Rooms and 2 suites, all with fireplace and Jacuzzi for two, $195/$415 B&B. Peak season premiums apply. Open year-round. See website for specials. Number of Rooms: 10

**Cuisine**
Nationally-acclaimed breakfasts served in the magnificent Conservatory with its wall of windows facing the mountains. "...a breakfast that'll knock your socks off..." *Yankee Magazine's Travel Guide.* "...perhaps the best breakfasts in Vermont," says *New England Travel.*

**Nearest Airport(s)**
Albany, New York

**Directions**
In Manchester Center, at junction of Routes 11/30 and 7A, take Historic Route 7A South. The Inn is approximately 3 miles on the left.

# Inn at Manchester

www.innatmanchester.com
3967 Main Street, Manchester Village, VT 05254
**800-273-1793** • 802-362-1793 • Fax 802-362-3218
innkeeper@innatmanchester.com

*Member Since 2008*

*Vermont*

*Manchester Village*

*"Thank you for your Southern charm, delicious breakfasts and beautiful rooms.
We'll be back!"*

Innkeepers/Owners
**Frank and Julie Hanes**

Unforgettable personality and unlimited possibilities await you at one of Vermont's most
inviting getaways, The Inn at Manchester. Tucked away in the breathtaking landscape
of the Taconic and Green Mountains in Vermont's cultural haven, Manchester – where
there's something for everyone year round. Golf, skiing, hiking, fishing, shopping, theatre
or art, Manchester and the Mountains has something for every taste. As always, there is
no rule you ever have to leave the inn! Unwind beside the hearth in the living room, or
over a game of chess in the cozy den. Maybe take a stroll around our beautiful grounds, a
dip in the pool, or just relax in a rocker on the porch. Then drop in for a cocktail in the
Nineteenth Room, our fully licensed pub ? one of the places where guests gather to relax
and socialize. We look forward to welcoming you to the Inn at Manchester, a Gem in the
Green Mountains.

**Rates**
Our rates run from $155 to $295. Number of Rooms: 18

**Cuisine**
At the Inn at Manchester, we pride ourselves on a full
traditional breakfast that is guaranteed to start your day off in
the right way! Try our famous cottage cakes with hot apricot
sauce, tomato-mushroom or spinach quiche, or a savory
omelet -- to name just a few of our popular dishes. Sneak into
our guest pantry and help yourself to refreshments and fresh
baked treats!

**Nearest Airport(s)**
Albany, New York (Approximate time: 1 1/2 hours)

**Directions**
In Manchester, take a left at the junction of Routes 11/30 and
7A.We are just one mile on your right.

SelectRegistry.com

# Reluctant Panther Inn & Restaurant

www.reluctantpanther.com
39 West Road, P.O. Box 678, Manchester Village, VT 05254
**800-822-2331** • 802-362-2568 • Fax 802-362-2586
stay@reluctantpanther.com

*Member Since 2008*

*"Fabulous relaxing getaway - loved the double Jacuzzi!"*

Innkeepers
**Liz and Jerry Lavalley**

Southern Vermont's newest small luxury inn is situated at the foot of Mount Equinox in historic Manchester Village. The inn and its renowned fine dining restaurant have been transformed into a chic boutique hotel offering elegant accommodations and a remarkable culinary experience in a sophisticated setting. All suites are newly refurbished with in-room fireplaces (some with two), hydrotherapy spa tubs (most designed for two persons), luxurious linens and free high-speed wireless Internet access. Some rooms offer exceptional mountain views or a private porch entrance. Each is uniquely designed to evoke an individual experience as well as the Reluctant Panther's signature pampering style. Inn guests will enjoy proximity to world-class spa, golf, designer outlet shopping and four-season activities, including hiking, biking, skiing and horseback riding. Relax and rejuvenate in a quintessential New England setting conveniently located within easy driving distance from both New York and Boston.

**Rates**
16 Rooms from $259; 4 Suites from $449; rates vary according to season. Number of Rooms: 20

**Nearest Airport(s)**
Albany (ALB) 1.5 hrs; Boston (BOS) 3.0 hrs; NYC Airports 3.5 hrs; Hartford (BDL) 2.5 hrs.

**Cuisine**
Sophisticated culinary experience--refined American cuisine with emphasis on local, seasonal ingredients and supreme presentation; outstanding wine list, generous selection of wines by the glass; cozy tavern features award-winning cocktails and variety of local microbrews and imported beers.

**Directions**
At the intersection of Historic Rte 7A, Seminary Ave. and West Rd. in Manchester Village, Vermont.

*Vermont*

*Manchester Village*

# West Mountain Inn

www.westmountaininn.com
144 West Mountain Inn Road, Arlington, VT 05250
**802-375-6516** • Fax 802-375-6553
info@westmountaininn.com

*Member Since 1984*

*"A wonderful ambiance where the warmth extends beyond the fireplace."*

Innkeepers/Owners
**The Carlson Family**

Imagine a time when a visit to the country meant a luxurious room, splendid meals, refreshing outdoor pursuits, relaxing afternoons and convivial evenings - now imagine having your own Country Estate and you will understand what a visit to the West Mountain Inn is like. Set high on a mountainside overlooking the historic village of Arlington and the Green Mountains beyond, the century-old West Mountain Inn has been hosting guests for over thirty years. Visitors to the Inn are surrounded by spacious, antique-filled guest rooms, fantastic views, and 150 acres of gardens, lawns, woodlands and meadows. Without having to leave the Inn's property, guests can hike or snowshoe on miles of trails, flyfish, swim or canoe in the famous Battenkill River and read or relax in the Adirondack chairs on the front lawn. The Inn's wood-paneled diningroom provides the perfect setting for the lavish country breakfasts and sumptuous 5-course dinners created daily by our award-winning chef. The Inn also offers private rooms and a wonderful old barn for the unique celebration of weddings, birthdays, anniversaries, reunions or business meetings.

**Rates**
12 Rooms, 3 Suites, 3 Townhouses $165/$323 B&B,
$240/$398 MAP. Service charges included in all rates.
Number of Rooms: 20

**Cuisine**
A lavish country breakfast and splendid 5-course dinner are
prepared daily. Seasonal menus focus on local VT products
and organic produce. Weddings and rehearsal dinners a
specialty. Full bar, premium beers and exceptional wine list.

**Nearest Airport(s)**
Albany, NY

**Directions**
Vermont Route 7 N, exit 3, L off ramp, take access road to end,
R on Rte. 7A into Arlington. One mile then L on Rte. 313 for .5
mile, L on River Rd., green bridge over river, Inn's driveway on
the L, Inn at top of driveway.

SelectRegistry.com

# Three Mountain Inn

www.threemountaininn.com
3732 Main Street Route 30/100, P.O. Box 180, Jamaica, VT 05343
**800-532-9399** • 802-874-4140
stay@threemtn.com

*Member Since 1982*

*"Great hosts, wonderful rooms with a beautiful Vermont setting." "Jamaica Vermont...Vermont as one hoped it would be..." Travel & Leisure*

Innkeepers/Owners
**Jennifer and Ed Dorta-Duque**

The Three Mountain Inn, located in the small, unspoiled village of Jamaica, Vermont is a perfect choice to spend a few days of rest and relaxation. Peacefully set among Vermont's Green Mountains, the Inn overlooks the woodlands and trails of Jamaica State Park and is just minutes away from Stratton, Bromley and Magic Mountain Ski areas. Our individually decorated rooms - named after nearby towns - feature luxurious linens, relaxing robes, period pieces, fabulous featherbeds, private baths, queen or king beds, air conditioning and WiFi. Most have fireplaces while some have private decks, whirlpool tubs and TV/DVDs. With its wide-planked pine walls and multiple fireplaces, the Three Mountain Inn has an abundance of history and a sense of luxury. Whether you enjoy a romantic dinner in our Dining Room, relax by one of the many fireplaces, indulge in our incredible three-course breakfast, or explorer the various outdoor possibilities; the Three Mountain Inn will revive your senses.

**Rates**
$165 to $360 Seasonal Packages available.
Visit www.threemountainn.com. Number of Rooms: 15

**Cuisine**
Southern Vermont's only AAA Four Diamond restaurant, offers elegant dining experience, showcasing contemporary Vermont Fresh Cuisine.

**Nearest Airport(s)**
Hartford, CT (1.5 hours); Albany, NY (1.5 hours)

**Directions**
Jamaica is located on VT Rt 30, 1/2 hr. NW of Brattleboro, VT (I-91, Exit 2) and 1/2 hr. South of Manchester, VT

ĦOĦ ĦOĦ ĦOĦ ♀

# Windham Hill Inn
www.windhamhill.com
311 Lawrence Drive, West Townshend, VT 05359
**800-944-4080** • 802-874-4080 • Fax 802-874-4702
windham@sover.net

*Member Since 1989*

*"We have reached total peace, many thanks!"*

Proprietor - **US Hotels**
Innkeeper - **Katja Matthews**

Windham Hill Inn, a "...place that touches your soul.." sits on 160 acres at the end of a Green Mountain hillside country road, surrounded by rock-wall bordered fields and forests, and breathtaking views. Friendly innkeepers and staff welcome you to this country estate with its sparkling rooms, memorable gourmet meals, extensive and award winning wine list, relaxing ambiance and closeness to nature. Relax with a glass of wine in our lounge with wood buring fireplace or enjoy our living room with beautiful mountain views. Guest rooms feature antiques, locally crafted furnishings, hardwood floors and oriental rugs. Most rooms have soaking or whirlpool tubs, gas fireplaces or Vermont Castings stoves. Some have private decks. Centrally air-conditioned throughout. Close to abundant Southern Vermont events and activities. A true destination property, the Inn is "....as good as it gets, especially if you're in search of a romantic getaway." *Frommers* 2006. Seasonal packages & Windham Hill Wine Series are not to be missed!

**Rates**
21 Rooms, $215/$415 B&B; Peak season premiums apply.
Open year-round, except the first two weeks of April. Number of Rooms: 21

**Cuisine**
Full breakfast and afternoon refreshments. Light Lunch avail.
Award-winning Fine Dining by reservation every evening. Fully Licensed. Winner *Wine Spectator* Best of Award of Excellence.

**Nearest Airport(s)**
Hartford (Bradley International 1.5 hrs)

**Directions**
I-91 N to Brattleboro exit 2, follow signs to Rte. 30, 21.5 miles NW to West Townshend. Turn R opposite Post Office onto Windham Hill Rd., 1.3 miles, follow sign to Inn.

# Four Columns Inn

www.fourcolumnsinn.com
P.O. Box 278, 21 West Street, Newfane, VT 05345
**800-787-6633** • 802-365-7713 • Fax 802-365-0022
innkeeper@fourcolumnsinn.com

*Member Since 2000*

*Vermont*

*Newfane*

*"If romance requires a stage set, Four Columns is the theater of choice!" - Country Home*
*"Quintessential New England!" - Daily Candy*

Innkeepers/Owners
**Debbie and Bruce Pfander**

The Four Columns Inn was lovingly built in 1832 by Pardon Kimball to replicate the childhood home of his southern wife. Today that home is an elegant country inn with 15 delightful guest rooms ranging from 6 charming traditional rooms to 9 beautifully refurbished suites, all featuring private baths, individual heat and air conditioning, period antique furnishings, complimentary telephone usage, and afternoon tea and cookies. Gas fireplaces are the focal point in 11 rooms, and the suites deliver grand scale bathrooms with spa tubs and separate showers. High speed Internet is available throughout the inn. Select rooms also offer televisions with DVD players plus a huge library of complimentary movies. A hearty country breakfast, complete with a selection of morning newspapers, is included for all house guests. Situated on the historic Newfane Green unchanged since the 1830s, the property includes 150 acres of rolling hills, an inviting stream, ponds and exquisite gardens. Guests will enjoy the lovely pool and rustic hiking trails in summer, plus access to all the seasonal outdoor activities in Southern Vermont only a short distance away. "Why go anywhere else?" - Sandra Soule.

**Rates**
$170/$390 includes full breakfast. Special Packages in some seasons. 11 rooms with fireplaces, 9 suites with whirlpool/ soaking tubs. Open year round. Number of Rooms: 15

**Cuisine**
And not to be missed is dinner in the Inn's fine dining restaurant, where Chef Greg Parks has led the culinary team for over 25 years and has a well-earned reputation for his creative regional cuising. Awards: James Beard Foundation, *Wine Spectator*. Dinner nightly except Tuesday. Extensive wine list.

**Nearest Airport(s)**
Bradley, Logan, JFK

**Directions**
I-91 to VT Exit 2. Turn L at end of ramp. Go 1 mile to traffic light, turn L on Main St. Follow signs to Rte.30 N. Go 12 mi. to Newfane. Village Green on the L-Inn is just behind Courthouse.

# Deerhill Inn

www.deerhill.com
14 Valley View Road, P.O. Box 136, West Dover, VT 05356
**800-993-3379** • 802-464-3100
innkeeper@deerhill.com

*Member Since 1999*

*Vermont*

*West Dover*

*"Beautiful, charming, great touches everywhere - food incredible - just what we were looking for!! Thank you!!"*

Innkeepers/Owners
**Chef Michael Allen & Stan Gresens**

Once chosen "one of the most romantic places in the world," the elegant, but unpretentious, Deerhill Inn is nestled on a hillside overlooking the quintessential Vermont village of West Dover. Panoramic views of the Green Mountains provide a breathtaking backdrop for the full country breakfasts and romantic candlelit dinners. Perfectly located in the middle of Southern Vermont, Deerhill has access to the best of Vermont and Northern Massachusetts. Museums, theaters, antiquing, shopping, hiking, boating, and of course skiing. Fourteen uniquely decorated guest rooms with private baths, designer linens, French toiletries, microfiber robes, and private porches. Three comfortable sitting rooms, art gallery, gift shop, secluded "grotto" pool, lush gardens and the "amazing" cuisine of Chef Michael Allen complete the experience. Chef-owned and operated and only four hours from Manhattan and two and a half from Boston.

**Rates**
12 rooms, 2 suites $145/$355. Special packages and off-season discounts. Open nearly all year, except late April/early May. Number of Rooms: 14

**Cuisine**
Full, made to order, Country breakfast; the "amazing" Seasonal American Cuisine of Chef Michael Allen; and a *Wine Spectator* awarded, New World wine list. Chosen one of the 25 best Chef-Owned Inns in the U.S. by *Conde Nast Traveler* April 1999. Full liquor license.

**Nearest Airport(s)**
Albany, NY - 1.5 hours Hartford, CT - 2 hours

**Directions**
From I-91, Vt. exit 2 (Brattleboro); to Rte. 9W 20 miles to Rte. 100N 6 miles to Valley View Road, up hill 200 yards.

# Inn at Sawmill Farm

www.theinnatsawmillfarm.com
P.O. Box 367, 7 Crosstown Road, West Dover, VT  05356
**800-493-1133** • 802-464-8131 • Fax 802-464-1130
sawmill@sover.net

*Member Since 2007*

*Vermont*

*West Dover*

> *"The Inn at Sawmill Farm is an oasis of elegance - also a magnet for lovers of fine dining and even grander wining."... Gourmet Magazine*

Chef/Proprietor
**Brill Williams**

We warmly invite you to experience the Vermont we cherish, and to delight in the romance and well-designed sophistication of The Inn at Sawmill Farm.  Nestled on 20 acres in the foothills of the Green Mountains, this charming country inn with 20 individually appointed guest rooms, including cottages and suites with wood burning fireplaces, Jacuzzi baths and beautiful views, exudes comfort. The Inn has been the recipient of numerous awards and accolades through the years, including selection by the Oprah Winfrey Show to host Oprah's Book Club.  "The Inn is known far beyond Vermont for its fine cuisine." ... *Bon Appétit*.  Located in the center of historic West Dover village, the Inn is just down the road from two 18-hole championship golf courses, and within sight of Mount Snow Ski Area.  Nearby, Manchester is a shopping mecca with many fine art galleries and antique shops. On property, guests can enjoy the use of the tennis court, swimming pool and two trout ponds.  Packages available include romantic getaways, skiing, golf, and Orvis-endorsed fly-fishing and sporting clays.  The Inn at Sawmill Farm extends to you, our guest, the magnificent colors of autumn, a rushing brook after a summer rainfall, the tranquility of silence after a winter snow and the amazing clarity of the night sky.

### Rates
Rates starting at $325 Midweek; 10% meals/lodging tax and 15% service fee are NOT included. Inclusive of full country breakfast and 5-course dinner for two.  Number of Rooms: 20

### Cuisine
Our award-winning dining room features French-inspired cuisine using local ingredients. *Wine Spectator* has awarded the Inn's extensive wine cellars the Grand Award for the past 15 years for its 1300 selections and 15,000 bottles.  In addition, DiRōNA has honored the dining room with its award for culinary excellence.

### Nearest Airport(s)
Albany International - 68 miles
Bradley International - 117 miles

### Directions
From Albany: NY Rte 7E to VT Rte 9E through Bennington to Wilmington. Left onto Rte 100N.* From Bradley: I-91N to Brattleboro, VT exit 2. VT Rte 9W to Wilmington. Right onto Rte 100N.* *6 miles to W. Dover.First left, Crosstown Rd, after church. Inn is on left.

# *Virginia*

**"The Old Dominion"**

Famous for: Blue Ridge Mountains, Mount Vernon, Monticello, Arlington National Cemetery, Skyline Drive, Manassas National Battlefield Park, Colonial Williamsburg, Jamestown Settlement, Virginia Beach, Yorktown, Chesapeake Bay.

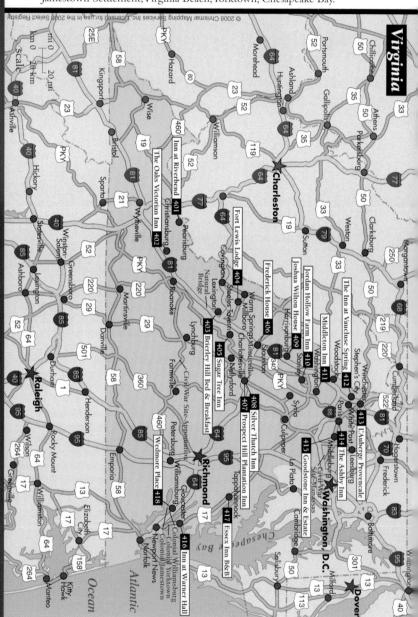

© 2008 Chrismar Mapping Services Inc. Licensed for use in the 2008 Select Registry

# Inn at Riverbend

www.innatriverbend.com
125 River Ridge Drive, Pearisburg, VA 24134-2391
**540-921-5211** • 540-599-6400 • Fax 540-921-2720
stay@innatriverbend.com

🍽️ 🍽️ 🍽️ 🍷

*Member Since 2005*

*Virginia*

*Pearisburg*

*"In our 14 years of marriage, we have stayed at over one hundred Bed and Breakfasts or Inns and Inn At Riverbend is, by far, our favorite."*

Innkeepers/Owners
**Linda and Lynn Hayes**

Newly constructed in 2003, Inn at Riverbend sits on 13 acres overlooking the oldest river in the United States, the New River. Designed to view the mountains and river from the great room, TV room and each guestroom; spacious, decks and terraces provide plenty of space to enjoy the panoramic views, bird watch and even spot a deer or two in the lower meadow. The distant sound of the train sets the tone for a restful sleep. Perfect for romantic getaways, outdoor enthusiasts, retreats and family gatherings. All rooms feature private baths, large closets, pressed sheets, robes, satellite TV, WiFi, CD Players w/MP3 connections and thoughtful amenities. Enjoy afternoon refreshments, the endless cookie jar, and a sumptuous breakfast each day. A casual supper is available on Sunday evening and a candlelight dinner is offered on Friday, both with 72 hour notice. Located just two miles from the Appalachian Trail so let us help plan a hike, a trip down the river or pack a picnic for the Cascades Waterfalls! Follow your outdoor experience with in-room massage. Ask for details on seasonal packages and our "Just the Few of Us" Wedding package.

**Rates**
$135/$250 Two night min. for all weekends and holidays.
Corp rate available. Number of Rooms: 7

**Cuisine**
Full plated breakfast included with Riverbend roast coffee, teas and juices. Complimentary 24 hour beverage bar. Friday casual supper and candlelight Sunday dinner w/advance reservation. Wine available. Casual dining at "The Bank Food and Drink" 3 mi. away

**Nearest Airport(s)**
Roanoke-ROA

**Directions**
Located between I-81 and I-77, 2 mi. off Hwy 460. Exit 460 Bus. at SR 636/Ripplemead/Pearisburg to 1st light (Wal-Mart, turn left, and left again onto Virginia Hts, continue 1.3 mi. to Riverbend Dr, turn left at River Ridge Dr.

# The Oaks Victorian Inn

www.theoaksvictorianinn.com
311 East Main St., Christiansburg, VA 24073
**800-336-6257** • 540-381-1500 • Fax 540-381-3036
stay@theoaksvictorianinn.com

*Member Since 1993*

*Virginia*

*Christiansburg*

*"Nights are soft and mornings come gently to the Blue Ridge. Attitudes are tranquil and the air smells clean. Come and replenish your soul and spirit."*

Owners and Hosts
**Lois and John Ioviero**

Listed on the National Register of Historic Places, our award-winning Four Diamond, Queen Anne Inn is located in the small town of Christiansburg, near Roanoke just 2 miles off I-81; 3 miles from Blacksburg, home of Virginia Tech and Radford University. Whether you are planning a "romantic getaway," a reunion, a historic trip to the New River, Roanoke and Shenandoah Valleys or the majestic Blue Ridge Parkway or Virginia wineries; come and enjoy the glorious setting in relaxed elegance, while feeling as comfortable as you would in your own home. Fireplaces and beautiful private baths with Jacuzzis for romantics. Private telephones, wireless DSL, cable TV, DVD/VCR/CD/MP3 players and stocked refrigerators in all rooms. Beautiful surroundings, luxurious guest rooms, a dedication to detail, warm hospitality and memorable breakfasts are the hallmark of The Oaks. The region provides the best in bike trails, hiking, antiques, local crafts, live music, boating and golf...or just relax on the world class wrap around porch!

**Rates**
6 Rooms, 1 Cottage, $139/$219; $99 Corp. rate Sun. though Thu., Sgl. Only. Extended stay suites/7 days + (EP) (check rates). Open year-round. Number of Rooms: 7

**Cuisine**
3-course gourmet breakfast by candlelight, excellent restaurants for dinner nearby.

**Nearest Airport(s)**
Roanoke, 30 miles

**Directions**
From I-81 Exit 114 (Main St.) just 2 miles on the corner of E Main & Park. From Blue Ridge Pkwy.: Take Rt. 8 (MP165) west 28 miles to The Oaks. 2 miles off US 460 East. 38 miles north of I-77 and I-81 Interchanges.

# Brierley Hill Bed & Breakfast

www.brierleyhill.com
985 Borden Road, Lexington, VA 24450
**800-422-4925** • 540-464-8421 • Fax 540-464-8925
relax@brierleyhill.com

*Member Since 2007*

*"We will remember your beautiful home, the stunning views, the delicious food and the most important, your hospitality."*

Innkeepers/Owners
**Ken and Joyce Hawkins**

Brierley Hill offers the best of both worlds...spectacular views of the Shenandoah Valley and Blue Ridge Mountains only minutes from the center of historic downtown Lexington, Virginia. Our individually decorated rooms - named for the Pati Bannister print that graces each - feature private baths, fireplaces (gas or electric), 350+ count linens, TV/ DVD combinations, wireless Internet access and CD / MP3 / radio alarm clocks. The suites additionally offer whirlpool tubs with bathrobes, refrigerators and separate sitting areas. Both the main house and Magnolias cottage feature central air conditioning / heat for our guests' comfort. The common area consists of two rooms where you can meet other guests or just curl up with a good book. These rooms have a television, snack area, 24-hour hot beverage machine, refrigerator and a guest computer with high-speed Internet access. Guests are welcome to stroll through the award-winning gardens and enjoy our panoramic views of the Shenandoah Valley.

**Rates**
$120 / $295. open year round  Number of Rooms: 6

**Cuisine**
Full 3-course country breakfast, snacks available in common area. Excellent restaurants in downtown Lexington.

**Nearest Airport(s)**
Roanoke (1 hr.)

**Directions**
Our GPS Coordinates are: Lat: 37 deg. 47.41' / Log:-79 deg. 28.12'  Traveling on I-81: Take exit 188B (60 West)  Drive three (3) miles to Lexington and continue on 60 West (Nelson Street)  Cross Main Street and go approximately a half mile  Turn left on Borden Road (60 West residence development on left corner)  Continue one mile to Brierley Hill (on the left, white sign)

# Fort Lewis Lodge

www.fortlewislodge.com
603 Old Plantation Way, Millboro, VA 24460
**540-925-2314** • Fax 540-925-2352
info@fortlewislodge.com

*Virginia*

*Millboro*

*"We didn't bring much - bathing suits, sensible walking shoes, tons to read and expand-o-waist pants. Eating is a recreational activity here. Believe me."*

Innkeepers/Owners
**John and Caryl Cowden**

Centuries old, wonderfully wild, uncommonly comfortable. A country inn at the heart of a 3200-acre mountain estate. Outdoor activities abound with miles of river trout and bass fishing, swimming, extensive hiking trails, mountain biking, and magnificent vistas. Fort Lewis is a rare combination of unpretentious elegance and unique architecture offering a variety of lodging choices where every room has a view. Three "in the round" silo bedrooms, three hand-hewn log cabins with stone fireplaces, and Riverside House are perfect for a true country getaway. Evenings are highlighted by contemporary American-style cuisine served in the historic Lewis Gristmill. Like most country inns, we trade in a change of pace, romance and exceptional fare. But over the years, we've come to understand that Fort Lewis has an asset that very few others have. Our wilderness - the mountains, forests, fields and streams and all the creatures that call this their home.

**Rates**
13 Rooms, $190/$210 MAP; 3 Family Suites, $210 MAP; 3 Log Cabins, $245/$295 MAP. Open April to early November. Number of Rooms: 19

**Cuisine**
Full dinner and breakfast included in the daily room rate. Evening meals offer a vibrant mix of fresh tastes, just plucked vegetables and interesting menus. The aroma of hickoy smoke rising from the grills will leave you yearning to hear the dinner bell.

**Nearest Airport(s)**
Roanoke, VA (1.5 hrs.); Charlottesville, VA (2 hrs.)

**Directions**
From Staunton, Rt. 254 W to Buffalo Gap; Rt.42 to Millboro Spgs.; Rt. 39 W for .7 mi. to R onto Rt. 678, 10.8 mi. to L onto Rt. 625, sign on L.

# Sugar Tree Inn

www.sugartreeinn.com
P.O. Box 10, Hwy 56, Steeles Tavern, VA  24476
**800-377-2197** • 540-377-2197 • Fax : please call
innkeeper@sugartreeinn.com

*Member Since 1998*

*Virginia*

*Steeles Tavern*

> *"What a Mountain Inn should be: elegantly rustic, historic but comfortable, convenient but worlds away.... our best B&B experience to date...."*

Innkeepers/Owners
**Jeff & Becky Chanter**

Recently featured as one of *Washingtonian* Magazine's "Most Romantic Inns" and called "Mountain Magic" by *Hampton Roads* Magazine! High above the Shenandoah Valley in the Blue Ridge Mountains, less than a mile from the Blue Ridge Parkway, is our haven of natural beauty. Set on twenty-eight wooded acres at 2800 feet, Virginia's Mountain Inn is a place of rustic elegance, peace, and tranquility. Enjoy our 40-mile views, which are complimented by spring wildflowers, cool summer nights and brilliant fall colors. Each elegantly rustic room has a WOODBURNING FIREPLACE, incredibly comfortable bed, private bath, coffee maker, CD player, and is decorated with a colorful country quilt. A full breakfast is served in our glass-walled dining room and you can savor our fine evening dining by reservation.

### Rates
1 Luxury Cabin, $248; 9 Rooms, $148/$198; 2 Suites, $178 & $198; Creek House with 2 bedrooms, bath & full kitchen, $178. Rates include our full country breakfast for 2.  Number of Rooms: 13

### Cuisine
A full counrty breakfast is served daily. Nicely prepared three course dinners with a choice of entrees available Friday & Saturday. Casual fare most weekdays.

### Nearest Airport(s)
Roanoke

### Directions
From I-81: Exit 205. East on Hwy 606 to Steeles Tavern. Turn Left on Hwy 11 and then immediately Right on Hwy. 56. Go up the mountain 4 1/2 miles to our sign. From Blue Ridge Parkway: (MP 27) West on Hwy. 56 approx. 3/4 mi. to our sign.

# Frederick House
www.frederickhouse.com
28 North New Street, Staunton, VA 24401
**800-334-5575** • 540-885-4220 • Fax 540-885-5180
stay@frederickhouse.com

*"You are TOPS! We were made to feel very welcome. The rooms were choc-full of antiques & felt like going back in time to a slower pace of life. Lots to do."*

Innkeepers/Owners
**Karen Cooksey & Denny Eister**

Frederick House's five beautifully restored 19th Century residences offer 23 spacious rooms and suites in award winning buildings. The buildings date from 1810 and offer guests an escape into the relaxed atmosphere of a bygone era. All rooms are individually decorated with antiques and period furniture. All offer private bathrooms, cable TV, telephone, internet access, alarm clocks, hair dryers and bathrobes. Wi-Fi is also available. Frederick House is located in culturally rich historic downtown Staunton, the oldest city in the Shenandoah Valley. Staunton's historic downtown includes over 60 shops, restaurants, museums, galleries, concerts, the American Shakespeare Center's Blackfriars Playhouse, Woodrow Wilson Presidential Library, Mary Baldwin College and Stuart Hall. For that leisurely getaway, park your car and enjoy strolling downtown. From the Frederick House, explore the historical, cultural, and recreational opportunities that surround Staunton in the Shenandoah Valley. Visitors are always amazed at the variety of options to explore.

**Rates**
12 Rooms, $99/$179; 11 Suites, $159/$259. Shakespeare Theater Package, Romance Package available year-round. Golf, Horseback Riding and other packages available seasonally. Open year-round. Number of Rooms: 23

**Cuisine**
11 Restaurants available within walking distance; Fine Dining, Seafood, Steaks, American, Italian, Mexican, Ribs, Gourmet Deli, Southern Home Cooking, Casual and Coffee Shops.

**Nearest Airport(s)**
Shenandoah Valley Regional Airport or Charlottesville Albemarle

**Directions**
From I-81 exit 222 follow Rt 250 West. Right on Greenville Ave. First left after railroad overpass. Right on New St. 1 1/2 Blocks left into parking.

# Prospect Hill Plantation Inn

www.prospecthill.com
Box 6909, Charlottesville, VA 22906
**800-277-0844** • 540-967-0844 • Fax 540-967-0102
Innkeeper@prospecthill.com

*Member Since 1979*

*Virginia*

*Charlottesville*

*"Our favorite inn. Fantastic food!" "Been coming every year for 21 years." "Wonderful food! What a GREAT inn!" "Our favorite getaway" "We love it here!"*

Innkeepers/Owners
**The Sheehan family since 1977**

Award-winning country inn and restaurant on historic 1732 plantation complex located just 15 miles East of Charlottesville, VA. Romantic candlelight dining daily with 12 rooms, suites and cottages featuring breakfast-in-bed, working fireplaces, double Jacuzzis (in eight rooms), outdoor swimming pool, gazebo on over 40 acres of beautiful grounds in the serenity of the countryside near Jefferson's "Monticello" and four other presidents homes. Nearby are many excellent wineries and other historic sites. B&B rates from $195 and also offering dinner at $49pp which includes pre-dinner wine reception and candlelight dining at private table for two. All guests have the choice of full country breakfast-in-bed served on a tray to their room or in our dining room. Corporate, meeting, MAP package and other special rates available. Go to www.prospecthill.com for descriptions, rates, virtual tours of all rooms, sample menus to get an idea why so many romantics choose Prospect Hill for their getaway. Selected many times over the past 31 years as one of America's most romantic getaways. Uncle Ben's "10 Best Country Inns" award three times (max).

**Rates**
12 rms/suites from $195 - 350 B&B, $49 pp for four course prie-fixe dinner. Number of Rooms: 12

**Cuisine**
Elegant Continental-American four course prie-fixe dining by candlelight daily at $49pp. Wine and snacks in room on arrival, pre-dinner wine reception, full country breakfast-in-bed (or served in dining room).

**Nearest Airport(s)**
Charlottesville-Albemarle or Richmond International

**Directions**
From C'ville (15 mi) East via I-64, exit 136 at Zion Crossroads. From Wash, DC (approx 100 mi) I-66 West to Hwy #29 S, to Hwy #15 South just past I-64, turn Left on Hwy #250E & go 1 mile, left on Poindexter Rd, go 3 mi to Prospect Hill on left.

# Silver Thatch Inn

www.silverthatch.com
3001 Hollymead Drive, Charlottesville, VA 22911
**800–261–0720** • 434–978–4686 • Fax 434–973–6156
info@silverthatch.com

*Virginia*

*Charlottesville*

*"I wanted to stay forever."*

Innkeepers/Owners
**Jim and Terri Petrovits**

This historic inn began its life as a barracks built in 1780 by Hessian soldiers captured during the Revolutionary War. As wings were added in 1812 and 1937, it served as a boys' school, a tobacco plantation, and a melon farm. It has been providing gracious lodging in antique-filled guest rooms and elegant candlelit dining since the 1970s. Relax and unwind in our intimate pub. Enjoy contemporary cuisine from our menu and wines from a list which has consistently won the *Wine Spectator* Award of Excellence and the *Wine Enthusiast* Award of Unique Distinction.

**Rates**
7 Rooms, $165/$200 B&B. Open year-round. Number of Rooms: 7

**Cuisine**
Breakfast for houseguests; Sunday Brunch; Dinner served Tues. - Sat., specializing in contemporary cuisine, featuring local produce when available and eclectic sauces. Open to the public. Great English Pub, outstanding selection of wine and spirits.

**Nearest Airport(s)**
Charlottesville/Albemarle Regional Airport, 2 miles.

**Directions**
From S: 6 miles N of intersection of US 29 & US 250 bypass, turn R on North Hollymead Dr. From N: 1 mile S of Airport Rd., turn L on North Hollymead Dr.

# Joshua Wilton House Inn

www.joshuawilton.com
412 S. Main St., Harrisonburg, VA 22801
**888-294-5866** • 540-434-4464 • Fax 540-432-9525
info@joshuawilton.com

*Member Since 1985*

*Virginia*

*Harrisonburg*

*"The best overnight we've ever had in a B&B."*

Owners
**Sean Pugh, Ann Marie Coe and Mark Newsome**

Located in an elegantly restored Queen Anne Victorian, **Joshua Wilton House Inn & Restaurant** offers guests an oasis of quiet charm and gracious living in the heart of the Shenandoah Valley. The home is within walking distance of historic downtown Harrisonburg and the campus of James Madison University. The Inn features five non-smoking bedrooms that have been decorated and furnished with beautiful antiques and reproductions. All rooms have one queen size bed, private baths, individually controlled thermostats, telephones, clock radios and hair dryers. Premium AVEDA amenities and luxurious terry cloth bathrobes are provided for your use during your stay. High-speed wireless internet service is available throughout the house. The first floor lounge is tastefully decorated and furnished with roomy high-backed leather chairs, a perfect place for a cocktail before dinner or a brandy by the fire after dinner.

**Rates**
5 Rooms, $75/$150 B&B. Number of Rooms: 5

**Cuisine**
The Restaurant offers an exquisite a la carte menu that changes with the seasons and an award-winning wine list. Featured are the food products of many small local farms and producers who supply our kitchen with high quality ingredients that simply cannot be found elsewhere. During the warmer months, seating is available on the outdoor brick patio. The restaurant is open from 5:00 PM, Tuesday through Saturday.

**Nearest Airport(s)**
Dulles - Washington, D.C.

**Directions**
412 S. Main St. I-81, exit 245, W on Port Rd. to Main St. N approx. 1 mi. To Joshua Wilton House located on R.

# Jordan Hollow Inn

www.jordanhollow.com
326 Hawksbill Park Road, Stanley, VA 22851
**888-418-7000** • 540-778-2285 • Fax 540-778-1759
jhf@jordanhollow.com

*Member Since 1985*

*Virginia*

*Stanley*

*"Unpretentious and Totally Relaxing" "Great Hospitality!"*
*"What a Gem!" "Super Food!"*

Innkeeper
**Angela Fernandes**

Jordan Hollow Inn established in 1983, is probably Virginia's besk kept secret. If your in need of a private romantic getaway, this place will pamper and indulge you passionately. Located at the foothills of the Blue Ridge Mountains where sheer beauty of your surroundings will overwhelm you. The luxurious suites and private cabins are laced with tranquility and are gracefully furnished with soaking tubs and fireplaces. A few days spent here leaves you with a "never wanting to leave" sense that is ingrained into your memory. The enchanting Farmhouse Restaurant with it's quaint and characteristic dining rooms have a history that dates back to the 1700's. The nearby attractions are numerous and exciting, what with horseback riding, golfing, kayaking and scenic drives. Planned weddings and honeymoon packages will bring dreams to life. Bring romance back into your life with a visit to Jordan Hollow Inn.

**Rates**
$190/$300 B&B; All rooms have fireplaces, hydro-thermo massage spas, whirlpool baths or soaking tubs. Number of Rooms: 8 Suites, 6 Rooms and 6 Luxury cabins

**Cuisine**
Full restaurant breakfast, dinner, American Regional features Virginia wines and local produce. Picnic Baskets available for Lunch. Extensive Wine List and full service bar available.

**Nearest Airport(s)**
Dulles, Reagan National, Shenandoah Valley Regional

**Directions**
From Luray: Take VA Route 340 Business South for 6 miles, turn Left onto VA Route 624, turn Left onto VA Route 689, continue .5 mile and turn Right on VA Route 626 for .25 mile, Jordan Hollow Inn will be on the Right.

# Middleton Inn

www.middletoninn.com
176 Main Street, P.O. Box 254, Washington, VA  22747
**800-816-8157** • 540-675-2020 • Fax 540-675-1050
innkeeper@middletoninn.com

*Member Since 2006*

*Virginia*

*"There are 5 B&Bs in the village. The most deluxe is Middleton Inn where no expense was spared on detail and comfort." The Washington Post*

*Washington*

Innkeeper/Owner
**Mary Ann Kuhn**

Middleton Inn is AAA's highest rated bed and breakfast in the Mid-Atlantic and in "Little" Washington, Virginia, where it is a pleasant stroll on a village street to dinner at the world renowned restaurant of the Inn at Little Washington. Middleton's 1840s elegant manor house and other original buildings-summer kitchen, smokehouse, slaves' quarters and log cabin-sit high on a grassy knoll on a six-acre estate in the Historic District. Only 67 miles from "Big" Washington, DC, the inn provides a rural, tranquil setting with horses grazing in the paddocks while sterling silver trays carrying complimentary wine and cheese are served to guests sitting on the front porch, enjoying the spectacular views of the Blue Ridge Mountains. The inn has four exquisitely appointed bedrooms in the manor house, a romantic cottage for two and an historic log house for two to four guests. Working fireplaces are in all the accommodations, and most have mountain views. Enjoy a scrumptious, complimentary four-course breakfast served on fine china and silver in the beautifully restored dining room. The inn is owned and operated by journalist Mary Ann Kuhn.

**Rates**
4 rooms, $195/$475, one guest cottage, $375/$575 and the log house, $525-$725 per room. Rates vary depending on room, season, day of week. Call for rates or visit Web site. Number of Rooms: 7

**Cuisine**
Scrumptious 4-course breakfast on fine china and silver and afternoon wine/hors d'oeuvres included. Walk to dinner at the Inn at Little Washington or drive to other fine dining.

**Nearest Airport(s)**
Dulles, Reagan National

**Directions**
From I66 W take Exit 43A to Gainesville. Follow 29 S to Warrenton, Take 211 W for 23 mi. to Washington, Va. At first stop sign turn L onto Main St for 2 1/2 blocks.

🍽 🍽

# The Inn at Vaucluse Spring

www.vauclusespring.com
231 Vaucluse Spring Lane, Stephens City, VA 22655
**800-869-0525** • 540-869-0200 • Fax 540-869-9546
mail@vauclusespring.com

*Member Since 2000*

*Virginia*

*Stephens City*

*Southern Living* Magazine says "Perhaps The Inn at Vaucluse Spring was our best total experience. The best news? This place is an unbelievable value."

Innkeepers/Owners
**Barry & Neil Myers**

Set amidst 100 scenic acres in the rolling orchard country of the Shenandoah Valley, this collection of six guest houses is the perfect country retreat. Experience the elegance of the gracious 200 year old Manor House or the warmth and charm of an 1850s log home. For the ultimate in peace and privacy, stay in the old Mill House Studio at the water's edge, the Gallery Guest House with views of the meadow, or the Cabin by the Pond. Relax beside Vaucluse Spring's cool, crystal clear waters. Savor the region's bounty at the delicious breakfasts and weekend dinners. Ideally located for enjoying nearby activities.

**Rates**
12 Rooms/Suites: $155/$250 B&B. 3 Private cottages: $275/$315. Beautifully furnished, queen or king beds, all have fireplaces, 14 with Jacuzzis, some water/mountain views. Number of Rooms: 15

**Cuisine**
Full 3-course breakfast served daily. A 3-course 'Southern Comfort' Friday night supper and a romantic 4-course Saturday dinner are available by advance reservation. Wine and beer available.

**Nearest Airport(s)**
Dulles International

**Directions**
From I-66W, take exit 1B to I-81N. Go 1 mile to exit 302. Turn L on Rte 627, go .5 mile. Turn R on Rte 11, go 2 miles. Turn L on Rte 638, go 3/4 mile to Inn on L. Follow signs to check-in.

# L'Auberge Provencale

www.laubergeprovencale.com
P.O. Box 190, 13630 Lord Fairfax Highway, White Post, VA 22663
**800-638-1702** • 540-837-1375 • Fax 540-837-2004
info@laubergeprovencale.com

*Member Since 1988*

*"If you're not happy about life after a meal here you haven't got a pulse." Washington Post*
*"5 hearts, my top prize for Romance." Washingtonian*

Innkeepers/Owners
**Chef Alain & Celeste Borel**

Experience the Essence of Provence in the Shenandoah Valley. L'Auberge Provencale is a destination for the discerning traveler and gourmand. You will feel you are in Provence when you enjoy our nationally acclaimed cuisine. Zagat and USA today rated L'Auberge Provencale as one of the top 100 hotel dining rooms in the country. Indulge yourself in one of the guest rooms or suites at our quintessential French Country Inn. We feature cheerful yet elegant decor with faux walls, French fabrics and antiques to create an atmosphere of a true "Auberge", blending French country comfort with modern luxury. Dine evenings at the main manor house at Mt. Airy (circa 1753) in one of the three intimate dining rooms. Orchards, flower, vegetable and herb gardens supply the best and freshest for our cuisine. The inn uses locally produced and sustainable food. Our Villa La Campagnette offers a swimming pool, luxury suites and privacy. The two inns offer a special experience for discerning guests with exquisite food and courteous, attentive service. If you can't go to France this year visit L'Auberge Provencale.

**Rates**
8 Charming French Country Rooms, $155/$250; 6 Romantic Suites, $295/$325. Some with Fireplaces, steam showers & Jacuzzi. Welcome bowl of fresh fruit cookies & chocolates in your room. Number of Rooms: 14

**Cuisine**
Elegant, Romantic Dinners with Provencale flair served Wed. thru Sunday, breakfast of one's dreams, gourmet picnics & the best bistro lunch on Sunday. Full extensive wine list of French Chateaux & American Wines, liquor.

**Nearest Airport(s)**
Dulles

**Directions**
1 hour W of DC Beltway. One mile S of Rt. 50 on Rt. 340, Inn is on the Rt. 45 minutes West of Dulles Airport. 10 miles E of Winchester in the Shenandoah Valley.

# The Ashby Inn & Restaurant

www.ashbyinn.com
692 Federal St., Paris, VA 20130
**866-336-0099** • 540-592-3900 • Fax 540-592-3781
celebrate@ashbyinn.com

*Virginia*

*Paris*

*"Back here in paradise. Warm, elegant, exceptional. Don't change a thing."*

Innkeepers/Owners
**Jackie and Charles Leopold**

This 1829 Inn finds its character in the small village of Paris and its heart in the kitchen. The menu is guided more by tradition than trend-with great attention paid to seasonal foods like asparagus, shad roe, softshell crabs and game. Much of the summer produce, herbs and flowers come from its gardens. Guest rooms furnished in period pieces (half with fireplaces and balconies) have views stretching beyond the formal perennial gardens to the hills of the Blue Ridge. The four dining rooms are as intimate as they are distinct - from an enclosed porch, to a converted kitchen with walnut beams and fireplace, to a cozy room with booths set against faux painted walls and striking paintings. Summer dining on the covered patio overlooking the lawn attracts a wide Washington following.

**Rates**
6 guest rooms at the Main Inn, $155/$195 and 4 guest rooms at the School House, $275. Sun.-Thurs. discounts on all rooms. Closed Jan 1, July 4, Dec. 24 & 25. Number of Rooms: 10

**Cuisine**
Full country breakfast inclusive for our inn guests. Dinner is available Wednesday-Saturday offering traditiional American cuisine. Sunday afternoon brunch. On-site special events. Wine and liquor available.

**Nearest Airport(s)**
Winchester Regional Airport Washington/Dulles International

**Directions**
From Wash DC Rte 66 W to exit 23 - Rte 17 N, 7.5 miles L on Rte 701 for .5 miles or Rte 50 W thru Middleburg, L just after light at Rte. 17.

# Goodstone Inn & Estate

www.goodstone.com
36205 Snake Hill Road, Middleburg, VA 20117
**877-219-4663** • 540-687-4645 • Fax 540-687-6115
information@goodstone.com

*Member Since 2008*

*"I can't think of one amenity that was missing. Our room was beautifully decorated, spacious and comfortable. Dinner was superb and the staff so gracious."*

General Manager
**Simon Smith**

The Goodstone Inn & Estate, a luxurious country retreat in Middleburg, Virginia, is situated in the heart of the state's renowned Hunt & Wine Country 45 minutes from Washington, D.C. The historic property features five star-quality lodging in five distinctive dwellings, including the main building - the elegantly converted Carriage House, The Dutch Cottage, The Manor House, The French Farm Cottage and The Spring House. The Goodstone Inn & Estate provides superb cuisine in Hilltoppers restaurant, an impressive wine cellar dining room featuring an extensive selection of vintages from Virginia and around the world, an elegant afternoon English Tea, and facilities for corporate and social events. Wireless Internet access is available throughout the property. Recreational opportunities abound with a unique outdoor pool nestled within the Wisteria-covered ruins of the estate's original mansion, an all-season Jacuzzi, walking and hiking trails, mountain biking, stables for boarding guest' horses, canoeing, in room spa treatments, and superb shopping in Middleburg. Goodstone is a member of the Small Luxury Hotels of the World.

**Rates**
$235/$610. Individual cottages can be rented. Call for details.
Number of Rooms: 17

**Cuisine**
The imaginative epicurean menu is American fare with a European flare. Sample wine from the cellar, which feature more than 100 wines from all over the world, including Virginia's wine country. The menu changes regularly and seasonally.

**Nearest Airport(s)**
Dulles Airport, 45 minutes away.

**Directions**
Located in Middleburg, VA, just off Rt. 50, 1 hour from Washington, D.C.

*Virginia*

*Middleburg*

# Inn at Warner Hall

www.warnerhall.com
4750 Warner Hall Road, Gloucester, VA 23061
**800-331-2720** • 804-695-9565 • Fax 695-9566
info@warnerhall.com

*Member Since 2006*

*Virginia*

*Gloucester*

> *"All we can say is WOW! Unbelievable food & hospitality…What a beautiful, romantic place…something magical. We WILL be back!"*

Innkeepers /Owners
**Theresa and Troy Stavens**

Old world charm and new world amenities create the perfect balance between luxury and history in this beautifully restored romantic waterfront retreat.Established in 1642 by George Washington's Great, Great Grandfather, Warner Hall beckons guests to relax and enjoy. Comfortable elegance, fabulous food and attentive, friendly service are the essence of Warner Hall.Spacious guest rooms combine sumptuous antiques, fabrics and art with modern conveniences.Many rooms offer fireplaces, Jacuzzis or steam showers ? all have spectacular views. Experience Chef Eric Garcia's delicious cuisine paired with a bottle of fine wine. Explore the historic triangle of Williamsburg, Yorktown and Gloucester, or simply relax at the Inn's charming boathouse. Ideally situated at the head of the Severn River surrounded by 500 acres of fields and forest, Warner Hall resonates with tranquility and southern hospitality. National Register of Historic Places. Recommended by *Travel + Leisure, Hampton Roads Magazine, Virginian Pilot* and *Free Lance Star.*

**Rates**
$150/$220 Mon.-Thurs. $170/$245 Fri-Sun.  Number of Rooms: 11

**Cuisine**
Extraordinary breakfasts included. Chef's Tasting Dinners Fri./Sat., or by special reservation. Cocktail and wine bar. Gourmet supper baskets Sunday-Thursday. Box lunches daily.

**Nearest Airport(s)**
Nearest Airports Richmond / Norfolk

**Directions**
I-64 to Williamsburg area. Follow signs for Colonial Pkwy/Yorktown. Exit Rt. 17 N. Cross York River, proceed 6.5 mi. Turn R onto Rte. 614/Featherbed Lane. Go 2.3 mi. and turn R onto Warner Hall Rd/Rt. 629. Go 1 mi. Inn on R.

# The Essex Inn

www.EssexInnVA.com
P.O. Box 2038, 203 Duke Street, Tappahannock, VA 22560
**866-ESSEX-VA** • 804-443-9900
info@EssexInnVA.com

*Member Since 2008*

*"Your attention to detail is amazing, nothing was forgotten!" "We loved the privacy the innkeepers gave us, available when needed, but not hovering."*

Innkeepers
**Reeves and Melodie Pogue**

"Rivah', Romance, Revival". Experience the grandeur of this Greek Revival Inn located one block from the Rappahannock River in Tappahannock. Explore the Northern Neck's wineries; visit historic museums and birthplaces; kayak one of the many rivers; bike or hike the many birding trails or enjoy day trips to Yorktown, Williamsburg or Fredericksburg. The romantic bedrooms in the Main House feature four-posted beds custom made from wood salvaged from piers made of 300-year-old Cyprus trees and have working gas fireplaces or electric stoves. The "Quarters" is a separate building that was once used as the servants' quarters and is perfect for extended stays, guests with pets and guests needing outside access to smoke. It features suites that can sleep up to 3 guests each. Revive and relax in the Music room with its baby grand piano or the Library complete with games, movies, puzzles and fireplace; the screened-in porch overlooking the garden, the back porch with rocking chairs; or the private brick courtyard. The Inn is a Certified Virginia Green Inn. Special events included "Weekend with a Writer." Business travelers enjoy WIFI, special rates and flexible breakfast schedules.

**Rates**
$149/$189. Two night minimum stay on weekends. Number of Rooms: 8

**Cuisine**
A full three-course gourmet breakfast with specialties including Grapefruit Brulee, Crab N'Grits, Belgian Waffles with seasonal toppings and our signature coffee. Guests staying in suites may opt for extended continental breakfast served en suite. Butler's pantry offers beer on tap, wine, assorted beverages and snacks available at all hours.

**Nearest Airport(s)**
Richmond International Airport (RIC)- 1 hour.

**Directions**
Located one block from the river on the corner of Duke St. and Water Lane in Historic Tappahannock. See website for specific directions.

# Wedmore Place

🍽 🍽 🍽 ♀

Member Since 2007

www.wedmoreplace.com
5810 Wessex Hundred, Williamsburg, VA 23185
**866-WEDMORE** • 757-941-0310 • Fax 757-941-0318
info@wedmoreplace.com

*"We were fortunate enough to have the Tuscany suite. We were reminded of our travels through Italy. The property is beautiful and the staff are excellent."*

Proprietors
**The Duffeler Family**

Wedmore Place is an enchanting and elegant European Country Estate Hotel, in the middle of a 300-acre winery farm and is located just 3 miles from Colonial Williamsburg. Whether business or pleasure, the hotel offers a highly luxurious and relaxing atmosphere. The decor of each room is inspired by the culture and traditions of 28 different European provinces. Each is furnished and decorated in the style of the province after which they are named; all rooms have wood burning fireplaces. In the hotel's delightful cobblestone courtyard you'll find an impressive stone fountain imported from Spain. Exquisite dining is available in the Cafe Provençal, where fine Mediterranean cuisine is served daily. The dining room overlooks the pool terrace offering guests a romantic and relaxed setting. Guests at the hotel can also make use of the massage facilities, fitness room, British Club style Library and wine cellar. While no stay is complete without a walk next door to The Williamsburg Winery for a tour and wine tasting and shopping in the retail store. Things to enjoy: Restaurant, pool bar, massage treatments, fitness room and Library.

**Rates**
Classic Rooms-Sun-Thur $190/$235 Fri-Sat $235/$275
Superior Rooms-Sun-Thur $235/$295 Fri-Sat $295/$365
3 Suites available: from $300/$750  Number of Rooms: 28

**Cuisine**
Fine Mediterranean Cuisine. European-Style dining.

**Nearest Airport(s)**
Newport News/Wmbg Airport (PHF) - 26 Miles
Richmond, VA (RIC) - 50 Miles
Norfolk, VA (ORF) - 65 Miles

**Directions**
From Newport News/Wmbg Airport - Turn left on Jefferson Ave south to I-64 West 22 miles- To RT 199 West Exit 242 go 5.5 miles to the 3rd stoplight and turn left on to Brookwood Dr one block- Turn left on Lake Powell Dr 1 mile. Entrance to Wedmore Place and The Williamsburg Winery on the left.

# Washington

## "The Evergreen State"

Famous for: Mount St. Helens, Redwoods, Olympic National Park, Grand Coulee Dam, Space Needle, Pike Place Market, Puget Sound, San Juan Islands, Mount Rainier, Kettle Falls, Cascade Mountains, Apples, Jets, Hi-Tech.

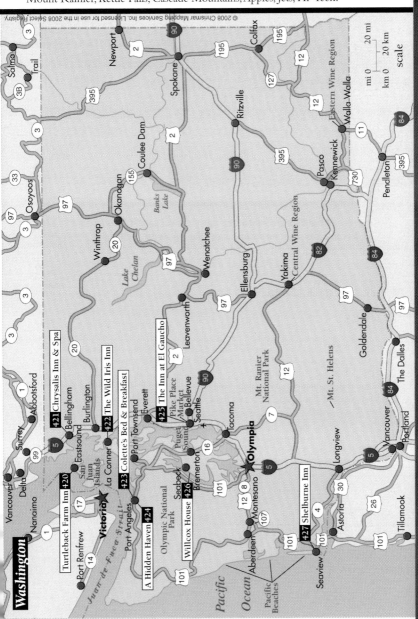

Washington

420 Turtleback Farm Inn
421 Chrysalis Inn & Spa
422 The Wild Iris Inn
423 Colette's Bed & Breakfast
424 A Hidden Haven
425 The Inn at El Gaucho
426 Willcox House
427 Shelburne Inn

Eastern Wine Region
Central Wine Region

Pike Place Market

Olympic National Park

Mt. Ranier National Park

Mt. St. Helens

Puget Sound

Juan de Fuca Strait

Pacific Ocean

Pacific Beaches

Lake Chelan

Banks Lake

scale
mi 0    20 mi
km 0    20 km

# Turtleback Farm Inn and Orchard House

www.turtlebackinn.com
1981 Crow Valley Road, Eastsound, WA 98245
**800-376-4914** • 360-376-4914 • Fax 360-376-5329
info@turtlebackinn.com

*Member Since 1991*

*Washington*

*Eastsound*

*"A marvel of bed and breakfastmanship full of tasteful personal touches and tender care. You are a model by which other innkeepers could use."*

Innkeepers/Owners
**William C. & Susan C. Fletcher**

THE FARMHOUSE and ORCHARD HOUSE is located on Orcas Island, the loveliest of the San Juan Islands. This graceful and comfortable Inn is considered one of the most romantic places in the country. Highlighted by a spectacular setting, the Inn is a haven for those who enjoy breathtaking scenery, comfortable accommodations and award-winning breakfasts. The island offers unique shopping, fine dining and varied outdoor activities: hiking, swimming, sea-kayaking, whale watching, sailing, fishing, birding, golf and bicycling. The newly opened Turtleback Mountain Preserve includes 1,576 acres of forest, grasslands and Garry Oak woodlands. Its high meadows and rocky ledges provide unparalleled views of the San Juan and Canadian Gulf Islands. The main trailhead is a short walk to the north. Turtleback Farm Inn is the perfect spot for the discriminating traveler to experience a step back to a quieter time. *Karen Brown's "Pacific Northwest Guide", "1000 PLACES TO SEE BEFORE YOU DIE." "Northwest Best Places"*

**Rates**
$115/$265 B&B. Open year-round. Number of Rooms: 11

**Cuisine**
Full breakfast, beverages anytime, fruit, freshly baked treats and complimentary sherry. Picnic baskets. Luncheons and dinners catered for private parties. BYOB.

**Nearest Airport(s)**
Eastsound - 4 miles

**Directions**
Orcas Island is accessible by ferry or airplane. The Washington State Ferry terminal is located in Anacortes, 90 mi. N of Seattle: I5 to Hwy.20. Ferries run through the day. From Orcas Ferry Landing: Follow Orcas Road N 2.9mi, turn L, .9 mi to first R, continue N on Crow Valley Road 2.4 mi. to Inn

# Chrysalis Inn & Spa

www.thechrysalisinn.com
804 10th St., Bellingham, WA 98225
**888-808-0005** • 360-756-1005 • Fax 360-647-0342
info@thechrysalisinn.com

*Member Since 2003*

*"What a way to celebrate life." "We love it here."*
*"Beautiful, indulgent, wonderful."*

Innkeepers/Owners
**J. Michael and Lisa Keenan**

Situated on Bellingham Bay, just blocks from Historic Fairhaven, The Chrysalis invites guests to relax and unwind. From the moment you enter you sense a special place as you view the bay from the floor to ceiling windows in the living room. Enjoy the shops and restaurants in Fairhaven, stroll along the waterfront in Boulevard Park or just relax on your windowseat and watch the activity on the bay. Our spa offers massages, facials, body treatments, manicures and pedicures, all designed to rejuvenate the body, mind and soul. Perfect for small business meetings and retreats, we can accomodate groups up to 45 in our two meeting rooms, and we offer on site catering.

**Rates**
34 Deluxe Rooms, $199/$249, 9 Suites, $269/$325. All have fireplaces, window seats, 2 person tubs. Breakfast is included. Number of Rooms: 43

**Cuisine**
Fino is our full service wine bar and restaurant featuring classic foods and wines of Europe. Lunch and dinner daily, room service and outdoor dining.

**Nearest Airport(s)**
Bellingham Airport

**Directions**
Bellingham is 90 miles north of Seattle and 50 miles south of Vancouver BC, Canada. Take exit 250 off of I-5 and head west to stop light at 12th St. (about 1.2 miles). Turn right on 12th and proceed approximately 1/2 mile to Taylor, turn left. Turn right on 10th.

# The Wild Iris Inn
www.wildiris.com
121 Maple Avenue, P.O. Box 696, LaConner, WA 98257
**800-477-1400** • 360-466-1400
info@wildiris.com

*Member Since 2003*

*"This is an amazing place. The attention to detail and warm hospitality made us feel truly pampered. We loved everything about our stay!"*

Innkeepers/Owners
**Stephen & Lori Farnell**

The award winning Wild Iris Inn and LaConner, Washington, an outstanding year-round destination, are a short drive from Seattle and Vancouver, British Columbia, but "miles" away. The Inn's convenient location is perfect for your exploration of the Pacific Northwest; located just 20 minutes from the ferry terminals that lead to the San Juan Islands, Victoria, BC and points beyond. Each season brings wonderful changes to LaConner. In winter, swans and snow geese cover the fields in a sea of white. The farmlands are brightly colored with daffodils in March, world famous tulips in April, iris in May, and dahlias in August. In summer, whale watching cruises leave LaConner each day and follow magnificent orcas in the North Puget Sound. The highlight of your stay, however, will be the hospitality, service and amenities of The Wild Iris Inn. Guest suites feature spa tubs, fireplaces and decks facing the Cascade Mountains, as well as all of the amenities you would expect from a Select Registry property.

### Rates
12 Guest Suites w/King beds, spa tubs, fireplaces & private decks $159/$209 B&B. 5 Casual Guest Rooms w/King beds and 1 with 2 twin beds $119/$139 B&B. Open Year Round. Number of Rooms: 18

### Cuisine
A full breakfast including fresh baked goods, homemade granola, hot entrees and fresh fruits is served each morning at tables for two. In-room and early departure breakfast options.

### Nearest Airport(s)
Seattle & Vancouver

### Directions
By Land: 1 hour N of Seattle. 1 1/2 hours S of Vancouver, BC. 9 mi. W of I-5. By Sea: 20 min. from the San Juan Islands & Victoria, BC ferry in Anacortes.

*Washington*

*LaConner*

# Colette's Bed & Breakfast

www.colettes.com
339 Finn Hall Road, Port Angeles, WA 98362
**877-457-9777** • 360-457-9197 • Fax 360-452-0711
colettes@colettes.com

*Member Since 2003*

*Fodor's Pacific Northwest "Top Choice" - considered the very best.*
*Best Places to Kiss Pacific Northwest "Highest Rating" - 4 Kisses.*

Innkeepers/Owners
**Lynda & Peter Clark**

Colette's is a breathtaking 10 acre oceanfront estate nestled between the majestic Olympic Range and the picturesque Strait of Juan de Fuca. This unique area is the gateway to Olympic National Park, a world of stunning coastline with booming surf, wave-manicured beaches, and sweeping vistas in every direction.

Each perfect day at Colette's starts with a gourmet multi-course breakfast. Luxurious King Suites with magnificent oceanfront views, romantic fireplaces, and indulgent Jacuzzi spas for two rejuvenate guests at the end of the day. Stroll through Colette's 10 acre outdoor sanctuary which includes enchanting gardens, towering cedars and lush evergreen forest.

Fodor's Pacific Northwest - "Top Choice" for the Olympic Peninsula - considered the very best. Karen Brown's Guide Pacific Northwest - "Top Pick". Best Places to Kiss Pacific Northwest "Highest Rating" - 4 Kisses.

**Rates**
Luxury King Suites $195/$395  Number of Rooms: 5

**Cuisine**
Our chef has created an exciting variety of culinary delights. Enjoy your multi-course, gourmet breakfast served with a panoramic view of the Strait of Juan de Fuca and the San Juan Islands.

**Nearest Airport(s)**
Seattle and Port Angeles

**Directions**
Two hours from Seattle via the Bainbridge ferry. Hwy 305 to 3 to 104 to 101 around Sequim. Travel 4.8 miles past the Sequim Ave. exit, R on Kitchen-Dick Road. Drive 1.5 miles to Old Olympic Hwy, turn L drive 2.5 miles to Matson road and turn R. Drive .5 to Finn Hall Road and turn L, drive .9 miles.

# A Hidden Haven

www.ahiddenhaven.com
1428 Dan Kelly Road, Port Angeles, WA 98363
**877-418-0938** • 360-452-2719 • Fax 360-417-7585
stay@ahiddenhaven.com

*Member Since 2007*

*Best Places To Kiss, Organic Magazine's "Top Choice" Treasures In Western Washington, Featured In "My Perfect Wedding Venue."*

Innkeeper/ Owner
**Chris and Jodi Jones**

Nestled in the lush forest at the foothills of the Olympic Peninsula, Hidden Haven is 20 acres of perfectly private woodsy seclusion and a Water Garden Retreat. From our central location explore some of the most fantastic and pristine wilderness beaches in America with incredible tide pools, rain forest, hot springs, alpine mountains, birding, kayaking, thousands of hiking trails, whale watching and more! Nature-Luxury and Romance exist harmoniously at Hidden Haven, a naturalist paradise and a delight to birders, this magical piece of heaven provides an ambience full of enchantment and wonder. With waterfalls, koi ponds, gardens, plants, wildlife, meandering streams and nature trails to explore, we believe you will find Hidden Haven an ultimate experience like no other! Our casually elegant and luxuriously charming new cottages include fully equipped kitchens, romantic fireplaces, king/queen beds, two-person Jacuzzis, and all luxury amenities. End a spectacular day with a fireside massage for an unforgettable getaway!

**Rates**
5 Luxury King/Queen Cottages $189/$379. 2 Luxury Suites/$189/$299. Watch For Our Winter Specials! Number of Rooms: 7

**Cuisine**
Experience a perfectly private light continental breakfast in your luxuriously appointed cottage or suite. Savor a morning cup of coffee by waterfalls, koi/trout ponds and abundant gardens.

**Nearest Airport(s)**
Seattle and Port Angeles

**Directions**
3 hours from Seattle via the Bainbridge ferry Hwy 305 to 3 to 101 past Sequim thru Port Angeles on Hwy 101 going W to Hwy 112W left on Dan Kelly Rd. 1.5 miles on the R.

# The Inn at El Gaucho

www.inn.elgaucho.com/inn.elgaucho/
2505 First Avenue, Seattle, WA 98121
**866-354-2824** • 206-728-1133 • Fax 206-728-1132
dcalle@elgaucho.com

*Member Since 2008*

*"Elegantly Comfortable Inn with Personal Service."*

Proprietor
**Paul Mackay**

The Inn at El Gaucho® is located at First Avenue and Wall Street, in the Belltown district, above the renowned El Gaucho® steakhouse. Minutes away from the Seattle Aquarium, Pike Place Market, Space Needle and downtown shopping. As well as Seattle's many sports venues, museums, theaters and other cultural attractions. The guest suites are decorated with handmade furnishings, in the same "retro-swank" fifties style synonymous with the El Gaucho® name. You'll find Anichini linens and bathrobes and we proudly feature L'Occitane and Philip B products. In addition, you'll enjoy the ultimate in modern conveniences: plasma screen TV with full high-definition digital cable, Bose Wave music system and high speed Internet, both wired and wireless. And of course, room service comes from the Inn's namesake restaurant, the incomparable El Gaucho®. The Inn's 24-hour concierge service is available to assist you with procuring tickets, town car service, and any other arrangements to help you relax and fully enjoy your stay.

**Rates**
$175 to $345 US  Number of Rooms: 18

**Cuisine**
Complimentary fresh fruit, local speciality baked muffins and pastries for Breakfast in Lobby or room. Award-winning El Gaucho Steakhouse® with live music nightly. Dinner only.

**Nearest Airport(s)**
Seattle-Tacoma International

**Directions**
From 1-5 (South Seattle/SeaTac Airport) Take I-5 North Exit at Seneca St. Turn right on Fourth Ave. Turn left on Cedar St. Turn left on First Ave. The Inn at El Gaucho is on the right 2505 First Ave. From 1-5 (North Seattle) Take I-5 South Exit at Mercer St. Turn right on Fairview Turn left on Valley Turn left on Second Ave. Turn right on Cedar Turn left on 1st Ave. The Inn at El Gaucho is on the right 2505 First Ave.

🍽 🍽 🍷

# Willcox House Country Inn

www.willcoxhouse.com
2390 Tekiu Rd. NW, Seabeck, WA 98380
**800-725-9477** • 360-830-4492

*Member Since 1993*

*A jewel within an emerald forest.*

Innkeepers/Owners
**Cecilia and Phillip Hughes**

With spectacular views of Hood Canal and the Olympic Mountains, this waterfront Country House Inn is situated in a forest setting beween Seattle and the Olympic Peninsula. The historic 1930s mansion estate offers beautiful gardens with fish ponds. Walk our oyster-laden saltwater beach. Enjoy the peace and serenity. Period pieces and antiques are featured in guest rooms, the great room, billiard room, pub, library, theater, and dining room. *Country Inns* magazine award: One of the top twelve inns in North America. Featured on *Great Country. Inns* T.V. series. Golfing, birding, and hiking nearby. The combination of Native American, Scandanavian, Military and world class garden attractions makes Kitsap an easy-to-tour destination rich in history and diversity.

**Rates**
5 Rooms, $169/$259 B&B. Open year-round. Number of Rooms: 5

**Cuisine**
Breakfast, afternoon wine and cheese included. Dinner available. Complimentary hot beverages. Large selection of wine and beer.

**Nearest Airport(s)**
Seattle

**Directions**
From Silverdale exit Hwy 3 at Newberry Hill Rd and go west to the end of the road (3.5 miles) and turn right on Seabeck Hwy. Drive 13.3 miles to fork right on Old Holly Hill Rd (just after 35 MPH sign), drive 200 yards and turn right on Tekiu Rd. Continue on Tekiu for 1.2 miles, stay left at the paved forks. Enter through the gate house into the circular drive.

# Shelburne Inn & China Beach Retreat

🍽️ 🍽️ 🍽️ 🍷

www.shelburneinn.com or www.chinabeachretreat.com
P.O. Box 250, 4415 Pacific Hwy, Seaview, WA 98644
**800-INN-1896** • 360-642-2442 • Fax 360-642-8904
innkeeper@shelburneinn.com

*Member Since 1988*

*Washington*

*"I want to commend you for having a place where people can come and forget the world and partake of the beautiful scenery that you are nestled in."*

*Seaview*

*Three Diamond Award*

Innkeepers/Owners
## David Campiche and Laurie Anderson

An unspoiled 28-mile stretch of wild Pacific seacoast is just a short walk through rolling sand dunes from this inviting Country Inn, built in 1896. Art Nouveau stained glass windows and period antiques highlight the decor. A sumptuous gourmet breakfast featuring the best of the Northwest is complimentary. nnovative cuisine and a discriminating wine list have brought international recognition to the restaurant and pub. Wireless Internet. Outdoor activities abound, including The Discovery Trail which parallels the majestic Pacific Ocean. Explore the western end of the Lewis & Clark trail from China Beach Retreat and its Audubon Cottage near Cape Disappointment State Park and two 100-plus-year-old lighthouses. Selected as one of the 'West's Best Small Inns', by Sunset Magazine, 2/01. Featured in *Martha Stewart Living* Magazine in January 2003. "Breakfast to the Shelburne is like art to the Louvre," from the *St. Louis Post Dispatch*. Three Stars *NW Best Places*. AAA Three Diamond-rated.

## Rates
13 Rooms $135/$175 B&B; 2 Suites $195 B&B. Off-site waterside B&B; two Rooms $199 B&B; 1 Suite $229 B&B. Audubon Cottage: $279 B&B. Number of Rooms: 19

## Cuisine
Gourmet Regional Cuisine features the best seasonal and local ingredients. Restaurant and Pub offer breakfast, lunch and dinner featuring fine NW wines, microbrewed beer and liquor. Innkeepers' Breakfast served daily and offers creative preparations to choose from.

## Nearest Airport(s)
Portland International

## Directions
From Seattle, I-5 (S) to Olympia, Hwy. 8 & 12 to Montesano & Hwy. 107 then 101(S) to Seaview; From OR coast, U.S. 101N across Astoria Bridge L. to Seaview.

# West Virginia

### "The Mountain State"

Famous for: Appalachian Mountains, Monongahela National Forest, White Sulphur Springs, Harper's Ferry National Historical Park, Smoke Hole Caverns, Apple Butter Festival, Grave Creek Burial Mounds, Country Music, Coal, Oil, Gas.

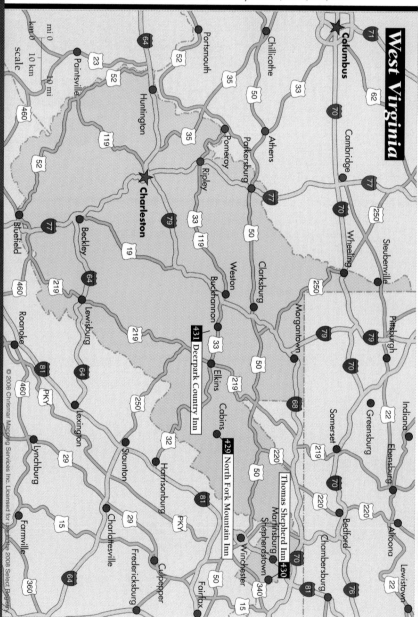

© 2008 Christman Mapping Services Inc. Licensed for use in the 2008 Select Registry.

SelectRegistry.com

# North Fork Mountain Inn

www.northforkmtninn.com
P.O. Box 114, Smoke Hole Road, Cabins, WV 26855
**304-257-1108**
info@northforkmtninn.com

*Member Since 2007*

*"Thank you for a wonderful weekend getaway! The inn is warm and inviting, but you two truly made the experience unforgettable."*

Innkeepers/Owners
**Ed & Carol Fischer**

Come marvel at the breathtaking scenery at an Inn described as "an outpost of luxury in the wilderness." We invite you to come and enjoy the natural beauty of the area in a quiet, relaxing atmosphere. Enjoy a gourmet breakfast as you start your day. Whether you spend the day hiking in the Monongahela forest adjacent to the Inn or enjoying the spectacular view of the mountains and valleys from a rocker on the Inn's wraparound porches, it is like taking a journey back in time to a simpler, slower paced world. Located only three hours from the Washington DC area. Escape for a romantic getaway! The Inn is located 7.6 miles up a paved mountain road with a view of Smoke Hole Canyon and six different mountains. The three story log Inn is of white pine construction with native field stone fireplaces. Each guest room is uniquely decorated with rustic elegance. Guest common areas include comfortable chairs & sofas, book & movie libraries, DirecTV, billiard table, microwave, refrigerator, and board/card games.Excellent fishing located nearby. Birdwatching also popular. Finish your day relaxing in the hot tub under a blanket of stars.

**Rates**
6 Rooms (some with Jacuzzi tubs & fireplaces), $130/$180. Also a 1 Bedroom cabin with full kitchen, $175. All rates include gourmet breakfast for two. Number of Rooms: 7

**Cuisine**
Gourmet breakfast, fine dining with wine tasting on Saturday evening, casual dining available on other evenings, gourmet picnic baskets available for lunch or dinner.

**Nearest Airport(s)**
Washington Dulles

**Directions**
From DC: West on I-66, South on I-81, West on Hwy 55 thru Petersburg, Left on Smoke Hole Road, 7.6 miles to Inn.

*West Virginia*

*Cabins*

# Thomas Shepherd Inn

www.thomasshepherdinn.com
300 W. German Street, P.O. Box 3634, Shepherdstown, WV 25443
**888-889-8952** • 304-876-3715
info@thomasshepherdinn.com

*Member Since 2006*

> *"Great room, great hospitality and good food. I enjoyed every moment; I will recommend you to my associates and friends!"*

Innkeepers/Owners
**Jeanne Muir & Jim Ford**

We invite you to stay in our bed & breakfast inn, with six 'inviting, well kept and beauti-fully decorated' guest rooms with private bath, central air and wi-fi, all located on the 2nd floor. Built in 1868, the Inn offers gracious hospitality to guests for over 25 years. Relax in front of the living room fireplace or on the back porch overlooking the garden; start your day with a generous homemade breakfast. Room amenities include comfy robes, plush towels, and bedside chocolates. Shepherdstown, a hidden gem for weary urbanites, is less than two hours from Washington, DC or Baltimore. The town has a vibrant cultural scene, ranging from premiere plays at the Contemporary American Theater Festival to indepen-dent movies at the Opera House to music and crafts festivals featuring local and nation-ally-known artists. A variety of locally-owned shops and over a dozen restaurants serving flavorful meals fill the historic buildings on German Street one block away. Rich U.S. history is only a few minutes away at Antietam Battlefield or Harpers Ferry. Biking, hiking and rafting abound along the C&O Canal Path, the Potomac or the Shenandoah.

**Rates**
$115/$195 per night double occupancy; lower rates apply Mon-Thurs and may be available off-season. 2-night min. stay on Saturdays & holidays. Senior & corp. discounts available most weekdays. Number of Rooms: 6

**Cuisine**
Full hot homemade breakfast daily w/fruit, entree, meat, baked goods; early beverage service with signature spice biscotti. Walk to several locally-owned fine dining restaurants.

**Nearest Airport(s)**
BWI & Dulles airports-70 miles.

**Directions**
Corner of German & Duke Streets at 4-way stop sign-intersec-tion of Routes 230, 45 & 480. See website/call for area directions. Parking beside & behind Inn.

 SelectRegistry.com

# Deerpark Country Inn

www.deerparkcountryinn.com
P.O. Box 817, Buckhannon, WV 26201
**800-296-8430** • 304-472-8400 • Fax 304-472-5363
deerpark@deerparkcountryinn.com

*Member Since 1999*

*"A great discovery! Worth every inch of a 500 mile trip."*

Owners
**Liz and Patrick Haynes**

Liz and Patrick Haynes invite you to surround yourself with 100 acres of rejuvinating country ambiance that reflects a by-gone era. The inn includes an 18th Century log cabin, a post-Civil War farm house and a newly constructed Victorian wing. Detailed period architecture is featured throughout. About 400 feet from the inn is the two story lodge, a 19th Century log cabin with attached wing, offering three gracious bedrooms, a fireplace as large as a man is tall, and french doors that open onto two wrap around porches...perfect for watching fireflies or shooting stars or snowflakes falling on deep pine forests. All the rooms and suites of both buildings are richly furnished with fine antiques and collectibles, ferns and fresh flowers and crisp cotton linens; each presents its own personality as well as central air, private bath and other amenities. Mist rises from the pond that invites you to fish under the watchful eye of resident mallards and clannishly arrogant geese. Let us design a special getaway package for you.

**Rates**
DBL occupancy, 4 Rooms and 2 Suites. $125/$185. B&B, private baths, phone, A/C, TV, VCR/DVD. Open year-round. Number of Rooms: 6

**Cuisine**
Gourmet breakfast daily. Full bar (honor system) on premises. Dinner service by request 8 or more persons. Several fine dining restaurants in the area. Catered events on-site weddings and reunions.

**Nearest Airport(s)**
Buckhannon Airport

**Directions**
From I-79: Exit 99, US 33-E, go 4 miles past Buckhannon, turn R at Keesling Mill SIGN, turn left on 151-E. When on 151-E, turn L and travel .7 mile to Heavener Grove Rd., turn R. 1.3 miles to Deerpark sign on R.

Famous for: Wisconsin Dells, Apostle Islands, National Lakeshore, Lake Superior, Mirror Lake State Park, House on the Rock (a 1940s retreat built on a 60-foot rock outcropping overlooking a 450 ft drop), Dairy, Beer, Cranberry Fest.

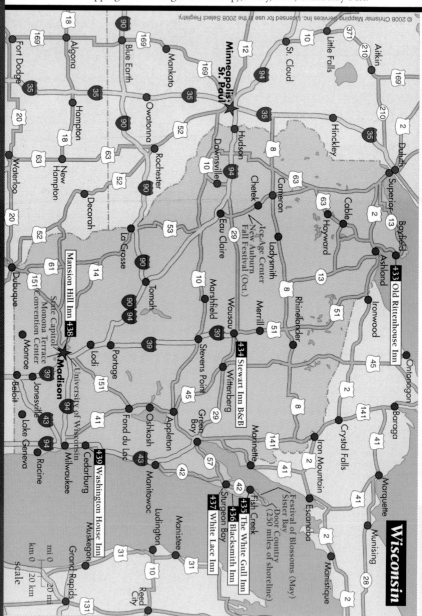

SelectRegistry.com

# Old Rittenhouse Inn

www.rittenhouseinn.com
301 Rittenhouse Ave., P.O. Box 584, Bayfield, WI 54814
**888-560-4667** • 715-779-5111 • Fax 715-779-5887
Gourmet@RittenhouseInn.com

*Member Since 1980*

🍽️ 🍽️ 🍽️ 🍷

*Wisconsin*

*Bayfield*

*"This Queen Anne-style mansion claims the dual distinction of being Bayfield's best-known bed & breakfast and most renowned restaurant."*

Innkeepers/Owners
**Jerry & Mary Phillips**

Standing proudly in the heart of Bayfield, Wisconsin, the Old Rittenhouse Inn enjoys a reputation as one of the premier Country Inns of the Midwest. Located four blocks from majestic Lake Superior and the gateway to the Apostle Islands, the Inn offers 20 guest rooms and suites in three historic buildings. Each room offers individual d...cor ranging from understated elegance to opulent third floor suites. Guest rooms are appointed with comfortable furnishings and antiques. Each has a private bath, and most have wood burning fireplaces, whirlpool tubs, and/or breath-taking views of Lake Superior. House guests and visitors alike will enjoy the spectacular view from one of the world's best front porches: a large wraparound veranda filled with geraniums, petunias, a porch swing, and comfortable wicker furnishings. Old Rittenhouse Inn is also home to a nationally recognized gourmet restaurant serving breakfast and dinner year-round, with seasonal lunch and brunch. The Inn offers weddings and business retreats, as well as wine, beer, and margarita weekends, wassail dinner concerts, mystery dinners, chocolate weekends, and more.

**Rates**
9 rooms $115/$225 B&B; 10 rooms/suites with whirlpools $195/$315 B&B; 1 Cottage, $275/395 B&B; All rooms have private baths. Most have fireplaces, many with lake views. Number of Rooms: 20

**Cuisine**
Serving a creative regional menu featuring Bayfield peninsula's freshest ingredients. Breakfast, brunch, Victorian luncheons, and dinner available. Featured in *Gourmet Magazine*, and *Bon Appetit*.

**Nearest Airport(s)**
Madeline Island - 4 miles

**Directions**
Duluth E on Hwy 2 for 60 miles, to N on Hwy 13 for 21 miles. Located on Rittenhouse Avenue and Third Street in the heart of Bayfield.

# The Stewart Inn Bed and Breakfast

www.stewartinn.com
521 Grant Street, Wausau, WI 54403
**715-849-5858** • Fax 715-845-3692
innkeeper@stewartinn.com

*Member Since 2005*

*Wisconsin*

*Wausau*

*"You remain our standard for B&B and Inn stays, and we have yet to find anything close. Your hospitality made the marvelous setting even better."*

Innkeepers/Owners
**Paul and Jane Welter**

Located in the historic downtown Wausau River District, the Stewart Inn offers upscale accommodations in an authentic National Register Arts and Crafts masterpiece. Public rooms on the first floor of this Prairie Style mansion retain the incredible architectural detail created 100 years ago by Chicago architect, George W. Maher, a contemporary and associate of Frank Lloyd Wright. The second floor serves as an exclusive five-room boutique hotel where the owners take pride in providing guests with exceptional, unobtrusive service. Each of the newly renovated guest rooms has an extraordinary ensuite bath and tasteful combination of modern amenities and historic charm, sure to please even the most discriminating travelers. The Inn is fully equipped for the business traveler and offers a comfortable, secure alternative to conventional lodging. Restaurants, shops, museums, and entertainment are all within walking distance. If you're traveling with a dog, you'll find the accommodations extremely pet-friendly.

**Rates**
$150/$195 weekdays, $170/$215 weekends. Business rates available. Closed April. All rooms have private bath, steam shower, air conditioning, premium bedding, cable TV/DVD/CD, desk, telephone, wireless Internet. Number of Rooms: 5

**Cuisine**
Full gourmet breakfast, afternoon wine and cheese, evening cookies and milk.

**Nearest Airport(s)**
Central Wisconsin Airport

**Directions**
From I39/Hwy 51 take Exit 192, to Hwy 52 East. Go 2 miles and cross the Wisconsin River. Turn left (North) on 1st Street and go 4 blocks to Grant Street. Turn right (East) and go 4 1/2 blocks to 521 Grant Street.

# White Gull Inn

www.whitegullinn.com
4225 Main Street, P.O. Box 160, Fish Creek, WI 54212
**800-625-8813** • 920-868-3517 • Fax 920-868-2367
innkeeper@whitegullinn.com

*Member Since 1979*

*Wisconsin*

*Fish Creek*

*"We loved it from start to finish. Your beautiful accommodations, delicious breakfasts and fish boil and your warm hospitality made our stay perfect,"*

Three
Diamond Award

Innkeepers
**Andy & Jan Coulson**

Established in 1896, this white clapboard Inn is tucked away in the scenic bayside village of Fish Creek on Wisconsin's Door Peninsula. Antiques, fireplaces and meticulously restored and exquisitely decorated rooms, suites and cottages provide a warm and romantic atmosphere. Several suites feature double whirlpool baths. Renowned for hearty breakfasts, sumptuous lunches and candlelit dinners, the Inn is famous for its traditional Door County fish boils, featuring locally caught Lake Michigan whitefish cooked outside over an open fire. With its back to a bluff and its face to the bay of Green Bay, Fish Creek today is a stroll around village with historic buildings housing numerous art galleries, shops and restaurants. A natural harbor filled with majestic yachts in summer separates the village from Peninsula State Park, Wisconsin's largest and most beautiful park. Within a few minutes of the inn, guests will find spectacular sunsets, summer stock theater, music festivals, antique stores and every imaginable recreational activity, from golf and fishing to wind surfing and kayaking, from hiking and biking to cross country skiing.

**Rates**
6 Rooms, $152/$215; 7 Suites, $225/$285; 4 Cottages (1, 2 and 4 bedroom), $237/$465. Includes full breakfast. Winter and Shoulder Season, Romance, Spa and other packages. Open all year. Number of Rooms: 17

**Cuisine**
Hearty full breakfast included, lunches daily & dinner from the menu or traditional Door County fish boil served nightly. Wine and beer available. Dining room open to the public.

**Nearest Airport(s)**
Austin Straubel Field, Green Bay (75 miles)

**Directions**
Milwaukee I-43 for 98 mi. to Green Bay, then Rte. 57 N for 39 miles to Sturgeon Bay; N on Rte. 42 for 25 mi. to Fish Creek, L. at stop sign for 3 Blks.

# Blacksmith Inn On the Shore

www.theblacksmithinn.com
8152 Highway 57, Baileys Harbor, WI 54202
**800-769-8619** • 920-839-9222 • Fax 920-839-9356
relax@theblacksmithinn.com

*Member Since 2002*

*Wisconsin*

*Baileys Harbor*

*"To fall asleep to the sound of that water is heavenly!"*

---

Innkeepers/Owners
**Joan Holliday and Bryan Nelson**

Awaken to the sound of waves lapping the shore as the morning sunlight glistens on the water. Linger over breakfast on our sun-washed porch. Kayak in summer, snowshoe the harbor edge in winter. Step out our door to hike the nearby Ridges Wildlife Sanctuary. Laze in your hammock. Bike a sleepy backroad to explore Cana Island Lighthouse. Bask in your whirlpool as you take in the warm glow of the fire. Stroll to nearby village restaurants and shops. Revel in an extraordinary view of the harbor any time of year. Complete privacy with all the amenities including, serene water views, private balconies, in-room whirlpools, fireplaces, canopied beds, fine linens, down pillows, satellite TV/DVD/CD with in-house DVD library, phones, individually controlled heat & air conditioning, free wireless internet, ipod hook-up, in-room refrigerators and a bottomless cookie jar! Door County offers art galleries, antiquing, music, theater and miles and miles of shoreline. Romance & relaxation are yours at the Blacksmith Inn On the Shore, located in the heart of the Door County Peninsula.

**Rates**
May through Oct., Rooms $215/$265, Cottage $255/$425; Nov. through April, Rooms $135/$235. All rooms have whirlpool, fireplace, & balcony w/view of the harbor. Open year round, smoke-free. Number of Rooms: 16

**Cuisine**
Guests enjoy a homemade continental breakfast from the balcony overlooking the harbor. "There is nothing simple about the view that beckons each guest every morning." Jill Cordes, Food Network.

**Nearest Airport(s)**
Green Bay

**Directions**
From Airport; Hwy 172 E 8 mi. to Hwy 43 N, 5 mi. to Hwy 57 N, 63 mi. to the inn at the north end of the village on the shore, 90 minutes drive time.

 SelectRegistry.com

# White Lace Inn

www.WhiteLaceInn.com

16 N. 5th Ave., Sturgeon Bay, Door County, WI 54235

**877-948-5223 (toll free)** • 920-743-1105 • Fax 920-743-8180

Romance@WhiteLaceInn.com

*Member Since 1988*

*Wisconsin*

*"This Whimsical Victorian Inn doesn't merely pamper its guests, it envelops them in comfort..expected amenities are here, but the unexpected set it apart."*

*Sturgeon Bay*

Innkeepers/Owners
**Dennis & Bonnie Statz**

Romance and relaxation in Door County begin as you follow winding garden pathways to your beautifully appointed room or suite. Four lovingly restored historic homes surround a 'central back yard' with a beautiful large gazebo, and are nestled in a friendly old neighborhood, bordered by a white picket fence. Guest rooms and suites are furnished for a special getaway and feature period antiques, down comforters on wonderfully ornate beds, oversized whirlpools and inviting fireplaces. Fifteen of our rooms have a fireplace, twelve rooms have a whirlpool and nine of our rooms/suites have both a fireplace and whirlpool - several with king sized beds. Mornings start with a delicious full breakfast served in the sunlit parlor of the Main House. Bonnie, Dennis and their staff invite you to enjoy the hospitality that has made their Inn a Door County tradition since we first opened in 1982. We've had over 1,100 small weddings performed at White Lace Inn - usually in the Gazebo. Door-CountyNavigator.com's User's Choice Award, Best B&B in Door County, 2003. Top 10 Romantic Inns of America, 1998, 2004 & 2005, American Historic Inns. AAA Three Diamond Award.

**Rates**
13 Rooms, $120/$195; 5 Suites, $200/$235. Late October-Mid June, Weeknights, Rooms $70/$130, and Suites $150/$160. Open year-round. Full breakfast included. Number of Rooms: 18

**Cuisine**
A delicious full breakfast is served to our guests daily. Afternoons and evenings include hot cider, hot cocoa, lemonade, iced tea, popcorn, and homemade cookies.

**Nearest Airport(s)**
Green Bay airport is a one hour drive, Milwaukee 2 1/2 hours, Chicago 3 1/2 hours. Door County Cherryland Airport is 5 miles from the inn.

**Directions**
Hwy 42 or 57 N to Sturgeon Bay. Business route 42/57 into town across Historic Bridge. Left on 5th Ave, 1/4 block on 5th Ave to Inn on right.

SelectRegistry.com

# Mansion Hill Inn
www.mansionhillinn.com
424 N. Pinckney Street, Madison, WI 53703
**800-798-9070** • 608-255-3999 • Fax 608-255-2217

*Member Since 1997*

*Wisconsin*

*Madison*

*"Madison's most gracious and intimate seclusion..."*
*"Thank you all so very much! We will certainly be back soon."*

General Manager
**Tania Worgull**

Elegance, luxury and charm await you at The Mansion Hill Inn. The Inn's warm hospitality has made it a favorite of business and leisure travelers alike. Lovingly restored and lavishly decorated, Mansion Hill Inn is the American Automobile Association's only 4 diamond rated accommodation in Madison. A masterpiece of Romanesque Revival style built in 1857, it abounds in fine architectural detail and period furnishings. Each of the ten guest suites and rooms are individually and exquisitely decorated to provide the best of antique ambience and contemporary amenities. Many rooms have marble fireplaces and balconies as well as views of the State Capitol building. The Inn is conveniently located on a quiet corner in the heart of downtown Madison and boasts luxurious accommodations, amenities, and a convenient location. We're close to the campuses of the University of Wisconsin, Madison Area Technical College, Edgewood College and within walking distance of State Street. Valet parking is complimentary.

**Rates**
Ten Beautiful Guest Rooms including 2 Suites, 4 Grand Standard Rooms and 4 Standard Rooms, ranging from $200 to $375 on special event weekends. Number of Rooms: 10

**Cuisine**
Many fine restaurants within walking distance. Complimentary wine service every evening. Continental-plus breakfast in our Breakfast Parlour.

**Nearest Airport(s)**
Dane County Regional Airport

**Directions**
Hwy. 151 to State Capitol, turn Right on Wisconsin, 4 blocks turn Right on Gilman 1 block turn Right onto Pinckney.

# Washington House Inn

www.washingtonhouseinn.com
W62 N573, Cedarburg, WI 53012
**888-554-0515** • 262-375-3550 • Fax 262-375-9422
whinn@execpc.com

*Member Since 2007*

*Wisconsin*

*Cedarburg*

> *"Elegant antiques give the inn a look of distinguished comfort...whirlpool baths are a delightful extra."* Better Homes and Gardens / Country Home

Innkeeper
**Wendy J. Porterfield**

Listed on the National Register of Historic Places, The Washington House Inn successfully blends the charm and romance of days past with the amenities and conveniences expected by today's discriminating travelers. 34 luxurious guest rooms include whirlpool and steam baths, fine antique furnishings, and fireplaces. Guests are invited to enjoy a complimentary evening wine and cheese tasting featuring award-winning wines from local Cedar Creek Winery, and a sampling of Wisconsin cheeses. For those who would like to indulge in a little extra pampering, the inn offers on-site massage for individual or couples. Located in the heart of Cedarburg's Historic District, the inn offers elegant lodging within walking distance of festivals, unique shops, antiquing, galleries, fine and casual dining, local winery, brew pub, the Cedarburg Cultural Center, and the Ozaukee Interurban Trail (30 miles of paved trail for hiking or biking). Within a 15 minutes drive are five golf courses, including The Bog, an Arnold Palmer-designed course. This inn is able to host private parties in the formal Gathering Room, or business meetings in its multi media Conference Room.

**Rates**
Guest rooms $95-$245. Whirlpools, steambaths, fireplaces, wireless internet. Number of Rooms: 34

**Cuisine**
A sumptuous continental breakfast buffet is thoughtfully prepared for you each morning by staff bakers and is sure to be one of the highlights of your stay.

**Nearest Airport(s)**
General Mitchell International

**Directions**
20 miles north of Milwaukee exit 89 off of I-43. West on County Highway C to Washington Avenue. North to Center Street. Left onto Center Street for parking.

# Wyoming

Famous for: Yellowstone National Park, Grand Teton National Park, Devils Tower National Monument, National Elk Refuge.

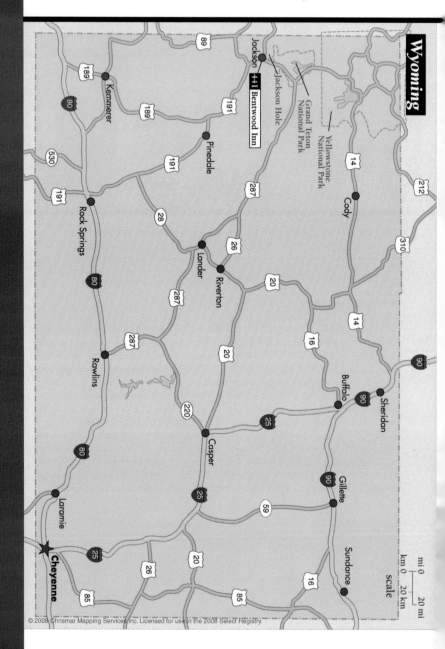

Wyoming

Jackson

+1 Bentwood Inn

Jackson Hole

Grand Teton National Park

Yellowstone National Park

Kemmerer

Pinedale

Cody

Rock Springs

Lander

Riverton

Rawlins

Buffalo

Sheridan

Casper

Gillette

Laramie

Sundance

Cheyenne

scale

mi 0    20 mi
km 0    20 km

© 2008 Chrismar Mapping Services, Inc. Licensed for use in the 2008 Select Registry.

SelectRegistry.com

# Bentwood Inn

🍽️ 🍽️ 🍷

www.bentwoodinn.com
P.O. Box 561, 4250 Raven Haven Road, Jackson, WY 83001
**307-739-1411** • Fax 307-739-2453
info@bentwoodinn.com

x

*Member Since 2008*

*Wyoming Jackson*

> *"One of the Top Ten Inns in the Country" Country Inns Magazine*
> *"...an Architectural Marvel!" Frommers Travel Guide*

Innkeepers
**Peter and Jennifer Tignor**

The Bentwood Inn is a luxury bed and breakfast in Jackson Hole, Wyoming, nestled on three acres of solitude, not far from the Snake River, Jackson Hole Mountain Resort, the south entrance to Grand Teton National Park, and the town of Jackson. The inn was built in 1995 with 200 year old logs from Yellowstone National Park, recycled from the fire of 1988. The Bentwood Inn is a welcoming, intimate lodge, focused on food, hospitality, and creating an unbelievable experience for each of its guests.

The Bentwood Inn boasts more than 6,000 square feet of luxurious space, including a three-story river rock fireplace in the Great Room and remarkable craftsmanship throughout. Each of the five guest rooms has a private fireplace, king bed, jetted tub, and personal balcony. The large, expansive decks are perfect for relaxing and socializing in warm weather. Majestic old-growth cottonwoods and pines offer privacy and serenity year round.

The Bentwood strives to offer our guests a balance between luxury and adventure, healthy food and sumptuous celebration, and outstanding hospitality, in a valley that offers world-class recreation.

**Rates**
Room rates vary by season and room type. Please visit our website to view our "Rates At A Glance" page. Number of Rooms: 5

**Cuisine**
At the Bentwood Inn we strive to use local and organic ingredients while preparing our innovative seasonal menus. Unique presentations with creative twists on old favorites will satisfy the appetite needed for our active guests.

**Nearest Airport(s)**
Jackson Hole Airport: 18 miles. Idaho Falls Airport: 85 miles.

**Directions**
The Bentwood Inn is located on Rte. 22 (Teton Village Road), just off Rte 390, 1/3 mile on the left. We're 5 miles from Jackson Town and 7 miles from the South Entrance to Grand Teton National Park.

*"We've experienced all four seasons in Canada—and we can't pick a favorite!"*

From California to Nova Scotia, SELECT REGISTRY represents the finest inns, B&Bs, and unique small hotels North America has to offer. We are proud to include among our members a number of exceptional Canadian properties. To our Canadian guests, we say, "Our innkeepers stand ready to welcome you during your travels, whether it is to the States or within Canada." To our American guests, we say, "Why not see what Canada has to offer?"

In these uncertain times, when crossing oceans is worrisome, nothing beats the exhilarating feeling of visiting an exciting new country in the security and comfort of your own car. Yes, for many millions of Americans, Canada is just a short drive away—and yet it is a whole new world!

No wonder Americans love to travel to Canada: not only do their U.S. dollars go a lot further there (which means a lot more holiday for the same amount of money), but they also get to choose between a multitude of completely different experiences.

*De la Californie à la Nouvelle-Ecosse, le SELECT REGISTRY représente plusieurs auberges, cafés-couettes et petits hôtels des plus distingués en Amérique du Nord. Nous sommes fiers de pouvoir compter parmi nos membres plusieurs des plus beaux établissements canadiens. À tous les voyageurs, canadiens-français, nous vous souhaitons de merveilleux séjours dans les auberges de prestige du SELECT REGISTRY.*

*"Unbelievable natural beauty, exceptional food and wine,
and our friendly neighbors to the North...perfect!"*

There are the breathtaking vistas, mountain wildlife, Asian food and totem poles of British Columbia, the "foodie" paradise of the Niagara Peninsula (Canada's Napa Valley) and the Eastern Townships of Quebec, replete with friendly wineries and raw milk cheeses. There are festivals galore, museums, parks and world-class shopping in Toronto and Montreal as well as the fascinating culture of the Province of Quebec where French-Canadians take food and fun very, very seriously. And, never to be forgotten, the bucolic seaside charm and legendary hospitality of Canada's maritime provinces, New Brunswick, Prince Edward Island and Nova Scotia.

Many travelers have experienced all four seasons of the Northland (the winters are sunnier and less cold than you think). Traveling east to west, it would be hard to declare a regional winner. Some Canadians modestly claim to be the most hospitable of innkeepers, and a critic can't easily challenge that assertion.

Superb food, wine and service can be expected at the Canadian inns of the SELECT REGISTRY. Understated luxury, too. But above all, they offer you an exclusive glimpse of the best of Canada: its forests, crystalline lakes, affordable golf and skiing and cosmopolitan, secure and friendly cities. The Northland beckons!

# Alberta

## "Canada's Rocky Mountain Playground"

Famous for: Camping, Wildlife, Skiing and Winter Fun (Lake Louise), Mt. Columbia, Hiking, Kayaking, Canoeing, Banff National Park, West Edmonton Mall, Birding, Bison, Olympic Hall of Fame, Calgary Stampede.

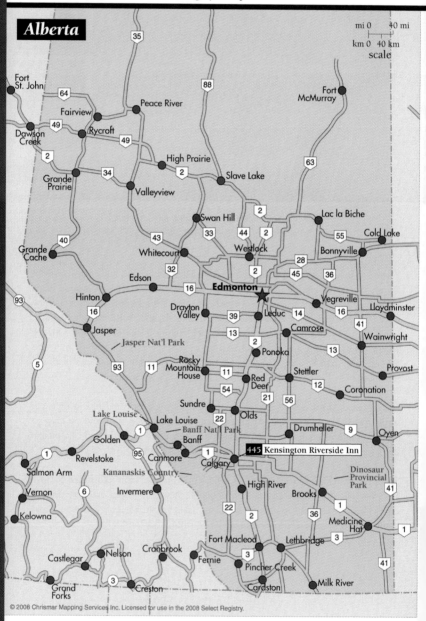

**445** Kensington Riverside Inn

# Kensington Riverside Inn

www.kensingtonriversideinn.com
1126 Memorial Drive NW, Calgary, AB T2N 3E3
**877-313-3733** • 403-228-4442 • Fax 403-228-9608
info@kensingtonriversideinn.com

*Member Since 2005*

*"The most comfortable stay I've ever had!" (Phoenix) "You have thought of everything to make your guests comfortable - you're #1 on our list." (Florida)*

Operations Manager - **Denis Barghshoon**
Maitre d' - **Andrew Stewart**
Executive Chef - **Theo Yeaman**

In the midst of Calgary's trendy Kensington district, just a short walk from the business centre of town, the Kensington Riverside Inn is Alberta's only AAA Four Diamond Inn. The Inn is traditional in style and gracious in atmosphere, with 10-foot ceilings, cornices and columns throughout, and a wood-burning fireplace and bar in the living room. Guests are treated to a magnificent view of the Bow River and the downtown skyline, exceptional accommodations, first-class service and amenities galore. Shops, restaurants and a theatre are close by, as well as the Light Rail Transit System, making many of the city's attractions readily accessible. Comfort and convenience are the way in each of the 19 guest rooms, from balconies or patios to gas fireplaces and Jacuzzis, to Egyptian cotton sheets, warm Frette towels, goose-down duvets and Aveda bath products. Video and book lending library, voice mail and wireless Internet. There's lots to do in and around Calgary, and the Canadian Rockies are only an hour away. With the recent opening of Chef's Table, an intimate upscale restaurant with an open kitchen design, as well as a new 30-seat lounge, the Inn is becoming a dining destination for food and wine lovers alike.

### Rates
19 Guest Rooms. $294/$454 CDN (approx. $259/$399 US). Lower rates on weekends. 5 room types featuring fireplaces, balconies, patios or Jacuzzis. Number of Rooms: 19

### Cuisine
A coffee tray is delivered to your room w/ the morning newspaper, followed by a gourmet breakfast in our dining room. In the evening, hors d'oeuvres are served in the living room. Chocolates by the bedside & cookies 24 hours a day. Light meals available at any time.

### Nearest Airport(s)
Calgary International Airport.

### Directions
From Downtown: W on 4th Avenue SW, N on 10th Street SW, W on Memorial Dr. for one block.

# Atlantic Provinces

New Brunswick: "The Picture Province"
Nova Scotia: "The Land of Evangeline"
Prince Edward Island: "The Garden Province"

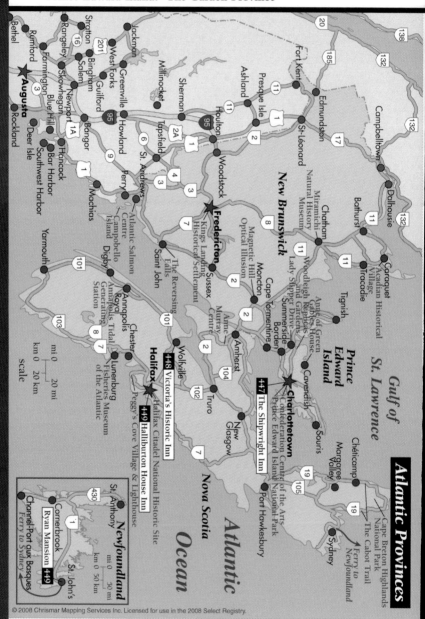

© 2008 Chrismar Mapping Services Inc. Licensed for use in the 2008 Select Registry.

# Shipwright Inn B & B

www.shipwrightinn.com
51 Fitzroy Street, Charlottetown, PEI, Canada  C1A 1R4
**888-306-9966** • 902-368-1905 • Fax 902-628-1905
innkeeper@shipwrightinn.com

*Member Since 1999*

*"The outside of the Inn looks like a storybook cottage and the inside is even better! An unforgettable experience."*

**Innkeepers/Owners**
**Judy & Trevor Pye**

Enjoy a "Unique Experience" at the award winning 5 Star Shipwright Inn. Relax, unwind and take in all that our "Gentle Island of Rejuvenation" has to offer you with its tranquil beaches, red soil and rolling countryside. This Victorian, Anne of Green Gables style, heritage home was built in 1865 by shipbuilder James Douse. Nautical theme antiques and artwork have been lovingly collected for your enjoyment. All bedrooms have polished pine floors, en-suite bathrooms, some with double Ultra Air Tubs, whirlpools and fireplaces. The Inn is located in historic Olde Charlottetown within a 3 minute walk of cultural sites, waterfront, live theatre and shopping. Seafood lovers experience the very best of lobster, mussels, oysters and more! A Golfer's Paradise. Beautiful English garden, safe, free parking, peaceful, comfortable and quiet. We pride ourselves on delivering warm Island hospitality, attentive service and believe in pampering our guests and exceeding their expectations. Frommer's Best on PEI, Canada Select Five Star Award.

**Rates**
3 Executive, 5 Premium suites, 1 Apartment. $149/$299 CAD. Open year-round. Off-season rates availab  Number of Rooms: 9

**Cuisine**
Afternoon refreshments. Memorable full served hot breakfast of four courses (if you have the appetite!!!)

**Nearest Airport(s)**
Charlottetown Airport - approximately a 10 minute drive.

**Directions**
From Confederation Bridge: TCH1 East to Charlottetown. Turn R on Fitzroy St go 1.5 blocks. From Wood Islands Ferry: TCH1 West to Charlottetown, cross Hillsborough Bridge, L into Water St. 5 blocks then R Queen St, 7 blocks L onto Fitzroy St. On R look for red/gold sign with gold ship on top.

🍽  ♀

# Victoria's Historic Inn

www.victoriashistoricinn.com
600 Main Street, Wolfville, NS, Canada B4P 1E8
**800-556-5744** • 902-542-5744 • Fax 902-542-7794
victoriasinn@eastlink.ca

*Member Since 1998*

*"Came for one night, stayed five - perfect!"*

Innkeepers/Owners
**The Cryan Family**

The Cryan family has worked tirelessly to achieve the first B&B five-star Canada Select rating in the province. Now perhaps the finest Victorian home in Nova Scotia, the Inn's professionally decorated rooms lend an intimate and first-class atmosphere, all with ensuite baths; some offer double Jacuzzis and fireplaces, with balcony or sweeping view. Travel writers say, "It is the attention to detail and the softly decorated rooms, as well as the sincere care of the innkeepers, that draw people back to Victoria's again and again for peace and relaxation in a pampered environment." Nestled in the picturesque and historic town of Wolfville, travelers are surrounded by a choice of activities. Hiking trails, scenic vistas, historic sites, award-winning dining, golf and wineries are all minutes away.

**Rates**
14 Rooms, $128/$189. 2 Suites, $245 CDN B&B. Open year-round. Number of Rooms: 16

**Cuisine**
Hot breakfast included in room rate. Award-winning restaurants within walking distance. Selection of wines available.

**Nearest Airport(s)**
Halifax International Airport 1 hour driving distance.

**Directions**
From Yarmouth: 101 E to exit #11. L off exit ramp. R onto Hwy 1. Just inside town limits on L. From Halifax Airport: Hwy. 102 S towards Halifax to exit 4B onto 101 W and Annapolis Valley (approx 15 min.) Take exit 10. Follow Hwy 1 to town. Located on R after downtown.

 SelectRegistry.com

# The Halliburton

www.thehalliburton.com
5184 Morris Street, Halifax, NS, Canada  B3J 1B3
**888-512-3344** • 902-420-0658 • Fax 902-423-2324
information@thehalliburton.com

*Member Since 1998*

*Nova Scotia*

*Halifax*

*"So pleased that we found this 'gem' in Halifax!
The flavours and food presentation are second to none."*

Manager
**Robert Pretty**

Downtown Halifax's historic boutique hotel.  The Halliburton features signature dining and
individually appointed guestrooms in a trio of heritage townhouses.  Twenty-nine rooms
and suites of various sizes, complimentary breakfast, and wireless Internet access.  'Stories' restaurant offers inventive regional cuisine in intimate dining rooms.  In the summer
months guests enjoy cocktails and light fare in the garden courtyard.  In the autumn and
winter a crackling fire invites from the cozy library.  The Halliburton, was built in 1809 and
was home to Sir Brenton Halliburton, the first Chief Justice of the Nova Scotia Supreme
Court.  More recently, the building housed Dalhousie University's prestigious law school.
A short stroll from popular shops, restaurants and the Halifax waterfront.   AAA/CAA
Three Diamond Award.  Canada Select Four Star Award.

### Rates
29 rooms including 4 suites, rates from $150 CDN, plus tax,
includes breakfast. Open year-round. Number of Rooms: 29

### Cuisine
An extensive continental breakfast is served each morning
from 7-10. 'Stories' offers relaxed fine dining from 5:30 until
10:00, reservations are recommended. Fine wine, local beer
and cocktails are served after 4:00 in the Library or garden
courtyard.

### Nearest Airport(s)
Halifax International -- CYHZ

### Directions
Downtown Halifax, Barrington at Morris Street. Use Hwy #102
from Halifax International Airport or Hwy #103 from Yarmouth.

# Ryan Mansion

www.ryanmansion.com
21-23 Rennies Mill Road, St. John's, NL  A1C 3P9
**709-753-7926** • Fax 709-753-7992
ryanmansion@gmail.com

*Member Since 2008*

*Newfoundland*

*St. John's*

*"5 Best Hotels to Open in 2007." "Guest rooms are exquisitely decorated with fireplaces, marble baths, and cushy beds that you can float on..."*

Proprietors
## Robert Hall and Kevin Nolan

Built during the exact time (1909-1911), the Ryan Mansion shares a unique connection with Titanic.  Carved from English White Oak and imported from the Old World, the staircase at Ryan Mansion was crafted by the same masters who fitted the world famous liner, Titanic. To celebrate this unique connection, Ryan Mansion offers a "Weekend Getaway of Titanic Proportions" (see website for details).  Located in the affluent heritage district, Ryan Mansion is steps from downtown, prime tourist attractions, historic sites, and the Provincial Art Gallery. Guestrooms are lavishly fitted with designer furnishings, luxurious Italian linens by Frette, and luxe European amenities by L'Occitane en Provence. Marble en suite baths feature heated floors and therapeutic tubs for two. Extravagant suites are arranged over 3 rooms and offer the ultimate in guest accommodation including en suite baths featuring personal steam/shower rooms and century old tubs carved from granite! A collection of local, national, and international artworks, sculpture and artifacts are exhibited throughout the mansion, and a cozy library offers a selection of books & games.

**Rates**
$185 CDN to $485 CDN.  Number of Rooms: 14

**Nearest Airport(s)**
St. John's International

**Cuisine**
Enjoy gourmet breakfasts featuring traditional favourites served with a twist.Always included are locally prepared preserves made from wild blueberries and partridgeberries.  Ask about our "Memories of Titanic" dinner. Selections from the actual menu served during the last meal on the Tiantic are recreated and served on accurate replica china from the Titanic!

**Directions**
From Airport: Left on Portugal Cove Road (heading South) You simply remain on Portugal Cove Road which eventually runs directly into Rennies Mill Road.

# British Columbia    "The Pacific Province"

Famous for: Canadian Rockies, Ferries, Vancouver Island, Spiral Railway Tunnels, Butchart Gardens.

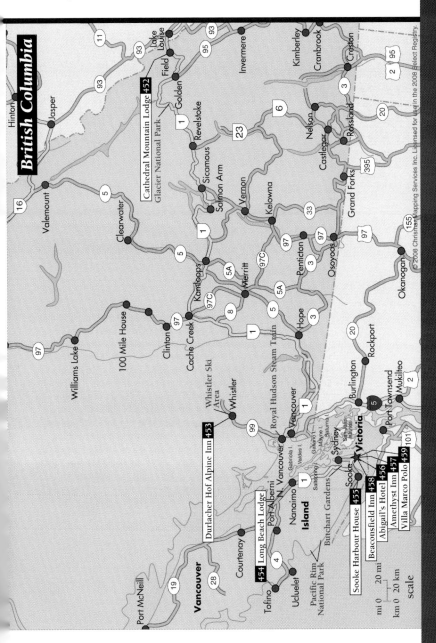

British Columbia

Cathedral Mountain Lodge 452
Glacier National Park

Durlacher Hof Alpine Inn 453

Long Beach Lodge 454

Sooke Harbour House 455
Beaconsfield Inn 458
Abigail's Hotel 456
Amethyst Inn 457
Villa Marco Polo 459

Vancouver Island

Pacific Rim National Park

Butchart Gardens

mi 0   20 mi
km 0   20 km
scale

© 2008 Christman Mapping Services Inc. Licensed for use in the 2008 Select Registry.

🍽️ 🍽️ 🍽️ 🍷

# Cathedral Mountain Lodge

www.cathedralmountain.com
Yoho Valley Road, P.O. Box 40, Field, BC, Canada V0A 1G0
**866-619-6442** • 250-343-6442 • Fax 250-343-6424
info@cathedralmountain.com

*Member Since 2003*

*British Columbia*

*Field*

*"Truly amazing - great time spent with our friends from France. You have done Canada proud. Thank you for your hospitality and attention to detail."*

General Manager
**Chris Bates**

Imagine your own log cabin in the heart of the Canadian Rocky Mountains; a stocked wood burning fireplace, down duvets, deep soaker bathtub, tranquil sitting areas and a generous private deck with commanding views of the magnificent Rocky Mountains and the glacier fed Kicking Horse River. Wake up to the song of wild birds and the call of an alpine river, to the scent of fresh pine and the beauty of mountain wildflowers. There is no television or telephone to disrupt your mountain escape. Your purpose is to replenish and revive - because tomorrow you can hike, climb, raft, canoe, bike, fish, golf and horseback ride! From leisurely strolls to day-long expeditions, an endless array of hiking trails are just outside your door. This is an authentic Rocky Mountain retreat surrounded by other-worldly alpine meadows, abundant wildlife, towering peaks and epic waterfalls. Close to all the attractions and activities of Yoho National Park, Lake Louise and Banff National Park, there is so much to do! Come to Cathedral Mountain Lodge - a place where every day is like no day anywhere else.

**Rates**
Rates vary according to season & cabin type. From $160 - $635 per night. Number of Rooms: 31

**Cuisine**
Complimentary continental breakfast is served daily. Packed hikers lunch is available. Dinner features the best of local producers, emphasizing fresh in season regional ingredients.

**Nearest Airport(s)**
Calgary International Airport

**Directions**
Located 200km (125 mi.) from Calgary, Alberta. Travel west on the Trans Canada Highway 1. Go past Canmore, Banff and Lake Louise before crossing into B.C. 5 km into B.C., the highway starts a steep descent; at the bottom take a right on Yoho Valley Rd. This will take you directly to the lodge

# Durlacher Hof Alpine Inn

www.durlacherhof.com
7055 Nesters Rd., Whistler, BC, Canada V0N 1B7
**877-932-1924** • 604-932-1924 • Fax 604-938-1980
info@durlacherhof.com

*Member Since 1998*

*"Breakfast 'par excellence.' Upon first site, we knew Durlacher Hof would be our official return destination. We feel refreshed & refueled. Memorable."*

**Innkeepers/Owners**
**Peter & Erika Durlacher**

Nestled in the spectacular Coast Mountains of British Columbia lies Whistler Resort, home to the Durlacher Hof, an enchanting mountain retreat. Durlachers' reputation as Whistler's most welcoming and generous innkeepers is legendary. The Hof serves up the complete authentic Austrian experience from ornate exterior trimmings to the Kaiserschmarren served at breakfast. Painstaking attention to detail is evident in the cozy guest lounge and the immaculate pretty rooms all with mountain views, goose-down duvets, luxury linens and ensuite baths with jacuzzi. Durlacher Hof is part of a place that mixes old world charm with romance and a natural beauty with inviting warmth and hospitality. The natural setting of Whistler offers a bounty of outdoor activities, a quaint village, which hosts art, culture events, and intriguing shops along with a wide spectrum of international cuisine. Host location of the 2010 Winter Olympics and Paralympics.

**Rates**
Summer $139/$299 CDN. Winter $179/$499 CDN. Ski & Golf packages. 10 days summer, 30 days winter cancellation policy, min. German spoken, Canada Select 4 1/2 Stars. AAA 3 Diamond. Seasonal Discounts. Number of Rooms: 10

**Cuisine**
Re-awaken your senses to the pleasures of fresh local healthy cuisine. The Inn serves up European Dinners in Winter on selected evenings. Special culinary events in Summer and Fall. Licensed Lounge

**Nearest Airport(s)**
Vancouver International 2.5 hrs.

**Directions**
75 miles/125 kilometres N of Vancouver on Hwy 99 (approx. 2 hours). 7 traffic lights on Hwy 99 from the 'Whistler Welcome' sign to Nesters.

# Long Beach Lodge Resort

www.longbeachlodgeresort.com

P.O. Box 897, 1441 Pacific Rim Highway, Tofino, BC  V0R 2Z0

**877-844-7873** • 250-725-2442 • Fax 250-725-2402

info@longbeachlodgeresort.com

*Member Since 2005*

*British Columbia*

*Tofino*

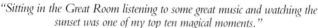

*"Sitting in the Great Room listening to some great music and watching the sunset was one of my top ten magical moments."*

Owner - **Timothy Hackett**

General Manager - **Carly Hall**

Experience the natural beauty, exceptional amenities and handcrafted gourmet cuisine at our luxurious beachfront resort on the West Coast of Vancouver Island. Our relaxed and inspirational coastal setting offers a perfect escape from your everyday responsibilities. Choose between accommodation in our beachfront Lodge with spectacular oceanviews or retreat to one of our tranquil, two bedroom Rainforest Cottages with full kitchens and private outdoor patios with hot tubs. You will begin to relax as soon as you enter the Lodge Great Room with its massive granite fireplace and its Douglas fir post and beam construction. Sink into an overstuffed chair, put your feet up, and gaze out at the sandy beach with the crashing surf to the lighthouse beyond. You will appreciate the attention to detail that has been lavished on each of our guest rooms, including luxurious bath amenities, bath robes, cozy duvets, decadent chocolates and waterproof rain jackets for those rainy day beach walks!

**Rates**

40 Lodge Rms $169/$569 CDN. 20 Cottages $269/$469 CDN. Seasonal.  Number of Rooms: 60

**Cuisine**

The Resort's dining room is a relaxed, informal space where the emphasis is placed on fresh food, superior service & meticulous attention to detail. Our chef captures the intricate flavours of sea, field & forest with his inventive & memorable gourmet cuisine.

**Nearest Airport(s)**

Tofino Airport, 10km

**Directions**

Take Hwy 1 North from Victoria past Nanaimo. Turn west, onto Hwy 4 at the Qualicum Beach/Port Alberni exit and follow signs. Drive will take approx. 4.5 hours. Direct flights available from Vancouver and Seattle.

# Sooke Harbour House

www.sookeharbourhouse.com
1528 Whiffen Spit Road, Sooke, BC, Canada  V9Z 0T4
**800-889-9688** • 250-642-3421 • Fax 250-642-6988
info@sookeharbourhouse.com

*Member Since 2003*

*Canada Select 5 Star Rating "Bliss defined."*

Innkeepers
**Sinclair and Frederique Philip**

Cozy and enchanting, Sooke Harbour House was rated, "One of Canada's Top Five Hotels" by *Travel + Leisure* Magazine, Jan. 2008 and "Best Vancouver Island Restaurant" by *Vancouver* Magazine Restaurant Awards, April 2008. Its restaurant specializes in West Coast Canadian cuisine, especially seafood, and much of its produce comes from the Inn's organic gardens. The rooms feature stunning ocean views, wood burning fireplaces, original art, and soaker or Jacuzzi tubs. Some offer steam showers for two. Step onto your private balcony, the perfect location for watching sea lions, river otters, seals and eagles play. Activities include: kayaking, whale watching, cycling and fishing.

**Rates**
28 Guest Rooms from $289/$640 (low/high) Incl. breakfast. Gourmet, Spa, and Romance Getaway Packages available. Open year-round. Number of Rooms: 28

**Cuisine**
Re-awaken your taste buds to the pleasures of fresh, local, seasonal culinary creations. Wine pairings from our cellar, one of the 75 best in the world, add to the adventure.

**Nearest Airport(s)**
Victoria, BC

**Directions**
23 miles W of Victoria. Take Hwy. 1 north to exit 14. Turn right onto Hwy.14 to Sooke. Turn left 2 miles past Sooke's third traffic light onto Whiffen Spit Road. We're at the end of the road, on the beach.

# Abigail's Hotel

www.abigailshotel.com
906 McClure Street, Victoria, BC  V8V 3E7
**800-561-6565** • 250-388-5363 • Fax 250-388-7787
innkeeper@abigailshotel.com

*British Columbia*

*Victoria*

*"When I think about our stay at Abigail's Hotel, I cannot help but smile.
Amenities, unparalleled service and location set Abigail's apart."*

Innkeeper/Owner
**Ellen Cmolik**

Intimate, elegant and exclusive... Abigail's delivers 'Romance and the City' with its heritage ambiance and modern conveniences. Located in a peaceful cul de sac 3 blocks from downtown and the Inner Harbour. Each luxurious room has antique furnishings, cozy down duvets, air conditioning, flat-screen televisions, wireless high speed internet and fresh flowers; most rooms have wood-burning fireplaces and jetted tubs. To enhance your experience, enjoy breakfast in bed or select from Celebration, Spa and Dinner Packages. Whether it's pampering yourself with a spa service in our comfortable Spa treatment room "The Pearl", whale watching, golfing, kayaking, hiking, dining at any number of gourmet restaurants or simply relaxing in our luxurious guestrooms, it's a perfect balance of adventure and luxury you'll find only at Abigail's Hotel.

**Rates**
$139/$450 CDN. Honeymoon Suites, King beds, fireplaces, double Jacuzzi tubs. Charming Sunflower and Country rooms, Queen beds with soaker tubs and shower. Seasonal discounts available. Open year-round, reservations available 24 hrs. Number of Rooms: 23

**Cuisine**
Our famous gourmet breakfast and complimentary evening appetizers served every evening in our fireside library. Licensed premises.

**Nearest Airport(s)**
Victoria International Airport

**Directions**
From Airport S on Hwy 17, L on Fort St., R on Vancouver St. and R on McClure St. From Downtown E on Fort St., R on Vancouver St. and R on McClure St.

# Amethyst Inn at Regents Park

www.amethyst-inn.com
1501 Fort Street, Victoria, BC, Canada  V8S 1Z6
**888-265-6499** • 250-595-2053 • Fax 250-595-2054
innkeeper@amethyst-inn.com

*Member Since 2003*

*British Columbia*

*Victoria*

*"We have traveled far and wide and never enjoyed an experience as delightful as Amethyst Inn. Our stay was one of those 'Beautiful Memories'..."*

Innkeepers/Owners
**Abel and Shelley Cheng**

Amethyst Inn at Regents Park is a heritage jewel and Victoria's most historically significant Inn. An award winning 1885 Victorian Mansion, which retains many original architectural features and is furnished with antiques. The preferred Inn for guests celebrating special occasions and cozy retreats. Comfortable, romantic, individually appointed accommodations offer a king or queen bed and sitting area with a fireplace. Bathrooms offer luxurious two person Jacuzzi Spa Tubs, deep soaking tubs or claw foot tubs. Mornings begin with coffee service followed by an elegant full breakfast. Enjoy visiting in the Parlor in the evening and gracious hospitality. The Inn is surrounded by heritage estates, beautiful gardens and tree lined streets. Conveniently located in the heart of Victoria and walking distance to Craigdarroch Castle, Antique Row and central to attractions. Concierge service for city and Butchart Garden tours, dining reservations, whale watching, golf and nature exploring. Best Breakfast in Canada 2005 *Inn Traveler*. Five Star Canada Select.

## Rates
16 romantic rooms and suites. $119/$399 CDN ($110/$330 US) Anniversary, Wedding, Elopement, Honeymoon, Spa & Sightseeing Packages. Seasonal Discounts. Open year-round. King or Queen beds, ensuite baths, two-person jacuzzi Spa tubs, fireplaces. Number of Rooms: 13

## Cuisine
Enjoy morning coffee and an elegant full breakfast. Organic, farm fresh and seasonal as available. Dining Room tables are set with linen, fine china and crystal.

## Nearest Airport(s)
Victoria Int'l (YYJ) - 20 miles

## Directions
HWY17 (Douglas St): L on Fort, R on St CharlesINNER HARBOUR: L on Government, R on Fort, R on St Charles. Free on-site Parking.

# Beaconsfield Inn

www.beaconsfieldinn.com
998 Humboldt St., Victoria, BC, Canada  V8V 2Z8
**888-884-4044** • 250-384-4044 • Fax 250-384-4052
info@beaconsfieldinn.com

*British Columbia*

*Victoria*

*"The Beaconsfield is...the standard by which we judge all others...," Special Places*
*"5 Star Luxury complemented by Historic surrounds." International Traveller*

Proprietors
**Mark and Diana Havin**

We invite to our Award-winning Edwardian Inn built in 1905 located only four blocks from Victoria's Inner Harbor, the Beaconsfield Inn is the ultimate in charm, luxury and romance. Enjoy antique furnishings, stately guest and common rooms, spectacular stained glass windows, feather beds with down comforters and fireplaces in all rooms. Jacuzzis in most every room. The Beaconsfield Inn is situated on a quiet, tree-lined street a short 10 minute stroll to downtown and the inner harbour with all it's shopping, restaurants and tourist attractions. Evening sherry hour, late evening coffee and cookies. Awake to our gourmet full breakfasts. *The Beaconsfield Inn has been awarded a 5 star rating from Canada Select.*

**Rates**
5 Deluxe Rooms, $109/$295 CDN; 4 Suites, $199/$299 CDN.
Open year-round.  Number of Rooms: 9

**Cuisine**
Full breakfast, Evening sherry. Late night cookies and freshly brewed coffee.

**Nearest Airport(s)**
Victoria International. Or downtown inner harbour - Float Planes from Vancouver.

**Directions**
Located Downtown From North: Hwy. 17 to City Centre, L on Humboldt St.; From Inner Harbor: Government St. N to Humboldt St. turn R for 4 blocks.

# Villa Marco Polo

www.villamarcopolo.com
1524 Shasta Place, Victoria, BC  V8S 1X9
**250 370-1524** • 877 601-1524 • Fax 250 370-1624
enquire@villamarcopolo.com

*Member Since 2007*

*British Columbia*

*Victoria*

*Have I dreamed this place? This escape from the ordinary? Thank you, Marco Polo, for this brief sojourn in the land of enchantment.*

Proprietors
**Eliza Livingston, Clarke Bingham
& Liam Morton**

Escape from the ordinary...to the Villa Marco Polo Inn, Victoria's first choice for the discerning traveler. Built in 1923 as a gift to a young bride, the Villa Marco Polo is an Italian Renaissance mansion that continues to be a romantic setting for special vacations and celebrations, especially weddings and honeymoons. A reflecting pool visited occasionally by bald eagles, Coopers hawks, and blue herons is the focal point of a classical Italianate garden. Our guest suites feature double soakers, fireplaces, fine linens, luxurious beds, down pillows, hardwood floors and Persian carpets. In our stunning Spa and Healing Space, guests can schedule treatments such as facials, manicures, and aromatherapy  Generous gourmet breakfasts featuring locally grown produce are served in our lovely sun-splashed dining room. Enjoy afternoon tea or Italian Amarone either in the garden, or in front of the fire in our wood-paneled library. Whether a business meeting requiring wireless internet access and private telephones, or a celebration requiring the services of an events planner, your experience at the Villa will be memorable!

**Rates**
Rates range from $190 to $325.  Number of Rooms: 4

**Cuisine**
Gourmet breakfasts feature locally grown organic produce, house-made preserves, organic maple and birch syrup from Quebec and the Yukon, organic fair trade coffee from Bolivia, and fresh eggs from island farms. With prior notice, we also offer vegetarian, vegan, low carbohydrate, gluten free, and diabetic breakfasts.

**Nearest Airport(s)**
Victoria International Airport is 28 km from the Villa.

**Directions**
From Blanshard Avenue, turn east onto Fort St., right onto St. Charles, and left onto Shasta Place.

# Ontario

Famous for: Wine Country, Niagara Falls, Toronto, the Shaw Festival, Forests, Lakes.

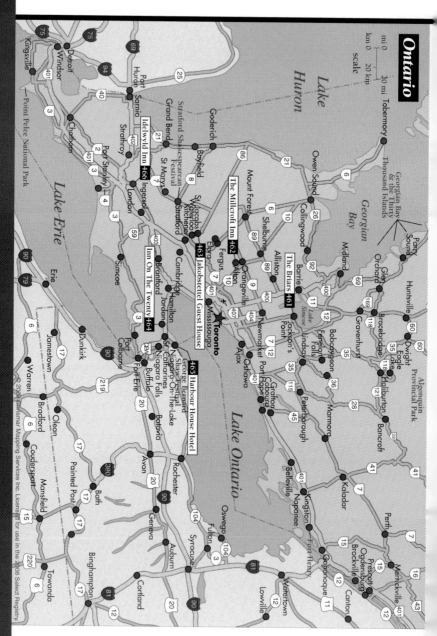

# The Briars Resort & Spa

www.briars.ca
55 Hedge Rd., R.R. #1, Jackson's Point, ON, Canada  L0E 1L0
**800-465-2376** • 905-722-3271 • Fax 905-722-9698
info@briars.ca

*Member Since 1980*

> *"The property and activities available, the surroundings, food, comforts and amenities, happy and pleasant staff - all outstanding!"*

Innkeepers/Owners
**The Sibbald Family**

The Briars is situated on Lake Simcoe just an hour from Toronto. With its lush gardens, gracious accommodation, memorable dining and warm hospitality, The Briars is the perfect destination for any occasion. Guests enjoy rooms or suites in the inn with views of the gardens and lake, or private lakeside cottages. Three meals daily are served in the inn. Fine country dining features traditional favourites, contemporary flavours and fresh pastries prepared in The Briars kitchens. This spacious property features the warmth of an inn with the recreation of a resort. Championship golf, biking, tennis and kayaking; billiards, ping pong and exercise room; yoga and guided walks; dancing Saturday evenings. The Briars Spa provides luxurious treatments, a solarium pool, sauna and whirlpool. In winter there's also cross-country skiing and horse-drawn sleigh rides. Nearby there's antiquing, shopping, fishing and southern Ontario's many attractions. An Ontario Heritage property. Member Ontario's Finest Inns and Premier Spas of Ontario.

**Rates**
57 guest rooms, 3 private lodges, 14 private cottages/suites. $149/$275 CDN($140/$270 US approx) per person/night with all meals. Open Year Round  Number of Rooms: 90

**Cuisine**
Fine Country Dining: traditional and contemporary favourites; fresh herbs & fruits from the gardens. Luncheons can be packed for excursions. Light meals and entertainment in Drinkwaters Lounge and on the patio.

**Nearest Airport(s)**
Toronto Pearson Int'l

**Directions**
From Toronto: 404(N)to Green Lane. R.(E)to Woodbine Ave; L.(N)past Keswick, curve R.(E)on Base Line to Sutton; L.(N)on Dalton Rd. to Jacksons Pt;(R)to Briars. From W of Toronto: take ETR 407 to 404.

*Ontario*

*Jackson's Point*

# The Millcroft Inn & Spa

🍴🍴🍴 🍷

www.millcroft.com

55 John Street, Village of Alton – Caledon, ON, Canada L7K 0C4

**800-383-3976** • 519-941-8111 • Fax 519-941-9192

millcroft@millcroft.com

*Member Since 1995*

Ontario

Alton

> *"Hospitality, fine dining and its country setting make the Millcroft a perfect getaway!"*

Innkeeper
**Wolfgang Stichnothe**

Less than an hour from Toronto, the unparalleled refinement and a tranquil location amid the rolling Caledon Hills make the Millcroft Inn & Spa the Definitive Country Retreat. The serene surroundings and historic charm provide a balm for the city-weary. The riverside setting, fifty-two beautiful guestrooms (some featuring a wood burning fireplace, a Jacuzzi tub, patio, or a private outdoor hot-tub) and 100 wooded trail-lined acres combine with the appeal of AAA/CAA Four Diamond cuisine and vintage wines in a warmly appointed dining room for an extraordinary getaway experience. The full-service Millcroft Spa, Centre for Well-Being features fine European products and pampers guests with a broad range of services, including hydrotherapy, massage, Infrared Sauna and special detoxifying packages. It is also the first and only spa in Canada to offer beer-based treatments. Whether you choose to read by the lounge's wood-burning fireplace, hike a sun-dappled wooded trail, or relax in the Spa, the Millcroft is ready to make your next escape the best yet. Visit www.millcroft.com or call 1-800-383-3976 Toll Free for more details.

**Rates**
From $274/$354 CDN per room. GUARANTEED 20% rate of exchange on US currency. B&B & Packages available. Golf nearby. AAA/CAA 4 Diamonds. Number of Rooms: 52

**Cuisine**
International cuisine. Breakfast, lunch & dinner menus. AAA/CAA 4 Diamonds. Extensive selection of wines & spirits.

**Nearest Airport(s)**
Pearson International (YYZ) 40 minutes away.

**Directions**
Hwy. 401W or 401E to Hwy. 410N to Mayfield Rd., W (L) to Hwy. 10 (Hurontario St.), R on Hwy 10 to Caledon Village, L on Hwy. 24 (Charleston Sideroad) to Peel Regional Rd 136 (Main St), then R, follow to 4-way stop, L on Queen St. and continue until the Millcroft entrance on right side.

# Jakobstettel Inn

www.jakobstettel.com
16 Isabella St., St. Jacobs, ON, Canada  N0B 2N0
**800-431-3035** • 519-664-2208 • Fax 519-664-1326
info@jakobstettel.com

*Member Since 1995*

*"Thank you for a wonderful escape from reality."*

Owner
**Daniel P. Reeve**

The Jakobstettel Inn is St. Jacobs' finest retreat. From the moment you walk in through the front door our welcoming staff will show you the best comfort outside your own home. Built in 1898, this grand Victorian home rests on five acres crowned by a century of towering trees and accented by groomed gardens.

Enjoy a myriad of activities on the back lawn. Take a dip in our cabana lined swimming pool, serve up an ace on the tennis court and hit the walking trails along the banks of the Grand River. Explore St. Jacobs, one of Ontario's premier shopping villages with boutiques, craft studios, restaurants and theatre within walking distance of the Inn. Or, do nothing at all. Grab a lounge chair and find your perfect spot in the sun. And for those autumn nights when a slight chill enters your world, warm up in front of one of our fireplaces. Make business a pleasure by meeting at Jakobstettel Inn. We offer a luxurious setting that encourages fresh thinking outside the box or let our grounds be the perfect backdrop for your wedding photographs. Why not have your nuptials last the whole day as you and your guests enjoy the splendor and luxurious hospitality of the Inn and the staff.

### Rates
We have 10 distinctly decorated guest rooms for your accommodations. All silver suites are $199 per night and Presidential suite is $399 per night plus applicable taxes.  Number of Rooms: 10

### Cuisine
Continental breakfast, evening dessert cart is served each day in our in-house dinning room. Lunches can be served to small groups by our very own chef only when pre-arranged.

### Nearest Airport(s)
Kitchener-Waterloo Regional Airport
Toronto Pearson International Airport

### Directions
From Hwy. 401 exit Hwy. 8 W to Kitchener then Hwy. 85 N through Waterloo, choose Rd. 15 or Rd. 17 exit; in St. Jacobs turn W on Albert St.

🍽️ 🍽️ 🍽️ 🍷

# Inn on the Twenty

www.innonthetwenty.com
3845 Main Street, Jordan, ON, Canada L0R 1S0
**800–701–8074** • 905–562–5336 • Fax 905–562–0009
info@innonthetwenty.com

*Ontario*

*Jordan*

*"Thanks to the gracious hosts at the Inn...it's not necessary to name individuals since each and every person offered the same welcoming presence."*

Innkeeper/Owner
**Helen Young**

DiRoNA

This is the heart of Ontario's wine country! Renovated winery buildings boast twenty-six suites, all with fireplaces and Jacuzzi tubs; antiques and unique art abound. The Inn is located in a charming village with artisans and antique shops. Great golf, walking and bicycling opportunities as well as the sophistication of Niagara's famous Shaw Theatre and the not-to-be-missed Falls. Our restaurant, On the Twenty, is a DiRoNA award winner and a leader in regional cuisine. Our full service Spa enhances any stay too. The Niagara wine route beckons with up to forty diverse wineries within a fifteen minute drive of the Inn. Cave Spring Cellars, one of Ontario's most recognized premium wineries, is our partner and is right across the street from the Inn. Special tasting offers are available to Inn guests. A visit to Canada is a fresh experience and we are thrilled to welcome so many of our US neighbours. We are just 25 minutes from the borders at Niagara Falls and make a great on route stop to Toronto.

**Rates**
26 Suites: 7 two-story, 20 one-level, 5 with private garden.
$171/$353 US (exchange approximate) $189/$389 CDN Open year-round. Number of Rooms: 28

**Cuisine**
On the Twenty is a DiRoNA Award restaurant with regional focus. Private Dining Rooms available for up to 135. Ontario wines and beers. Full bar. Cave Spring Cellars Winery on site. Tours and tastings available daily.

**Nearest Airport(s)**
Buffalo, Toronto

**Directions**
QEW Hwy. to Victoria Ave. (Vineland Exit 57). L off the Service Road, S to Regional Rd. 81 (King St.). Turn L and go through the valley; first L at top of the hill onto Main St. 5 minutes from QEW.

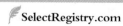

# Harbour House Hotel

www.harbourhousehotel.ca

Box 760, 85 Melville Street, Niagara-on-the-Lake, ON, Canada  L0S 1J0

**866-277-6677** • 905-468-4683 • Fax 905-468-0366

inquire@harbourhousehotel.ca

*Member Since 2003*

*"What sets Harbour House apart is its friendly yet impeccable service, its serene atmosphere and those heavenly beds." - Frommer's Niagara Region*

**Innkeepers/Owners**
**Susan Murray**

Harbour House is a wonderful blend of intimacy, quality, personality, professionalism, sensuous comfort and attention to every detail. Overlooking the Niagara River and within walking distance of the Shaw Festival, many intriguing shops and more than a dozen fine restaurants, Harbour House is just a short drive from the wonder of Niagara Falls, Niagara's world class wineries and dozens of top-flight golf courses. Perched beside Niagara-on-the-Lake's pretty yacht harbour, Harbour House has been designed in the spirit of maritime life in the 1880s?elegant simplicity, quality finishes, carefully selected antiques and unique accents. Each bedroom and suite offers whirlpool baths, fireplaces, DVD players, down duvets and featherbeds, WiFi internet access and much more. Harbour House captures the flavour of historic Niagara. Member of Ontario's Finest Inns and CAA/AAA Four Diamond. Named best hotel in Canada by travellers on the world's largest consumer-based hotel review site, www.tripadvisor.com. Recipient of top rating of 3 Stars by Frommer's.

**Rates**
31 Deluxe Rooms & Riverview Suites from $199 CDN. Dinner Packages & seasonal rates.  Number of Rooms: 31

**Cuisine**
Harbour House features a classic European-style buffet breakfast, an afternoon wine and cheese sampling and cookies at bedtime. A shuttle service is available for dozens of local restaurants.

**Nearest Airport(s)**
Buffalo, 45 min; Toronto, 60 min.

**Directions**
Queen Elizabeth Way (QEW) to Exit #38 (or 38B from Toronto). R on Glendale, follow signs for Route #55. R on East-West Line to Niagara Pkwy. L on Niagara Pkwy to Wellington St. R on Wellington to Ricardo St. R 1/2 block.

*Ontario*

*Niagara-on-the-Lake*

🍴 🍴 🍴 🍷

# Idlewyld Inn
www.idlewyldinn.com
36 Grand Avenue, London, ON N6C 1K8
**877-435-3466** • 519-433-2891
info@idlewyldinn.com

*Member Since 2008*

*"Idlewyld Inn...the perfect escape."*

Innkeeper, Proprietor
**Christine Kropp**

Experience victorian surroundings, exquisite fine dining and service as it was meant to be at London's spectacular boutique hotel. The Idlewyld's signature ambience of quiet elegance has been captured in the spectacular dining room ~ featuring a menu that is imaginative and inspired ~ and continues into the garden courtyard. Each of our 23 individually-designed rooms offers its own special atmosphere reflective of the Idlewyld Inn experience. Our guests will enjoy complimentary with their stay wired hi-speed Internet service, on-site parking, nightly turndown service, and morning coffee service with national newspaper. There is so much to discover in London. You can venture into London's past, which has seen the emergence of a big band legend and the discovery of insulin or go back further and witness an archaeological dig. To satisfy your artistic interests there is The Grand Theatre, Orchestra London, the London Regional Art and Historic Museum plus an array of special events focused on the visual and performing arts.

**Rates**
Dinner & Breakfast $255/$325; Night only $135/$225.
Number of rooms: 23  Number of Rooms: 23

**Cuisine**
Our chefs maintain the tradition of using only the finest locally-produced meat, vegetables, fruits and herbs, including AAA Ontario beef, award-winning lamb and pork and the full bounty of garden and orchard. Serving breakfast, lunch, dinner daily and weekend afternoon tea.

**Nearest Airport(s)**
London International Airport (YXU)

**Directions**
From Detroit or Toronto: Exit Highway 401 at Exit 186 (Wellington Road North). Follow Wellington Rd N to Grand Avenue. Turn left, proceed through one stop light and a four way stop sign.

# *Ontario Inn Style*

Discover over 40 of Ontario's Finest Inns and Spas including several Select Registry properties. All of the innkeepers share the Select Registry's philosophy and promise of excellence.

Enjoy true Canadian hospitality along the sparkling Great Lakes, in vibrant, clean cities and throughout quaint villages and quiet rolling countryside.

*Attention Spa Goers* –Ontario's Finest now offers quality assured spas that feature distinctly Ontario treatments and therapies.

We look forward to welcoming you this season.

ONTARIO'S *finest* INNS · SPAS

*Ask for a complimentary map & guidebook at 800-340-4667 or visit*

www.ontariosfinestinns.com · www.ontariosfinestspas.com

*See you soon in Ontario, Canada!*

Famous for: St. Lawrence Seaway, French Culture, Maple Syrup, Winter Sports, Apples, Camping.

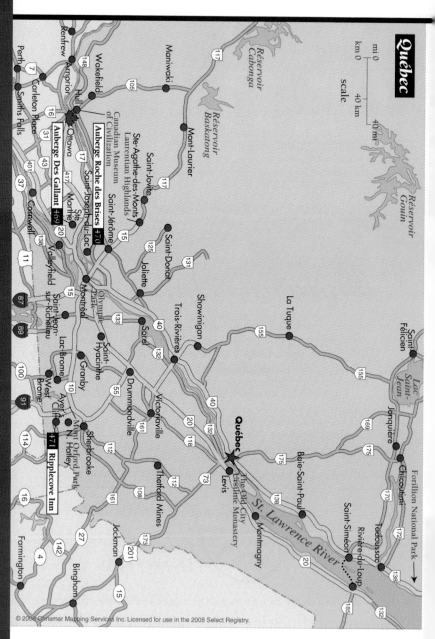

# Auberge des Gallant

www.gallant.qc.ca
1171 St - Henry Rd., Ste-Marthe, Rigaud, QUE, Canada J0P 1W0
**800-641-4241** • 450-459-4241 • Fax 450-459-4667
res@gallant.qc.ca

*Member Since 1998*

*"My home away from home!"*
*"Very friendly, warm, professional. Excellent food and service."*

Innkeepers/Owners
**Linda, Gerry & Neil Gallant**

Garden and SPA lovers will enjoy romantic **Auberge des Gallant (The Gallant Inn)** nestled on Rigaud Mountain, between Montreal and Ottawa in the heart of a bird and deer sanctuary. Enjoy award-winning French cuisine and wine list, as well as our gourmet spa! We offer wine, chocolate, and even maple sugar body wraps and facials. Elegant spacious rooms with real wood-burning fireplace and balcony overlook our five acres of beautifully appointed gardens, which in summer attract a multitude of birds and butterflies, while winter promises sleigh rides, cross country skiing and down hill skiing. Fall foliage is at its best in October, and our maple sugar house with its 10,000 taps is open from late February to the end of April for traditional maple meals. Maple syrup is available all year round! Next time you are visiting Québec, Montreal, Hudson and St-Lazare, make sure to stop in and stock up on our maple syrup.

**Rates**
24 Rooms with wood-burning fireplace & balcony, from $150, MAP pp. for a country room and $175, MAP pp. for a honeymoon suite. Open year-round. Number of Rooms: 24

**Cuisine**
Breakfast, lunch, gourmet 5 course dinner, Sunday brunch. Extensive wine list and liquor. Maple products available all year.

**Nearest Airport(s)**
Montreal, Trudeau, 30 miles. Ottawa 70 miles.

**Directions**
Between Montreal and Ottawa, Rte. 40 W, Exit 17, Left on Rte. 201, 3 miles & Right on St-Henri 5 miles.

*Quebec*

*Ste-Marthe, Rigaud*

# La Roche des Brises

www.rochedesbrises.com
2007, rue Principale, St-Joseph-du-Lac, QUE  J0N 1M0
**450-472-2722** • Fax 450-473-5878
info@rochedesbrises.com

*Member Since 2005*

*Quebec*

*St-Joseph-du-Lac*

*Award winning Gold Medal of the Laurentians Tourist Association.*

Innkeeper/Owner
**Gina Pratt**

The Inn is located on the outskirts of Montreal overlooking rolling hills, orchards and our vineyard with a spectacular view of Montreal. Beautifully decorated with antiques, the Inn has been awarded the Five Sun top rating by Quebec Tourism for the Laurentians. Our rooms all have King size beds and private baths and air conditioning. We also offer our guests the luxury of hot stone and grape seed massage in a relaxing ambiance. The Inn has its own pool and is close to beautiful Lake of Two Mountains. And if you take a little stroll through the vines and experience our charming fine dining restaurant or wine tasting room, revealing our renowned award winning wines, you shall feel the true nature and magic of this unique ambiance. Location: Downtown Montreal is located 30 minutes away by car or commute by train to avoid traffic. "Auberge Roche des Brises" offers a unique lodging experience in a country setting, close to the heart of Montreal.

**Rates**
5 suites, $120/$180 CDN double occupancy. Open February through December 31.  Number of Rooms: 5

**Cuisine**
Elegant full breakfast included. Award winning fine dining with a french twist. World wines available. Roche des Brises winery on site. Tours and tasting available daily.

**Nearest Airport(s)**
Dorval/Pierre Eliot Trudeau Airport, 50 minutes

**Directions**
From South: Highway 13 North to Highway 640 West, Exit 2 Left on "Chemin Principal" for 4.7 km

SelectRegistry.com

# Auberge Ripplecove Inn & Spa

🍴 🍴 🍴 🍷

www.ripplecove.com
700 Ripplecove Road, Lake Massawippi, Ayer's Cliff, QUE, Canada  J0B 1C0
**800-668-4296** • 819-838-4296 • Fax 819-838-5541
info@ripplecove.com

*Member Since 1995*

*Quebec*

*Ayer's Cliff*

*"One of the most beautiful Inns we have ever stayed at! Keep up the good work!"*

**Innkeepers/Owners**
**Debra and Jeffrey Stafford**

Since 1945, Ripplecove Inn has been chosen by sophisticated travelers from around the world to get away from it all in an atmosphere of romance, privacy, refined service and luxury. The Inn resides on a beautifully landscaped 12 acre peninsula alive with English gardens, and century-old pines. Guests can choose from 34 designed decorated rooms, suites and lakeside cottages, many with lakeview balcony, fireplace and antiques galore! New since 2004, a full service Spa facility offering massage, hydro therepy, facials, private salons and a four season outdoor hot tub have been added. A private beach, boating, biking, tennis, heated outdoor pool and lake cruises are also all on site! Rated as one of Quebec's top 10 best places to dine, our victorian dining room and lakeside terrace offer refined cuisine and vintage wines accompanied by the strains of live piano music and sterling silver service. American visitors don't forget; Ripplecove Inn is a perfect stop over on route to either Montreal or Quebec city via Interstate 91 through Vermont.

**Rates**
34 Rooms, Suites and Cottages, US $129/$355MAP/person/ day including dinner, breakfast and service. All rooms offer TV, TEL, A/C and designer decor Most rooms offer fireplace, private lakeview balcony and whirlpools.  Number of Rooms: 34

**Cuisine**
Four Diamond Award cuisine in our Victorian dining room & lakeside terrace. 6000 bottle wine cellar and pub.

**Nearest Airport(s)**
Pierre E Trudeau, Montreal

**Directions**
From New England take I-91 N to the Canadian border then follow Rte. 55 N to exit 21. Follow signs to Inn which is 3 miles from exit 21. Distances: Montreal 1.5 hrs, Boston 3 hrs, New York City 7 hrs.

# Index by Inn

# Index by Inn

 SelectRegistry.com

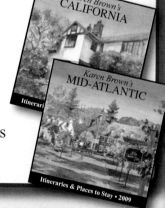

Our family pottery was established in 1972, in Minnesota, just as you see here, by Peter Deneen sitting down at his potter's wheel.

The process of hand making pottery is time consuming and labor intensive.

Over twenty-four pairs of hands will touch each piece during its production process until it is ready to be shipped.

While each item is uniform in size and shape, every one is created on a wheel by a master potter, making it unique.

You can find our mugs at over 170 of your favorite Select Registry Inns.

When you purchase a mug made by Deneen Pottery, know that you are supporting a family business that holds true to a craft that is rich in tradition and history.

DENEEN POTTERY

DENEEN POTTERY.COM
ST. PAUL, MN USA 08
HANDTHROWN

Look for our stamp on the bottom of our stoneware

1889
WhiteGate Inn
& Cottage

To learn more about our company and our stoneware visit us on line at : www.deneenpottery.com

SELECT REGISTRY is, first and foremost, a marketing association comprised of independently-owned, unique inns. Our members include diverse styles, locations, and property sizes, and we cater to travelers who enjoy the finer things in life—and who expect comfort, hospitality, and most importantly, value when they travel.

Our target audiences appreciate, recognize, and rely on various other brands and organizations, and SELECT REGISTRY often co-markets or connects with such groups. For example, many of our member properties belong to the educational arm of our industry—**PAII** (Professional Association of Innkeepers International), an organization with 20 years of experience guiding aspiring, novice, and experienced innkeepers.

**Karen Brown's Guides** have long featured SELECT REGISTRY member properties as part of their itineraries in locations throughout North America. For many years, Karen Brown was, herself, the owner of a SELECT REGISTRY member inn.

We continue to value our co-marketing relationship with **DiRoNA** (Distinguished Restaurants of North America).

The ultimate hospitality experience for new owners of "The Ultimate Driving Machine®": This year, in partnership with **BMW of North America**, SELECT REGISTRY® is pleased to offer new BMW owners a special reward: a complimentary night's stay at one of our 409 quality-assured member properties!

We are pleased to support the **American Heart Association**'s efforts to encourage individuals to Learn and Live.

SELECT REGISTRY does modest, targeted print advertising, in addition to earned media efforts. We are particularly pleased to regularly appear in *Inns Magazine* and *Executive Traveler*.

Fine food—and particularly breakfast—is an important part of today's complete hospitality and lodging experience. Last year, SELECT REGISTRY held its inaugural "Inn-credible Breakfast Cook-off" culinary competition, with more than 100 of our members submitting breakfast recipes to a panel of culinary judges. The five finalists competed before a live audience in Coeur d'Alene, Idaho last May, with the winner receiving a new **TurboChef** range. Event sponsors included: **Eggland's Best, Starbucks, Le Creuset, Steelite, and Workman Publishing**. This year, we will be staging the finals of the second annual "Inn-credible Breakfast Cook-off" in Williamsburg, Virginia. Stay tuned to our website (www.selectregistry. com), where you'll find recipes and news flashes regarding the competition.

SELECT REGISTRY values its association with all of these organizations and brands, and we look forward to continuing to provide introductions to exceptional lodging and hospitality experiences for these diverse audiences.

FOODSERVICE